A HISTORY OF CHRISTIANITY *in* PITTSBURGH

GARY SCOTT SMITH

THE History PRESS

Published by The History Press
Charleston, SC
www.historypress.com

First published 2019

Manufactured in the United States

ISBN 9781467141093

Library of Congress Control Number: 2018952868

Notice: The information in this book is true and complete to the best of our knowledge. It is offered without guarantee on the part of the author or The History Press. The author and The History Press disclaim all liability in connection with the use of this book.

This book is dedicated to the many faithful Christians who strove to make Pittsburgh as famous for God as for steel.

CONTENTS

ACKNOWLEDGEMENTS

I would not have been able to write this book without the help of the head pastors, CEOs and numerous other staff members of the churches and parachurch organizations profiled in the book. The information and insights provided by athletes and sports chaplains also greatly enriched my study. The names of all these individuals are provided in the chapters to which they contributed. I especially thank my two assistants—Alexia Soriak and Sarah Gibbs, both students at Grove City College at the time—who did research on varied topics and accompanied me on visits to the nine profiled congregations. I thank my mother, Arlene Smith, who proofread the text for me. As always, I thank my wife, Jane, for her help with research, technical matters and stylistic advice. I owe an immense debt of gratitude to Bruce Barron, a Christian author and professional editor, who painstakingly read my manuscript and helped me update numerous matters, correct some factual errors and improve the prose. Finally, I appreciate the professionalism and excellent work of acquisitions editor Banks Smither and senior editor Ryan Finn, who did the copy editing for my book.

INTRODUCTION

The untapped conviction and belief in this city means more to it than all the coal in the hills and all the steel in the mills. If we could train and mobilize that force, Pittsburgh would become a spiritual pilot plant for America.
—Samuel Shoemaker, TIME, *1955*

There is no part of society in Pittsburgh that has not been created or strongly influenced by faith.
—David Zubik, bishop of the Diocese of Pittsburgh

Pittsburgh is one of America's most maligned, industrial and diverse cities. It is the Steel City, the City at the Point, the "Gateway to the West," America's Most Livable City and the City of Bridges (its 446 bridges are more than those in Venice).

Thanks to the success of its three major sports teams—the Pirates, Steelers and Penguins—Pittsburgh has also been called the City of Champions, beginning in the 1970s when the Pirates won two world championships and the Steelers won four Super Bowls led by their Steel Curtain defense. Since 1965, of all American cities with at least two professional sports teams, only Boston has won more championships—10 percent of the total titles in which its teams have played—than Pittsburgh with 9 percent.[1] The Pirates have won the World Series five times (losing only twice), the Steelers are 6-2 in the Super Bowl (the most wins of any team) and the Penguins have won five Stanley Cups (losing only once) since they entered the National

Hockey League in 1967.[2] Moreover, some of the greatest stars in these three sports have played for Pittsburgh teams: Honus Wagner, Arky Vaughan, Pie Traynor, Paul Waner, Ralph Kiner, Roberto Clemente and Willie Stargell in baseball; Mario Lemieux, Sidney Crosby, Jaromir Jagr and Evgeni Malkin in hockey; and Joe Greene, Mel Blount, Jack Ham, Jack Lambert, Terry Bradshaw, Franco Harris, Lynn Swann, Rod Woodson and Jerome Bettis in football. Only the Bears, Packers and Redskins have more players in the NFL Hall of Fame, and the Steelers have placed more players there since 1980 than any other team. The Pittsburgh area has also produced a plethora of stars for other teams, most notably Cardinal slugger Stan Musial in baseball, several of the NFL's superior quarterbacks—Johnny Unitas, Joe Namath, Joe Montana and Dan Marino—and outstanding running back Tony Dorsett. Finally, Pittsburgh has been rated the no. 1 Sports City by *Sporting News* and as having the best (most passionate) football fans by ESPN.[3]

Pittsburgh is also the home of individuals who made impressive contributions in numerous other fields: songwriter Stephen Foster; painter Mary Cassatt; playwright George S. Kaufmann; authors Willa Cather, Gertrude Stein, Anne Dillard and David McCullough; environmentalist Rachel Carson; dancer and choreographer Martha Graham; dancer and actor Gene Kelly; scientist Jonas Salk; artist Andy Warhol; singers Perry Como, Bobby Vinton, Lena Horne and Christina Aguilera; actors F. Murray Abraham, Michael Keaton and Jeff Goldblum; television children's program host Fred Rogers; playwright August Wilson; and producer David O. Selznick.

Pittsburgh was long one of America's major industrial centers. By the 1850s, it led the nation in iron production, and in 1901, when J.P. Morgan created U.S. Steel, Pittsburgh produced 64 percent of America's structural steel.[4] Its leadership in the steel industry made Pittsburgh the epicenter of the national, violent railroad strike of 1877, the bloody Homestead Strike of 1892 and the Great Steel Strike of 1919. By this latter date, "Pittsburgh's working-class population of Catholics, blacks, and Jews made it culturally more diverse" than almost any other American city.[5]

Perhaps no other American city has been more ridiculed than Pittsburgh. Literary luminaries have outdone one another in denouncing its smoke, squalor, political corruption and ugliness. For more than one hundred years, historian Roy Lubove claimed, journalists competed to describe its repulsiveness. Pittsburgh was repeatedly compared with hell.[6] In 1842, renowned English novelist Charles Dickens labeled the city "hell with the lid lifted." James Parton agreed, calling Pittsburgh "Hell with the lid off" in an 1868 *Atlantic Monthly* article. After visiting Pittsburgh in 1887, prominent British philosopher Herbert Spencer joked that six months' residence in Pittsburgh "would justify suicide." In 1903, muckraker Lincoln Steffens declared that Pittsburgh "looked like hell, literally." Describing the city around 1900, a British economist deplored its "grime and squalor," "ferocious contests between labor and capital" and scramble for money. In 1913, another English visitor lamented Pittsburgh's befouled streams, piles of trash, hovels and black mills that covered everything "with a film of smoke." Even steel magnate Andrew Carnegie admitted that "Pittsburgh is the smokiest place in the world....The soot gathered in the hair and irritated the skin." Pittsburgh's soil, journalist H.L. Mencken claimed, was a combination of "coal dust, grease and garbage"; the city was "so dreadfully hideous, so intolerable, bleak and forlorn that it reduced...human aspirations to a macabre and depressing joke." "No sane man would be a Pittsburgher," he added, "if he could help it." As late as the 1940s, author John Gunther decried Pittsburgh as "one of the most shockingly ugly and filthy cities in the world." Comedian Johnny Carson, host of NBC's *The Tonight Show*, quipped in the 1960s that Pittsburgh was "like Newark without the cultural advantages."[7]

By the mid-1950s, however, boosters were touting Pittsburgh's remarkable renaissance. The *Sun-Telegraph* boasted that Pittsburgh was the nation's eighth-largest metropolitan area and that only six other areas employed more workers. The city was a great industrial center and had five colleges and universities, forty-four research laboratories and two hundred cultural enterprises.[8]

Amazingly, given its earlier reputation and post-1975 economic struggles in the wake of its declining steel industry, Pittsburgh has since 2000 been named America's most livable city numerous times, including by *Places Rated Almanac*, Forbes.com and *The Economist*. Its medical facilities, educational institutions, cultural amenities and cost of living have enabled Pittsburgh to capture many other accolades. Thanks to its theatrical productions, dance and ballet performances, symphony, top-flight museums (especially the Carnegie Museum of Art, the Andy Warhol Museum, the Carnegie Science Center and the Carnegie Museum of Natural History) and the Phipps Conservatory and Botanical Garden, Pittsburgh is a major cultural center.[9] *American Style* magazine named Pittsburgh the "best arts destination for midsize cities," while *New York Magazine* called it a great city for "culture hunters." Both *National Geographic Traveler* and *Frommer's* categorized Pittsburgh as a best travel destination, and the Brookings Institution branded it one of the nation's "most walkable cities." Strikingly, *Forbes Magazine* rated Pittsburgh as one of "the world's cleanest cities."[10] Pittsburgh has also recently been named "America's smartest city" based on its colleges, libraries, media and museums per person; average resident's educational level; and public school rank.[11] In 2015, *Metropolis Magazine* ranked only two American cities—Pittsburgh and Indianapolis—among the world's "best cities to live, work, and play in."[12]

CHRISTIANITY IN PITTSBURGH

While Pittsburgh is known for its steel industry, sports teams, ethnic diversity, earlier deplorable social ills and recent physical makeover and cultural renaissance, it is much less recognized as one of the nation's most religious metropolitan areas or for its rich faith heritage. The Pittsburgh region is known more for its "steelworkers and sports teams" than for its church steeples. Although Pittsburgh's religious history is deeply intertwined with its "economic growth, community-building, politics, and ethnicity," scholars have generally ignored the importance of its religious leaders, churches and parachurch organizations to the city, region and nation.[13]

Presbyterians played a principal role in founding Pittsburgh, and for the first seventy-five years, they dominated its religious landscape because of their numbers and social prominence. First Presbyterian Church was established in 1787, and in 1842, forty-six of the city's seventy-six congregations were Presbyterian. Of Pittsburgh's founding families, 52 percent were Presbyterians, and Presbyterians long served as "guardians of the city's public morals" and "put a firm cultural stamp on the life of the city." In 1869, Presbyterians—who had divided in 1837 over theology, polity and slavery—reunited at a General Assembly held in Pittsburgh. Between 1850 and 1890, Presbyterians constituted about 40 percent of Allegheny County's church members. In 1900, Presbyterians still surpassed all other Protestant groups, constituting 13 percent of the religiously affiliated.[14]

Although Catholics substantially outnumbered them by the late nineteenth century, a Presbyterian journal argued in 1914 that Presbyterian congregations were "the most influential [ones] in the city" and contended that "Pittsburgh is the greatest center of Presbyterianism in the world."[15] While both points are disputable, members of Presbyterian congregations controlled three-fourths of Pittsburgh's industry during the Progressive years and Pittsburgh Presbytery was the largest presbytery in the world, so the region was arguably at least "America's center of Presbyterianism."[16] The United Presbyterian Church of North America had its headquarters in Pittsburgh for a century. In 1958, when the United Presbyterians and the Presbyterian Church in the United States of America merged, Pittsburgh became the heart of the new denomination and the "greatest concentration of Presbyterian strength in the world." About one-seventh of the congregations and one-fifth of the members of the new communion lived within two hundred miles of Pittsburgh.[17] At this point, Presbyterians composed 22 percent of the Protestants living in Allegheny County.[18]

Pittsburgh has also been home to sizable numbers of Methodist, Baptist, Lutheran, Episcopal and other Protestant communicants. Methodists founded their first church in the city in 1788 and, twenty years later, built an edifice on the corner of Smithfield Street and Seventh Avenue that was dubbed the Brimstone Corner because of its pastors' fiery denunciations of sin over the years. Pittsburgh had twenty-six Methodist congregations in 1860 and forty-six in 1928. The city's Baptists increased substantially between 1830 and 1860 and had twenty-one congregations by the latter date. Lutherans grew rapidly between 1830 and 1880, at which time they were Allegheny County's third-largest Protestant denomination.[19] William Passavant, who served prominent congregations from 1844 to 1879, was the region's most influential Lutheran during this period. Strongly committed to helping the poor, he founded Passavant Hospital in McCandless, an orphanage that became Glade Run Lutheran Services in Zelienople and several other institutions.[20] In 1917, Pittsburgh had forty-seven thousand Methodists, twenty-eight thousand Lutherans and twenty-two thousand Baptists.[21]

Because of their wealth, social prominence, reforming zeal and recent efforts to safeguard biblical orthodoxy, Pittsburgh's Episcopalians have also had a substantial influence in the city and beyond the region. Led by rector George Hodges and several key laymen, most notably H.D.W. English, Calvary Episcopal Church in Shadyside spearheaded numerous efforts to remedy social and civic ills between 1890 and 1915. In the 1950s, under charismatic pastor Samuel Shoemaker, the congregation promoted spiritual revitalization and increased interdenominational cooperation in the Steel City. In the early twenty-first century, Pittsburgh became the nation's center of evangelical Episcopalianism because of the work of Trinity Episcopal School for Ministry in Ambridge and the transfer of many congregations to the Anglican Church in North America. Robert Duncan, who served as the Episcopal bishop of Pittsburgh from 1997 to 2008, argued that the influence of the seminary and the strength of the diocese made Pittsburgh the "center of biblical Anglicanism in North America."[22]

The first Catholic Mass was held in Fort Duquesne in 1754, and Pittsburgh's first Catholic church (St. Patrick's) began worshiping in 1808. A diocese was established in 1843, headquartered in Pittsburgh, to serve Catholics in a six-county region. Beginning in the 1880s, thousands of Catholics came to the Steel City, primarily from eastern Europe. From 1900 to 1930, both the number of priests and nuns and the Catholic population of the Pittsburgh Diocese more than doubled (280,000 to 581,327); between 1904 and 1921, the diocese built a new church every month, and by 1950, 448 Catholic schools were educating pupils in Allegheny County.[23] The Pittsburgh metropolitan area today is home to 632,000 Roman Catholics. Between 1880 and 1920, Pittsburgh also became one of the largest American centers of non-Roman Catholic parishes, most notably the Byzantine Rite Catholic Church. Eastern Europe also sent many Orthodox Christians to Pittsburgh, and the city became a major hub for Eastern Orthodoxy after the St. Nicholas Carpatho-Russian Greek Church was established in Duquesne in 1890.

Bethel African Methodist Episcopal Church, which began as a Sunday school in the Hill District in 1808, is the oldest black congregation in Pittsburgh.[24] Before the Civil War, the city's African Americans established several other congregations, as well as four benevolent societies, a school, a newspaper and a temperance society.[25] African Americans came in sizable numbers during the late nineteenth century to work in Pittsburgh's burgeoning steel industry. Their arrival accelerated during the "great migration" between 1910 and 1930. African Americans founded dozens of congregations (forty-five in the Hill District alone by 1930), including Euclid Avenue AME, Ebenezer Baptist and John Wesley AME Zion, which often doubled as community centers, providing social, economic and spiritual benefits. During the 1950s and 1960s, many of the city's African American congregations participated enthusiastically in the civil rights movement.

Pittsburgh has been home to five seminaries—three Presbyterian, one Episcopal and one Byzantine Catholic—four of which are still operating. In addition, United Presbyterians, Reformed Presbyterians, Byzantine Rite Catholics, the Russian Orthodox Greek Catholic Church of America and the Greek Archdiocese of North and South America have all had their national headquarters in Pittsburgh. Today, according to one survey, Pittsburgh is the nation's fifth most religious city after Salt Lake City, Birmingham, Memphis and Oklahoma City with 57,695 religious adherents per 100,000 residents; it has hundreds of thriving congregations and parachurch ministries.[26]

Several other significant religious developments occurred in Pittsburgh. Its first synagogue opened in 1855, and a major branch of the Jewish faith—Reform Judaism—grew out of a conference held in the city in 1885. Charles Taze Russell founded Jehovah's Witnesses, a group that today claims to have more than 8 million members worldwide, in Pittsburgh in the 1870s. Today, large Hindu temples grace Penn Hills and Monroeville, and Muslims worship at mosques in Oakland and the Hill District.

In 1940, Pittsburgh had 635 churches belonging to 45 different denominations and 34 Jewish synagogues. Among Protestants, Baptists had the most congregations, followed by Methodists, Presbyterians, Lutherans, United Presbyterians and Episcopalians. Catholic churches were 14 percent of the city's congregations in 1940 and 18 percent in 1960.[27] In 2010, Allegheny County had 179 Catholic congregations, 145 Presbyterian Church (USA) congregations, 100 Methodist congregations, 93 Evangelical Lutheran Church of America congregations, 85 nondenominational congregations, 42 American Baptist congregations, 30 Assemblies of God congregations, 24 Anglican Church in North America congregations, 22 American Methodist Episcopal congregations, 19 Episcopal congregations and 18 Christian and Missionary Alliance congregations. City-Data.com lists the membership numbers for Allegheny County as follows: Methodist 44,204, PCUSA 42,808, nondenominational 33,103, ELCA 24,718, American Baptists 17,148, Assemblies of God 12,398, Episcopal 7,780, African Methodist Episcopal 6,375 and Christian and Missionary Alliance 6,171. This site and two other recent analyses of religion in Pittsburgh disagree about the city's religious composition. City-Data and Best Places estimate Catholics to be about 62 percent of the Christians in Allegheny County (more than double the percentage of Catholics nationwide), while a Pew survey projects them to be 41 percent. While City-Data puts the county's mainline Protestants at 19 percent, Pew projects them to be 25 percent. City-Data estimates evangelical Protestants to be 10.5 percent of the county's Christians, while Pew found them to be 15 percent. Both these organizations list black Protestants as 2.5 percent and Orthodox Christians as about 1.5 percent of the county's Christians.[28]

While all these religious developments and communities are significant, this book analyzes the history of Christianity in Pittsburgh. Moreover, while Pittsburgh's entire religious history is important and interesting, I focus principally on the years from 1950 to today. Numerous developments have contributed to the flourishing of Christianity in the Steel City during these years. The 1952 Billy Graham Crusade, the creation of the Pittsburgh Experiment in 1955, the coming of Young Life to Pittsburgh in 1956 and the thriving ministry of First Presbyterian Church were major events. The 1960s saw the founding of Youth for Christ clubs, Youth Guidance and the Pittsburgh Offensive, conferences for college students at Oglebay Park and Atwood Lake and the charismatic renewal movement at Duquesne University. Shoemaker, Don James, Reid Carpenter, Paul Everett, Robert Lamont and Bill Winston played key roles in founding and leading these organizations.

In the 1970s, Pittsburgh experienced a religious renaissance. During this pivotal decade, the Coalition for Christian Outreach, the Pittsburgh Power and Light Company, the Ligonier Valley Study Center, Trinity School of Ministry, Summer's Best Two Weeks camp, the Pittsburgh Leadership Foundation and the Labor-Management Prayer Breakfast were created. Carpenter, John Guest, John Howe, Bob Letsinger, R.C. Sproul, Bob Long, Wayne Alderson and Dora Hillman established, led or funded these enterprises. The conviction grew among many Pittsburghers that God was doing a mighty work in the city and that Christians should claim the power of Christ to advance God's kingdom.

The 1980s were a difficult decade for Pittsburgh, as the steel industry laid off thousands of workers and the region's population declined. Nevertheless, religious revival continued with the founding of Alderson's Value of the Person program, The Pittsburgh Project, Garfield Jubilee, the Pittsburgh Coalition Against Pornography, East Liberty Family Health Care, the Pittsburgh Youth Network and many other important ministries, as well as North Way Christian Community by Jay Passavant and Orchard Hill Church in Wexford. Since 1990, many of these ministries have increased in size and influence and collectively have helped make Pittsburgh better known for God.[29]

This book describes the role Christianity has played in Pittsburgh, especially the quest to make the city "as famous for God as for steel." In 1917, the newly formed Pittsburgh Council of Churches conducted a survey of the city's demographic, religious, industrial and social conditions. In a book detailing its findings—*The Challenge of Pittsburgh*—Methodist pastor Daniel Marsh exhorted Christians to transform the metropolis into a "city of God" where individual and social righteousness flourished.[30] Shoemaker did the most to popularize this slogan, and he created two influential organizations to help promote it.

My first chapter analyzes the impressive efforts of Pittsburgh Christians to reform social ills between 1900 and 1930. The second and third chapters appraise the history of Pittsburgh's Catholics and African American Christians, respectively. The fourth chapter assesses Shoemaker's vision and ministry and the creation and accomplishments of the Pittsburgh Experiment, the Pittsburgh Offensive and the Pittsburgh Leadership Foundation. The fifth and sixth chapters describe the work of four exceptional parachurch organizations: the Coalition for Christian Outreach, the Urban Impact Foundation, the Light of Life Rescue Mission and The Pittsburgh Project.

The seventh, eighth and ninth chapters profile nine of the city's most influential congregations, primarily those that today have large numbers of parishioners and a significant impact: First Presbyterian Church, Calvary Episcopal Church, St. Paul Cathedral (the mother church of the Diocese of Pittsburgh), North Way Christian Community, Allegheny Center Alliance Church, The Bible Chapel, Victory Family Church, Mount Ararat Baptist Church and Macedonia Baptist Church. One of these churches is located downtown (First Presbyterian), two in East Liberty (Calvary and Mount Ararat), one on the North Side (Allegheny Center), one in Oakland (St. Paul), one in the Hill District (Macedonia) and one in the North Hills (Victory), while two congregations have campuses in several locations in the Pittsburgh area (North Way and The Bible Chapel). Four are nondenominational, two are Baptist and one each is Presbyterian, Episcopal, Catholic and Christian and Missionary Alliance. Mount Ararat and Macedonia are predominantly African American. Collectively, they provide a good snapshot of the vibrancy and impact of Christianity in Pittsburgh today.

The tenth, eleventh and twelfth chapters discuss a sizable number of Christian Pirates, Steelers and Penguins who have been vocal about their faith. The Pirates have been hosting a "Faith Night" after a game each year since 2013 at which thousands of fans have heard the testimonies of various players. Since the 1970s, many Christians have coached or played for the Pirates, Steelers and Penguins, most notably Pirates manager Clint Hurdle, Andrew McCutchen, Mark Melancon, Neil Walker, Jay Bell, Sid Bream, Steelers head coach Mike Tomlin, Jon Kolb, Donnie Shell, Mel Blount, Terry Bradshaw, Tunch Ilkin, Antwaan Randle El, Jeff Hartings, Troy Polamalu, Ben Roethlisberger, Penguins head coach Dan Bylsma, Jordan Stahl, Matt Cullen, Eric Fehr and Matt Cooke. The concluding chapter assesses the results of the crusade to make Pittsburgh as famous for God as for steel.

Reading widely, combing through archives, visiting churches and parachurch organizations and interviewing numerous pastors, parachurch leaders, sports chaplains and athletes has enabled me to tell this exciting, inspiring story of Christianity in Pittsburgh. As I was completing this book, I learned that Bruce Barron, a scholar in American religion who has lived in Pittsburgh for more than thirty years, was writing a book titled *Famous for God: Great Christian Endeavors in Pittsburgh, 1952–2018*. While his book covers four of the topics I do—Samuel Shoemaker, the Pittsburgh Leadership Foundation, the Pittsburgh Steelers and North Way Christian Community—it focuses on different aspects of their lives and ministries. The two books complement each other and enrich our understanding of Christianity in twentieth- and twenty-first-century Pittsburgh.

CHAPTER I

PITTSBURGH AND THE SOCIAL GOSPEL, 1900–1930

Jesus moves to save the city, and to rights its many wrongs;
Purifying individuals, and uplifting throbbing throngs.
And His march is one of triumph, let us join the Victor's songs
For Pittsburgh shall be saved
—Daniel Marsh, "He Beheld the City," 1914[1]

The first quarter of the twentieth century was an "age of crusades," characterized by numerous noble causes and "unusual moral idealism." Inspired by their belief that "God wills it," millions of Americans strove to pass Prohibition, promote world peace, reform society or win "the world for Christ in this Generation."[2] During these years, Christians and Jews played key roles in Progressive campaigns to purify politics, make government more representative and responsive and improve industrial conditions, schools and social services. They also helped lead efforts to alleviate poverty; reduce prostitution, drunkenness and crime; provide better housing, sanitation and medical facilities; furnish more parks and playgrounds; and construct a more just society. While scholars have closely examined how residents of New York City, Chicago, Boston, Philadelphia, Columbus and Rochester strove to reform their cities, little attention has been paid to the quest of Pittsburghers to achieve similar goals.[3] Moreover, studies of Pittsburgh have often falsely assumed that its Protestants protected the city's robber barons while ignoring their victims who endured long hours and horrible working conditions in the mills and abysmal living accommodations in immigrant hovels. Although most Pittsburgh-area clergy and churchgoers did not openly confront the ruling capitalist class, many of them worked to alleviate the suffering of immigrants, African Americans and other working-class residents of the city.[4]

Through two interdenominational bodies, the Christian Social Service Union and the Pittsburgh Council of Churches; numerous organizations, most notably the Methodist Episcopal Church Union, Pittsburgh Presbytery and the Lutheran Intermission; and the ministries of various Methodist, Presbyterian, United Presbyterian, Baptist, Episcopal, Lutheran and Catholic congregations, thousands of Pittsburghers worked energetically to remedy the city's social ills. Keith Zahniser argued that reformers wanted to demolish "the growing profitability of the saloon, the brothel, and corrupt politics because this alliance was ruining lives" and preventing Pittsburgh from becoming "more like the Kingdom of God."[5] The city's religious groups founded several social settlements (most notably Kingsley House, the Irene Kaufmann Settlement and Morgan Community House), rescue missions and community centers to aid newcomers and the indigent. Protestants joined forces to evangelize to city residents and ameliorate social conditions through a crusade called the "Challenge of Pittsburgh." They established a morals court to redirect youthful offenders and adjudicate cases dealing with moral issues. From 1900 to 1930, thousands of Pittsburghers significantly improved spiritual, social and material life as they strove to create a "city of God."[6]

As the twentieth century dawned, Pittsburgh was America's "great industrial capital"; "the home of magnificent schools, museums, literature, art and music"; a "pious, church going city"; and the nation's center of "staunch, uncompromising Presbyterianism."[7] Nevertheless, Pittsburgh's social problems were plentiful. While the Pirates won their third consecutive National League Championship in 1903, critics vilified the city as a human and physical inferno. Many maligned Pittsburgh as the city of smoke, purportedly controlled by corrupt politicians, filled with callous millionaires and totally bereft of culture.[8] Nationally known journalist H.L. Mencken lampooned Pittsburgh as "one great forest of smokestacks, one solid gob of grime" inhabited by "a wretched and degraded proletariat."[9] Other commentators accentuated the sharp contrast between the conspicuous consumption of the city's elites and the grinding poverty of its manual laborers. In *The Shame of the Cities* (1904), muckraker Lincoln Steffens called Pittsburgh "A City Ashamed" because its millionaire industrialists had formed a corrupt alliance with the Republican machine to further their interests.[10]

In 1908, when Pittsburgh celebrated its 150th birthday, it was the nation's sixth-largest metropolitan area, with a population of 521,000 (Allegheny County had a population of about 1 million). That year, a major survey of its social conditions was completed. Financed by the Russell Sage Foundation and conducted by some of America's most respected social welfare specialists, the Pittsburgh Survey filled six fat volumes published between 1909 and 1914. The study documented the city's widespread political corruption, abominable housing, rampant disease and dangerous working conditions.[11] The survey's authors decried the low wages of millworkers and the destruction of their families caused by disease, the excessive demands of work and industrial accidents that killed and crippled thousands.[12] Its labor unrest, widespread poverty, ethnic stratification, poor sanitation, dilapidated housing and high death rates from infectious diseases, smog, grime and crime made Pittsburgh ripe for reform.

Investigators criticized the response of Pittsburgh's religious communities to these problems. John Fitch complained that the preoccupation of the city's clergy with preserving the sanctity of the Sabbath and reducing drunkenness and crime kept them from working to improve industrial and social conditions. Pittsburgh religious leaders enforced Sabbath and liquor laws more strenuously than any other American city, Robert Woods protested, but they ignored the "appalling" amount of Sunday work in steel mills. Pittsburgh's churches had a "large, devout [and] loyal" following, but they were "not a conquering army of righteousness." Echoing these criticisms, historian Linda Pritchard argued that for most clergy, "curbing drinking, dancing, and other personal vices" took priority over eliminating "crowded and filthy housing," abolishing child labor or working to provide livable wages.[13] Keith Zahniser countered that Calvary Episcopal Church, Christ Methodist Church and numerous other Pittsburgh congregations had long striven to limit working hours, end municipal corruption, improve housing conditions and provide clean water.[14] While numerous elites and middle-class suburbanites, including some Christians, saw neighborhoods with high concentrations of African Americans, Russian Jews, Hungarians, Poles, Croatians and Italians as beyond redemption because of their dirt, vice, domination by political machines and alien religiosity, other Christians sympathized with their problems and labored to alleviate them.[15]

Two decades after the Pittsburgh Survey was conducted, Fred B. Smith, an internationally known social reformer, declared that the leaders of the Federal Council of Churches viewed Pittsburgh as a "laboratory of interchurch community work." Pittsburgh's "powerful church forces," he trumpeted, worked diligently to remedy problems that were merely discussed in other cities. Council executives closely watched what Pittsburgh's religious agencies did and then tried to copy their methods and programs in other cities.[16] Smith's testimony affirmed that in the twenty years following the survey's completion, Pittsburgh's religious forces waged an extensive campaign to improve the social and material conditions of their region.

In this crusade, the Christian Social Service Union (founded in 1913), the Pittsburgh Council of Churches (which began in 1917) and the "Challenge of Pittsburgh," an interdenominational, county-wide initiative conducted in 1917, played a principal role. Also very important were the social ministries of various denominations and congregations. The four Pittsburghers who did the most to support the survey's work—William Matthews and three Episcopalians, H.D.W. English, George Guthrie and Joseph Buffington—were staunchly committed Christians; they also led efforts to combat the Steel City's social ills. Matthews was the director of Kingsley House. Founded by Calvary Episcopal Church rector George Hodges in 1893 in the Hill District, Kingsley House furnished clubs and classes for youth, cooking and parenting classes for mothers and a playground, library, lectures and movies for neighborhood residents. Matthews took pictures to publicize the abysmal accommodations in numerous city neighborhoods, spoke at dozens of clubs and churches and brought in famed author and photographer Jacob Riis to help improve the city's housing and health.[17]

English was the manager of an insurance company, the president of the Pittsburgh Chamber of Commerce, the chair of the city's Civic Commission and the vice-president of both the Voters' League and the National Housing Association. He served as the warden of Calvary Episcopal Church for twenty-nine years, chaired the Social Service Commission of the Pittsburgh Council of Churches and the Episcopal Diocese of Pittsburgh's Commission on Social Service and was president of the Allegheny County Sunday School Association. In 1922, the *Pittsburgh Christian Outlook* called him a "champion of the application of the principles of Jesus" to "economic and industrial problems" who combined "large business interests" and "wide civic influence with earnest devotion to the Church and the Kingdom of God."[18]

Attorney George Guthrie was also a member of what some Pittsburgh politicians derisively labeled the "damned Calvary crowd."[19] As the city's mayor from 1906 to 1909, Guthrie cleansed politics, instituted civil service exams for employees and instituted other reforms. He created the Pittsburgh Civic Commission to help remedy such problems as industrial accidents, substandard housing, inadequate education, an ineffective judicial system and deficient public hygiene and sanitation.[20] A third Calvary member, Joseph Buffington, who spent thirty-two years as a circuit court judge, served as the president of the Kingsley House Association and on several other reform commissions and organizational boards.[21]

The Christian Social Service Union

Pittsburgh's Protestants created the Christian Social Service Union in 1913 to carry on work initiated by the Men and Religion Forward Movement the previous year. The MRFM sponsored eight-day campaigns in seventy-five North American cities in 1911 and 1912 to promote evangelism and social action and to motivate men to play a larger role in churches.[22] The Pittsburgh campaign inspired many participants to combine their resources to remedy their city's problems. Its organizers persuaded almost four hundred ministers to preach on the theme of social service on one Sunday in December 1911. The MRFM campaign increased the social activism of many congregations and inspired the creation of the CSSU.[23] The CSSU's roots lay in the Pittsburgh Ministerial Union, formed in 1900 to abate the liquor traffic, eradicate prostitution and political corruption, alleviate poverty and assist the homeless and addicted.

The CSSU was established by more than four hundred Pittsburgh-area congregations belonging to fourteen different denominations, which had a combined membership of about 150,000.[24] Its leaders were some of the city's most prominent laymen (English, United Presbyterian judge James Gray and Methodist businessman H.G. Samson) and some of its most respected ministers (W.E. McCulloch, pastor of the Homewood United Presbyterian Church, and Presbyterian Charles Zahniser, the CSSU's general secretary). To redeem Pittsburgh, the Union created six departments: publicity, social education, surveys, social purity, civics and legislation and industrial relations. Its members partnered with the Ministerial Union to close saloons, abolish brothels and reduce graft and poverty. They also encouraged Christians to vote; supplied information about candidates and issues; strove to improve the police force, the city council, judges and juries; and persuaded the mayor to appoint a morals bureau to combat vice.[25]

In addition, the CSSU published a newspaper to educate Pittsburghers about social ills, conducted social surveys and sought to develop close relationships between the city's religious and labor leaders. Its members promoted "social evangelism" through preaching sermons, teaching Sunday school lessons and offering special courses in congregations, including a three-month course in "Bible Studies in Social Christianity" based on Zahniser's *Social Christianity* (1911). Although commercialized vice continued to plague Pittsburgh, the Union enabled Protestants to combine their human resources to alleviate social ills and paved the way for a more enduring and influential organization.[26]

The Pittsburgh Council of Churches

The Pittsburgh Council of Churches began its work in 1917 when the CSSU merged with two other interdenominational enterprises—the Evangelism Committee, which had been sponsoring revivals in the city since 1904, and the City Missions Council, established in 1914 to coordinate Protestant efforts to minister to recently arrived southern blacks and European immigrants. By 1919, the council represented thirteen denominations, which included 83 percent of Allegheny County's Protestants.[27] The council sponsored evangelistic campaigns and strove to strengthen the evangelistic programs of individual congregations. It also enabled the county's Protestants to speak more powerfully about Pittsburgh's moral, social and civic problems.[28]

The council's Social Service Commission established committees on education, public morals, legislation, civic action and industrial relations. During the next twelve years, English, James Gray, Harry Samson, W.E. McCulloch, Church of the Brethren educator Carman Johnson and Ambrose Hering, the head of the Lutheran Inner Mission of Pittsburgh, led the commission's many endeavors.[29] In 1918, English challenged Christians to mobilize "spiritual and social resources" to remedy Pittsburgh's civic and moral problems and make it "a city set upon a hill." To accomplish this objective, they must provide a "righteous minimum standard of living" and job security for manual laborers, improve housing and working conditions, make "Christian principles dominant in politics" and reduce vice, intoxication and gambling.[30] By 1926, the Council of Churches had helped to significantly improve management-labor relations, industrial conditions, housing and recreational facilities; supply care better for delinquents and dependent youth; reform municipal politics and courts; and establish ministries to assist African Americans and eastern European newcomers.[31]

Soon after it was founded, the Council of Churches undertook a major study of industrial, social, moral, material and religious conditions in Allegheny and adjacent counties. Led by Daniel Marsh, pastor of the Smithfield Methodist Episcopal Church and superintendent of the Methodist Episcopal Church Union, the organizers published *The Challenge of Pittsburgh* in the fall of 1917 to "lay the foundation-stones" for a new city.[32] Marsh envisioned what Jesus would observe and say about Pittsburgh if he visited. Boosters would emphasize that the city led the world in manufacturing steel, glass, aluminum, pickles, preserves and other products. They would stress Pittsburgh's flourishing educational, social, artistic and religious institutions. Boosters would *not* point out, however, the low wages of the working class, the unchristian principles underlying the city's industries, the city's wretched housing or its 1,256 retail establishments that sold intoxicating beverages. Seeing the incongruity between Pittsburgh's phenomenal wealth and its numerous social and moral ills, Jesus would exhort residents to repent and care for the victimized and vulnerable. If Pittsburghers did not work zealously to eliminate the city's "unchristian social conditions," the book warned, God would punish them.[33]

The Challenge of Pittsburgh lamented that the city's ethnic communities had to endure overcrowding, low wages and discrimination. Authors urged Christians to implement the 1912 Federal Council of Churches' "Social Creed" to help improve their quality of life. They stressed people's right to have a job, protecting workers from industrial accidents and occupational diseases and abolishing child labor. Council leaders called for using conciliation and arbitration to settle industrial disputes, applying Christian principles in acquiring and using property, dividing the products of industry more equitably and reducing the hours of manual laborers. The poor, the authors protested, were 65 percent of Pittsburgh's population but had only 5 percent of its wealth.[34]

The book denounced the "brutalizing poverty" that forced many to "go hungry and wear shabby clothes," robbed them of dignity and caused them to "feel discouraged, bitter [and] hopeless." Its authors challenged Christians to build relationships with the destitute, provide more affordable housing, care for convalescents and reduce communicable diseases.[35] Thankfully, they noted, the city's congregations and their many allies—the public schools, the Civic Club, the Associated Charities of Pittsburgh, the YMCA, the YWCA and the Allegheny County Sabbath School Association—had substantial resources to accomplish these aims.[36]

The authors asserted that Pittsburgh could be transformed into the city of God only if believers promoted both aspects of "true Christianity": prayer and worship and service to humanity. Christ's method for transforming society was to redeem individuals and use them to change institutions. Society could be reformed only as individuals experienced "a thorough" personal conversion and then attacked the causes, not the symptoms, of social ills.[37]

To inspire Christians to make Pittsburgh "a city of the great King," the council formed forty-five district committees, each composed of one minister and one representative of the Allegheny County Sabbath School Association, the Women's Home Missionary Union and the Young Peoples' Societies of these districts. The council used seminars, sermons and eight-week courses to train and motivate Allegheny County Protestants to implement the campaign's agenda.[38]

The response to *The Challenge of Pittsburgh* was enthusiastic. Many newspaper articles discussed the campaign, and numerous religious and civic leaders praised the book. Hundreds of sermons discussed the book's themes, and many Sunday school classes, youth groups and women's circles studied its topics. Its popularity led the editors of the *National Liquor Dealers' Journal* to denounce the book and exhort its constituency to vigorously combat the "Rev. Daniel Marshes of the country."[39]

During the next decade, the council worked diligently to achieve the campaign's reform agenda. In the early 1920s, the council worked vigorously to ensure that Prohibition laws were strictly enforced. Council leaders argued that excessive drinking contributed to the poverty, unemployment, sickness and crime afflicting many workers and recent immigrants. In 1923, hundreds of Pittsburghers demanded that state senators and representatives pass a prohibition enforcement law Governor Gifford Pinchot submitted to them. They deplored the "open and notorious bootlegging and illegal use of liquor" in their city, resulting in "bribery and corruption of public officials," "tampering with juries" and widespread disobedience to the law.[40] The council also strove to educate citizens about political issues and equip them to vote intelligently. During the "Red Scare" of 1920, the council adopted a "Statement on Civil Liberties" to oppose "any legislation, rules, regulations, or executive action" that curtailed "the fundamental rights" of freedom of speech, press, assembly and worship. Council leaders frequently tried to influence the Pennsylvania legislature, opposing bills to authorize gambling on boxing matches and supporting bills to restrict prostitution and give laborers a day of rest every week.[41]

The council also worked to end the exploitation of factory and millworkers. From September 22, 1919, until January 7, 1920, more than 300,000 steelworkers—most of whom resided in Pittsburgh—went on strike to protest the industry's twelve-hour days and seven-day weeks, low pay and refusal to acknowledge labor unions. The council formed a committee to investigate the competing claims of U.S. Steel and its employees, educate the public about the issues involved and ensure that the workers received a fair hearing. Council leaders also supported efforts to prevent union meetings from being shut down, strikes from being prohibited and public opinion from being manipulated to favor owners.[42]

The Council of Churches' most significant accomplishment during its first decade, in the judgment of Charles Zahniser, who served as the organization's executive secretary from 1917 to 1929, was persuading the city to establish a Morals Court to adjudicate all cases involving offenders under age twenty-one, female offenders, crimes of a sexual nature and almost all domestic relations cases. Before the founding of this court, the city had to either incarcerate the nearly five thousand youth arrested each year for minor crimes or reprimand and return them to their original surroundings.[43] Both dispositions were harmful, argued Judge Tensard De Wolf, because the typical jail or reform school in Pittsburgh taught youth to be professional criminals, while youth who were merely admonished received no help in coping with their adverse circumstances or changing their behavior or peer groups.[44] The Morals Court, by contrast, strove to offer offenders a second chance and worked to transform environments that had "overpowered them." De Wolf sought to eliminate the causes of crime: dysfunctional families, negative peer influences, deviant subcultures, lack of recreational opportunities and improperly directed youthful energies. To accomplish this objective, he partnered with social workers to assess why youth had committed crimes and devise a course of action to reorient their lives. Many youthful offenders were assigned "big brothers" or "big sisters" who belonged to hundreds of Pittsburgh congregations to counsel them, supervise their activities and help them improve their behavior. These mentors took their wards to movies and baseball games and brought them into their own homes. They visited their residences, helped them find jobs, brought them to church and monitored their compliance with the schooling, work and daily conduct requirements the court mandated.[45]

Unfortunately, many youthful offenders still eventually ended up in criminal courts, reformatories and prisons. Nevertheless, the Morals Court did help redirect hundreds of troubled and delinquent youth. Its work, rejoiced De Wolf's successor, Judge A.D. Brandon, was conducted entirely by church members who took Christ's words literally: "I was in prison and ye visited me."[46] The *Literary Digest* reported that during its first six years of operation, the number of male offenders under age twenty-one who appeared before the court declined from 6,000 to 2,500. An investigator from *Harper's Magazine* concluded that the court was helping to instill "a social conscience that may spread to other cities."[47]

The Council of Churches engaged in many other enterprises. It sponsored several surveys of social, economic and religious conditions to assess the needs of various neighborhoods and groups and devise programs to aid them. The council created a room registry in 1917 to help people find "respectable and reliable accommodations." It developed a system to ensure that all patients at city hospitals received a visit from either a pastor or layperson who shared their religious affiliation and lobbied for prison reform.[48]

In 1920, the council created a Department of Women's Work to expand its ministry, coordinate the community service provided by women's organizations of local congregations and oversee the Morals Court's work with female offenders. Its members strove to convince women to register to vote and improve the city's moral climate to enable "good homes, active churches, and uplifting schools" to flourish. Before, during and after the Progressive era, the women's auxiliaries of many congregations made gifts for destitute children and raised money to provide food, clothing and medicine for the indigent.[49]

The council deplored the overcrowded and unsanitary accommodations that many southern blacks who had migrated to Pittsburgh to find jobs were forced to occupy, and it urged the city to help provide more moderately priced houses they could rent or buy. The council called for giving African Americans more job training and employment opportunities and allowing them to join labor unions and vote.[50] Three major enterprises that aided African Americans during the 1910s and 1920s were the Provident Rescue Mission, the Centre Avenue Branch of the YMCA and the Morgan Community House. Founded in 1914, the mission provided temporary accommodations for black men and tried to help them obtain jobs. By the early 1920s, it housed forty-eight men at a time, aided about four hundred men per month and helped hundreds of men procure employment each year. The YMCA, located in the Hill District where sixteen thousand of the city's thirty-eight thousand African Americans lived in 1920, furnished numerous social and religious services. By the early 1920s, Morgan Community House operated a kindergarten, a nursery school and a medical clinic and provided free legal services, clubs for boys and girls and classes in dressmaking, first aid and automotive repair.[51]

During its first decade, the council compiled "an impressive record of voluntary service and reform advocacy."[52] Two other organizations led by Christians labored arduously to improve life in Pittsburgh: the Civic Club and the Voters' League. The Civic Club strove to abolish child labor and improve housing, established a Legal Aid Society to assist low-income Pittsburghers and helped build parks and playgrounds. The Voters' League worked to curb corruption in the Pittsburgh City Council and improve the council's structure and efficiency.[53]

Denominational Associations and Congregations

Between 1910 and 1926, numerous congregations also worked individually or through their denominational associations to improve social conditions. In 1880, the Methodist Episcopal Church Union was formed to devise cooperative evangelistic, home missions and social service programs. Under Daniel Marsh's energetic leadership from 1913 to 1926, the Union expanded its ministries to help win "Pittsburgh for Christ."[54] By 1926, the Union, composed of 103 congregations, was operating the Pittsburgh branch of Goodwill Industries; a children's home; missions to Poles, Italians and African Americans; four social settlements; and a rescue mission. It was also conducting extensive programs in evangelism, church planting and hospital visitation. The Union employed 90 people to run its programs, and its periodical, the *Pittsburgh Methodist*, had a circulation of 14,500. Goodwill Industries restored and refurbished furniture, clothing, shoes and other items and sold them at low prices throughout the city. Goodwill Industries provided temporary jobs for the downtrodden and permanent ones for widows, the disabled and the elderly and enrolled 1,200 individuals in sixty-three clubs or classes in 1924. At Trinity Temple in the Strip District, Smithfield Street Church in the downtown area and Calvary Community House on the North Side, Methodists provided classes for immigrants and the impoverished, sponsored clubs, provided recreational facilities and operated a baby clinic.[55]

Most of the ministers and members of the Presbyterian Church (USA), Pittsburgh's largest and most prominent Protestant denomination, prioritized evangelism over social service. The fact that Presbyterians controlled about

75 percent of Pittsburgh industry in the 1910s and owned many other businesses in the city undoubtedly contributed to the conservative approach most PCUSA pastors took toward social issues. In 1915, Pittsburgh Presbytery created three committees—Sabbath, Temperance and Public Morals; Work for Men; and the Church and Social Problems—to address social issues.[56] The social programs Pittsburgh Presbyterians conducted during the first quarter of the twentieth century—most notably their Presbyterian Missionary Training School; their ministry in more than ten languages in hospitals, jails and immigrant communities; and the Market Street Mission that aided the poor and homeless—all contained a strong evangelistic component. Led by Maitland Alexander, Hugh Thompson Kerr and Peter Snyder, First, Shadyside and Homestead Presbyterian Churches, respectively, sponsored many social ministries. Under Alexander's leadership from 1899 to 1927, First Presbyterian provided industrial training for boys and sewing and millinery classes for girls, a nursery, a club for adolescent girls who worked at nearby retail outlets, a gymnasium for exercise and recreation and a job placement program. The author of many books, Kerr served Shadyside from 1913 to 1945 and oversaw its ministries to the impoverished through mission churches it established in McKees Rocks and the South Side. Snyder, who pastored the Homestead church from 1905 to 1921, created the "most ambitious" institutional church (one that provided a wide variety of social programs and services) in Pittsburgh. Presbyterians advanced education and medicine in the city by founding the Pennsylvania College for Women (later Chatham College) in 1869, Shady Side Academy in 1883 and Presbyterian Hospital in 1894.[57]

Many adherents of the United Presbyterian Church of North America (UPCNA) were very active social reformers. In 1920, about 25 percent of the denomination's 130,000 members lived in Allegheny County. Hundreds of articles and editorials in the UPCNA's weekly newspaper exhorted congregations and members to combat intemperance, municipal corruption and poverty; improve the workplace; and support labor unions.[58] United Presbyterians founded a home for the aged and a hospital in Wilkinsburg and an orphanage on the North Side and ministered to immigrants throughout the city. In 1917, First UPC on the North Side opened a six-story community house that featured a large gymnasium, a swimming pool, bowling alleys, a rooftop playground and a dining room and sponsored lectures, concerts, classes and clubs for adults and youth.[59]

Pittsburgh's Baptists also worked energetically to reform the Steel City. Baptists founded a residence for the elderly, a children's home and Provident

Mission to aid African Americans. They established fifteen missions to assist non-English-speaking immigrants.[60] Their most significant social ministry was the Rankin Christian Center, which opened in 1923 to meet the physical, social and religious needs of the community's 7,300 residents who did not have a single park, playground, ball field, public library or lyceum. To give Christ "a commanding place in the life of the individual, the home and the community" and to regenerate all life, the center operated a chapel, a gymnasium, baths, club rooms, a nursery, a kindergarten, a free medical clinic, a library and a playground.[61] First Baptist Church, the denomination's principal institutional church in Pittsburgh, offered its parishioners numerous opportunities to engage in social service.[62]

Numerous Episcopalians also participated in social ministries. Following in the footsteps of George Hodges, who pastored Calvary Episcopal Church from 1881 to 1894, its rectors during the Progressive years, W.D. Maxon and James McIlvaine, inspired many parishioners to promote social reform. McIlvaine belonged to the Civic Club and the Pittsburgh Civic Commission. The significant contributions of four Calvary members—H.D.W. English, George Guthrie, Joseph Buffington and Tensard De Wolf—have already been discussed. Five others—attorneys Edwin Smith, George Wallace, Congressman James Brown, manufacturer Reuben Miller and businessman H. Kirke Porter—were also prominent social activists. Moreover, Calvary laypeople constituted almost 20 percent of the initial membership of the Voters' League, and nine of them belonged to the Civic Club.[63] Pittsburgh Episcopalians founded the Saint Margaret Memorial Hospital in 1898 and the Saint Barnabas Free Home to care for convalescent and incurably ill men and boys in 1900.

Although Lutherans did not belong to the Pittsburgh Council of Churches, many of their members also worked to combat the city's social evils. The county's more than one hundred Lutheran congregations founded many institutions to meet people's physical and social needs, including Passavant Hospital in the Hill District, a downtown hospice for young women, a community house, four residences for orphaned and neglected children and three facilities for the aged. The Lutheran Inner Mission, established in 1907, aided Lutherans who moved to urban areas, strove to reform offenders and provided pastoral care and lay visitation to residents of correctional and charitable institutions. The mission created a training school to prepare laypeople to engage more effectively in evangelism, Christian education and social ministry.[64]

Conclusion

Christian and Jewish businessmen, professionals and civic reformers played a key role in founding, shaping and carrying out the mission of the Christian Social Service Union, the Pittsburgh Council of Churches, the Federation of Jewish Philanthropies and other agencies that ministered to immigrants, African Americans and the destitute. Although these individuals and their clergy colleagues wanted to increase economic productivity, improve Pittsburgh's public image, elevate morality and inhibit social protest, most of them were staunchly committed to their faith and cared deeply about people's spiritual, physical and material welfare. Few of them defined well-being as members of the working class did, but both groups strove to improve industrial conditions, housing, health, civic affairs and social institutions. The city's religious forces did not eradicate Pittsburgh's political corruption, prostitution, poverty, racial discrimination or abuse of alcohol, but they did diminish these social ills. In 1890, few Pittsburgh congregations made upgrading the city's physical, social and environmental conditions a priority, and efforts to help the poor and provide justice for workers were limited and uncoordinated. By 1920, all Protestant denominations had joined forces to combat the city's social ills, especially aiding the impoverished.[65] Although Christians did not "redeem" Pittsburgh through their civic reforms, church programs and community outreach, they made it a better place to live, work and raise families. Weathering the challenges of World War I, the 1919 Steel Strike and the fundamentalist-modernist controversy, they also established "patterns and precedents that came to fruition in later generations."[66] Their commitment to Christ and efforts to help the "least of these" and make Pittsburgh known for God were impressive.

Chapter 2

CATHOLICISM IN PITTSBURGH

"A CHURCH ALIVE"

For Pittsburgh, faith is a very big thing. God isn't on the back burner.
—David Zubik, bishop of the Diocese of Pittsburgh, 2010[1]

The history of Catholicism in Pittsburgh is multifaceted, complex and rich. Jesuit Joseph Bonnechamps is believed to have celebrated the first Mass in Western Pennsylvania when he accompanied French Canadian explorer Pierre-Joseph Céloron de Blainville to the area in 1749.[2] Franciscan friar Denys Baron established the region's first Catholic church in the 1750s at the Point where the Allegheny and the Monongahela join to form the Ohio River; he ministered to French soldiers at Fort Duquesne, Native Americans and people of Irish and English descent. Pittsburgh's first Catholic parish, St. Patrick's, opened in the Strip District in 1808, and the Sisters of St. Clare founded the first Catholic school in 1828 on the North Side.

By 1843, the large number of Catholics in the Pittsburgh region led to the establishment of the Diocese of Pittsburgh.[3] St. Paul Church, which had opened in 1834 at the corner of Grant Street and Fifth Avenue, was named the Cathedral Church. It was destroyed by a fire in 1851 and rebuilt at great expense in 1855. The difficulty of paying the debt incurred in constructing the church and the area's significantly rising property values prompted Bishop Richard Phelan to sell the property to industrialist Henry Clay Frick in 1901 for $1,325,000. The new Cathedral Church—St. Paul Cathedral, a large Gothic Revival structure in Oakland designed by Chicago architects James Egan and Charles Prindeville and costing $1.1 million—opened in 1906.[4]

Pittsburgh's Catholics, like their coreligionists across the country, clashed with Protestants during the 1850s over temperance legislation, Sunday closing laws and the curriculum of public schools. Protestants, especially ones who supported the Know-Nothing Party, discriminated against Catholics. In the 1850s, Pittsburgh's Republicans shared an evangelical worldview that "collided with the distinctly ritualistic or liturgical mindset of the city's Catholic voters." Efforts to make public schools more explicitly Protestant prompted the city's Catholics to create parochial schools to preserve their values.[5]

The diocese faced many challenges in the Gilded Age as thousands of Catholics from Central and eastern Europe poured into Pittsburgh looking for jobs in the steel mills, factories and shops to improve their lives. Ethnic and labor strife was commonplace, anti-Catholicism continued and poverty was pervasive. During these years, the diocese worked diligently to construct parishes and schools, help newcomers adjust to life in America and strengthen its position in Pittsburgh.

From 1904 to 1921, J.F. Regis Canevin, the first native son and the first American-born priest to serve as the diocese's bishop, strove energetically to improve spiritual and material conditions in the Pittsburgh region. He fortified the finances of Catholic institutions by raising large sums to endow Duquesne University, which was established by the Congregation of the Holy Spirit in 1878, and to fund Catholic Charities, which began during his tenure.[6]

Since the 1870s, Pittsburgh has been the home to a diverse group of Catholics. St. Paul of the Cross Monastery is the American headquarters of the Passionist religious order, whose members have been in Pittsburgh since 1852. The first Polish Catholic church in Pittsburgh, St. Stanislaus Kostka Church, founded in 1875 in the Strip District, grew rapidly. By 1920, 125,000 Polish Catholics lived in Pittsburgh, which had the third-largest number of Poles of any American city. Italians, Slovaks, Croatians, Carpatho-Russians and Ukrainians who came in droves to work in Pittsburgh's industries in the late nineteenth and early twentieth centuries also established their own ethnic Catholic churches. By 1930, more than 100,000 Slovaks had settled in the Pittsburgh area, making it the country's chief Slovak enclave. About 225,000 Croatians and Slovenes migrated to steel-producing towns in Pennsylvania in the 1910s and 1920s, and Pittsburgh became known as Croatia's "Second City" and Slovenia's American capital.[7] Moreover, by this date, Italians constituted 8 percent of Pittsburgh's population. In addition, Pittsburgh has served as the seat of the Byzantine Rite Catholic Church since Czech immigrants organized St. John the Baptist Church in 1890 on the South Side. By 1920, Pittsburgh was one of the principal centers for non–Roman Catholic parishes in the nation. The archeparchy operates Byzantine Catholic Seminary of Saints Cyril and Methodius on the North Side, which educates priests for all Byzantine Rite Catholic eparchies in North America.

The influx of immigrants from eastern Europe more than doubled the number of Catholics in Allegheny County between 1900 and 1930, from 280,000 to 581,000. Priests and nuns kept pace, also more than doubling to 3,920. By 1910, Catholics outnumbered Protestants in Pittsburgh, although Protestants had substantially greater wealth and social status. Between 1904 and 1921, Catholics established 204 new congregations, an average of one per month.[8] The Slavs (the collective name for all the ethnic groups from eastern and southern Europe) were more religiously devout than Catholic immigrants from western Europe who came prior to World War I, and the Catholic Church strove to strengthen their faith by providing spiritual nurturing, religious education and wholesome recreational activities. Hugh Boyle, who served as the diocese's bishop from 1921 until 1951, sought to renew Italians' ties to the Catholic Church by recruiting Italian-speaking priests, and under his leadership, the diocese opened 58 new parochial schools. Most of these Catholic groups lived in "segregated ethnic enclaves, worshipped in their own congregations and married within their religious and cultural groups."[9]

From 1900 to 1930, many Catholics worked diligently to supply the spiritual, social, physical and material needs of Pittsburghers and to improve the city's living and working conditions. Polish and Italian congregations served as social centers, charity agencies and employment bureaus, and they offered classes in English, cooking, sewing and industrial skills. At Sacred Heart Parish in Shadyside and many other congregations, Catholics cared for children, fed and clothed the indigent, assisted the elderly and strove to prevent evictions, keep families together and arrange adoptions. Many Catholic women engaged in social and charitable projects under the auspices of the Catholic Women's League of Pennsylvania. The city's Catholics founded South Side Hospital, St. Joseph's Hospital and St. Rita's Home for babies. Father Thomas Devlin, who helped establish these three institutions, led Catholic social activism during these years. As the pastor of the Holy Cross Church on the South Side for forty years, superintendent of the Pittsburgh diocesan schools and the organizer of the diocese's Catholic Charities, he directed numerous social ministries and motivated many other Catholics to participate. In December 1914, he partnered with other Christian leaders to organize a "bundle day" that received so much donated clothing that it took one hundred volunteers nearly two weeks to sort and distribute it to the city's impoverished residents. In addition, Devlin cofounded the Allegheny League for Mothers' Assistance. After becoming the pastor of St. Peter's Church on the North Side in 1923, he created an organization to furnish various social services to neighborhood residents. The energetic and enthusiastic priest also worked to combat intemperance and elevate public morality and mediated several labor disputes.[10]

A Catholic New Deal

In 1940, the Pittsburgh Diocese had 662,000 parishioners who belonged to 366 parishes, the diocese was the nation's seventh largest and Pittsburgh Catholics were more ethnically diverse than their counterparts in Boston and New York. When World War II began, 55 percent of the city's Catholics were working class, but many other Pittsburgh Catholics lived in poverty. Working conditions and wages in the steel industry had long been deplorable. A sixty- to seventy-two-hour workweek was typical, industrial accidents occurred frequently and few workers earned enough to provide for their families, forcing many of their children to stop attending school and take jobs to supplement their families' income.

The Great Depression made the plight of steel workers even worse; at its nadir in 1933, Pittsburgh's steel industry was operating at a mere 10 percent of its capacity, 40 percent of the city's steel workers had been laid off and the wages of those who still had jobs had been reduced by 30 to 60 percent. In the 1930s and 1940s, numerous Pittsburgh-area "activist clergy and laity championed a distinctively Catholic vision of social justice," and Pittsburgh became "a hotbed of Democratic politics, industrial unionism, and Catholic social activism."[11]

Motivated by biblical teaching and the unwillingness or inability of politicians and corporate executives to alleviate the suffering of the urban poor, five men led a campaign to improve the lives of Pittsburgh's workers: Father James Cox, Bishop Hugh Boyle, John Collins (the editor of the *Pittsburgh Catholic*), Father Carl Hensler and Father Charles Owen Rice. Cox was a Pittsburgh native who toiled in a steel mill before graduating from Duquesne University and Saint Vincent, the diocese's seminary. He was ordained as a priest in 1911 and served in a hospital on the front during World War I. Following the war, Cox completed an MA in economics at the University of Pittsburgh and was assigned to Old St. Patrick's Church in the Strip District, the diocese's poorest parish, which was surrounded by factories and dingy warehouses. Using innovative methods, including sponsoring plays and boxing matches, Cox rejuvenated the church. From 1930 to 1934, the church's soup kitchen served 2 million meals to the indigent and unemployed and built shelters on its property out of wooden crates to house 250 previously homeless men, earning Cox the title of the "Mayor of Shantytown, Pennsylvania." In January 1932, Cox led 25,000 unemployed men, mostly from the Pittsburgh region, on a march to Washington, D.C., and met with reluctant President Herbert Hoover, whom Cox chastised for ignoring the plight of workers. After returning home, Cox organized a rally that attracted 65,000 city residents to the University of Pittsburgh's football stadium to protest Hoover's policies. In 1932, Cox ran for the presidency as candidate of the Jobless Party to bring "disillusioned, apathetic people back into the political process." He eventually dropped out and campaigned for Franklin Roosevelt, who became the first Democratic candidate to carry Allegheny County since 1856, largely because of the votes of Catholics.[12]

Bishop Boyle staunchly supported Cox's initiatives to aid the poor, effect political change and organize labor unions. He exhorted the diocese's parishioners to give generously to the Catholic Welfare Fund to aid destitute families. On the national level, Boyle championed the cause of organized labor through the auspices of the National Catholic Welfare Conference and exhorted Congress to guarantee workers the right to bargain collectively. Boyle helped organize a Catholic Conference on Industrial Labor in Pittsburgh in 1934, attended by one thousand union, business and church representatives.[13] Boyle also supported the effort of Catholic politicians to procure civil rights and jobs for African Americans.

In numerous articles in the *Pittsburgh Catholic*, Collins urged readers to work to remedy the city's social ills. He also commended Roosevelt's 1934 message to Congress for endorsing several of Pius XI's points in his 1931 encyclical *Reconstructing the Social Order* and pledging to fight "the ruthless exploitation of all labor." In 1936, Collins castigated Republicans for promoting "rugged individualism," greed and other evils that thwarted social justice.[14]

Hensler, the son of a coal miner, grew up in Carnegie, graduated from Saint Vincent Seminary, attended the North American College at Rome and served as an assistant pastor in Braddock from 1924 to 1930. After working for four years in China to establish the Catholic University of Peking, he served as a priest in Lawrenceville. Because 60 percent of Americans did not have enough income to live a healthy life, Hensler argued, society must be restructured.[15] Relief programs, job training and banking reforms, he insisted, were insufficient to give the working poor "a decent livelihood." Moreover, people who worked for years at subsistence wages and then were forced to retire because of disability or infirmity did not have enough savings to cover their basic needs. Therefore, Hensler asserted, businesses, unions and the government must partner to create a pension system to assist them.[16]

Charles Owen Rice, a graduate of Duquesne University and Saint Vincent Seminary, was ordained as a priest in 1934 and served various parishes in the Pittsburgh area for seven decades. Rice, one of America's best-known priests in the 1930s and 1940s, and Hensler exhorted Catholics to vote for candidates who promoted a progressive agenda. In 1937, the two priests—whose commitment to social activism was inspired by both Dorothy Day's Catholic Worker movement and Father John Ryan and the National Catholic Welfare Council—founded a House of Hospitality in the Hill District to support the labor movement and upgrade the morals of the poor; its clientele included unemployed steel workers and alcoholics who had never had a steady job. African Americans and European immigrants lived and ate together; the house served one thousand meals daily and provided beds for 250 men who learned that poverty should not entail degradation. That same year, Rice and Hensler created the Catholic Radical Alliance to devise a just and Christian social order and to teach laypeople how to engage in social action.[17] The combination of the nation's unjust economic system, racial and ethnic discrimination and self-destructive lifestyles, they insisted, produced poverty. Government programs and laws could help reduce the first two causes, but families, churches and communities must work together to change people's attitudes, habits and mores. Rice and Hensler affirmed the principle of subsidiarity championed in *Reconstructing the Social Order*—Catholics should work to build societies that promoted the common good by utilizing the help of every sector of society.[18] The best way to defeat communism, Rice argued, was "by striving tooth and nail for social justice." If American Christians obeyed Christ's teachings on justice and charity, the country would have no Communists.[19]

As they promoted social justice, Pittsburgh Catholics helped increase the membership and strengthen the power of unions. The harshness of the Depression, the high percentage of workers who were Catholics and "the flowering of Catholic social activism in Pittsburgh" led to the founding of the Congress of Industrial Organizations in Pittsburgh in 1936. Philip Murray, an ardent Catholic, established the Steel Workers Organizing Committee in 1936, and he served as president of the CIO from 1940 to 1952. By December 1937, the SWOC had almost 500,000 members who belonged to 1,080 lodges. Many Pittsburgh Catholic leaders endorsed the activities of the SWOC and the CIO. Catholic clerical and lay advocates of social justice, Kenneth Heinemann contended, joined with the Democratic Party and the steel workers union to forge an "Iron City Trinity" to promote the New Deal. This coalition governed more successfully and benevolently in Pittsburgh than in most other cities, and Catholic priests, unions and the Democratic Party were stronger allies in Pittsburgh than in Chicago, Cleveland or any other urban center.[20]

Changes in Catholic Culture and Practices, 1950–70

Many Catholics today, argues historian Timothy Kelly, view the 1950s as a time of "social cohesiveness, family stability, economic expansion, and political consensus in which American Catholics understood and observed clearly defined and widely shared modes of behavior." Many Catholics in Pittsburgh, as in other American cities, however, were concerned about the efforts of Protestants to change them either directly through evangelistic crusades (like the four-week one Billy Graham conducted in the Steel City in 1952) and interfaith marriages or indirectly through cultural norms and customs. Pittsburgh's Catholic hierarchy sought to create a separate culture—a Catholic enclave—where the faithful could avoid both the pressure of Protestant mores and practices and the immorality of the larger secular culture, especially its indecency, sensuality, unrestrained capitalism and commercialism. Catholic officials strove to provide a distinctly Catholic milieu in which parishioners could conduct almost all their activities—"education, health care, marriage, social life, union membership, retirement, and old age care."[21] This parallel culture sought to protect Catholics from the contamination of mainstream culture rather than to try to change it.[22]

To achieve this objective, Bishops Hugh Boyle and John Dearden and *Pittsburgh Catholic* editors John Collins and John Ward staunchly promoted both Catholic social and cultural separatism, including sending children to parochial schools, and Catholic devotionalism. Boyle and Collins also fervently strove to "create a just society based upon the principles of Catholic social teaching." Pittsburgh's diocesan leaders prohibited Catholics from attending Protestant and interfaith services and from marrying Protestants. They also required Catholic parents to educate their offspring at Catholic elementary schools, high schools (the diocese had more than twenty in the 1950s) and colleges.[23]

This quest to create a separate religiously based culture was only moderately successful. Four factors contributed to this outcome: the American suburban emphasis on family activities, the increase in women working outside their homes, the growing social interaction of Catholics and Protestants and the inadequate number of parochial schools. Devotional activities that took individuals away from their spouses or children became less appealing, and working women had less time to participate in them. Consequently, by 1960, far fewer Catholics engaged in "the devotional ethos that had resonated so profoundly for decades." While Masses continued to be packed, the number of attendees of traditional devotional exercises such as novenas, perpetual Eucharistic adorations and group rosary recitations, as well as the Stations of the Cross, declined significantly in the 1950s. One attempt to address this problem was the organization of the Christian Family Movement in 1953. It sought to adapt Catholic devotional activity to the suburban context by focusing on the home and family. By 1959, four hundred couples belonging to twenty-five Pittsburgh-area parishes were participating in the movement. They sought to carefully observe the surrounding culture, analyze it in light of the mind of Christ and conform it more fully to biblical ideals by supporting fair housing and gender equality and promoting international peace and justice.[24]

By 1960, Pittsburgh-area parochial schools did not have nearly enough spaces to accommodate all the children Catholic parents wanted to send them. Moreover, the rationing system established to select children for the schools paid little attention to the religiosity of parents. Parochial schools could not keep up with the growing Catholic population, especially in Pittsburgh's suburbs. In 1951, only three of five suburban Catholic children attended parochial schools, and the percentage declined during the decade. Meanwhile, laypeople largely replaced Catholic priests, brothers and sisters as teachers in parochial schools, reducing their distinctive Catholic perspective on education.[25]

Yet another indicator that, by 1960, many Catholics no longer lived in their own social world was the shift in attitude toward movies. In the 1950s,

Bishops Doyle and Dearden required all Pittsburgh-area Catholics to publicly pledge each year at a December Mass that they would not attend movies the Legion of Decency judged to be immoral. By the late 1950s, however, many Pittsburgh Catholics were confident that they could determine "whether particular films put their souls in danger." This led the Legion to pitch its pledge and guidance as a means of helping Catholics "who might not be sophisticated or savvy enough to resist the dangers mature films posed."[26]

During the 1950s, Catholic leaders also sought to combat three major social problems: the exploitation of workers, "the commercialization of social and cultural interactions" and racial prejudice and discrimination. The Catholic Radical Alliance continued to fight to improve the working conditions and pay of laborers. Catholic officials complained that shopping on Sundays and the commercialization of Christmas and Easter violated biblical teaching and demeaned these major religious holidays. Editor John Deedy used the *Pittsburgh Catholic* to accentuate the discrimination and poverty plaguing the city's black citizens. He exhorted his coreligionists to oppose racial inequality, especially by supporting efforts to pass and enforce fair housing legislation. The Holy Name Society also worked to reduce racial discrimination.[27]

Catholics played a significant political role in Pittsburgh during the 1950s, principally because David Lawrence, an Irish Catholic heir of the New Deal coalition, served as mayor for most of the decade. After World War II, as journalists were penning "obituaries for a polluted, decaying city," he partnered with the Mellon family to create the "Pittsburgh Renaissance." This $632 million project reduced the Steel City's smoke, replaced the downtown's deteriorating warehouses and substandard housing with skyscrapers and condominiums and rejuvenated the city's economy and reputation.[28]

In short, the 1950s were a pivotal decade for Pittsburgh Catholics. To cope with a variety of economic and social changes that threatened traditional Catholic norms and practices, church leaders promoted spiritual development, "a separate Catholic social and cultural world" and social justice. At the beginning of the decade, many Catholic laypeople followed the prescriptions of diocesan officials by participating in church rituals and devotionals, sending their children to parochial schools and working to reduce economic exploitation. By 1960, however, fewer Pittsburgh Catholics engaged in devotional activities, and many more of their children attended public schools. In addition, a higher percentage of Catholics married outside the faith, socialized more frequently with Protestants and saw few problems with the flourishing consumer culture.[29]

Because of Pittsburgh's hills, rivers, ridges and valleys, European ethnic groups often lived together, producing a proliferation of Catholic churches in numerous neighborhoods. This pattern continued in Pittsburgh into the 1960s, decades after it stopped in Detroit, Chicago and many other major cities. For example, Polish, Italian and Slovak churches thrived within neighborhoods that were primarily Irish and German territorial parishes. This ethnic concentration has contributed to Catholic parishes in urban areas often being much larger than most Protestant congregations. The average Catholic parish in Pittsburgh had 1,488 parishioners in 1940, 2,001 in 1951, 2,901 in 1960 and 2,844 in 1980.[30]

Vatican II, held from 1962 to 1965, had a powerful impact on Catholics in Pittsburgh, as it did on many of their coreligionists around the world. Vatican II initiated "a new era in Christian history" and produced a "new Catholicism."[31] As more laypeople became college-educated and middle-class and gained greater social, political and cultural influence, they demanded a more active role in the church, and the reforms of Vatican II were necessary to "keep pace with the laity's changing religious and broader social and cultural sensibilities." Unfortunately, Timothy Kelly argued, church officials did not know how to relate effectively to "a highly educated, confident and increasingly independent laity who wanted" to exercise leadership in their parishes and Catholic organizations. In the 1960s, however, the leaders of the Diocese of Pittsburgh began to recognize that the laity had valuable insights into the church's ministry and started to listen to their opinions instead of simply telling them what to believe and how to behave.[32] Vatican II, Kelly contended, helped create a church that was more responsive to the needs of parishioners and the problems of society. It inspired laypeople in Pittsburgh and other locales to bring their religious convictions "more fully into the public sphere and to let that engagement inform their theology" on race relations, changing gender roles, economic inequality, war and other issues.[33]

In conjunction with Vatican II, the Pittsburgh diocese's Liturgical Commission strove to reform church liturgies, especially by transforming the Mass from "a mysterious remembrance" of Christ's atoning sacrifice on the cross that "parishioners observed passively or actively ignored, to a celebration of Christ's resurrection from the dead in which all participated." To help shift the focus from sin to redemption, commission members devised sermon outlines for priests to use during Lent, produced materials for children to study in parochial schools and discussed this new emphasis on television programs.[34]

As Vatican II encouraged greater lay involvement, ecumenical relationships and deeper spirituality, a weekend retreat involving twenty-five students, two professors and a chaplain at Duquesne University in February 1967 gave birth to the Catholic charismatic renewal movement. Today, an estimated 120 million people around the world participate in this movement, and many scholars refer to the Catholic Church's "charismatic wing." The Catholic charismatic movement had roots in the Pentecostal movement that began in the United States in 1901 and accentuated emotional worship, prophetic messages, physical and spiritual healing, speaking in tongues and the neo-Pentecostalism embraced by some mainline Protestant leaders and congregations in the 1960s.

The two Duquesne faculty—theology professor Ralph Keifer and history professor Bill Storey—actively participated in the Cursillo movement, which strove to help Catholics know God more intimately through three-day retreats. After attending several prayer meetings with Protestant neo-Pentecostals in Pittsburgh and receiving the baptism of the Holy Spirit (a dramatic infilling and empowering of the Spirit), Keifer and Storey invited twenty-five devout Catholic students who belonged to Duquesne's Chi Rho society, an organization that promoted spiritual development and social action, to a weekend retreat to study Jesus' Sermon on the Mount. At the retreat, many of the students had a deep experience with God and spoke in tongues. They returned to campus and widely shared what had happened. Word spread to the University of Notre Dame, Michigan State University and other locales, leading many Catholics to have similar encounters with the Holy Spirit. After examining Catholic charismatic renewal in 1969, the U.S. Catholic Bishops' Committee on Doctrine concluded that the movement should be allowed to develop. Four books published by respected Catholics between 1969 and 1971 helped justify the movement theologically, and a 1973 Catholic charismatic conference at Notre Dame attracted thirty-five thousand people. By the early 1970s, sixty weekly ecumenical prayer groups were meeting in the Pittsburgh area, ranging in size from a dozen people to several hundred participants.[35]

The 1960s were a challenging decade for Pittsburgh Catholics. Bishop John Wright, who had no previous connection with either the Pittsburgh area or working-class Catholics, alienated many of the diocese's leading clergy and laity. Although he was a respected intellectual and a rising star in the church, by 1969 he had become the diocese's most controversial bishop. Some detractors hung effigies of him outside the cathedral office, and many parishioners refused to give money to their local churches until he was removed from office. Meanwhile, the "Holy Trinity" of Pittsburgh Catholics, unionists and Democratic politicians who had joined forces in the 1930s fell apart in the 1960s. Rice, who was assigned to Holy Rosary Parish, located in a predominately black neighborhood in Homewood, and Father Donald McIlvane, who served St. Richard's Parish in the Hill District, antagonized many Pittsburgh Catholics by their opposition to the Vietnam War and support of civil rights activism, including some of the tactics of black militants. McIlvane's acts of civil disobedience made him the diocese's first Catholic priest to be arrested, and by 1970, Rice had become a pariah to Democratic politicians and Catholic unionists whose counterparts had greatly admired him in the 1930s. Most Pittsburgh Catholics, like their coreligionists throughout the country, continued to support the Vietnam War, and they had little contact with the city's black citizens. Ministering in Homewood and the Hill District, Rice and McIlvane understood black poverty and black-on-black crime differently from most other white Catholics. In the 1960s, Rice, McIlvane and some other Catholic social activists argued that systemic racial discrimination "trapped blacks in low-paying jobs in rotting neighborhoods." Believing that these problems had multiple causes, many other Pittsburgh Catholics rejected their argument that they could be remedied only through federal legislation and anti-poverty programs.[36]

Challenges to Pittsburgh Catholicism, 1990–Present

The 1990s was a difficult decade for Pittsburgh. By 1990, all the city's steel mills had closed, and its population declined as 100,000 unskilled manufacturing jobs that had paid good wages disappeared after 1970. Because many Catholics either left the Pittsburgh area or moved to suburban communities near interstate highways, the diocese was forced to close many of the churches that eastern European, Italian and other ethnic groups had constructed near factories and rivers when they came to the Pittsburgh region decades earlier. The consolidation of urban parishes and parochial schools, led by Bishop Vincent Leonard, the son of a working-class Pittsburgh family, caused many older laypeople to complain bitterly.[37] In Ambridge, for example, seven ethnic parishes were consolidated into the Good Samaritan Parish. Donald Wuerl served as the diocese's bishop from 1988 to 2006. He staunchly promoted Catholic education and catechesis for people of all ages through diverse types of media, including a television program based on his popular adult catechism, *The Teaching of Christ*.

After being appointed as the Pittsburgh diocese's twelfth bishop in 2007, David Zubik—who graduated from a Catholic high school in Ambridge and Duquesne University and served in various pastoral, educational and administrative roles in Pittsburgh—announced his plan to create a "Church Alive!" He challenged Catholics to be enthusiastic and joyful about their faith, "to grow the church of Pittsburgh" and to be a servant community. Zubik sold the diocese's mansion in Squirrel Hill where several of his predecessors lived and resides in a modest apartment in East Carnegie. Zubik explained that an encounter on a plane changed his approach to ministry and guides his work in Pittsburgh today. His seatmate told the bishop that he grew up Catholic but became a Buddhist. "I believe in Jesus," the man confessed, but he had never "seen a Christian who really tries to be like Jesus." This experience prompted Zubik to try to "get people excited about their faith," to know and reflect Jesus so as to help people get to heaven. Zubik reorganized the diocesan offices to serve the needs of its parishes more effectively and strove to energize the laity. The diocese today, one of the largest in the United States, consists of 632,000 Catholics, which is 34 percent of the population of southwestern Pennsylvania.[38]

Zubik has promoted the gospel in Pittsburgh and beyond in diverse ways. He meets regularly with professors and students at the diocese's three Catholic colleges—Carlow, Duquesne and LaRoche—to learn about their lives and goals, and he participates actively in Christian Associates of Southwest Pennsylvania, which coordinates the work of Protestant, Catholic and Orthodox groups in the region. Zubik's name is associated with a 2016 U.S. Supreme Court case, *Zubik v. Burwell*, in which he and other plaintiffs contended that religious charities and schools should not be forced to participate in the Affordable Care Act mandate that healthcare plans pay for female employees to receive contraceptives. The Supreme Court returned the case to lower courts, and settlement negotiations are continuing. The bishop has also opposed attempts by Republicans to repeal the act if it reduces the number of Americans who can purchase reasonably priced healthcare and has defended beleaguered immigrants and refugees.[39] Zubik exhorts Pittsburgh Catholics to evangelize—"to bring others to God" through their words and deeds. The faithful should share God's good news with those who have left the Catholic Church, the unchurched "who have no or little religious upbringing" and "the already churched" to help deepen their relationship with God.[40]

Because Roman Catholic parishes are organized geographically to avoid competition, Catholic churches are by far the largest ones in Pittsburgh. Today, twenty-nine of the thirty largest congregations in the Pittsburgh area are Catholic, almost all of which are in the suburbs. Four churches have more than 10,000 members—St. Ferdinand Parish and St. Kilian Parish both in Cranberry Township, St. Benedict the Abbot Parish in McMurray and St. Bernard Parish in Mount Lebanon. The only Protestant church among the largest thirty congregations, ranked seventh, is Mount Ararat Baptist Church in East Liberty, an African American congregation that has 9,000 members. In 2013, Mount Ararat had the largest average weekly attendance at 4,800; St. Ferdinand's was second at 3,443.[41]

Since Vatican II, American Catholics, including those in Pittsburgh, have undergone substantial changes. The percentage of Catholics who attend Mass weekly has declined from 65 in 1968 to less than 40 today. Moreover, many laypeople have relied more on their own consciences than on church officials to determine their positions on the use of contraceptives and other moral questions. Nevertheless, Kelly argued, most Catholics still approach social issues "from a perspective shaped powerfully by their understanding of Catholic values and mores." Laymen and laywomen have continued to be concerned about moral questions, but they have viewed church leaders, especially after clergy sex abuse scandals became widely known in the 1980s, as less reliable guides than did earlier generations in deciding how to live in ways that please God and benefit others.[42] This will undoubtedly be exacerbated by the Pennsylvania grand jury report in August 2018 that accused 301 priests in the state of sexually abusing more than 1,000 victims over seventy years.[43]

Recognizing another type of ethnic diversity, the Pittsburgh diocese hired Jorge Vela in 2017 as its coordinator of Hispanic ministry. The Mexican native, who previously worked to help Latinos better integrate into the Catholic community in Milwaukee, serves as a spiritual guide for the region's Hispanic Catholics, especially congregations that celebrate Mass in Spanish as part of their ministry.[44]

In 2017, a diocesan planning commission recommended consolidating the Pittsburgh area's 188 Catholic parishes into 48. The proposal was prompted by a decline in the region's Catholic population (from 914,000 in 1980 to 632,000 in 2017) and average weekend Mass attendance (from 246,896 in 2000 to 138,888 in 2017), as well as the lower number of marriages, baptisms, parochial school students and confirmands (which have all decreased by about 50 percent in the twenty-first century). Moreover, half of the parishes in the Pittsburgh region had operating deficits, and during the first seventeen years of the century, the number of active priests in the Pittsburgh region decreased from 338 to 211. Because 86 priests are older than the retirement age of seventy or are planning to retire within five years, the diocese is projecting that it will have only 112 priests by 2025. Although numerous other archdioceses and dioceses in the Northeast and Midwest closed and consolidated parishes during the past three decades, no other diocese has changed as dramatically as the Pittsburgh plan proposed. The commission emphasized that it did not seek to reshuffle parishes but rather to take bold action to reverse the decline of "priests and Catholics in the pews" and to move from "maintenance to mission." Although the region's economic problems contributed to the decrease of Catholics in the diocese by causing many of them to move to other places, in recent decades, thousands of other Catholics have simply stopped participating in formal religious practices. To address these concerns, the commission called for forming larger parishes from currently existing ones to equip them to evangelize and minister to their people more effectively. The diocese envisions creating parishes of between 7,000 and 60,000 members, some of which would have multiple churches. The goal is for every parish to have between 2,000 and 4,000 worshippers at Mass every weekend and at least one priest for every 2,400 parishioners.[45]

Zubik made some alterations before releasing a final reorganization plan in April 2018, which would create 57 new parishes from the region's 188 parishes. Implementation began in October 2018 and will take five years to complete.[46] The bishop wants to create centralized parishes that have a pastor, a youth minister and a chaplain.[47] Diocesan leaders contend that by having greater financial resources, these larger parishes can minister better to youth and young adults, many of whom are not currently practicing Catholics. To compensate for the lower number of priests and enable other Christians to fulfill their vocational mandate, the Catholic Church since Vatican II has trained and appointed lay ecclesial ministers to serve as youth ministers, catechetical administrators, liturgical and music ministers, pastoral associates, social service ministers and business managers in parishes.

The history of the Diocese of Pittsburgh since its creation in 1843 is impressive. Its leaders, priests and laypeople have helped hundreds of thousands of immigrants adjust to American society and millions of members grow in their faith and lovingly serve their communities. In countless ways, its parishioners have helped make the Steel City more famous for God. By striving to win souls for Christ, "build up the Body of Christ," aid the marginalized and vulnerable, practice biblical sexual ethics and live "consistently and persistently" for Christ, they have displayed God's kingdom at work.[48] The diocese has also helped produce numerous prelates who have faithfully led the American Catholic Church, including Cardinal Sean O'Malley of Boston and Cardinal Daniel DiNardo of Galveston-Houston. The diocese's legacy is certainly worth celebrating.

Chapter 3

THE AFRICAN AMERICAN CHURCH IN PITTSBURGH

PROMOTING THE GOSPEL, ECONOMIC ADVANCEMENT AND RACIAL JUSTICE

Free African Americans began to arrive in Pittsburgh in the early nineteenth century, and in 1808, some of them created Bethel African Methodist Episcopal (AME) Church, which is the oldest African American congregation in Western Pennsylvania. Over the years, Bethel planted many flourishing daughter congregations in the Steel City, including Brown Chapel, St. James AME, Chartiers Street and St. Paul's on the South Side. By the 1830s, Pittsburgh's 1,500 black residents were living in a segregated community and prohibited from participating in the city council, public schools, white churches, theaters and social clubs. In 1833, convinced that education was the key to self-reliance and social advancement, Bethel's pastor, Lewis Woodson, and three businessmen—Abraham Lewis, John Vashon and John Peck—founded The African School at the church. Among the students educated there were George Vashon, the first black graduate of Oberlin College; David Peck, the first black graduate of a U.S. medical school; and Martin Delany, an author, newspaper editor, physician and Civil War major.[1]

During the 1830s, prominent abolitionist Theodore Weld spent several weeks speaking to groups in the Pittsburgh vicinity and convinced many individuals to support the antislavery cause. The Pittsburgh Antislavery Society, founded in 1835, soon merged with the Antislavery Society of Western Pennsylvania and published a newspaper called the *Christian Witness*.[2] Bethel's members worked energetically to abolish slavery and help black residents gain civil rights. In 1841, Bethel hosted Pennsylvania's first statewide convention to help black men gain the right to vote. Woodson, Vashon and Peck all served on the organization's executive committee. Numerous Bethel parishioners helped southern slaves escape through the Underground Railroad. Bethel also held prayer services to beseech God to end slavery, including one on the eve of Abraham Lincoln's Emancipation Proclamation on December 31, 1862.[3]

Many white Protestants, however, continued to defend slavery. The pastor of the Third Presbyterian Church, for example, strongly endorsed the fugitive slave law of 1850 in a sermon in which he cited passages that exhorted slaves to obey their masters and Paul's returning Onesimus to his master. Thousands of copies of the sermon were distributed in Pittsburgh. Such actions prompted leading black abolitionist Frederick Douglass to complain, "What a commentary on the religion of Pittsburgh it is, that every church in the place was closed against us. All were too holy to plead the cause of our common humanity."[4]

During the Gilded Age, the life of the black community revolved around the church, which provided numerous fellowship activities and social services. Black Baptists established thirty congregations in the Steel City before World War I. The two most prominent ones, Metropolitan and Ebenezer, founded in 1868 and 1875, respectively, both had more than one thousand members by the early 1910s. Grace Memorial Presbyterian Church, which opened in the Hill District in 1868, was Pittsburgh's most important black Presbyterian congregation. St. Benedict's, the city's only black Catholic church, held its first services in the Hill District in 1890. In the early twentieth century, Ebenezer's minister, George Howard, served as the African American representative on several Pittsburgh boards and advised the city on civic issues. During World War I, Grace's pastor, Charles Trusty, helped plant the Bidwell Street Presbyterian Church on the North Side and the Bethesda Presbyterian Church in East Liberty.[5]

The "Great Migration" between 1910 and 1930 swelled the ranks of African Americans in Pittsburgh, producing a chronic housing crisis among black residents that has continued to the present. Blacks were forced to create makeshift neighborhoods "in hollows and ravines, on hill slopes and along riverbanks, by railroad tracks and in mill-yards." Predominantly black communities arose in East Liberty, Homewood and the South Side, but the Hill District, next to downtown, became the commercial and social center of the city's African American life.[6] In the early 1900s, many migrants searching for work in coal and steel mills lived on the Hill, which was "a rich ethnic stew of blacks, Jews, Irish, Italians, Lebanese, Syrians and other groups."

By 1930, as thousands of black southerners seeking a better life came to Pittsburgh, the neighborhood had become mostly African American.[7]

The blacks who settled in Pittsburgh between 1880 and 1910 were primarily from Virginia, often over thirty and typically brought other family members. Significant numbers of them owned businesses or were lawyers, physicians, journalists and other professionals. Their homeownership rate was average for the city, and most black teenagers attended high school in the early 1900s.[8] African Americans who came as part of the Great Migration were dramatically different: 51 percent came from the Deep South, about the same percentage were under age thirty, 40 percent were single and most of them lacked vocational skills, forcing them to take jobs as menial laborers.[9] Moreover, African Americans suffered from two forms of discrimination—racial stereotypes and competition from immigrants—that limited their wages. Judging them to be "inefficient," "unstable" and "unsuitable" to perform mechanized tasks, many employers refused to hire them. Moreover, they had to compete with thousands of white immigrants from eastern Europe who objected to working with blacks and prohibited them from joining their trade unions.[10]

Their churches in Pittsburgh affected all facets of black life. They served as community centers and helped neighborhood residents obtain education, find jobs and pay their bills in times of crisis. Black clergy strove to shape the behavior of their parishioners through sermons and newspaper articles that exhorted blacks to work hard, be punctual and follow workplace orders. By eschewing dancing, drinking excessively, gambling, prostitution and other sinful practices, pastors argued, blacks could conform to biblical norms, improve their life circumstances and gain greater respect. Racial discrimination would end, a black pastor naïvely promised, when African Americans acquired "morals, mind, and manners."[11]

During the 1910s and 1920s, black pastors and laypeople worked through the Pittsburgh Council of Churches, the Alliance of Negro Churches and their individual congregations and vocations to improve the quality of life for the city's black residents. In 1918, the council published "The New Negro Population," which increased sympathy for the struggles of Pittsburgh's African Americans, urged labor unions to stop excluding black workers, "expressed fears about machine politicians who might exploit these newly-arrived migrants, and called for the creation of wholesome social outlets to undercut the influence of seedy pool halls and saloons."[12] Formed in 1918 to address these problems, the alliance represented all the city's African American denominations and most of its leading black ministers. Led by its president, William R. Brown, the longtime pastor of Metropolitan Baptist

Church on the North Side, the alliance created committees on evangelism, social service, comity and Christian education and launched a campaign to improve housing for Pittsburgh's blacks.[13]

In 1927, the Council of Churches established a Department of Work Among Negroes, consisting initially of fifty-eight African American congregations. Led by Brown, an executive committee composed of both African Americans and whites directed this department's efforts to upgrade accommodations, amusements and industrial opportunities for Pittsburgh's black community and to protect its most vulnerable members.[14] Describing the challenges this department faced, a Hill District YMCA executive lamented that most African Americans, who constituted 21 percent of Pittsburgh's steel workers, were denied employment in the skilled trades; 90 percent of blacks in the Pittsburgh area worked at the lowest-status and lowest-paying jobs in mines and mills or as custodians. He urged the city's banks to employ African Americans to teach them how to provide banking, insurance, real estate and other financial services for the black community. He also argued that the congested, unsanitary living arrangements of many Pittsburgh blacks contributed to their health, social and moral problems.[15]

THE HILL DISTRICT

By the 1930s, Pittsburgh's 55,000 African Americans, 85 percent of whom had arrived after 1917, comprised 8 percent of the city's population. Baptist and Methodist congregations absorbed most of these newcomers, which led to "internal class and cultural tensions and conflicts." Meanwhile, Pittsburgh's black elite belonged primarily to Presbyterian, Congregationalist and Episcopal congregations or to Bethel AME Church.[16] By 1930, black residents had established forty-five churches in the Hill District, including seventeen Baptist ones. The combined membership of the largest twenty-five of these congregations was 12,400, and about 10,000 people worshipped regularly at their Sunday services. The most prominent congregations were Ebenezer Baptist with 3,000 members, Central Baptist Church with 1,750 members, Euclid Avenue AME with 1,500 members and Euclid Avenue AME with 1,500 parishioners. Impressed by his emphasis on racial pride, promotion of black unity and battle against discrimination, the pastors of Ebenezer and John Wesley AME Zion invited Marcus Garvey, the founder of the Universal Negro Improvement Association, to speak at their churches in the 1920s. Black congregations on the Hill sponsored numerous community activities, including youth athletic teams, youth clubs, orchestras and organizations to help black residents find homes and adjust to urban life. They focused more, however, on saving souls and nurturing believers in the faith than on trying to change social conditions, a pattern that continued until the 1960s. While some sermons by black pastors dealt with social issues such as segregation and poverty, most of them discussed spiritual themes such as God's blessings, changed hearts and the ministry of the Holy Spirit.[17]

During the first half of the twentieth century, African Americans "built one of the nation's most vibrant urban communities" in the Hill District.[18] The Hill was known for its jazz, newspaper and baseball team. Famous musicians, including Duke Ellington, played at the Savoy Ballroom and other jazz hot spots. The *Pittsburgh Courier*, for a while America's most influential black weekly newspaper, was produced there. The Pittsburgh Crawfords, a Negro National League baseball team that included three of its greatest stars—Satchel Paige, Josh Gibson and Cool Papa Bell—played there. The Hill was home to a prosperous black middle class whose members by the 1930s were attorneys, judges and city legislators. African American physicians, lawyers and business owners met in prestigious social clubs and established several organizations to aid the poor. Robert Vann, the editor of the *Courier*, served as an advisor on race in Franklin Roosevelt's "black cabinet." So great was the Hill's creative and intellectual stature between 1930 and 1950 that Harlem Renaissance poet Claude McKay called it "the crossroads of the world."[19]

On the other hand, poverty and crime plagued the Hill District, and its residents endured much discrimination. The Hill had forty-five of Pittsburgh's fifty-six historically black congregations, but they did not have enough influence or funding to arrest the "social corrosion poverty wrought."[20] Meanwhile, throughout the city, department stores, restaurants, theaters, swimming pools, skating rinks and other public facilities either excluded blacks or subjected them to segregated, inferior service. In the 1920s, J.C. Austin, the pastor of the Ebenezer Baptist Church, served as the president of Pittsburgh's NAACP branch and spearheaded efforts to increase black teachers, enable black students to attend previously all-white schools, pass a state civil rights act, permit blacks to join labor unions and end police harassment experienced by the community.

Many black clergymen also held jobs in industry to supplement their income, and their congregations—consisting mainly of steelworkers, factory laborers and coal miners employed by local industrialists—

benefited from their periodic philanthropy. This led most black pastors to emphasize the work ethic and avoid directly attacking the rampant discrimination against blacks in hiring, job assignments and promotion. During the 1930s, however, "some courageous black preachers criticized industrial employers for their discriminatory treatment of black workers and for their hostility toward organized labor." T.J. King, pastor of the Ebenezer Baptist Church, AME Zion Church bishop William Walls and several other black clergy endorsed the efforts of the National Negro Congress and the CIO, which held a conference in Pittsburgh in 1937 to open unions to black steelworkers. Some black clergy offered to let union organizers meet at their churches and encouraged their parishioners to join these new unions.[21] Nevertheless, in 1942, half of Pittsburgh firms still either refused to hire blacks or "relegated them to the lowest rungs of their employment ladder."[22] Some Hill residents and their black allies in other Pittsburgh neighborhoods combatted these deplorable conditions. Four years before Rosa Parks refused to give up her seat on a bus in Montgomery, Alabama, two black citizens tried to swim in a pool in Highland Park but were forcibly expelled by a large group of whites shouting racial slurs. After this episode, several black attorneys filed a lawsuit that led to the facility being desegregated, but other city pools were either converted to different purposes or filled with cement to prevent co-racial swimming.

Renaissance I, which began in 1946, sought to make Pittsburgh a "progressive, vital American city." It revitalized the downtown, built a new airport and renovated parts of East Liberty, the North Side and the Hill District. By the 1950s, the Hill had deteriorated economically and socially. Deplorable apartment buildings and other dilapidated structures on the lower Hill, many of which lacked hot water or central heating and could be seen from downtown, were demolished to build a cultural center that included the Civic Arena, which opened in 1961. More than eight thousand residents of this area and many small businesses were displaced, "ripping the heart out" of the Hill's low-income black community.[23]

African Americans continued to push for integration, and some barriers slowly crumbled in the 1950s and 1960s. A significant triumph occurred in 1967 when Robert Lavelle, who operated a bank and sold real estate in the Hill District, won a lawsuit forcing the all-white Greater Pittsburgh Multilist to provide blacks with access to properties in historically white neighborhoods. This decision, which brought Lavelle "death threats, crude epithets, and general intimidation," enabled minority realtors across the nation to become multilist members. It also prompted many banks and building and loans associations to agree to lend money to all qualified applicants without regard to race or religion.[24]

After the assassination of Martin Luther King Jr. in 1968, riots erupted in the Hill District and other black neighborhoods, expressing the frustration and fury of many inhabitants. For eight days, looting, firebombing and other acts of violence destroyed buildings and disrupted life. In the aftermath of these riots, many of the city's African Americans worked valiantly through their congregations and religious and civic associations to help blacks win and exercise their civil rights.[25] White Protestants, Catholics and Jews all created organizations to help reduce racial tensions and violence. The largest umbrella organization was the Citizen-Clergy Coordinating Committee, a coalition of about thirty community groups that worked with the NAACP and other black associations to improve racial relations, housing and social and economic conditions for the city's African Americans.[26] In the mid-1980s, the Metropolitan Pittsburgh Crusade for Voters, led by Thomas E. Smith, pastor of the Metropolitan Baptist Church in the Hill District, filed a federal lawsuit to elect representatives by districts rather than at-large voting to increase the black voice in the city government.[27]

Sadly, the riots in black communities in the late 1960s increased the flight of more prosperous African Americans to the suburbs and damaged previously vital neighborhoods. Those who remained were largely an "underclass" of urban poor, plagued by unemployment, crime and chronic dependence; they were inadequately educated, politically powerless and generally ignored by the city government.[28] Streets that had earlier bustled with commerce were filled with drug dealing, gambling and prostitution. This version of the Hill served as a basis for Stephen Bochco's acclaimed 1980s television police drama *Hill Street Blues*.[29]

Robert Lavelle and Dwelling House Savings and Loan

Some African Americans, however, strove diligently to arrest the Hill District's drain of human and financial resources and revitalize the community. Robert Lavelle, born in Cleveland, Tennessee, in 1915, led these efforts during the last thirty years of the twentieth century. His minister father died when Robert was nine, and he and his seven siblings dealt with great adversity as they grew up in Pittsburgh. Their poverty forced Lavelle to drop out of high school to work as a dishwasher to help support the family. He eventually graduated from Schenley High School and spent twenty-one years working with the *Pittsburgh Courier*, interrupted by a three-year stint in the army during World War II. While employed by the newspaper, Lavelle earned his BS at the University of Pittsburgh (funded by the GI Bill) and an MA at its Katz Graduate School of Business. In 1951, he started his own real estate company in the Hill District, and five years later, he left the *Courier* to work full time in this business.

In 1957, Lavelle sought to help black clients obtain a mortgage for a house. Although they could put down one-third of the selling price, no bank would loan them the remainder of the money. At this point, the frustrated real estate agent noticed a small bank in the Hill District that appeared to be ready to close its doors. After this bank also refused to give the family a mortgage, Lavelle explained to its board of directors how approving such loans could help the bank stay in business. Not only did the directors agree to provide the loan, but they also appointed Lavelle as their new CEO. He quickly changed the bank's mission and gave it new life.[30]

Renamed Dwelling House Savings and Loan, the bank strove to serve the poor, increase family stability, promote civic responsibility and racial reconciliation and practice economic justice and mercy. Its motto was "We exist to serve your need, not our greed."[31] The Hill, Lavelle explained, was a "conglomeration of everything and everybody," and blacks "loved and cherished it because it was all we had."[32] Through his real estate agency and the bank, he worked virtually alone for more than three decades to increase homeownership and businesses on the Hill. Several times during the 1980s, I took students from my Social Problems class at Grove City College to tour the Hill District and learn about his work. Lavelle, who was then in his sixties, bounded aboard our bus, served as our guide and passionately described his quest to improve the Hill's spiritual, moral and economic conditions.

Many of the Hill's inhabitants were poor and lived in public housing, and drug usage was widespread. Its residents declined from fifty thousand in 1950 to only fifteen thousand in 1990. At that point, Pittsburgh's percentage of black female-headed households with children (62 percent) was higher than any other American city (it was 70 percent in the Hill District, where the median income was a paltry $10,665). The lack of education, skills and jobs, coupled with racism and personal irresponsibility, contributed to poverty, family instability, social ills and political powerlessness.[33]

Lavelle, a journalist wrote, "was as much preacher as banker in his evangelistic crusade to increase homeownership among the low-income residents of Pittsburgh who had trouble getting loans from mainstream banks." Lavelle considered DHSL to be "a Christian mission" through which he spread the gospel. Client bank statements included Bible verses. Lavelle often visited people whose mortgage payment was late at their home to counsel them on money management and to pray with them.[34] For Lavelle, business was not primarily about making money or even providing services; it was a tool for establishing caring relationships and acting righteously. His business was "a concrete way of practicing Jesus' call to love his neighbor and to live out God's vision for justice." Lavelle wanted to strengthen rather than dehumanize people through his marketplace interactions.[35] Robert Wauzzinski argued that DHSL combined "commerce and compassion, service and sensitivity, profits and people," "fiscal and social responsibility, business with love" and "personal responsibility with community solidarity." Its staff stressed that Jesus spent much of his ministry teaching the poor about how "reconciliation, mercy, and justice" "applied to daily life."[36]

DHSL provided mortgages at below-market interest rates to enable low-income individuals to buy homes. Homeowners, Lavelle argued, cared more about the appearance of their residences, the actions of city government and the quality of police services, garbage collection and neighborhood schools. Consequently, crime and filth decreased, property values rose and community life improved. Moreover, owning a home boosted people's "hope, self-respect, and responsibility." Increasing homeownership, Lavelle added, would attract businesses to the Hill District and enable every dollar to circulate three times throughout the community.[37]

As he strove to fulfill his mission, Lavelle faced substantial financial and security problems. For thirteen years, Lavelle took no salary at the bank; his maximum salary as the bank's CEO was $15,000. He and his wife even borrowed money on several occasions to keep the bank solvent. Before 1980, DHSL was robbed eight times. Nevertheless, Lavelle refused to install grills on the windows because doing so would send community members the wrong message. His actions told Hill residents, "I am not afraid," Lavelle asserted. "Because I love them, I trust them. My very vulnerability is my protection."[38] Eventually, the bank became so respected and its contribution to the community so valued that no one tried to hold it up.[39]

Lavelle's strategy worked. Homeownership in the Hill District rose from 13 percent in 1957 to 50 percent in 2006. His work also inspired members of Redeemer Church in San Francisco to found Dayspring Technologies Inc., a web and mobile development company, in 1997 to provide job training and employment for at-risk youth living in the city's Mission District.[40]

While some economists questioned the wisdom of Lavelle's approach, it succeeded because many embraced his mission. In the early twenty-first century, the bank had about five thousand savers and clients who lived in forty-six states and nine countries. Depositors, who received below-market returns on their investments, were "racially diverse, religiously ecumenical, and very disparate economically and educationally." Their agreement with its objectives led some businesses and organizations to also place their funds at DHSL. Pittsburgh Presbytery, for example, did so to help provide housing for the poor and to take a stand against racial discrimination. The bank's employees attributed its success simply "to the faithfulness of God." In the early twenty-first century, DHSL's median home mortgage loan was $32,500. DHSL was also one of a few American banks that allowed prisoners to open bank accounts.[41]

Lavelle was a longtime member of Grace Memorial Presbyterian Church in the Hill District, where he served for many years as an elder, a Sunday school teacher and the leader of a Wednesday night Bible study and worship service. His grandson, City Councilman Robert Daniel Lavelle, argued that "his thoughts and actions were based in the Word" and on his sense of the Lord's leading. "He was one of the godliest men I've ever met," declared a policewoman. "He loved the Lord," and his "faith in Jesus Christ" and "commitment to the community" are "his legacy."[42]

Lavelle served with several community organizations and on numerous boards, including Pittsburgh Theological Seminary, the United Presbyterian Foundation, the Salvation Army, the NAACP, the Urban League of Pittsburgh and the Katz Graduate School of Business. His pioneering work led the Thomas Merton Center to award him its Pittsburgh's Peace and Social Justice Center New Person Award in 1982.[43] Lavelle, State Representative Jake Wheatley asserted, "helped a lot of families build financial health and he always preached the word of God." "He was a giant and a trailblazer," insisted a program officer of the Heinz Endowment, who helped many obtain the "cornerstone of wealth [homeownership]."[44]

Sadly, cyber thieves broke into DHSL's computer system and electronically removed about $4 million. Despite a community rally to try to save the bank and extraordinary efforts by both the Office of Thrift Supervision and the FDIC to keep it open, bank regulators, after concluding that DHSL "had no reasonable hope of recovering," shut it down in 2009 and sold its assets to a PNC regional bank. After it closed, a *Pittsburgh Post-Gazette* article extolled DHSL as "a golden thread forever woven into the fabric of this city" and declared, "Well done, good and faithful servants."[45]

Through their congregations, companies, vocations and families, many other Christians have also worked to revitalize the Hill District and other predominately black Pittsburgh neighborhoods. As the new millennium began, many black professionals, corporate employees, artists, athletes, teachers and retirees moved to the Hill, hoping to recapture some of its colorful past and restore the economic vigor of an area that produced singers George Benson and Lena Horne, jazz greats Stanley Turrentine and Art Blakey, Pulitzer Prize–winning playwright August Wilson and NFL running back Curtis Martin. Other Christians joined Lavelle in the campaign to rejuvenate the Hill. Macedonia Baptist Church bought thirty-two properties, opened a counseling center and worked to increase low-income housing. "The Hill is Jericho Road," its pastor, Jason Barr Jr., declared in 2002. "Every day there is a challenge and opportunity to be a Good Samaritan."[46]

Conclusion

Pittsburgh has been the home to many influential black churches, two of which—Mount Ararat Baptist and Macedonia Baptist—are profiled in chapter 9. Another congregation discussed previously, Ebenezer Baptist Church, has arguably been the city's most important black church. Ebenezer has been "a cornerstone of Pittsburgh's black community" since the Gilded Age and a "driving force" in the nation's civil rights movement. It has significantly advanced black spiritual and material life in the city. Ebenezer was the first black church in the United States to transport people with physical limitations to its services and to install an elevator. Ebenezer lists its core values as worshiping God, making disciples, evangelizing, fellowshipping and "ministering the Social Gospel."[47] To facilitate the last objective, the 2,500-member church operates a personal care home, a large Christian life center and an eleven-story senior high-rise building with 101 apartments. It hosts numerous community programs, including Head Start, Alcoholics Anonymous and several Scout troops. In addition, Ebenezer ministers to prisoners and pairs mentors with many black middle and high school students to help them learn more effectively and aids them in obtaining college scholarships. It also holds an eleven-week summer academy to help students improve their academic performance. The congregation survived major fires in 1973 and 2004, the latter of which destroyed its church.[48] While established more recently and usually smaller in size and influence, dozens of other black congregations have promoted similar spiritual and social aims.

Pittsburgh's black Christians continue to work to remedy social ills, including AIDS and racial injustice. The Hill District Ministers Alliance, composed of nineteen church leaders, has played a leading role in this enterprise, including organizing a march in 2015 to help end violence against African Americans and create better relationships with the police.[49]

For more than two hundred years, countless African American Christians have labored persistently and courageously in the Steel City to proclaim the gospel, help individuals know Jesus personally, grow in their faith, develop stable and loving families and live as Christ's disciples. Despite immense challenges, they have created flourishing, Christ-centered churches, met the needs of their neighborhoods and worked to end racial discrimination. In both predominantly black communities and in ones where they are a minority, thousands of African Americans have incarnated the Christian message, attacked social ills and enriched the city's spiritual, social, economic and political life. Through dozens of congregations and numerous parachurch organizations, the city's black citizens have greatly advanced the quest to make Pittsburgh famous for God.

Chapter 4

SAMUEL SHOEMAKER, THE PITTSBURGH EXPERIMENT AND THE PITTSBURGH LEADERSHIP FOUNDATION

Although many have labored vigorously to make Pittsburgh known for its Christian faith, the coming of Samuel Shoemaker in 1952 to serve as the rector of Calvary Episcopal Church in East Liberty is a decisive moment in this quest. A graduate of Princeton University and General Theological Seminary in New York City, Shoemaker rejuvenated an inner-city parish in New York's garment district, also named Calvary Episcopal Church, while serving as its rector from 1926 to 1952. He revitalized the congregation by founding a rescue mission, developing a radio show and holding outdoor services.[1] He also founded Faith at Work in 1926 and helped establish Alcoholics Anonymous in 1935.[2] "A parish priest, a prophetic preacher, a prolific writer" and one of mid-twentieth-century America's "most popular radio personalities,"[3] Shoemaker pastored Pittsburgh's Calvary Episcopal Church from 1952 to 1961. By creating a variety of organizations, writing numerous widely read books, promoting personal evangelism and ministering to college students, Shoemaker had a significant impact on his era and laid the foundation on which many others built to make Pittsburgh famous for God. Shoemaker "was a parish parson with a deep concern for the urban poor" and an "unofficial chaplain to corporation executives" whose emphasis on the power of the Holy Spirit anticipated the charismatic renewal and evangelical revival of the 1970s and beyond.[4] No one in his generation, Billy Graham declared, had "a greater impact for God on the Christian world, than did Samuel Shoemaker."[5]

Samuel Shoemaker. *Courtesy of Calvary Episcopal Church.*

Calvary Episcopal Church, widely hailed as one of the nation's most beautiful Gothic-style buildings, had 2,500 members when Shoemaker arrived. The church's worship attendance, Sunday school enrollment, budget and activities all increased substantially under his leadership. Calvary rekindled its earlier passion for social ministry, as its members participated in numerous church and civic groups to help the poor and improve Pittsburgh's social conditions. KDKA aired Shoemaker's half-hour weekly radio program, and he gave a series of talks on *National Episcopal Hour* shows on both radio and television. Shoemaker also did three twelve-week series on the National Council of Churches' "Art of Living" program in the late 1950s and early 1960s that prompted hundreds of thousands of listeners to request copies of his talks. Calvary mailed as many as eight thousand copies of his sermons each week to interested individuals.[6] In 1955, *Newsweek* named Shoemaker one of the nation's ten greatest preachers. A national Episcopal magazine called Shoemaker "one of the greatest evangelists" in the denomination's history who believed deeply in the power of prayer and strove to convert everyone he met to Christ. "No man," asserted Norman Vincent Peale, "has excelled Sam Shoemaker in sheer spiritual depth and persuasive power." At his memorial service in 1963, Mayor Joseph Barr declared that Shoemaker helped many "see a shining future for Pittsburgh as a city under God."[7]

The Pittsburgh Experiment

Shoemaker especially sought to promote evangelism, create small groups of laypeople who shared their faith experiences and prayed together and motivate Christians to express their faith through their work. These priorities prompted Shoemaker to found the Pittsburgh Experiment in 1955 to "encourage people to bring Christianity into their normal daily dealings with each other," especially their business relationships.[8] The pastors of five prominent downtown churches belonging to five different denominations agreed to serve as its advisory board. The Experiment recruited its members primarily from church men's groups, Junior Chambers of Commerce, Lions Clubs, Rotary Clubs and lodges. It formed groups among secretaries, foremen, lawyers, insurance salespeople, executives and individuals in numerous other occupations to discuss how their faith was relevant to their jobs. The organization featured "experiments" through which members pledged to pray diligently about specific problems for thirty days. The Experiment focused principally on transforming individuals rather than society; moreover, its leaders argued that the best way to change society was to convert individuals.[9]

Describing its underlying philosophy, Shoemaker wrote in *The Experiment of Faith* (1957) that Christians are called to redeem "the body, money, work, amusements [and] statecraft." Going to the office, he insisted, is as spiritual as going to church "if you go both places to serve and obey God." Shoemaker exhorted Christians to live out their faith through their work, promote justice through their jobs and start a prayer or fellowship group at their place of employment. "Business," Shoemaker declared, can "be a channel of God's power"; as "the chief extension of the church in the world," it provided great opportunities to witness for Christ. The Experiment, announced *Parade* magazine, "preaches a message of practical, prayerful Christianity applied to everyday life and business. Its ambitious aim [is] to bring a whole city to God."[10]

As the Experiment's executive director from 1960 to 1969, Don James significantly expanded its ministry. A native Pittsburgher, James repudiated his childhood faith after both his parents died while he was a teenager. As a Marine in World War II, James drank excessively, had numerous sexual liaisons and brawled in bars. After earning a college degree in night school and marrying in his late twenties, in 1954 he started attending Calvary Church and meeting with a small group of businessmen led by Shoemaker. Four years later, James left his job as an insurance man to attend the Episcopal Seminary of Kentucky. The chain-smoking Episcopal rector who frequently used colorful language arduously advanced Shoemaker's objective to make Pittsburgh renowned for its faithfulness to God.

Shoemaker also profoundly influenced Reid Carpenter, a leader of Young Life, an evangelistic ministry to high school students. Carpenter described himself as "a disillusioned, rebellious" youth who had a life-changing experience as a teenager while attending a Young Life camp in Colorado. After ministering to gangs in New York City's Lower East Side through Young Life, the twenty-two-year-old Carpenter came to Pittsburgh in 1961 and spent many hours on the streets sharing the gospel with emotionally hurting kids. The number of Young Life clubs rapidly multiplied from five to forty and participants from 350 to 3,000.[11] Carpenter quickly progressed from being the Young Life area director for Pittsburgh to the regional director in Ohio, West Virginia, Pennsylvania and New York to the director of the organization's Northeast Division.

In 1961, Shoemaker took Carpenter and James to Mount Washington to pray. As they surveyed downtown Pittsburgh, Shoemaker proclaimed, "Behold your city," and cited Revelation 21:2: "I saw…the new Jerusalem, coming down out of heaven from God." This "mountaintop" experience transformed Carpenter's life and changed his calling. He concluded that Christians, as directed by the Lord's Prayer, must bring the kingdom of God, which was already flourishing in heaven, to earth. To do this,

Reid Carpenter. *Courtesy of the Pittsburgh Leadership Foundation.*

Christians must increase their collaboration and view cities as Jesus did. Just as Jesus had wept over the plight of Jerusalem, Carpenter sought to partner with like-minded souls who were weeping about Pittsburgh's high rate of drug usage, murder, school dropouts and poverty. Carpenter concluded that Shoemaker's *With the Holy Spirit and with Fire* supplied a blueprint for a reformation: Christians must admit they are powerless without the filling of the Spirit, become risk takers and work together to change their cities.[12]

This book, Shoemaker's most popular one, also exhorted Christians to improve business practices, upgrade housing conditions and increase wages.[13] Inspired by Shoemaker's social vision, James exhorted Experiment members to participate in community service. The Experiment created Unemployment Anonymous to help individuals find jobs, a prison ministry, a program to assist ex-convicts readjust to society and a ministry to reform juvenile offenders. During the 1960s, the Experiment also supplied marital counseling, spiritual guidance, food, clothing and legal aid to residents of federal housing projects. About ninety thousand people listened every week to the Experiment's *Faith at Work* program on KDKA radio. The Experiment sponsored numerous groups whose participants met at lunchtime in downtown Pittsburgh to pray, study Scripture and discuss how to put their faith in action in the business world. In 1961, the Experiment began hosting an annual retreat at Oglebay Park near Wheeling, West Virginia, that attracted hundreds of Pittsburgh businessmen and lay leaders and helped create an evangelical network in the city.[14]

The collaboration and shared convictions of James and Carpenter led them to establish the Pittsburgh Offensive in 1969 to mobilize Christians to win the city for Christ by more effectively meeting its residents' spiritual and social needs.[15] The Offensive's members—several prominent pastors and the leaders of Young Life, the Coalition for Christian Outreach, InterVarsity Christian Fellowship and the Ligonier Valley Study Center—met regularly to strategize about how to fulfill Shoemaker's vision. They strove to combat racism and improve labor-management relations by sponsoring a prayer breakfast directed by Wayne Alderson and helped found Trinity Episcopal School for Ministry in Ambridge to supply evangelical pastors for Episcopal congregations. As will be discussed in chapter 5, the Offensive also brought John Guest to Pittsburgh to work with college students, which led to the creation of the Coalition for Christian Outreach in 1971.[16]

Thanks to its talented executive directors, most notably Paul Everett, who served from 1969 to 1995, the Experiment has continued to supply spiritual resources to aid business, professional and working people and Pittsburgh-area congregations. Its primary mission has remained assisting residents of Allegheny County to "apply their faith in day-to-day business relationships." For more than sixty years, the Experiment has helped change the lives of thousands of Pittsburghers and improve the city's social conditions. It has also inspired groups in Cincinnati, Cleveland-Akron and Columbus; Jacksonville, Florida; Mobile, Alabama; Portland, Maine; Park Ridge, New Jersey; and Jackson, Mississippi, as well as in Canada, Sweden, East Africa, Zaire and Australia to establish similar organizations.[17]

The Pittsburgh Leadership Foundation

Seeking a broader platform to advance the gospel in Pittsburgh, Carpenter left his fruitful Young Life ministry in 1978 to establish the Pittsburgh Leadership Foundation.[18] Its board adopted Shoemaker's vision in its initial "Statement of Principles," committing the organization to labor to make Pittsburgh a "City for God."[19] Arguably, no one has done more to advance Shoemaker's dream of helping Pittsburgh become as famous for God as for steel than Carpenter, who served as the PLF's CEO for its first twenty-five years. Working with others who shared this goal, Carpenter raised $250,000 to strengthen Pittsburgh's Christian social fabric by providing connections among denominations and assistance to the addicted, abused and destitute. The time was ripe for such a venture. Pittsburgh was undergoing a civic renaissance as its center city was being revitalized and the region's economy was becoming more diversified. The PLF sought to spearhead a "spiritual transformation" to match Pittsburgh's "nascent physical renaissance."[20]

Driven by this bold vision and committed to a "theology of place"—a belief that God can transform churches, neighborhoods and cities that are committed to long-term kingdom ministry—the charismatic Carpenter has spent more than fifty years seeking to make Pittsburgh famous for God. Known for his enthusiasm and work ethic, Carpenter has been characterized as bilingual because he can fluently speak both the language of the streets and that of corporate America.[21] Since its inception, the PLF has created or aided more than forty ministries that have enriched the spiritual and physical health of thousands of Pittsburgh families and youth. To date, the PLF has helped raise $500 million to fund programs it created or has supported.[22]

The PLF currently defines its mission as equipping, mobilizing and connecting leaders from every sector of Pittsburgh to make it a place of "truth, beauty, goodness, justice, and human flourishing" (Jeremiah 29). The PLF's three key values are community (Ephesians 2:1–10), stewardship (Colossians 1:25) and integrity (Jeremiah 29:10). It strives to create communities of "intimacy, trust, accountability and love" to enable leaders to feel accepted, learn, grow, cultivate their gifts and contribute significantly to society. Its staff seek to build teams that can "accomplish great things in Kingdom service for the common good." The PLF works to equip leaders who are committed to promoting righteousness, grace and love to help Pittsburgh thrive. Its staff want to help individuals have lives that are integrated physically, emotionally, intellectually and spiritually and who further the flourishing and shalom of the city.[23]

Three key components differentiate the PLF from other leadership development organizations: its biblical worldview, focus on creating community among leaders and quest to transform culture for the public good. The PLF insists that leadership is best developed through a collaborative process that is rooted in a scriptural understanding of human beings and stewardship. "Inspiration, innovation, and learning happens best," the PLF asserts, "in a diverse group of people with common values." Leaders must seek not simply to advance the agenda and bottom line of their organizations but rather to reconstruct their city and world.[24] The PLF's vision, declared second president John Stahl-Wert, "is to transform the culture of Pittsburgh by building the character and the capability of its leaders" to glorify God. The PLF works with artists, business owners, teachers, bankers, homemakers, doctors and many others to "advance the reign of God's truth, beauty, goodness, love, justice and bounty" in Pittsburgh and beyond. It seeks to transform individuals, organizations and culture. The PLF supplies resources to help leaders think, exercise their leadership and build new enterprises as "Kingdom citizens" who act as "agents of cultural transformation" so "that God's will and God's way may increase in every city and in all spheres" of life.[25]

From its inception, the PLF has focused on equipping leaders to bring "Christ-centered solutions" to pressing urban problems, including youth development, drug and alcohol addiction, church divisions, neighborhood blight and educational inadequacies. By 2002, the PLF had created forty organizations and ministries, funded fifty additional ones, performed 131 case studies, equipped hundreds of leaders to work more effectively and "brought healing and hope to tens of thousands of men, women and children in Pittsburgh."[26] The PLF helped found Saltworks in 1981, the Pittsburgh Coalition Against Pornography and the East Liberty Family Health Care Center in 1982 and Garfield Jubilee in 1983. Saltworks, a professional theater company, produces and performs plays to enrich the lives of children. The PCAP worked for about thirty years to stop women, men and children from being exploited through pornography. The Health Care Center today provides varied medical services to more than thirty thousand residents of Pittsburgh's most destitute neighborhoods each year. Garfield Jubilee is a faith-based community development organization that operates programs to assist welfare recipients in the low-income Garfield area. It has helped thousands of families open savings accounts and hundreds of families purchase homes.[27] The PLF also partnered with World Vision to open an international distribution center in Ambridge and helped create the Pittsburgh Community Storehouse. The Storehouse provided clothing, health and household items and school supplies to needy families through a network of businesses nationwide that donate their surplus inventory. Justin Brown, who was the director of the Storehouse, created the Educational Partnership in 2009 to distribute school supplies at no cost to students and teachers who need them.[28]

From 1999 to 2002, the PLF operated the City as Parish (CAP) program. The brainchild of Stahl-Wert, it supplied training and resources to seventeen congregations it designated as "mission equippers." The program helped some six thousand church members discover their spiritual gifts and determine to which missions God had called them. Laypeople from CAP-participating churches engaged in about sixty ministries or projects to meet spiritual and material needs in Allegheny County.[29]

Since its founding, the PLF has focused on the spiritual, social and educational development of the city's youth. It created the Pittsburgh Youth Network to do research and provide training and networking opportunities for youth leaders, retreats for teenagers and citywide gatherings of youth. By 2002, the PYN was assisting the youth ministries of more than four hundred congregations and organizations and affecting one-third of the total young people in the Greater Pittsburgh Area each year.[30] Especially popular are the Laurelville Weekends, which draw two to three thousand middle and high school youth and their leaders twice each year from one hundred different congregations to introduce teenagers to Christ. In addition, each summer, more than one thousand middle-school youth attend Surf City, a weeklong summer camp at Silver Lake, Michigan, where they study the Bible, grow spiritually and enjoy recreational activities.[31]

Almost no problem in Pittsburgh escaped Carpenter's attention. He envisioned, initiated or helped found forty organizations and projects to reduce substance abuse and addiction among adults and youth; address homelessness, hunger, poverty, juvenile crime, racial discrimination and school dropout and truancy; assist the elderly; and provide healthcare for the poor. These include an affiliate of Communities in Schools, a national organization that tutors students to help them succeed academically; the St. Francis Adolescent Treatment Program, a facility that aids chemically dependent youth; Cross-Trainers, which equips college students to minister to youth in conjunction with inner-city churches during the summer; six Circle C Group Homes, community-based homes for juvenile delinquents; the Anti-Racism Institute, which works to help organizations eliminate racist attitudes and practices; and Houses of Worship, which facilitates collaboration among churches to increase resources for needy people.[32]

For many years, the PLF directly ran programs. In 2002, the PLF still coordinated sixteen projects, partnered with nine local affiliates and participated in three national partnerships. In 2005, the PLF was still operating seven major projects, including CLEAR (Coalition for Leadership, Education and Advocacy for Recovery)—a coalition of service providers, public health officials, criminal justice system leaders, advocates and concerned citizens who help individuals struggling with drug and alcohol addiction—and Amachi Pittsburgh, a mentoring program for children of prisoners. Founded in 1979, CLEAR operates as a referral service and advocates for these individuals. It created task groups for business people, clergy, counselors, psychologists, school administrators and teachers, criminal justice personnel, government representatives and healthcare workers to educate the public about both prevention and treatment.[33]

By 2004, the PLF had trained 2,000 youth leaders and helped 120,000 middle and high school students accept Christ as their savior and/or grow in their faith. Since 1978, through the ministries it had founded, the PLF had saved 300,000 low-income residents of Allegheny County an estimated $130 million by providing them with winter coats, school clothes, diapers, furniture, eyeglasses and other items, as well as free or reduced-cost medical services. Other organizations that the PLF spun off had mentored 30,000 public school students and counseled 15,000 families on housing issues. In its first twenty-five years, the PLF created one hundred community-based drug and alcohol task forces, trained the executives of ninety-five nonprofits in leadership development and helped pass fifty local ordinances to restrict pornography. During this period, through partnerships with other organizations, the PLF helped fifty thousand congregations gain Internet access and distributed $350 million in supplies across the globe.[34]

Lisa Slayton, the PLF's current CEO, grew up in a Catholic family in Rydal, a suburb north of Philadelphia. She attended Catholic elementary and secondary schools but put her faith on the back burner during her college and young adult years. Slayton attended Mount Holyoke College, majoring in anthropology, until 1981, was employed as a buyer and merchant in Colorado and then worked in the garment merchandising industry in New York City. After her husband took a position in Pittsburgh in 1993, she served for two years as a Kaufmann's business analyst and information systems manager. After her son was born in 1994, she became a stay-at-home mom. About that time, she became more serious about her faith, and she and her family began attending New Community Church in Wexford. In 2010, she and her husband felt a strong call to worship in the city and began to explore with several other families the possibility of joining or planting a church in downtown Pittsburgh. They soon joined a team from Memorial Park Evangelical Presbyterian Church in Allison Park that opened a church plant called New City Church and worshipped there until the spring of 2017, when it was folded back into Memorial Park and became a hub for prayer and outreach in the city.[35]

Lisa Slayton. *Courtesy of the Pittsburgh Leadership Foundation.*

Her passion for equipping leaders led Slayton to take a position with PLF in 2005 to establish its Leaders Collaborative Program. Her part-time work with an organization that focused on leadership development helped prepare her to direct this initiative. So did her visit to Redeemer Presbyterian Church's Center for Faith and Work in New York City and the books of R. Paul Stevens, especially *The Other Six Days: Vocation, Work, and Ministry in Biblical Perspective* (2000) and *Work Matters: Lessons from Scripture* (2012). While working at the PLF, Slayton completed an MA in social and civic entrepreneurship at the Bakke Graduate University in Seattle in 2012.[36] A longtime PLF board member calls Slayton an "insightful coach" who excels at pinpointing people's gifts to help them better perform their roles.[37]

The PLF, Slayton asserted, seeks to produce "transformed leaders" who help their organizations thrive. "PLF works to equip, connect and mobilize leaders" to serve God's "Kingdom-building business in every sphere of influence" in Pittsburgh. It enables leaders to identify their specific strengths, values, opportunities for influence and place in God's larger story. Transformed people and organizations can assist individuals and communities to experience the integral "wholeness—shalom—that God intended for the world."[38]

Echoing Shoemaker and Carpenter, Slayton declared that the PLF's purpose is to make Pittsburgh known for its devotion to God. To change a city, she argued, executives must operate their businesses in a biblically based way, and leaders of both businesses and nonprofits must strive to create "a healthy institutional culture." Many Christians, Slayton lamented, do not see their work as an opportunity to advance the kingdom of God. Instead, they simply try to do their jobs well and promote the gospel only through their involvement in churches or community organizations.[39]

In 2006, the PLF began to shift its focus from running programs to aid the homeless, addicted, poor and youth to equipping executives, pastors and nonprofit leaders to better mobilize their staff and parishioners to advance kingdom causes. For example, the director and staff of Light of Life Rescue Mission participated in a learning cohort to enhance their ability to minister to the indigent and homeless. By 2009, the PLF had transferred the oversight and operation of all the programs it helped create to the agencies themselves. This shift was necessary, Slayton contended, because the PLF's original strategy was untenable for both practical and financial reasons.[40]

Another example is that in 2008 the Pittsburgh Kids Foundation took charge of the PLF's work with youth. The PKF seeks to expand the kingdom of God in Pittsburgh and beyond by helping congregations and other groups that minister to youth do so more strategically and effectively with local churches, organizations and leaders to reach students with the life-changing love of Jesus Christ. To accomplish this goal, the PKF provides training for youth leaders and opportunities so that they can network and share ideas and resources through monthly citywide meetings and its annual Pittsburgh Youth Workers Conference. The PKF is widely recognized as "the largest and strongest youth collaboration" in any American city. Brad Henderson, an ordained minister in the Evangelical Church Alliance and the chaplain for the Pirates and the Penguins, is the president of the PKF. The organization also works to share the gospel and improve social conditions in Haiti. Henderson travels to Haiti regularly with teams from Pittsburgh, and under the auspices of PKF, youth pastors, youth groups and adult groups make twenty to twenty-five additional trips annually to build schools and medical clinics, provide clean water and improve sanitation, work with children in orphanages and evangelize.[41]

Today, the PLF uses cohort-based learning experiences and one-on-one coaching to train individuals to lead more effectively. Its Leadership Collaborative, which began in 2007, currently offers two twelve- to fifteen-member cohorts annually. Designed for senior-level executives of for-profit, public and not-for-profit organizations, this six-month experience includes intensive sessions, workshops, vocational coaching, classes and the development of a Breakthrough Goal to convince participants to embrace a philosophy of "leadership as stewardship" and learn how to apply it to their day-to-day business practices. Based on a theology of vocation, this program helps people better fulfill their callings by further developing their God-given gifts.[42] The PLF contends that "business is not merely a means to provide resources" to others who are "doing the 'real' work of the Kingdom of God—it is as much part of that 'real' work" as any other activity. Therefore, the PLF seeks to equip business executives to use their companies, resources and influence to fundamentally change "our broken world," provide justice, and promote "flourishing in God's creation."[43] By charging for the Leaders Collaborative it conducts for the managers of for-profit businesses and raising funds, the PTF can give nonprofit executives this service for free.[44] Bombardier TTS, NetHealth, CTR Systems, Akina, Prominent, ABC Anesthesia and Wabtec have all greatly benefited from the organizational development, consulting, training and coaching services the PLF furnishes.

The PLF's Urban Leaders project helps twelve- to fifteen-member cohorts consisting of faith-based nonprofit leaders and full-time ministry leaders working in urban environments to strengthen their leadership and management skills by providing six months of coaching and collaboration. In 2016, the PLF launched its Pittsburgh Vocational Learning Community. This shared one-year learning experience teaches two or three representatives of participating congregations (presently sixteen) how to instill "a robust theology of faith, work, and economics" into their culture. Slayton; Rick Wellock, the PLF's director of organizational development; Steven Garber, the principal of the Washington Institute for Faith, Vocation and Culture; Amy Sherman, senior fellow at the Sagamore Institute; Jay Slocum, the founding pastor of Jonah's Call; and Terry Timm, the lead pastor of Christ Community Church of the South Hills, facilitate the sessions. The PLF also currently works with about 150 executives who serve on leadership teams in a dozen companies. Darrin Grove, the founder and CEO of Truefit, a Pittsburgh-based technology company, argues that the PLF enables leadership teams to reach their potential. It helps executives make good decisions and develop valuable relationships with leaders of other companies.[45]

Since 2011, the PLF has sponsored the Jubilee Professional conference in partnership with the Coalition for Christian Outreach's Jubilee conference, where thought leaders and practitioners in integrating faith and work discuss biblical principles of leadership and their own enterprises to instruct and inspire the five hundred business, educational, church and community leaders who attend.

The PLF hosts similar smaller events each year.[46] For example, in 2015, the PLF hosted *Leadership Journal*'s Redeeming Work event. More than one hundred clergy and marketplace leaders from numerous cities gathered at PNC Park to hear local pastors, business executives and Pirates manager Clint Hurdle discuss the concept of servant leadership, learn about how Christians were integrating faith and work in Pittsburgh and discover how to do this themselves.[47] Over the years, the PLF has partnered with congregations, nonprofits and other faith-based organizations to sponsor numerous citywide endeavors, including prison outreach ministries, evangelistic rallies and worship services.[48] In addition, the PLF sponsors the annual Greater Pittsburgh Community Leaders Prayer Breakfast. The PLF also prods Catholic dioceses, Protestant denominations and congregations to place greater emphasis on discipleship and vocation. Slayton speaks to many groups to challenge Christians to let their faith direct all areas of their lives, including their business activities.[49]

Slayton argued that the PLF's greatest strengths are its ability to help clients understand the importance and interconnectedness of faith, vocation and culture; to persuade Christians living throughout Allegheny County to work together; and to apply ideas and practices gleaned from other people and places to improve religious and social conditions in Pittsburgh.[50]

Despite its solid scriptural foundation and sizable initial endowment, by 2012, Slayton explained, the PLF was in deep financial trouble because its approach was not sustainable. People knew about the organizations the PLF had created but not about the PLF itself, and it had spent its initial endowment investing in the many organizations previously mentioned. Consequently, as its new CEO, she sought to move the PLF forward in "a new, fresh way." Today, the PLF's greatest challenges are convincing Christians from different theological traditions and religious backgrounds to work together, equipping Christian leaders to work effectively in a post-Christian, pluralistic society and raising funds to support these vital activities. Fundraising is difficult, Slayton insisted, when your mission is not about some tangible cause such as helping babies or saving puppies. The PLF's ministry does not have the emotional appeal many other organizations do. The PLF is working for long-term, systemic transformation rather than a more immediate, short-term impact. Moreover, unlike many other nonprofits, the PLF has no annual fundraising gala event but instead relies on the gifts of donors who believe in investing in long-term change. Determining how best to promote the common good and create a more just society in an increasingly secular culture, Slayton insisted, is also very challenging.[51]

Jubilee Professional Conference. *Courtesy of the Pittsburgh Leadership Foundation.*

To date, more than three hundred community, church and business leaders have participated in PLF learning communities. Although these individuals understand relevant biblical principles, guide their organizations more effectively and train others to be leaders, Slayton wants the PLF to be even more intentional about helping program participants collaborate to meet the needs of Pittsburgh and building partnerships to help the city flourish. She wants to teach many more congregations how to promote "whole-life discipleship" and help them recognize that much more unites "people across faith traditions than divides them."[52]

The PLF has had a substantial impact well beyond Pittsburgh. Carpenter and other staff developed close personal relationships with civic leaders around the United States who shared their vision. In 1993, Carpenter founded the Council of Leadership Foundations (today called simply Leadership Foundations) to strengthen these relationships and help other cities establish enterprises like the PLF. Under the leadership of Dave Hillis, today it includes seventy member organizations (forty in the United States) and strives to "Connect Leaders, Change Lives, and Transform Cities." Some of these organizations, particularly ones in smaller cities, either directly operate or strongly support programs to assist specific groups as the PLF did initially. Other affiliates primarily fund these programs. A third group of organizations, like the PLF, focuses on developing leaders and organizing citywide initiatives to improve spiritual and material life. Leadership Foundations identifies leaders "who are making the greatest impact on their cities" and equips them to direct change more effectively, quickly and permanently. In cities around the world, these leaders have created and operate programs that are providing spiritual, social or economic opportunities and are transforming thousands of lives.[53] Leaders in many other cities view Pittsburgh as a place where the faith, work and vocation emphasis has had a huge practical impact and are seeking to follow its example.[54] "In the language of the prophet Jeremiah," Steve Garber declared, the PLF has promoted "the flourishing of the city" for years. Its energetic endeavors to achieve the hopes of Pittsburgh's Christians have been "remarkable."[55] No ministry has done more to help achieve Shoemaker's ambitious aim.

Chapter 5

THE COALITION FOR CHRISTIAN OUTREACH AND URBAN IMPACT FOUNDATION

The CCO: Transforming College Students to Transform the World

One of the most significant outcomes of Samuel Shoemaker's quest to make Pittsburgh as famous for God as for steel is the creation of the Coalition for Christian Outreach (CCO). This interdenominational campus ministry, headquartered in Pittsburgh, strives to transform "college students to transform the world." Since its modest beginning in 1971, it has grown to involve more than 300 staff who work on 143 campuses in 17 states and the District of Columbia. The CCO estimates that its ministry has touched the lives of 1 million college students by either introducing them to Christ or helping them grow in their faith.[1]

As the 1960s ended, a group of church youth leaders, pastors and parents in the Pittsburgh area were deeply disturbed that many young people were abandoning their faith while in college. Because of secular perspectives in their classes; the temptations of alcohol, drugs and sex; and the lack of attractive spiritual opportunities, thousands of college students who had been raised in Christian homes, participated in Young Life clubs and/or attended Bible-believing churches were not engaging in Christian fellowship or living by biblical values.[2] Led by English rock musician and evangelist John Guest; Bob Letsinger of the Pittsburgh Power and Light Company; Bob Long, a campus minister at Bellefield Presbyterian Church in Oakland; Young Life director Dick Shorthouse; Jim Welch, a pastor at Fox Chapel

Presbyterian Church; and InterVarsity Christian Fellowship staff member Carl Derk, these concerned individuals organized a conference in Pittsburgh in 1970 called Revolution + One to help connect freshmen with Christian fellowship groups on campuses in the metropolitan area. To enhance these efforts, the CCO was established the next year to partner with other campus ministries and local churches to evangelize to and disciple college students. Guest was named the CCO's first executive director.[3]

Its first year, the CCO employed only six campus missioners who worked with students at four institutions: the University of Pittsburgh, Carnegie Mellon University, Allegheny College and Indiana University of Pennsylvania. Graystone Presbyterian Church in Indiana became the CCO's first church partner by hiring David Diehl to minister to IUP students. Guest soon decided to accept a pastoral position at St. Stephen's Episcopal Church in Sewickley, and thirty-one-year-old Long replaced him as the executive director. Long accepted the leadership of the fledging organization because he was convinced that God was calling him and that he could have a great impact for His kingdom through the CCO. He was the perfect fit for the CCO's needs. A former University of Pittsburgh football player, a graduate of Gordon-Conwell Theological Seminary and an ordained Presbyterian Church (USA) minister, Long had the drive, tenacity and interpersonal and administrative skills to enable the CCO to fulfill its mission. Despite his young age, Long brought much valuable ministry experience to his role. He had helped lead Pitt's Fellowship of Christian Athletes chapter, worked for five summers through Young Life with inner-city youth in New York City and run a Young Life–style club in the Boston area while attending seminary. Guest, who had worked with Long on Revolution + One and observed his vibrant college ministry, was impressed with his character, organizational skills and attention to detail. Over the years, all staff, including Long, have raised funds from churches and individuals to pay their salaries.[4]

The CCO differs from other campus ministries—including InterVarsity, Cru, Navigators, Catholic Newman Centers and Ratio Christi—in three main ways. First is its locale. The CCO was initially created to minister to students attending colleges within a 150-mile radius of Pittsburgh. Over the years, the CCO has expanded its outreach to the Mid-Atlantic region of Pennsylvania, New York, West Virginia, Ohio, Indiana and Washington, D.C., and its suburbs. It has recently begun operating on campuses in eleven additional states, including Texas, Florida and California.[5] Pittsburgh, however, has always been the heart and soul of its ministry.

Bob Long. *Courtesy of the Coalition for Christian Outreach.*

Second, the CCO, more than other campus organizations, has sought to build coalitions among and establish relationships with other ministries, congregations and colleges themselves. Wherever possible, CCO staff hold multiple positions. They have served as both campus missioners and youth ministers in churches, residence hall staff, directors of student activities, college coaches, school nurses, adjunct faculty, career counselors and assistant chaplains. This has been a win-win arrangement. Colleges gain full-time staff for less money since CCO staff raise part of their own salaries. Christian schools have been eager to hire CCO staff because they agree with the organization's mission; both Christian and secular colleges appreciate the valuable work CCO personnel do. As colleges have increasingly demanded that their staff hold master's degrees, the CCO's focus has shifted more to working with local churches.[6] More than most other campus ministries, the CCO partners with churches and encourages students to participate in the life of local congregations. CCO staff have often persuaded the various Christian groups meeting on campus to join for fellowship, evangelism and service. Moreover, its flexible, multifaceted approach has enabled the CCO to design ministries to fit the needs of individual campuses.

The CCO's third distinction is its guiding philosophy. From its inception, the CCO has accentuated Christ's lordship over all aspects of life. Its staff have emphasized that Christians are called to be God's "co-laborers" in His work to restore His entire "good creation." This perspective, rooted in Reformed theology, has exalted God's sovereignty and directed all facets of the CCO's ministry—its Bible studies, fellowship and discipleship meetings, evangelistic efforts, student conferences and summer projects. The CCO declares, "We believe that Jesus Christ is Lord of all things and thus we are committed to the implementation of the social and cultural implications of God's commandments and grace for the transformation of society and the well-being of people." To fulfill this mission, the CCO seeks to inspire and equip students to passionately serve Christ through their studies and extracurricular activities while in college and in their jobs, congregations, communities and families after they graduate.[7]

Over the years, the CCO has steadily increased in geographic scope, staff and the campuses where it ministers. Three years after its inception, the organization employed 37 missioners who worked for 27 colleges in Pennsylvania, Ohio and West Virginia. By 1979, the CCO had 165 staff serving on 39 campuses. The CCO's size plateaued, and in 1996, the organization had 157 staff ministering to students on 43 campuses. Growth began again soon, and by 2000, the CCO employed 195 staff on 50 campuses. Expanding its territorial outreach, the CCO began a ministry to college students in Philadelphia in 2001, which included work on 14 campuses by 2011. In 2004, the CCO opened its first ministry in New York State at Elmira College, and the next year, it launched ministries in the Washington, D.C., area at George Mason University and Howard University. In 2010, the CCO initiated work in the state of Indiana by establishing connections between several churches and campuses in Indianapolis. As the CCO celebrated its fortieth anniversary in 2011, its 224 staff were working with students on 90 campuses. In addition, the organization was partnering with 36 congregations belonging to 17 different denominations; 60 percent of its staff had either earned or were currently pursuing graduate degrees. In recent years, the CCO has used part-time staff and associate staff to further expand its ministry. Today, the CCO's 300 staff work annually with more than 30,000 students on 140 campuses. Moreover, the Evangelical Presbyterian Church considers the CCO to be its campus ministry, and the CCO has begun establishing partnerships with Anglican Church of North America congregations.[8]

During its first decade, Pete Steen and R.C. Sproul played a leading role in helping staff understand and apply the CCO's "distinctive emphasis that Christ is Lord over everything."[9] A former religion professor at Geneva College, Steen served the CCO in the 1970s as an itinerant teacher and introduced many staff to the writings of the faculty who taught at the Institute for Christian Studies in Toronto, including James Olthius, Calvin Seerveld and Evan Runner. By holding informal classes at many colleges, Steen helped many CCO staff and students better understand the nature of God's kingdom and become zealous about building it. After teaching briefly at Westminster College in Pennsylvania and working at College Hill Presbyterian Church in Cincinnati, in 1971 Sproul founded the Ligonier Valley Study Center, which was modeled on Francis Schaeffer's L'Abri in Switzerland, sixty miles east of Pittsburgh.[10] By studying with Sproul at LVSC for two weeks each year and reading his numerous books, campus missioners became more deeply grounded in the Reformed faith and a holistic Christian worldview.

Several other talented individuals played a crucial role in the CCO's growth and fruitful ministry. Terry Thomas, who joined the staff in 1972, has taught at Geneva College and addressed thousands of students at CCO conferences, retreats and campus meetings. Jim Welch, like Long an ordained PCUSA minister, became the CCO's associate executive director in 1973. Before leaving in 1979 to found Summer's Best Two Weeks, a camp about sixty miles southeast of Pittsburgh, he arranged numerous partnerships between the CCO and churches and colleges. Following a productive ministry at IUP beginning in 1974, Bill Painter worked in the CCO office for more than twenty years, developing many new venues for CCO staff to reach college students. From 1976 to 1986, Tom McWhertor played a variety of important roles, including as a regional director, the director of the Jubilee Conference and the CCO's administrative coordinator. Paul Harbison has led the CCO's experiential education ministry since 1978, which currently includes twenty-two staff members. Harbison estimates that more than 100,000 students have participated in this ministry since its inception. The CCO joined the Wilderness Education Association and received an award in 2008 for its highly effective adventure education program. In the 1980s, Bill Romanowski (who later taught at Calvin College and wrote *Eyes Wide Open: Looking for God in Popular Culture*) performed a rock-and-roll show on many campuses to provide a Christian perspective of popular culture. To help equip CCO staff and students with valuable resources, former CCO staff worker Byron Borger and his wife, Beth, established Hearts & Minds

Bookstore near York, Pennsylvania, in 1979. For many years, Borger, known for his extensive reading, insightful analysis and passion for learning, has energetically promoted books at Jubilee conferences and staff training events. Graphic designer Bonnie Liefer created the CCO's greeting card ministry, which has blessed people around the world.[11]

Dan Dupee. *Courtesy of the Coalition for Christian Outreach.*

In 1999, Dan Dupee replaced Long as the CCO's president and CEO, and Long became the chair of the board. As CEO, Long's primary role had been raising money, and as board chair, he strove to increase planned giving and build an endowment to strengthen the CCO's financial position.[12] Dupee was converted to Christ at Jubilee while he was a freshman at Ohio Wesleyan University. After graduating, he served as a CCO missioner for three years at Penn State University. Following thirteen years at a family business in Cincinnati, Dupee returned to the CCO in 1997 as its vice-president of development. As CEO, Dupee helped the organization delineate its core purpose, "transforming college students to transform the world," and its core values: "All things belong to God. Jesus changes people's lives. We love college students. We embrace God's multi-ethnic Kingdom. Faithfulness is pursued together. We celebrate life." After serving seventeen years as CEO, Dupee became the chair of the CCO board in 2016; at that time, it consisted of thirty-three business leaders, community leaders and pastors.[13] Vince Burens, the CCO's executive vice-president, took over as president and CEO. Under his leadership, the CCO developed a more efficient infrastructure to enhance its impact.[14]

One of the highlights of the CCO's ministry is the Jubilee Conference, which it has sponsored in Pittsburgh since 1977. This unique conference, held at the Westin Convention Center since 2009, annually attracts three thousand or more participants, primarily students from the campuses where CCO staff work. Jubilee focuses on the theme of God's kingdom and challenges attendees to examine how their faith can direct their vocations. As Burens explained, "Jubilee seeks to equip students to serve Jesus Christ passionately" in their families, vocations, churches and communities.[15]

Over the years, many prominent Christian politicians, community activists, journalists, authors, educators and evangelists have delivered keynote addresses at Jubilee. Most notable are Oregon senator Mark Hatfield; U.S. Surgeon General C. Everett Koop; Prison Fellowship founder Charles Colson; evangelist Tom Skinner; Fuller Seminary president Richard Mouw; NFL player, coach and analyst Tony Dungy; Anglican theologian John Stott; Baptist theologian Carl Henry; Kay James of the Family Research Council; sociologist and author Tony Campolo; John Perkins, the founder of both Voice of Calvary Ministries and the Christian Community Development Association; Kelly Monroe Kullberg, author and creator of the Veritas Forum; artist Makoto Fujimura; author and social critic Os Guinness; Andy Crouch, the executive editor of *Christianity Today*; Gabe Lyons, author of *unChristian*; and Gary Haugen, the founder and president of International Justice Mission.[16]

The heart of Jubilee is the forty to fifty workshops that discuss the role of Christian faith on campus, in the workplace and public life and in fields ranging from the law, science and technology to the social sciences, music and the arts. Where else can people go to "talk about justice and beauty, architecture, and sports, medicine and hip-hop," Crouch asked, "all soaked in the good news of the Gospel? I've loved Jubilee for its energy, enthusiasm, and incredible depth." "There is simply nothing like the Jubilee conference," declared Australian Jon Tyson, founding pastor of Trinity Grace Church in New York City. "It is a powerful, theologically rich, Spirit-empowered, justice-oriented gathering with a rich vision for seeing the glory of God established in all of life."[17] Thousands testify that Jubilee has brought them to Christ, helped them better understand God's kingdom and the cultural implications of the gospel and stimulated them to think more deeply about their faith and vocation. Michael Worsley, who worked as a chaplain at Howard University for twenty-five years, explained that attending Jubilee gave him a passion for justice, a commitment to pursuing excellence and relationships with people who were changing the world. Douglas Lee, the president of Waynesburg University, insisted that going to Jubilee taught him to love God and his neighbors and helped prepare him for his work in law and education.[18]

Electricity filled the air and the excitement was palpable as almost 3,500 people filled the ballroom of the David L. Lawrence Convention Center for the Fortieth Jubilee Conference in 2017. Boisterous worship songs rocked the plenary sessions as participants expressed their praise to God. Banners proclaimed the conference slogan—"Every Square Inch"—taken from early

Jubilee Conference at the David L. Lawrence Convention Center. *Courtesy of the Coalition for Christian Outreach.*

twentieth-century Dutch prime minister Abraham Kuyper's declaration that "there is not a square inch in the whole domain of human existence over which Christ, who is sovereign over all, does not cry, 'Mine!'"

At every conference, dynamic keynote speakers discuss the themes of creation, fall, redemption and restoration. In 2017, Tyson and Lecrae, a hip hop artist, songwriter and actor, extolled God's creative work. Tyson argued that God gives people a cultural mandate to reorder their fallen world. Genesis provides "an alternative subversive narrative" to Americans' widespread focus on utility, treatment of people as commodities and sense of futility. God created people, Lecrae avowed, to demonstrate His goodness and glory. He urged students to "love God, love people, and do what you love" as a vocation. Three African Americans—theologian and author Ekemini Uwan, recording artist and activist Sho Baraka and poet Propaganda—delineated the tragic and devastating impact of the fall and sin. They emphasized that sin dehumanizes people by breaking their fellowship with God, creating strife between them and introducing illness, pain and death into the world. Leonce Crump Jr., an All-American wrestler, a star defensive end at the University of Oklahoma and a founding pastor of Renovation Church in Atlanta, explained the marvelous implications of redemption, while Anthony Bradley, a professor of religious studies at The King's College in New York City, described how God was working to restore all things to their original condition.

Workshops at Jubilee in 2017 discussed such topics as "Race and Faith," "How Women Can Make the Most of Their Ambition," "A Christian Response to the Refugee Crisis," "Finding Meaning after College," "How Should Christians View History?," "Can We Love Our Neighbors Through Politics?" (a panel that included George W. Bush's principal speechwriter, Michael Gerson, and Michael Wear, who directed faith outreach for Barack Obama's 2012 reelection campaign), "Serving God in the Trades and Engineering," "Art and the Church," "Making Music to the Glory of God," "How Christians Think About Origins," "Redeeming Social Media," "Handling Success and Failure" and "Transformation in Healthcare."

Since 2010, the CCO and the Pittsburgh Leadership Foundation have cosponsored a Jubilee Professional conference on the Friday afternoon preceding the Jubilee Conference. It features both nationally renowned and locally influential speakers who seek to help several hundred professionals of varied ages apply biblical truth to their vocations and understand more fully how their work can promote "the flourishing of their community, city, and world."[19] In 2017, for example, speakers included Katelyn Beaty, an editor for *Christianity Today*; Daniel Hall, a professor of surgery at the University of Pittsburgh and an ordained Episcopal priest; Dr. Greg Thornbury, the president of The King's College; Doug Wilson, the chair of Monon Capital LLC, a multidisciplinary investment, thought and conversation studio; and Dr. John Wallace, the senior pastor of the Bible Center Church in Homewood, a low-income African American Pittsburgh community.

Lisa Slayton, president of the Pittsburgh Leadership Foundation, opened the 2017 conference by declaring that the PLF and the CCO shared "the same spiritual DNA" because they were both birthed by the Pittsburgh Offensive, which Reid Carpenter created. Jubilee Professional, she insisted, focused on practice rather than theory. It enabled people to continue their Jubilee experience after they graduated from college and entered the work world. Beaty argued that many Christian women have failed to recognize what it means to be full image bearers of God. Wallace shared how his church was working to transform Homewood through its Oasis Project, which provides programs, starts businesses, creates jobs and repurposes vacant and abandoned property to empower community residents.[20]

During the 2015–16 academic year, the CCO piloted Jubilee Academy to provide a forum for the best and brightest students with whom its staff work to meet periodically to discuss politics, popular culture, work, spiritual disciplines and leadership development. The academy enables "mature and motivated students to explore vocation and whole-life discipleship" through "mentoring, instruction, and experiential learning." In 2016–17, cohorts of students met in four different areas—Pittsburgh, Northwestern Pennsylvania, Philadelphia and Ohio. Undoubtedly speaking for many participants, Jeff Schallick of the University of Pittsburgh declared that Jubilee Academy gave him "a concrete idea of how to glorify God through my work."

In addition to Jubilee, the CCO has sponsored other conferences to either present the claims of Christianity or nurture students in their faith. Its first evangelism conference, "RSVP: An Invitation that Demands a Response," was held in 1988. The event became so popular that in 1995 it was split into two conferences. Although many students accepted Christ as their savior at these conferences, they were discontinued in 2000 to enable the CCO to focus on other regional and on-campus evangelistic events.

To provide staff with additional education in theology, ministry, the Bible, higher education and student development, the CCO has established two partnerships. The first was a cooperative graduate program with Fuller Theological Seminary in Pasadena, California, in 1979. In 1986, this program was transferred to Gordon-Conwell Theological Seminary in South Hamilton, Massachusetts; in 2014, it was shifted to Trinity School for Ministry in Ambridge, Pennsylvania. In 1994, the CCO created a Master of Arts in Higher Education degree program in conjunction with Geneva College to enable its staff to better understand and serve both the colleges where they worked and the students to whom they ministered. Through these programs and its in-house training, CCO staff have received substantial education in theology, the Bible, practical ministry and student development; developed rich relationships with one another; and learned how to apply their faith to all areas of life. Moreover, every year since the award was introduced in 2003, the CCO has been recognized as the Best Christian Place to Work in the Parachurch and Missions category by the Best Christian Workplaces Institute.[21]

The CCO has created a variety of innovative ministries to reach diverse types of college students. In addition to its adventure programs, the CCO has devised specific outreaches to minority students, international students, athletes, art students, trade school students and even atheists. In 1982, Bill Saxton launched a ministry to international students at Penn State University that has produced a significant harvest. Gene Tibbs built a thriving ministry to black students at the University of Pittsburgh beginning in 1990. The next year, Ken Wagoner initiated a ministry to Chinese students studying at Carnegie Mellon University and the University of Pittsburgh. Since then, Wagoner has helped hundreds of Chinese students become Christians and/or grow in their faith, many of whom have become leaders in their home country. After being hired to serve as its director of multiethnic ministries in 2002, Wayne Younger devised a program to train CCO staff to minister more effectively to students of various races and cultures.[22] Today two full-time staff—Michael Chen and Michael Thornhill—work to encourage and equip CCO staff to engage in cross-cultural ministry.

CCO staff at several schools targeted student athletes because they are often key leaders on their campuses. Missioners sought to "help them to balance the challenges of academics, athletics, faith development and a healthy social life."[23] Ted Schumacher began working with athletes at Kent State University in 1986, and the CCO started a ministry to athletes at the University of Pittsburgh in 1992. In 2009, the CCO expanded its outreach to athletes by assigning All-American shot putter Sandie Starr Everhart and her husband to work with athletes at Edinboro University of Pennsylvania.[24]

The CCO developed programs to appeal to three other underserved student groups. Artist and CCO staff member Dayton Castleman established a ministry to students at Pennsylvania Academy of the Fine Arts and the University of the Arts in Philadelphia in 2005. In 2009, the CCO began a ministry to students at trade schools by sending staff to Wyotech Blairsville and the Williamson College of the Trades in Philadelphia. That same year, Steve Lutz and Jonathan Weyer devised a groundbreaking ministry at Big Ten sports rivals—Penn State University and The Ohio State University—aimed at presenting the claims of the gospel to atheist students.[25]

Over the years, the CCO has used several summer ministries to train student leaders to serve more effectively on their campuses. Its staff believe that giving students opportunities to lead and to invest in others' lives while in college helps equip them to play similar roles after they graduate.[26] Students have taken jobs in resort-oriented businesses—hotels, restaurants and shops—and received training from CCO staff to do evangelism, lead Bible studies and organize groups and meetings. From 1972 to 1975, CCO staff operated the College Club at Chautauqua Institute in southwestern New York and provided this training to about fifty students each summer. From 1983 to the present, the Ocean City Beach Project has brought twenty-eight Christians from various campuses to Ocean City, New Jersey, each summer for ten weeks of rigorous discipleship and leadership development. The Erie Summer Project ran from 1986 to 1992. Its eight to ten participants interacted with Pennsylvania congressman Tom Ridge (later governor of Pennsylvania and Secretary of Homeland Security) and other political leaders and discussed how to develop a Christian perspective in their future vocations. In addition, since 1995, the CCO has offered Leadership and Discipleship in the Wilderness as a summer experience. To date, more than two hundred students have participated in seventeen trips to Wyoming and Georgian Bay in Canada.

To enhance the spiritual development of college students, CCO staff have authored several books. In 1982, four campus missioners—Brad Frey, Bill Ingram, Tom McWhertor and Bill Romanowski—published *All of Life Redeemed: Biblical Insight for Daily Obedience*. Four years later, they wrote a companion volume, *At Work and Play*. Both books were widely used by CCO staff for many years to help students understand and apply a holistic gospel. In 1996, Steve Garber published *The Fabric of Faithfulness: Weaving Together Belief and Behavior*, which grew out of his experience ministering to college students with the CCO. In 2007, staff member Derek Melleby and staff alumnus Donald Opitz co-wrote *The Outrageous Idea of Academic Faithfulness: A Guide for Students*, which has been assigned in numerous college courses. Three years later, Melleby issued *Make College Count: A Faithful Guide to Life and Learning* to help high school seniors better prepare for college. In 2016, Dan Dupee published *It's Not Too Late: The Essential Part You Play in Shaping Your Teen's Faith* to teach parents how to guide their children's spiritual development in high school and college. Other important books by CCO staff include Erica Young Reitz's *After College: Navigating Transitions, Relationships and Faith* (2016) and Sam Van Eman's *Disruptive Discipleship: The Power of Breaking Routine to Kickstart Your Faith* (2017). The CCO also partnered with the Center for Parent/Youth Understanding to develop a seminar to better prepare Christian high school students for the spiritual and moral trials of college and help them remain grounded in their faith.[27]

Throughout its history, the CCO has faced many challenges, especially raising enough money to fund its staff and programs and finding and training enough talented individuals to fill all its positions effectively.[28] Nevertheless, the CCO has impressively fulfilled its mission to transform the lives of thousands of college students. After graduating, many of them have promoted God's kingdom through their diligent work as pastors, youth workers, educators, attorneys, artists, accountants, physicians, business people, entrepreneurs and in numerous other occupations, as well as through their devoted parenting and active participation in their congregations and community organizations. In addition, CCO staff, after

A student Bible study at the University of Pittsburgh. *Courtesy of the Coalition for Christian Outreach.*

completing their campus ministry, have served God faithfully and fruitfully in these and other capacities.

Although the CCO's ministry has had a significant effect well beyond Pittsburgh, its impact has been especially strong in Allegheny County. Many members of area congregations participated in CCO activities while in college. Motivated by the CCO's priorities, thousands of these individuals are working vigorously to be light and salt in their communities through their churches, marriages, parenting and vocations. Countless individuals converted and/or nurtured through the CCO's ministry are building God's kingdom and enriching life in Pittsburgh.[29]

Urban Impact Foundation: Holistic Transformation on the North Side

Ed Glover and his wife, Tammy, founded Urban Impact Foundation in 1995 to help youth become Christians and grow in their faith and to combat the problems facing urban communities, which they had witnessed firsthand for nine years as residents of Pittsburgh's North Side and through Ed's work as a pastor at Allegheny Center Alliance Church. The Glovers concluded that the difficulties confronting children and families on the North Side—drugs, crime, violence, prostitution, gangs, fatherlessness, the lack of jobs and quality education and physical and spiritual poverty—could be effectively tackled only through the "holistic development of the mind, body, and spirit through Christ." Rather than choosing to live in a safe, secure suburban neighborhood, the Glovers moved to Avery Street on the North Side, where half the houses were boarded up and drug deals were common on the sidewalks. They shared the gospel and Christ's love with their neighbors and took in numerous children who needed a place to stay. For many youth, their home became a refuge from the hostile, dangerous outside world. The North Side today has fifty thousand residents, including eleven thousand children, 15 percent of whom are involved in UIF's ministries.[30] The North Side has one traditional high school (Perry), a high school for students who get into trouble (Oliver), pre-K–8 (Pittsburgh King) and a K–8 charter school (Propel Northside).

Ed Glover grew up in a non-Christian home and graduated from Lambuth University in Tennessee, where he starred on the baseball team. He became a Christian at age twenty-two while trying out with the Pirates. He earned a Master of Divinity degree at Alliance Theological Seminary in Nyack, New York, and for several years served as an adjunct professor at Nyack College. Tammy, who earned a BA at Seattle Pacific University and a Master of Divinity degree from Alliance Theological Seminary, directs Urban Impact's performing arts program. In 1986, Ed began working as an outreach pastor at Allegheny Center Alliance Church and soon became its youth pastor.[31]

In creating and developing UIF, Ed Glover has been strongly influenced by Reid Carpenter; Art Erickson, a pastor at Central Community Church in Minneapolis; training he received from John Perkins and Wayne Gordon's Christian Community Development Association; the work of Dan Spader of Chicago; and his relationships with his father-in-law, Ken Backlund, pastor of the Chico Neighborhood Church in Chico, California, and John Guest.[32]

Its mission, UIF proclaims, is to help fulfill "Christ's Great Commission on the North Side of Pittsburgh by following His model of holistic ministry by investing in the lives of at-risk children, youth, and their families" to "develop responsible followers of Christ." Its vision statement declares, "We desire to see lives holistically transformed in our community one person, one family, and one block at a time" and to have "a powerful impact locally and globally for Jesus Christ."[33] UIF's seventy-eight full- and part-time staff and about four hundred volunteers help prepare North Side children for life after

Ed and Tammy Glover. *Courtesy of the Urban Impact Foundation.*

high school, whether they choose higher education, training in a trade, jobs, military service or ministry. The staff includes thirty-five urban missionaries who raise their own salaries and live on the North Side to develop close relationships with its residents. Volunteers must be committed Christians, have security clearances and be passionate about sharing their faith; they receive two hours of mission and vision training, primarily provided by Ed Glover.[34] More than 1,600 students in kindergarten to twelfth grade participate every year in UIF's academic, tutoring, options and performing arts programs, summer camps and athletic teams. UIF's slogan is, "We build relationships, and God changes people's lives." UIF staff and volunteers present the gospel and introduce children to Jesus through all their programs. In a typical year, 300 to 400 youth accept Christ as their savior or rededicate their lives to Him.[35]

Through various programs conducted in schools and at its own facilities, UIF helps hundreds of students improve their academic performance. UIF's longest-running program is its Summer Day Camp. This eight-week camp for students entering first through eighth grade costs only $170 and includes daily lessons in math, literacy and the Bible, as well as worship, swimming, field trips and skills development in dance, art, sewing, electronics, football and other areas. The camp, which employs forty-five summer interns, helps

Urban Impact Foundation summer campers. *Courtesy of the Urban Impact Foundation.*

prevent "summer slide"—academic regression—and some participants improve by as much as two grade levels. After graduating from high school, many campers have returned to work at the camp.

UIF also operates a tutoring center and literacy and math support programs for students in grades one through twelve for three hours every Monday. By supplying remedial assistance and reinforcing school lessons, the tutoring center helps children fulfill their academic potential. It provides individualized aid with homework in math, science and reading; prepares students to take the SAT and the Armed Services Vocational Aptitude Battery; and offers a job readiness class. Through UIF's Literacy Support program, both staff and volunteers furnish in-school tutoring in reading, writing and spelling for about 150 K–2 grade students at Pittsburgh King School and first-grade students at Pittsburgh Allegheny School for eight hours each week. UIF's Math Support program provides personalized instruction one or two class periods a week to sixth-grade students at Pittsburgh Schiller and ninth-grade students at Pittsburgh Perry who are struggling to perform at their grade level.[36]

Athletics are also very important at UIF. The ministry offers programs in basketball, baseball, soccer, swimming and athletic discipleship, and members of the Pittsburgh Steelers conduct a football clinic annually. Through these programs, UIF seeks to build relationships with youth, develop character and sportsmanship, promote physical fitness, provide constructive alternatives to gangs and street life and "communicate and demonstrate the Gospel of Jesus Christ." The basketball program features boys' and girls' intramural games, boys' and girls' middle school and high school travel teams and leagues for middle school and high school boys. UIF supplies coaches, feeds participants and presents an evangelistic message every night at intramural games. Coaches develop close relationships with and mentor the six hundred youth who participate each year.[37]

UIF partners with Ambassadors in Sport to teach boys and girls baseball skills, share scriptural principles and stories and help them memorize Bible passages. UIF sponsors a coed team of North Side sixth through eighth graders that plays in a citywide league. Participants develop positive relationships with peers and adults, grow spiritually and learn how to deal constructively with conflict. Practices include both baseball instruction and devotions, while games provide opportunities to enjoy the sport and build character. UIF collaborates with the Ambassador Football Club to provide soccer instruction and games for pre-K to fifth-grade boys and girls on Saturdays in the fall. Participants engage in interactive Bible lessons and memorize Bible verses. UIF's weekly swimming lessons teach students in grades K–3 how to swim. Bible lessons and Scripture memorization are also a key aspect of this program. Through UIF's Athletics Discipleship program, mentors and student assistants help participants become more dedicated disciples of Christ.[38]

Each June, more than four hundred K–8 grade students and their families attend a football clinic conducted by Pittsburgh Steelers. Kids eat, do football drills, learn new skills and play football with some of their heroes, while their parents are informed about community resources that can enrich their children's lives. In 2017, Steelers linebacker L.J. Fort shared about how coming to know Jesus personally transformed his life.[39] The Steelers contribute to UIF in other ways. For example, former Steeler Jeff Hastings served as the emcee for UIF's Play Ball for Kids Appreciation Dinner in 2015, where he was recognized for helping the program recruit more than forty sponsors and raise $3.5 million during its first twelve years. He and Steeler chaplain Chad Johnson interviewed current Steelers Will Allen, Maurkice Pouncey and Kelvin Beachum about their faith and football experiences.[40]

UIF's Options component includes four free programs to help high school students plan for their future by identifying their interests and preparing for one of five postsecondary tracks: college, trade school, job, military or ministry. Its Options Resource Center at Pittsburgh Perry assists high school juniors and seniors to decide which track best suits their aptitudes, abilities and aims and helps them take the steps necessary to achieve their goals. About 97 percent of those who regularly participate in this program graduate from high school, and 95 percent of these graduates get a job, go to college or trade school or enter the military or ministry. Options mentoring pairs high school juniors and seniors with staff or volunteers who equip them to succeed in one of the five tracks. UIF's year-round SAT prep program supplies students in grades ten through twelve with tutors in math and reading. Its Jobs 4 Life program enables ninth- to twelfth-grade students to cultivate the values prized in the work world, learn how to write résumés and interview for jobs and "discover God's plan and purpose for their lives." UIF awards about seven scholarships a year to help Options participants attend college.[41]

Each year, UIF's Performing Arts component offers more than twenty classes and numerous groups to enable students of all ages to develop their talents and perform in vocal and instrumental music, theater, dance, the visual arts and technical production. The flagship program is the Urban Impact Middle School/High School Choir. Its 120 members meet weekly to eat dinner, study the Bible and practice. Members of this talented ensemble glorify God by singing to thousands of people at various venues in Pittsburgh and beyond. The 100 participants in UIF's Children Choir, who are in grades one through five, receive individualized voice instruction and perform for audiences. The Urban Impact Singers, an invitation-only group for high school singers and instrumentalists, travels throughout the country during both the summer and school year to publicize UIF's ministries and testify about Christ's impact on their lives. The group's itinerary in 2017 included a three-day tour in Philadelphia and a ten-day tour in California. Through UIF's musical theater course, middle and high school students learn more about singing, dancing and acting to prepare them for roles in various public performances. UIF also offers a course on introduction to music to teach students in grades three through twelve rhythm, how to read music and hand coordination through playing chimes, recorders and buckets. In addition, UIF sponsors a jazz band for middle and high school

Urban Impact Foundation middle school/high school choir. *Courtesy of the Urban Impact Foundation.*

students that performs throughout the Pittsburgh area. Especially impressive is Urban Impact Shakes, which performs a Shakespeare play each year and helps middle and high school students develop their acting and leadership potential. This troupe performs at various venues in Allegheny County and beyond. Moreover, UIF sponsors a dance team that teaches middle and high school students about various forms of modern dance and offers a summer camp to improve the dance skills of students in grades three through twelve. Finally, UIF provides classes in visual arts, photography, industrial arts and stagecraft. All these performing arts programs also include Bible study, spiritual nurture and life skills instruction. Each year, UIF hosts the Performing Arts Showcase, at which about 120 students dance, sing, act, play instruments and exhibit artwork.[42]

To help children and youth grow spiritually, UIF employs a model designed by Dann Spader, which is detailed in his *4 Chair Discipling: Growing a Movement of Disciple-Makers* (2014). Spader emphasizes that Jesus' final words on earth included four specific instructions: go, make disciples, baptize and teach. The four chairs are Come and See (John 1:39), Follow Me (John 1:43), Become a Fisher of Men (Matthew 4:19) and Go and Bear Fruit (John 15:16). UIF regularly brings staff from Spader's organization, Sonlife, to train its urban missionaries how to use this approach in their work.

Since 2013, UIF has organized the ManUp conference. Sponsored by Chick-fil-A, Highmark Blue Cross Blue Shield, Dollar Bank, WORD-FM Christian talk radio and other companies and organizations, the conference challenges men to be the spiritual leaders in their families, parent their children in accordance with biblical principles and help children without fathers. The 2017 conference, held at Victory Family Church in Cranberry, drew 1,500 men and featured former Steeler Tunch Ilkin, head coach Mike Tomlin, defensive coordinator Keith Butler, Pirates manager Clint Hurdle and three of the pastors profiled in this book—Ron Moore, John Nuzzo and Rock Dillaman. Hurdle argued that God will not ask us at the final judgment how many games we won or lost, but rather how we used our gifts to serve Him. Tomlin, who has spoken at all five conferences, exhorted participants to serve as godly role models for vulnerable children.[43]

UIF's annual budget is about $3 million, which does not include its free building space, thousands of donated meals and the salaries of urban missionaries because they raise their own support. The largest gifts in UIF's history are several $100,000 grants from foundations. UIF's funding comes from individuals (30 percent), foundations (19 percent), Play Ball 4 Kids (12 percent) and three public events—ManUp, the Pittsburgh Marathon and

Light the Night (11 percent). Churches, businesses, the United Way and other entities donate smaller amounts.[44]

Glover argued that UIF has had such a substantial impact because it is incarnational and faithful to Jesus; UIF strives to imitate Christ. Second, its staff earn people's trust by living in North Side neighborhoods. Third, its commitment to prayer, passion, vision and leadership has enhanced its ministry. Fourth, UIF has invested primarily in the lives of youth. Fifth, it has created a solid organizational structure, used technology wisely and obtained adequate funding. During the next decade, Glover hopes to create a training center to teach Christians how to communicate the gospel more effectively, develop more associate staff who have other careers but volunteer long-term with UIF, expand its ministry into other neighborhoods and partner with more organizations.[45]

As with numerous other individuals and ministries based in Pittsburgh, Glover's influence extends well beyond the city. He founded another organization—Global Impact USA—six years before establishing UIF. During the next twenty-four years, fifty-five thousand youth from nineteen cities learned about the needs of and opportunities for service in the world through this annual one-day mission event. Their participation in this event has helped inspire an estimated one thousand pastors and missionaries to serve the Lord throughout the world. Moreover, since its founding, UIF has trained about one hundred missionaries who are currently serving in Pittsburgh or other cities. UIF also helped create programs in Toledo, Baltimore, San Diego and Aliquippa, Pennsylvania, to work with disadvantaged and troubled youth.[46]

The youth to whom UIF ministers have been taunted, harassed, bullied, threatened and even attacked by neighborhood gangs. Thousands of them, however, have benefited spiritually, emotionally and physically from its programs and have significantly improved their opportunities in life. The Glovers' fruitful ministry has been widely recognized. In 2003, Ed and Tammy were awarded the Alumni of the Year Award by both Alliance Theological Seminary and Nyack College. In 2011, Ed received the prestigious Restoring Places Award at the Epoch Missions Gala in Atlanta, which honors an individual for having a significant long-term impact on a specific region. The next year, the Chick-fil-A Foundation awarded UIF its inaugural True Inspiration Award for the Northeast region, for demonstrating "groundbreaking practices and visionary leadership" through its innovative education program.[47] For almost a quarter of a century, UIF has been transforming lives and improving conditions on Pittsburgh's North Side.

Chapter 6

LIGHT OF LIFE RESCUE MISSION AND THE PITTSBURGH PROJECT

Light of Life: Transforming Lives through Christ-Centered Care

Since 1952, the nondenominational Light of Life Rescue Mission has been ministering to a sizable number of homeless, transient and indigent individuals and families on the North Side. Originally called Harbor of Hope Rescue Mission, it started as a soup kitchen and a refuge for transient men. Programs were later developed to also assist women and children. Light of Life purchased several buildings in 1979 on the North Side, where many of its programs still operate.[1]

Light of Life's goal is to transform "lives through Christ-centered care." "Everything we do," insisted Director of Advancement Jessi Marsh, "is faith-based." The mission furnishes a haven "for the homeless and food for the hungry" and builds "disciples for the Kingdom of God among the poor, addicted, abused, and needy." Light of Life staff share the good news of Jesus gently and lovingly through their words and actions with all those to whom they minister.[2] They strive to create "a healing community," empathize with individuals they serve and develop "Spirit-filled disciples" of Christ. This "redemptive" community enables its residents to examine their failures, change their attitudes and behaviors and have a better life. The mission seeks to help its clients understand their identity as beloved children of God and receive the salvation Jesus brought by dying on the cross to atone for human sin.[3] Light of Life

The front of the Light of Life Rescue Mission. *Courtesy of the Light of Life Rescue Mission; photo credit to Michael Ray.*

provides services "to anyone regardless of age, race, creed, nationality, religious views or sexual orientation."[4]

Light of Life operates a Men's Program, a Women and Children's Program, a Food and Emergency Shelter Program, a Housing and Employment Program and a Street Engagement Program. The Men's Program seeks to equip men who are battling addiction, mental health issues and homelessness to "become self-sufficient, productive members of society." Its two tracks house up to thirty-eight men at a time. Men in the Life Recovery Program stay an average of twelve to eighteen months, and men in the Mental Health Program stay an average of three to five years. While living in a "Christ-centered community," men receive counseling and engage in work and group activities to overcome their addictions, gain essential life skills and set personal goals. Participants must be willing to continuously discuss and evaluate their conduct, as this is an indicator of deeper-heart issues that they work to uncover and deal with in a healthy way. Residents agree to follow the daily schedule, complete their assignments and duties around the mission (primarily preparing and serving food and doing laundry for shelter guests), communicate honestly and openly with staff and one another and be teachable and willing to change.

Care Team Leaders are staff members who each have about twelve men on their caseload. They help the men obtain medical and housing services, education and training so that they can find jobs and become lifelong learners. Residents also read books, play instruments, participate in classes and clubs (on such topics as the fundamentals of Christianity, coping with grief, healthy sexuality, twelve-step recovery, ethnic foods and tennis), play on teams in a local sports league and work out at the YMCA. These activities expand their minds, improve their social skills and help them grow in their faith. Chapel services, Bible studies and involvement in a local church also enhance residents' spiritual growth and facilitate their recovery and readjustment to society.[5] Men who test positive for drugs are required to leave the program, although they can stay in the emergency shelter center. If they admit they are struggling with drugs or alcohol and want to change their behavior, they can reenter the residency program. To achieve educational goals, participants can use self-guided GED programs and take classes at the Salvation Army or online college courses. Halfway through the program, men are assigned a mentor—usually someone who previously completed this program and/or has overcome addiction—and must have a place to live and a means of financial support. After they complete the program, they participate in aftercare activities.

The Women and Children's Program, which began in 1990, ministers to single mothers (and their children) and women without children who are suffering from homelessness, addictions and abusive relationships. The mission can accommodate thirty women who typically participate in the program for eighteen months. Women are usually referred to this recovery program by other community organizations. Most of them have little income, have used drugs and have lived on the street; some suffer from PTSD and other mental health issues. When they enter the program, most

Bunk beds in the emergency shelter at the Light of Life Rescue Mission. *Courtesy of the Light of Life Rescue Mission; photo credit to Michael Ray.*

women cannot function effectively as parents because of the impact of their addictions, physical and sexual abuse and poverty. Women who do not have custody of their children when they enter the program work with Light of Life staff and social services to regain custody and learn how to provide a safe, loving home. Participants live in subsidized apartments, take classes and receive job training, assistance with childcare and transportation and twenty hours of counseling a week. Light of Life's program staff typically have work experience with drug and alcohol recovery, have advanced degrees, are pastors or have personally experienced addiction recovery.[6]

Light of Life staff help women deal with the problems that brought them to the program and create stable lives. Enabling these women to improve their parenting and household management skills and reestablish strong bonds with their children is a major priority. The mission's programs, combined with outside resources such as counseling, seek to empower these women to develop a healthier lifestyle, become self-sufficient, prepare for jobs, improve their relational abilities and deepen their spiritual walk. Women learn life skills, work to overcome addictions, engage in Bible studies, receive training to use computers and study to pass the GED to help them obtain employment and live independently. Because they are recovering from traumatic life experiences, Light of Life first focuses on building a strong foundation before supporting them to go to school or get a job.[7]

While the mothers take classes and receive counseling, their young children learn, play and eat nutritious meals. Mothers and their children take field trips to the Pittsburgh Zoo and museums and engage in other educational and entertaining activities that strengthen family bonds. Light of Life also gives school-age children backpacks and clothes.[8] Women read various books to identify their talents, learn how to utilize their strengths and discover how they can best serve God and others. Before entering the program, women must have stopped using drugs or abusing alcohol, and by the time they finish the program they have significantly improved their relationships, are part of a supportive church community and can live independently. Some women whose children have been taken by social services regain custody.[9] Almost all women who complete this program continue to stay in touch with the mission.[10]

Light of Life operates two shelter programs: an Emergency Shelter open to any man who needs a bed for the night and a Housing and Employment Program for men whose primary problem is homelessness rather than substance abuse. The Emergency Shelter can accommodate twenty-six men per night. Men can come any night to escape rain, snow or cold weather. They sleep in clean beds and receive dinner and breakfast, the opportunity to shower and an invitation to participate in case management. If they need clothing, Light of Life can help them. The Housing and Employment Program, which can accommodate eight men, works to help them obtain housing, jobs and stable lives. Participants commit to an average of three months of case management and must take random drug tests.

All participants in Light of Life's residence programs must attend 9:00 a.m. chapel services throughout the week, led by staff and local pastors, and a community meeting following the services at which they share concerns and prayer requests and celebrate achievements. The mission treats program participants as adults and gives them the "freedom to fail." Shelter guests, staff and volunteers are encouraged to attend other chapel services at 7:00 a.m. and 6:30 p.m. Light of Life does not require its clients or volunteers to be Christians; all its staff, however, must affirm its statement of faith.[11] Its hundreds of volunteers come from diverse backgrounds. Most of them are committed Christians; some of them have life experiences similar to the program participants and community residents they seek to help. Army veteran Mike Gebhart, for example, served in Iraq until substance abuse forced him out of the military and into jail. Sober for more than seven years, he now assists at Light of Life.[12]

Light of Life began as a soup kitchen, and serving meals is still a major part of its mission. In 2017, it served more than 272,000 nutritious meals annually at its main facility on the North Side (with two dining areas that together seat about 40 people) and other locations. Staff cooks and volunteers prepare breakfasts and dinners for community members as well as lunch for the residents. Light of Life also supports the work of other local organizations; for example, it provides hot meals and snack bags for Urban Impact every week. During the Easter, Christmas and Thanksgiving holidays, Light of Life volunteers deliver meals to fourteen local senior care facilities. While serving the meals, staff and volunteers develop relationships with residents and lead worship services that primarily entail music and prayer.[13] Light of Life staff work with community partners and churches to identify individuals and families who most need Thanksgiving baskets; in 2017, volunteers packed and community partners delivered 1,060 baskets that included food for a Thanksgiving meal, a New Testament and community resource guide. On Thanksgiving Day, staff and volunteers serve a turkey dinner to hundreds of homeless and low-income people (1,261 in 2017). Trader Joe's, Giant Eagle and Target donate about three-quarters of the food served.

When my wife and I visited Light of Life, we met with Jessi Marsh, director of advancement since 2011, and Kate Wadsworth, manager of communications and special projects. Marsh previously worked at Community Human Services in Oakland. Wadsworth volunteered as meal server at Light of Life before joining the staff in 2011.

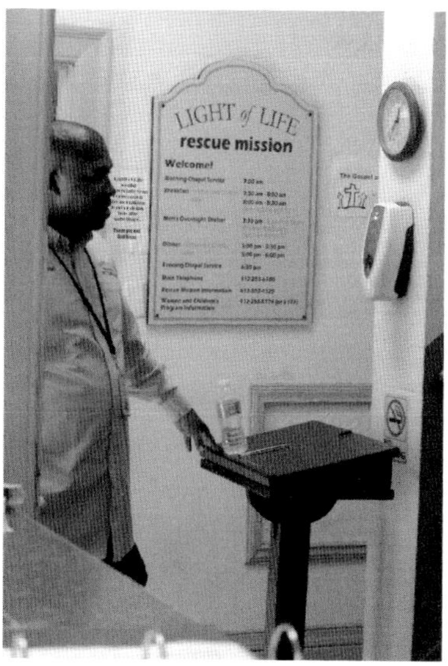

The entry to the Light of Life Rescue Mission. *Courtesy of the Light of Life Rescue Mission; photo credit to Michael Ray.*

Since 1994, Light of Life has made relocating from North Avenue a priority. Light of Life staff and community residents both favor a new North Side location away from the main business district, a local elementary school and a park. In 2012, the mission purchased a former vocational-technical school building on Ridge Avenue near the Community College of Allegheny County. The mission currently uses this property to store donations. Light of Life was granted approval in February 2017 by Pittsburgh's Zoning Board to build and occupy an additional building beneath the supports of the Veterans Bridge on the North Shore. Only one neighbor objected to the Ridge

Avenue site, and six community members and/or organizations protested the site under the bridge, claiming that it was still too close to homes. Light of Life wants to use both sites because of their relative isolation and the many homeless people staying in the vicinity. Opponents of the relocation argued that the move would bring more homeless people and drug addicts into the area. Mission staff counter that the properties are sufficiently far from people's homes and that Light of Life is helping reduce drug problems on the North Side.[14]

Some members of the community strongly support Light of Life; they value its ministry, efforts to improve the North Side and economic impact (staff and volunteers eat in local restaurants and pay for parking). Numerous local businesspeople have written letters commending the mission. For example, Kerry Kennedy, the owner of a flower shop, has been especially appreciative and helpful.[15]

The mission also sponsors several events to aid residents of the North Side. During the Christmas season, Light of Life gives warm clothing, hot chocolate and cookies to passersby as part of the Christmas Celebration Meal. Volunteer praise and worship teams hold services in the chapel to offer spiritual help and hope to anyone who comes through the doors. Every July, Light of Life hosts a Day of Hope Picnic in West Park. It features a community cookout and an initiative to clean North Side streets. Forty benevolent organizations furnish information about their programs and free services such as vision tests, and musicians and speakers from Allegheny Center Alliance Church, h2o Church, Urban Impact and City Reach share the good news of the gospel. For several years, Light of Life has sponsored a Community Cookout; in July 2016, it served 925 meals consisting of hot dogs, hamburgers, macaroni salad and watermelon to low-income North Side residents.[16] Each November, Light of Life partners with the Northside Homeless Alliance to provide winter coats, sweaters, blankets, gloves, scarves and bags of toiletries to low-income people. The mission also serves a Christmas banquet each year at which it distributes similar items.[17]

Light of Life works closely with numerous other local social service agencies, including Gateway Rehab, Bethlehem Haven, Mercy Behavioral Health, North Side Christian Health Center, Action Housing, St. Vincent DePaul, the Greater Pittsburgh Community Food Bank and Bidwell Training Center. The mission also partners with the Allegheny County Jail's Hope Pod program, which helps people readjust to life after incarceration.[18]

Light of Life Mission's 2016 budget was $7.1 million. About 56 percent of the 2016 budget came from individuals (thirty-three thousand in 2015) who donate between $60 and $10,000 per year. The remainder of the budget is supplied by in-kind donations (11 percent), foundations and trusts (8.3 percent), government grants (6.3 percent), fundraising events (4.2 percent), corporations and twenty-five to thirty congregations (which collectively give 2 percent).[19]

Light of Life uses a variety of special events to raise revenue. Since 2002, it has held Tunch and Wolf's Walk for the Homeless, named for two former Steeler players and current Steeler broadcasters—Tunch Ilkin and Craig Wolfley—who lead the event. In 2017, more than 1,000 walkers raised more than $110,000. For the past six years, Light of Life has put on the Yinzer 5k. Emceed by Pittsburgh radio personality Jim Krenn, the race encourages runners to wear costumes representing prominent Pittsburgh landmarks. People also provide funds for Light of Life by recruiting individuals to sponsor them in the annual Pittsburgh Marathon. In 2017, the mission recruited 154 runners and raised $94,000. Light of Life's primary fundraiser is its annual gala. Hosted by Ilkin and Wolfley, it includes a delicious dinner, a tour of the mission's facilities, silent and live auctions and videos of success stories. In 2017, 450 supporters attended and $185,000 was raised.[20]

Light of Life has changed the lives of thousands of Pittsburghers. For example, Clarissa testified that the Women and Children's Program "has provided a purpose to live again." It inspired her "to reflect on who I am, the issues I face, the changes that are needed, and the support to do it." It gave her "a safe environment to open up and dig deep through the pain that has plagued my life, thus ensuring a clean start and transformation to the woman and mother I know I am."[21] Light of Life estimates that 75 percent of families who have completed this program lived independently for at least five years.[22]

Kevin Hutchison, who spent eighteen months in the Men's Residential Program after his life fell apart, has worked in Light of Life's kitchen since 2006. Many of its residents and his coworkers, he explained, "have come from brokenness." They are inspired by seeing others who "have turned their lives around."[23] Hutchison greatly impressed employees from the Henderson Brothers Insurance Company who volunteered at Light of Life. He taught them how to prepare and serve breakfast and "a few life lessons" as well. Through faith and the mission's support, he told them, he "beat alcohol addiction and is now clean and sober."[24] After battling alcohol and drug addiction for years, Aleshia accepted Christ as her savior while participating in the Women's and Children's Program. She earned a BA in human services, is completing an MDiv and works as an intake counselor at

Light of Life. This mother of seven children who is celebrating ten years of recovery thanks the mission for turning her life around.[25]

For sixty-six years, Light of Life has faithfully obeyed Christ's admonition to aid the least of these. As Christ directs believers to do in His Sermon on the Mount, they have also been light and salt on the North Side. God has used them to transform the lives of thousands of troubled individuals and to preserve, flavor and improve life in one of Pittsburgh's most challenging communities.

The Pittsburgh Project: Aiding Vulnerable Homeowners and Developing Servant Leaders

Saleem Ghubril, who was born in Beirut, Lebanon, founded The Pittsburgh Project (TPP) in 1985 as a summer work camp for suburban teens to repair the houses of low-income city residents. His father, an accountant who worked for the U.S. embassy, got his family out of Lebanon soon after a civil war erupted there in 1975. Ghubril finished high school in Iowa and graduated from the University of Iowa with a major in religion. He planned to go to law school, but after volunteering with middle and high school students, he sensed God's call to a different vocation. Following a short stint as a youth pastor, at age twenty-five, he started TPP to renovate houses in Pittsburgh and minister to the residents of the troubled and turbulent Perry South neighborhood on the North Side. Seven years later, Ghubril moved his wife and two children into this high-risk urban neighborhood, causing his parents great consternation. They had sacrificed much to remove their son from similar conditions in Lebanon, where several of his cousins were killed, his brother was kidnapped and his friends brandished M16s. Nevertheless, convinced that "Christian faith must show itself in love that changes lives and brings reconciliation between enemies," Ghubril created and directed TPP. The North Side long had a high homicide rate, and in the mid-1990s, twenty-eight people were killed at an intersection near TPP. Both poverty and drug use have been prevalent since the 1960s.[26] Today, about 75 percent of the residents of the neighborhoods surrounding TPP are low income.

In establishing and developing TPP, Ghubril was influenced by Tony Campolo, an evangelical sociologist at Eastern University in Philadelphia, who operated a similar ministry in Camden, New Jersey; the Search Institute, a Minneapolis-based organization that provides research and resources

Saleem Ghubril. *Courtesy of The Pittsburgh Project.*

to help youth succeed; and the Christian Community Development Association (CCDA). John Perkins, an African American minister from Mississippi, created CCDA in 1989 to apply biblical tenets to aiding impoverished communities. CCDA accentuates "3Rs" of community development: remaining in or relocating to needy neighborhoods to do ministry; "reconciliation between God and people and among individuals across racial, ethnic and economic lines"; and the redistribution of resources to bring new skills, relationships and opportunities to people living in destitute communities. Following CCDA's model, TPP strives to affirm people's dignity, listen to community members, develop leaders and provide a holistic ministry to empower the poor.[27]

The Pittsburgh Project gradually expanded its activities beyond home refurbishing, and after buying a former Catholic school building in Perry South in 1993, it began providing tutoring, summer camps and leadership training for neighborhood youth. TPP also purchased a church building, built dormitories (an environmentally "green" facility that sleeps 324) and took control of a nearby park and swimming pool that the city could not afford to maintain. Today, its permanent staff of 26 (15 full time and 11 part time) and 50 summer staff run the home rehabilitation program and operate various afterschool and summer educational and enrichment programs, which are attended by more than 250 urban youth. While TPP staff want children to "do well in school and work," their primary goal is to introduce them to Jesus and enable them to "become who God wants them to be." TPP staff use the park—which also includes a basketball court, a playground, a peace garden and an amphitheater—to build relationships with neighborhood youth. About 2,500 people use the pool each year, and day camp participants can take free swimming lessons. TPP also serves catered meals in its dining hall and Garden Courtyard and operates a specialty coffee shop. Many TPP staff live near its campus, which has helped create cordial relationships and good will with neighborhood residents.[28]

Paraphrasing a biblical prophecy about Jerusalem, TPP's mission is "that Pittsburgh will be called a City of Truth, where once again men and women of ripe old age will sit in the streets each with cane in hand because of age, and where the city streets will be filled with boys and girls playing there (adapted from Zechariah 8:4–5)." TPP seeks to "develop servant leaders and uphold the dignity of vulnerable homeowners."[29]

Continuing its initial mission, TPP strives to improve the lives and affirm the worth of low-income homeowners by repairing their houses, visiting with them and connecting them with local churches and social services. TPP aids

The headquarters of The Pittsburgh Project. *Courtesy of The Pittsburgh Project.*

homeowners who are destitute, live in substandard conditions, face eviction, have limited social resources and/or have poor health because of advanced age or disability. Its volunteers work to ensure that these individuals live in "a safe, healthy, and accessible home" and have the social networks they need to experience "optimum living." Volunteers repair or renovate about 125 homes each year in Pittsburgh and nearby neighborhoods. They do painting, dry walling, carpentry, minor plumbing and masonry jobs and yard work. Volunteers also build wheelchair ramps, fortify retaining walls and replace doors, floors and windows.[30]

Much of this work is done by more than 1,500 youth who come each year from churches, schools, colleges and community groups across the United States for a day, weekend or week. At TPP, student volunteers are immersed in a cross-cultural setting where they interact with individuals from different locales, races, denominations and schools. These young volunteers spend their evenings reflecting, worshipping, learning about servant leadership and receiving encouragement to participate in ministries in their home communities.[31] TPP also sponsors fall and spring "one-day plunges," weekend retreats and custom trips. During the plunges, about fifty volunteers of all ages spend eight hours repairing houses in a Pittsburgh-area neighborhood and conclude with worship and debriefing. For the two annual weekend retreats, eighty to one hundred participants—including adult, college, family and youth groups—spend eight hours on Saturday and Sunday working at eleven to fourteen worksites. They listen to a speaker and have a time of worship and contemplation to connect their work with biblical teachings. Groups from some churches, including City Reformed Church, come every year. The custom trips typically involve groups of high school or college students who come for two to seven days during their spring break to repair houses.[32]

The weeklong summer camps feature homeowners' nights. All those whose houses volunteers have refurbished are invited to a dinner and worship service at TPP's facilities. "God has answered my prayers," an elderly woman testified at one of these events. "In two days, you have done more for me than my family has done my whole life."[33] This evening was "the best part of the trip," a high school sophomore insisted. "It was priceless to see how much everyone appreciated our work, and to see all the people we helped."[34]

Since its establishment, TPP has repaired and renovated more than 2,100 Pittsburgh-area houses. It has trained more than thirty-six thousand volunteers from thirty-five states and four countries to assist homeowners (TPP has a large map in the hall of its main building pinpointing all the locales from which volunteers have come). Collectively, they have worked more than 700,000 hours to help these homeowners. For example, First Presbyterian Church of Caldwell, New Jersey, has brought youth every summer and sometimes twice a summer for eighteen years. They do so because youth "grow in their faith and in their understanding of unconditional giving." TPP staff encourage volunteers to see homeowners as "respected elders for whom it is an honor to work." Many youth gain much more than they give.[35]

After Ghubril left in 2008 to found The Pittsburgh Promise to provide college scholarships for graduates of Pittsburgh Public Schools and charter schools, TPP experienced a financial crisis. Several factors contributed. The principal one was that organizations often have great difficulty replacing their highly respected, charismatic founders. Their successors are often treated like a "rebound girlfriend," and only after time passes can someone again provide effective leadership. Moreover, many organizations that funded TPP did so because of Ghubril's personal relationships with their executives rather than because of their commitment to its mission. As Bruce Bickel, a senior vice-president at PNC Wealth Management, explained, "In the world of philanthropy, people give to people. They don't give to programs." Exacerbating TPP's problems, some of the grants it had been

Youth working to renovate a house with The Pittsburgh Project. *Courtesy of The Pittsburgh Project.*

receiving from foundations ended in 2008, and new ones had not been procured to replace them. Making matters worse, the stock market crashed, and American charitable giving declined significantly. As a result, TPP had to slash its budget from $3.1 million to $2 million and reduce its staff from 50 to 29. The number of youth in its tutoring and life skills programs and the summer camp program declined from 450 to 300.[36]

Under the leadership of William Thompkins, who became executive director in 2014, TPP bounced back. Thompkins grew up in a working-class African American family on the North Side very near TPP's campus. Thompkins worshipped at the Mount Carmel Baptist Church on the North Side and graduated from Oliver High School. After spending three years in the army, including a tour in Vietnam, he completed a business degree at Point Park College by attending night classes while working full time. Prior to becoming head of the TPP, Thompkins served as executive assistant to Allegheny County chief Jim Roddey, CEO of the Urban League of Nebraska, vice-president for programs and services at the Urban League of Pittsburgh and, from 2004 to 2012, as TPP's director of community outreach.[37]

Thompkins identified TPP's greatest strengths as its Christian foundation, its staff's commitment and passion, its networking capability and its reputation. He argued that TPP has worked closely with law enforcement personnel to help prevent crime and retribution on the North Side. It provides a safe haven for many youth in a community where violence and gang activity are still widespread (the Crips, Original Gangsters and several other gangs operate on the North Side).[38]

TPP's after-school programs and summer day camps intellectually, socially, emotionally and spiritually enrich the lives of more than five hundred North Side children each year. These programs enhance academic achievement, foster healthy relationships, improve character, promote faith development, render service to others and seek to transform the neighborhood.[39] Through its "preventive and proactive asset-building program," TPP youth development programs have empowered more than seventeen thousand youth since 1985. TPP has also trained more than six thousand volunteers who collectively have spent more than seventy-five thousand hours tutoring, mentoring and building relationships with these youth.[40]

TPP's Leaders-in-Training program seeks to enable high school students to achieve their potential and become tomorrow's leaders. Participants receive individual and small-group mentoring, specialized tutoring, paid on-the-job training, opportunities to do community service, preparation for higher education and college scholarships. Since 2002, more than 95 percent of the students who have completed this program have entered institutions of higher education, the military or the workforce. Graduates of the program also often work as TPP summer staff. Some of them have received grants to do volunteer work and learn about business and culture in China and Brazil. Each year, twenty graduates receive $3,000 scholarships to study at local colleges. To qualify, students must earn high grades and take TPP classes in SAT preparation, college success strategies, writing and a Christian worldview.

Hundreds of these young people have been redirected through their relationships with TPP. Tevin Jones is using his scholarship to study nanotechnology at Indiana University of Pennsylvania. He testified that TPP helped him academically and spiritually. "We had Bible studies where we talk about life and how it connects to what God has done for you and how it benefits you to follow him and practice being a righteous man," he stated. As a result, "I want to find ways to improve technology" and make the world "more eco-friendly." Scholarship recipient Isaiah Reeves graduated from Grove City College, where he majored in exercise science and played varsity basketball, and he now works for Urban Impact. Undoubtedly speaking for many, Allison Arthur, a medical assistant, praised TPP for keeping her four children "off the streets" and out of trouble and helping them do well in school. Two of them attended college thanks in part to TPP scholarships.[41]

Lauren Pfeiffer, TPP's homeowner services manager, contended that TPP's more than thirty-year incarnational presence in the community makes it different from most other service organizations. TPP staff have built relationships with and carefully listened to the concerns of their North Side neighbors, enabling them to earn their trust and devise programs to effectively assist them. "First and foremost," Pfeiffer explained, "we want to introduce people to a Jesus" who is present in the places where they "don't expect to find Jesus." Student volunteers can see Him "in the house of a poor widow who lives day to day by her trust in God." TPP staff challenge students to commit their lives to serving others and to invest in and encourage the disadvantaged. Staff seek to "spark a fire for change in volunteers' hearts" as "they make decisions" about college, career, marriage and homeownership. "We strive," Pfeiffer asserted, to be "the hands and feet of Jesus," to not simply "talk about the love of God" but to demonstrate it. TPP wants to convince students to live sacrificially as Jesus did and to inspire church members "to love and serve in their own communities."[42]

According to Thompkins, TPP's greatest challenge is to raise adequate funds to conduct its ministry. It has $1 million in deferred maintenance and needs to upgrade its technology, but it has no endowment. TPP would also benefit, Thompkins argued, from greater racial diversity; presently, most of the youth it serves are African American, while most of its volunteers are Caucasian.

To fulfill its mission, TPP collaborates with many other organizations, including Urban Impact, Pittsburgh Kids Foundation, LIVING (Love Initiated Ventures Investing in Neglected Groups) Ministry, Northside Common Ministries and local churches such as Allegheny Center Alliance Church and Mosaic Community Presbyterian Church, which meets on TPP's property. For many years, TPP has worked with the Perry Hilltop Citizens Council and City Reach Church to host a spring Block Party. TPP partners with public schools to sponsor the Northside Open Spelling Challenge. LIVING Ministry, founded by several young men influenced by TPP, seeks to "address the root causes of the homeless by engaging in Christian discipleship, mentoring, counseling, and relational support." Since its founding in 2002, the organization claims to have aided more than ten thousand homeless individuals.[43] Northside Common Ministries operates a food pantry; provides housing for homeless men; offers free eye screenings, glasses and medical advice; and assists low-income individuals to prepare their taxes, pass the GED and search for jobs.[44] Urban Impact and the Pittsburgh Kids Foundation are described in chapters 4 and 5.

In March 2018, Wayne Younger became the new executive director of TPP. Younger, who grew up and lives on the North Side, has worked in social service and campus ministries for twenty years, most recently with PULSE, which seeks to develop young servant leaders to help transform Pittsburgh. A graduate of Asbury University in Wilmore, Kentucky, Younger is also a founding co-pastor of Cityview Covenant Church in Spring Garden. Because of Younger's gifts in "building bridges between races, ethnicities, and communities of differing educational, economic, and faith backgrounds," Ghubril is hopeful that TPP's "best days are ahead of it."[45]

Joanna Doven, the press secretary for former Pittsburgh mayor Luke Ravenstahl, called TPP "one of our city's greatest organizations" because it "provides positive activities and mentoring to hundreds of our city's young people" every year and has motivated many North Side residents "to take greater pride in their community."[46] TPP has also affected hundreds of volunteers by increasing their social consciousness, redirecting their priorities and influencing their choice of college majors; some volunteers have even started their own ministries to aid the destitute.[47] Moreover, TPP has helped inspire Christians in other cities to found similar ministries, including the Philadelphia Project; God's Helping Hands in Mechanicsburg, Pennsylvania; Impact Kalamazoo in Kalamazoo, Michigan; and Aliquippa Impact in Aliquippa, Pennsylvania.[48] TPP is helping make Pittsburgh a city of truth, a shining example of what God can do through staff and volunteers who are committed to emulating Christ and empowering the less fortunate.

Chapter 7

THREE HISTORIC PITTSBURGH CHURCHES

Among Pittsburgh's many congregations, three stand out for their substantial contributions to the city's spiritual, social and educational development. Founded in 1773, 1843 and 1855, respectively, First Presbyterian Church, St. Paul Cathedral and Calvary Episcopal Church have significantly influenced the city's religious life and helped fulfill Shoemaker's vision of making Pittsburgh renowned for its commitment to and service of God.

First Presbyterian Church: Pittsburgh's "Orthodox Center of Faith"

Founded in 1773, First Presbyterian Church in downtown Pittsburgh is the city's first and arguably most important congregation. It is Pittsburgh's oldest institution, predating any newspaper, school or business. Forty-eight men associated with FPC served as officers in the Revolutionary War. Prominent early members included James O'Hara, the first quartermaster general of the United States, and Major Ebenezer Denny, the first mayor of Pittsburgh, whose descendants played a prominent role in FPC until 1966. Under the leadership of pastor Samuel Barr, the church established the Pittsburgh Academy in 1787, which became the Western University of Pennsylvania in 1819 and was renamed the University of Pittsburgh in 1908. During the first decade of the nineteenth century, led by pastor Robert Steele, FPC opened a Sunday school and established the Pittsburgh Moral Society to promote education, temperance and social reform.[1]

During the pastorate of Francis Herron (1811–50), First Presbyterian ministered to thousands of Pittsburghers and sent dozens of missionaries overseas, most notably physician William Speer, who served for many years in China. When Herron arrived in 1811, its residents' "follies and social habits, gambling, drinking, and loose speech had made Pittsburgh the Vanity Fair" of Pennsylvania's western frontier. Some argued that Herron's preaching and personal influence did more to promote good moral conduct than the presence of the city's police force. Convinced that the gospel was relevant to all aspects of life, Herron energetically promoted Pittsburgh's spiritual, moral, economic, educational and social development. During Herron's tenure, First Presbyterian established the Western Foreign Missionary Society (the forerunner of the Presbyterian Church, USA's Board of Foreign Missions) and Western Theological Seminary (later Pittsburgh Theological Seminary). It also planted several other Presbyterian congregations in the city, including Third Presbyterian and First Presbyterian in Allegheny (today's North Side). Herron's fruitful ministry contributed to his selection as the moderator of the PCUSA General Assembly in 1827. By 1833, FPC had 422 members and was sponsoring twelve Sunday schools that met in stables, cellars, shops and warehouses throughout the city with a combined enrollment of 1,212 pupils. During Herron's tenure, the church experienced numerous revivals and added about 1,000 new members.[2]

William Miller Paxton served as FPC's pastor from 1851 to 1866. A Princeton Theological Seminary graduate, Paxton was a gifted preacher and scholar who taught preaching and pastoral theology at Western Theological Seminary (while pastoring FPC) and later at Princeton. FPC's growing numbers led the congregation to construct a much larger facility, which was completed in 1853. Meetings held at FPC in 1857 helped expand American missions to India and China, inspired efforts to minister to young men in Pittsburgh and increased opposition to slavery among city residents. Members of the Synod of Pittsburgh met for three days at FPC in January 1861 to pray that God would forgive guilty American citizens and prevent a war. During the Civil War, Paxton staunchly supported the Union cause, and a community meeting held at FPC raised $50,000 to aid the Sanitary Commission.[3]

During his pastorate from 1866 to 1883, Sylvester Scovel reorganized the church to minister more effectively, and FPC experienced considerable growth and enlarged its influence. In 1867, FPC hosted a "Christian Convention" led by Dwight L. Moody, which expanded its efforts to help needy and vulnerable Pittsburgh residents. For the first of several times, FPC was forced to deal with changing demographics, as many of the church's members moved out of the center city to surrounding neighborhoods, and few of those who took their places were Protestants. In the Gilded Age, FPC's Women's Christian Association conducted much of the congregation's practical ministry. During the 1877 railroad strike, large crowds of enraged workers and their supporters ripped up railroad tracks, set buildings on fire, looted stores and threatened to destroy the entire city. Scovel helped mediate the strike, restore order and gain some improvements for the strikers. By 1880, FPC was the largest congregation in Pittsburgh Presbytery, and in 1881, it added a Sabbath school chapel and lecture room.[4]

Following the pastorates of George Tybout Purves (1886–92) and David Breed (1894–98), who also both left FPC to teach at Presbyterian seminaries, Maitland Alexander became FPC's senior pastor. While most other downtown churches were fleeing to the suburbs, FPC remained in the center of the city, ministering to people working in offices, shops, banks and stores, and under his leadership until 1927, it flourished. Alexander was a Calvinist who, like Herron, sought to "make Pittsburgh truly a City of God." Three principles guided Alexander's effort to have FPC function as "a lighthouse in the heart of the city": prioritize preaching the gospel, welcome all socioeconomic groups and base FPC's social services on biblical principles. Dedicating the church's new building in 1905, Alexander affirmed FPC's commitment to the worship and service of Almighty God and "to the salvation of the men and women of this great city, through the Cross of Christ."[5]

During Alexander's tenure, First Presbyterian sponsored a wide variety of religious, educational and social programs and was open almost continuously. Led by Matilda Denny, FPC's Woman's Work Society taught boys and girls skills for the workplace and home. A parenting club attracted hundreds of mothers each week. FPC sponsored other classes and clubs for various groups, including ones on millinery, sewing, guitar, reading, singing, calisthenics, crocheting and business methods. FPC also helped the unemployed find jobs and furnished coal, clothing and other supplies to the indigent.[6]

Alexander advanced the cause of Christ in other ways as well. For almost twenty years, he taught homiletics at Western Theological Seminary while leading FPC. Alexander helped organize Billy Sunday's 1914 Pittsburgh

First Presbyterian Church. *Courtesy of First Presbyterian Church.*

campaign and strongly defended Christian orthodoxy during the theological battles between conservatives and liberals in the 1920s. He was elected moderator of the General Assembly in 1916 and led FPC to staunchly support American troops during World War I. Three hundred FPC members fought in the war.[7]

When Alexander retired in 1927, FPC called Clarence Macartney, a forty-eight-year-old bachelor who, as the pastor of Arch Street Presbyterian Church in Philadelphia, had answered Harry Emerson Fosdick's famous 1922 sermon "Shall the Fundamentalists Win?" with one titled "Shall Unbelief Win?" Macartney led the Presbytery of Philadelphia in bringing charges against Fosdick and served as the moderator of the General Assembly in 1924. Wedded to the theology of the Westminster Standards, Macartney strove to make the United States a Christian nation and was an ardent moral reformer. True revivals, he insisted, converted individuals and reformed society. Macartney denounced the nation's moral decline as evident in "widespread murder, rampant divorce, the decline of family religion, rising hemlines, blatant hedonism, and apostate preaching." He exhorted Christians to abstain from alcohol, arguing that its abuse was a major source of crime, a public health hazard and a primary cause of economic unproductivity.[8] The author of fifty books—including collections of sermons, a biography of Abraham Lincoln, a study of the Civil War and a history of Pittsburgh—Macartney adeptly led FPC until 1953, helping to maintain its theological orthodoxy and spiritual vitality.[9]

After Macartney retired in 1953, FPC called thirty-four-year-old Robert Lamont, who had pastored a congregation in Philadelphia and taught at Temple University School of Theology. In his first sermon, titled "The Heart of the Gospel for the Heart of the City," Lamont quoted John Wesley's journal entry: "I came to the city and offered them Christ." Wesley, Lamont argued, "could do no more. Under God, I hope to do no less." In 1954, KDKA began broadcasting FPC's Sunday services, which for several years garnered the second-largest radio audience to Norman Vincent Peale's services among national religious programs. As the Pittsburgh Renaissance worked to create the Golden Triangle, Lamont and FPC strove to make the downtown area "a Godly Triangle." In 1956, FPC completed a major expansion that added space for offices, Sunday school classes and church programs. By 1957, the Tuesday Noon Club, a meeting of businessmen that began in 1930, enrolled 2,400 members representing seven hundred congregations belonging to thirty-two denominations. Each week, more than 800 men came to hear a message by Lamont. FPC sponsored a similar club for women, which began in 1914 and, by the 1950s, had 1,200 members. Attendance at the Sunday morning service averaged 1,300 in the early 1970s, with worshippers traveling an average distance of ten miles.[10]

Other programs and activities abounded. In the late 1960s and early 1970s, FPC's Ligonier Camp and Conference Center, established in 1914 as an interdenominational outreach, completed a million-dollar expansion program to enhance its efforts to win young people for Jesus and "train them for Christian service and witness." During Lamont's tenure, FPC operated weekly boys' and girls' clubs that assisted participants with their schoolwork and offered courses in German, fencing, ceramics, carpentry, dressmaking, babysitting, the Bible and many other subjects. Lamont strongly encouraged his parishioners to actively serve their community and set a personal example by participating on the board of *Christianity Today*, two local hospitals, two colleges and two seminaries.[11]

Under Lamont's leadership, First Presbyterian strove to preserve the "relevance of Evangelical Christianity in the heart of Pittsburgh" and make the downtown fit for young people by eradicating strip-tease, decadent movies and obscene literature. Hundreds of its members served as publicists, counselors, ushers, singers and follow-up workers at the 1968 Billy Graham crusade held at Pitt Stadium. Partnering with the Pittsburgh

Experiment, FPC hosted the Pittsburgh Power and Light Company, which sponsored a restaurant, an arts and crafts studio, a library and a coffee house that used music and gospel presentations to minister to college students in the 1970s. Lamont's ministry helped equip hundreds of Christians to express and embody the gospel through their vocations and volunteer service in Pittsburgh.[12]

Lamont was succeeded in 1973 by thirty-three-year-old John A. Huffman Jr. Influenced to go into the ministry by Samuel Shoemaker, Huffman, like Macartney, was already well known before becoming FPC's senior pastor because President Richard Nixon had frequently attended his church in Key Biscayne, Florida. Huffman expanded the outreach of FPC beyond its weekly radio program on KDKA by hosting a live monthly television show that discussed ethical and spiritual issues with varied guests, including judges, politicians and prostitutes. In addition, his printed sermons were mailed to five thousand people each week. Huffman worked diligently to energize and empower the church's members to minister to city residents.[13]

After Huffman left in 1978, First Presbyterian faced many challenges, including the lack of pastoral leadership, whether to ordain women as elders and ministers and membership decline caused in part by Pittsburgh's economic struggles and population decline. Following a short pastorate by Ernest Lewis and two years without a senior pastor, FPC called Bruce Wheeler Thielemann in 1984. One of the nation's premier preachers, Thielemann had traveled to sixty nations to proclaim the gospel. Through his Sunday sermons, which were broadcast on KDKA radio, aired on several local television stations and disseminated to thousands of people as tapes (more clergy bought tapes of Thielemann's sermons than those of any other American minister), he reached a large audience for Christ. However, Thielemann suffered from heart problems, which forced him to limit his activity and led FPC to end its long-standing noon clubs for men and women. During Thielemann's tenure, which ended in 1993, FPC's active social ministry continued as its members compassionately counseled women on alternatives to abortion and energetically worked to help the unemployed, homeless and impoverished. FPC provided groceries for many low-income families, cleaned people's homes who could not do so themselves and replaced windows and did minor repairs for the elderly, disabled and impoverished.[14]

Because of Thielemann's health problems, restricted ministry and delayed resignation, FPC experienced another decline in membership, Sunday morning worship attendance and morale. Nevertheless, when Dr.

R. Leslie Holmes took the helm in 1993, FPC still had 1,031 members and enrolled 310 in its Sunday school. Born, raised and educated in Northern Ireland, Holmes, like Thielemann, was a gifted orator. Through well-crafted sermons that were heard by many on the radio and television as well as several books, Holmes strenuously strove to practice his motto of "Lifting Up Christ and Building Up People." FPC strongly supported the 1993 Billy Graham Crusade and conducted a successful youth ministry. However, Holmes was not able to duplicate the growth in membership and finances he had accomplished in his previous churches, and FPC continued to struggle.[15] After Holmes left in 2004, FPC went more than four years without a senior pastor, which brought even greater decline in its attendance, vitality and ministry.

First Presbyterian Church Today

In 2009, Tom Hall became FPC's fifteenth senior pastor. After earning a BS at the Air Force Academy and an MS at the University of Southern California, Hall spent thirty years in the air force, attaining the rank of full colonel. He served both in the United States and overseas and had assignments in flying operations, reconnaissance, intelligence activities and flight tests. Hall also taught courses in leadership for five years at the Air War College in Montgomery, Alabama, and had three command tours.[16]

For much of his life, Hall was not actively involved in a church, but in 1999, he concluded that his two teenage sons needed to see him actively living out his faith in Christ. After attending a Promise Keepers conference in Atlanta, he decided that Joshua 24—"as for me and my house, we will serve the Lord"—would be his guiding philosophy. Hall soon became deeply involved in Memorial Presbyterian Church in Montgomery, where he served as the head of its deacons.[17]

After retiring from the air force in 2004, Hall considered working as a motivational speaker or a government contractor. He felt called, however, to become a minister, and in 2005, Hall began attending Pittsburgh Theological Seminary; his son Sean joined him there the next year. Following his graduation, First Presbyterian's members, impressed by his gifts and life experience, called him to be their senior pastor.[18]

Hall's primary roles are preaching, furnishing a vision for the future and supervising the staff—which includes an associate pastor, a director of operations, a minister of youth and families, a director of faith development (Hall's wife, Jana), a music minister, an organist, a volunteer coordinator and a secretary. First Presbyterian's chief priority, according to Hall, is to faithfully proclaim the gospel as it has been doing for 245 years to "make a difference in the city." The church, Hall contended, has long been Pittsburgh's "orthodox center of faith." Its congregants' commitment to Jesus, he asserted, determines and drives everything the church does. First Presbyterian's mission is to transform Pittsburgh guided by five core values: confidence in God's Word, belief in God's faithfulness, a commitment to the city, obedience to God's direction and connection with and care of neighbors. A church flyer titled "What We Believe" affirms that "Jesus Christ is Lord; the Bible is God's Word; we all fall short of who God intended us to be; God loves us too much to leave us the way we are," as well as that people are created to worship, serve one another and live out their faith in the world. FPC's strengths, Hall argued, are its devotion to Scripture, Christ-centeredness, worship and preaching.[19]

Hall's preaching style is modeled on that of Tim Keller, a bestselling author and retired pastor of Redeemer Presbyterian Church in New York City—expository preaching that focuses on Jesus. Every sermon is based on texts that confront readers with a key problem: they should live to glorify God but fail to do so. One person, however, was completely faithful to God: Jesus. When a person is fully committed to Christ, he or she can begin to live as He did.[20]

What Hall loves most about the ministry is preaching the gospel from the grand pulpit of Pittsburgh's most historic church. He is especially energized by First Presbyterian's ministry to low-income city residents. Every Tuesday, twenty to sixty volunteers serve dinner to, talk with and share Christ's love with one hundred or so guests, most of whom are homeless. The meal is provided through FPC's partnership with Outreached Arms, a nonprofit whose members seek to build relationships with and care for the homeless and the hungry. Diners also often receive clothing, toiletries and snack packs. This partnership, Hall claimed, is changing many of his parishioners' approach to ministry.

Foreign and domestic missions have long been a priority at First Presbyterian. Today, about 12 percent of the church's budget ($100,000) goes to missions. During the summer of 2016, the church's youth group served residents of rural Kentucky. FPC supports fifty mission partners financially, including Hosanna Industries, the East Liberty Family Center, a local women's shelter and PRISM (an international student ministry).

Tom Hall. *Courtesy of First Presbyterian Church.*

The church also hosts a World Missions Weekend each year to enable numerous missionaries to share what God is doing around the world.[21] Partnering with Youth for Christ, since 2009 FPC has housed The Cellar, an after-school ministry for high school students. At The Cellar, which is open four days a week, students learn leadership skills, talk about life and faith and are mentored by caring adults.[22]

First Presbyterian was long one of Pittsburgh's most prominent churches, but it has been losing members for forty years and today has only 10 percent of the 2,500 members it had at its peak in the 1950s. Several factors have contributed to its recent decline in membership, attendance, programs and vitality. Its principal problem is the one experienced by hundreds of other downtown congregations in major cities—only a small number of people who live in its vicinity are regular church attenders, and numerous attractive alternatives exist in the suburbs. In addition, Hall explained that not having an installed senior pastor for more than four years and the temporary loss of its vision and mission significantly hampered First Presbyterian.[23]

On the brighter side, 2016 was the first year in the last forty when the church's average Sunday worship attendance increased (it is now about 140), and members are building stronger, more intimate relationships. Today's members live in sixty different zip codes. The average age of members is sixty-five, while the mean age of regular attenders is fifty. Most First Presbyterian members are professionals, some of whom are still working, while others are retired. Surprisingly, given the church's impressive heritage, only 10 percent of current members have a family history in the church. The twelve-person session (the church's governing body) is composed of both men and women.[24] The church currently offers five Sunday school classes for adults. FPC also sponsors a Tuesday noon Bible study, a ladies' Bible study on Mondays at a home in Millvale and activities for high school students on Sunday morning, Wednesday night and every other Saturday morning.[25]

First Presbyterian Church faces enormous challenges. Its congregants are a generation older than the people, mostly millennials, who live in the apartments and condominiums surrounding the church, and one-third of millennials have no religious affiliation. Hall asserted that years of decline have taken their toll on the church's ethos, leading many members to conclude that "our best days are behind us." He accepted the position at First Presbyterian, however, because he believed he could convince its parishioners to reimagine its ministry and make a difference for Christ in the city. In the spirit of Samuel Shoemaker, Hall's goal is to fulfill the church's slogan: to be "a dynamic, transforming church where all are welcome, lives are changed, and the gospel is lived and proclaimed."[26]

The Church Visit

My student assistant Alexia Skoria and I visited First Presbyterian Church on February 19, 2017. Located amid high-end retail shops, skyscrapers and high-rise apartment complexes is FPC's large and impressive English Gothic building, which was completed in 1905. It features a magnificent organ with 4,400 pipes and fourteen resplendent stained-glass windows, thirteen of which were designed by Tiffany Studios.[27] About 125 people of all ages were scattered throughout the large sanctuary seating 1,000 people.

The service included announcements, a responsive reading, a unison prayer of confession, an assurance of God's pardon, a children's message given to ten young ones, three traditional hymns (including "To God Be the Glory"), the reciting of the Apostles' Creed, a pastoral prayer followed by the Lord's prayer, an offering and a twenty-minute sermon.

Hall began the service by asking "where would you put the church?" and answering "right here in the middle of the fastest-growing neighborhood in America's most livable city. God is inviting us to be part of transforming this city." Using a text from I Corinthians 14, Hall concluded a series of sermons he had been preaching about Jesus and women. He argued that the Christians should not interpret the Apostle Paul's directive that "women should keep silent in the church" to mean that they could never speak in church services or play leadership roles in congregations. Misinterpretations of this passage, Hall lamented, had been used to oppress women for centuries and offended many people in twenty-first-century America. Paul did not intend to demean women or to teach that women must never speak or hold positions of authority in the church. Rather, Paul was striving to be sensitive to the cultural milieu. The Bible teaches, Hall contended, that women are the completion of men and that together women and men are the crown and glory of God. Moreover, some women—including Lydia, Priscilla and Phoebe—were church leaders, and women were the first witnesses to Christ's resurrection.

The God who in Jesus "ripped a hole in space and time," Hall proclaimed, wanted to spread His message as quickly and effectively as possible, which necessitated both men and women using their gifts to reach others for Christ. It is the same today: the church's ministry is most fruitful when both sexes work together to minister to those with physical and spiritual needs.

For 245 years, First Presbyterian has been Pittsburgh's flagship church. By conducting varied ministries, founding educational enterprises, planting other churches, operating the Ligonier Camp and Conference Center (which serves 1,800 campers each summer and hosts 8,000 people each year for conferences at its beautiful lodge about sixty miles east of Pittsburgh), sending hundreds of members into the ministry and mission field and supporting numerous interdenominational evangelistic and social reform campaigns, as well as by the outreach of its radio and television ministry, its Tuesday and Thursday Noon Clubs and its faithful witness to the Lordship of Christ, FPC has tremendously advanced Shoemaker's quest to make Pittsburgh as famous for God as for steel and has significantly promoted God's kingdom beyond the region.

St. Paul Cathedral: Shining the Light of Christ

St. Paul Cathedral, established in 1843, is the mother church of the Diocese of Pittsburgh, which currently consists of 632,000 Catholics. It is the home for Bishop David Zubik and the site of the diocese's major events, including ordinations to the priesthood and diaconate, an Easter blessing for families and the 2017 funeral of Steelers owner Dan Rooney. St. Paul celebrates Mass six times each week—at 6:00 p.m. on Saturday and at 6:30 a.m., 8:00 a.m., 10:00 a.m., noon and 6:00 p.m. on Sundays; the average total attendance is about 3,200. St. Paul Cathedral was originally located at the corner of Fifth Avenue and Grant Street in downtown Pittsburgh. After industrialist Henry Clay Frick bought this property, a spacious and beautiful church was constructed on Fifth Avenue in Oakland. It opened in 1906 and was renovated in 2006. Designed in fourteenth-century Gothic style and

St. Paul Cathedral. *Courtesy of St. Paul Cathedral.*

originally costing $1.1 million, the cathedral is 247 feet high and topped by a statue of the Apostle Paul. Located in a vibrant neighborhood in the Steel City's intellectual heart, the church is surrounded by universities, medical centers, museums, libraries and research centers, as well as restaurants, residences, offices and stores. Over the years, St. Paul has hosted many renowned Catholics, including Bishop Fulton Sheen, Pope John Paul II and Mother Teresa.[28] Since 1991, the cathedral's Mass has been televised. At present, its 8:00 a.m. Mass is televised three times every Sunday and viewed by a substantial audience.[29]

Father Kris Stubna, the current rector, was raised in a solidly Catholic family and attended Catholic schools. While at Holy Trinity High School in McKees Rocks, he began to feel God's call to become a priest. Two priests at his local parish in Robinson Township served as role models and helped confirm his call. In 1981, Stubna graduated from St. Paul Seminary in Pittsburgh and Duquesne University with degrees in psychology and philosophy. After completing his seminary studies at the North American College in Rome, Stubna was ordained in 1985. He briefly served parishes in Natrona Heights and the Allentown section of Pittsburgh and then returned to the North American College, where he completed a doctorate in fundamental theology in 1993. Following his work as the diocese's secretary for Catholic education from 1994 to 2012, he was appointed the rector and pastor of St. Paul Cathedral. Stubna has taught courses at LaRoche College and Duquesne and published numerous articles and books, including *What Catholics Believe: A Pocket Catechism* (1999), *Talking to Youth about Sexuality: A Parent's Guide* (2006) and *Take Five: On-the-Job Meditations with St. Ignatius* (2016). Stubna has served on several boards, including DePaul School for Hearing and Speech, the Homeless Children's Education Fund and Carlow University.[30]

Stubna sees his primary pastoral duty as shepherding God's flock at St. Paul. He strives to help all its members deepen their love for God, encounter "the Living Christ and his Church" and develop "a vibrant faith." To do this, Stubna preaches God's Word, administers the sacraments and seeks to motivate worshippers to commune with Christ. He celebrates Mass three times every weekday (at 6:45 a.m.; 8:15 a.m., which is televised; and 12:05 p.m.; a total of about 350 people typically attend the three Masses) and three times each weekend and hears about two hundred confessions each week. Every year, he officiates at many weddings, performs dozens of funerals and baptizes numerous children. Many Catholics, Stubna lamented, have been raised simply to attend Mass and give money to the church. He wants instead to develop a caring Christian community whose members serve others through the church's ministries and their daily activities.[31]

Compared with the profiled Protestant congregations, St. Paul has a small staff primarily because of its limited financial resources and the diocese's dearth of priests. St. Paul has a minister of music and an assistant organist, a parochial vicar who serves as an assistant, a business manager and two full-time administrative assistants in the office. A resident priest helps with the Masses and confessions as his schedule permits. The congregation also has a lay director of social and pastoral outreach.

The church's Pastoral Council has established four priorities—to provide inspiring worship that includes good music and preaching; to be a praying community; to promote spiritual formation through its worship, prayer, Bible study and specific programs for adults, young adults, children and families; and to welcome people of all races, ethnicities and socioeconomic statuses, as well as people with disabilities. "Empowered by the Holy Spirit and nourished by the Eucharist," St. Paul, the church's website states, "shares the Good News of Jesus Christ" with Pittsburgh residents.[32]

In his preaching, Stubna strives to faithfully explain Catholic doctrine and apply biblical teaching to people's lives. Through sermons based on scriptural texts, he seeks to get people "out of their comfort zones" and equip them to be faithful witnesses for Christ. Stubna described his preaching style as "engaging, optimistic, and joyful."[33] His twelve- to fifteen-minute sermons are considerably shorter than those of most of the other clergy highlighted in this book.

What Stubna loves the most about the ministry is "the impact that you can have on people" by "being an instrument of God's love" as they deal with life's challenges. He seeks to connect people to Christ and serve others. For Stubna, funerals provide especially powerful opportunities to present the gospel and deeply touch people's hearts. Many individuals have told him that the funerals he performed for their family members brought them closer to Christ.[34]

St. Paul provides a variety of venues to help parishioners deepen their faith. The church holds a weekly Bible study.[35] Its Family Faith Formation program meets monthly during the school year, as does a prayer group. Young adults gather each month at a local restaurant to eat and drink, become better acquainted and listen to speakers discuss aspects of Catholic faith.[36] Stubna hosts a monthly Wine, Cheese and the gospel discussion (which often attracts two hundred people) that deals with various moral, theological and social issues. Small groups that meet for Bible study, prayer and fellowship,

Kris Stubna. *Courtesy of St. Paul Cathedral.*

Stubna argued, greatly help individuals grow in their faith and connect more deeply with fellow believers. He encourages members to attend training the diocese offers to help them identify and develop their gifts and equip them to lead small groups.[37]

St. Paul partners with the Oratory—a national organization of priests and brothers who minister on college campuses—to sponsor Catholic Action. Its members organize about one hundred on-campus Bible studies in which several thousand University of Pittsburgh, Carnegie Mellon University and Chatham University students participate. The Oratory also holds weekly meetings in the church's parish hall following the 6:00 p.m. Sunday Mass that are attended by 80 to 120 students and feature pizza, ice cream and speakers who address timely religious and moral subjects.[38]

St. Paul is a very diverse congregation. Many of its worshippers are undergraduate or graduate students. While many older parishioners live in Oakland or the East End, a sizable number of members live in other Pittsburgh suburbs. The congregation has a growing number of families with small children. In 2016, the church had one hundred baptisms, which was twice the number of its funerals.[39]

St. Paul's Pastoral Council, consisting of fifteen members who serve three-year terms and can be renewed for another three years, provides guidance and support to Father Stubna to accomplish the parish's mission. Council members are a diverse group in terms of age, ethnicity and occupations. Including both men and women, the council meets quarterly, develops a strategic plan for the congregation and directs the church's ministry. A six-person Finance Council establishes the church budget, supplies fiscal oversight and oversees the physical plant.[40]

St. Paul has made local missions a priority. Its website emphasizes that all four gospels recount the story of Jesus feeding the five thousand to convey His miraculous power and teach that God expects us "to be the hands and feet of Christ on earth." The cathedral operates a food bank that serves several hundred people each week. Through its Annual Giving Tree, members provide toys to low-income children and support various social agencies to help the indigent and unemployed have "a meaningful Christmas holiday." The fifty women who belong to St. Paul's Ladies of Charity visit the local VA hospitals and church members who are in nursing homes or shut-ins. The cathedral's Race and Reconciliation Dialogue Group promotes human dignity, racial equality and social justice. It holds monthly discussion meetings, hosts a service to celebrate the philosophy and legacy of Martin Luther King Jr. and sponsors movies dealing with racial issues.[41] Through its Respect Life Group, St. Paul speaks "for those who are unable to speak for themselves." Its members work to protect people from conception to natural death by supplying information and going to Washington, D.C., every January to pray, protest and lobby "against the injustice of legal abortion" in conjunction with the March for Life. They also participate in an annual Life Chain and the biannual 40 Days for Life Campaign to protest against abortion.[42] Stubna noted that many of the young adults who attend St. Paul deeply deplore social injustice. They inspire the cathedral's older members with their passion, knowledge and service, especially to the two Catholic high schools in the parish.[43]

As the mother church of the Pittsburgh Diocese and the residence of the bishop, St. Paul plays a pivotal role in many Catholic campaigns and programs in the Greater Pittsburgh Area. The congregation has a rich history, a large, beautiful facility, a strong music program and powerful preaching. St. Paul's varied parishioners enjoy worshipping, learning and serving together.[44]

Stubna identified three major challenges confronting the congregation. First is to motivate members to actively live out their faith, to move them beyond simply attending Mass to participating in study and outreach. Second is the transient nature of the cathedral's flock, especially because it includes many college students and young adults who worship there for only a short period. Third, the church's physical plant is expensive to maintain, and its revenue is limited.[45]

St. Paul strives to be alive in the Spirit and to lovingly serve the surrounding community. Its highest priorities, according to Stubna, are to build a stronger congregation, win people to Christ, minister to the elderly and aid the poor. As American culture "pushes back against Christians," Stubna argued, believers must courageously and winsomely testify and live for Jesus by taking their faith into the schools and workplace.[46]

The Church Visit

Alexia Skoria and I attended the 6:00 p.m. Mass at St. Paul on Palm Sunday in 2017. I spoke briefly with the church's minister of music, who plays the church's massive, magnificent organ situated in the balcony at the rear of the sanctuary at all its Masses and directs its fifty-person choir at the Sunday noon service. About 500 worshippers of all ages, including numerous college students, were scattered throughout a sanctuary that seats 1,800.

Because this was a High Mass, Father Stubna sang much of the liturgy and dispensed a large amount of incense. As the service began, we faced the back of the sanctuary. Participants in the service, led by Father Stubna, stood in the rear of the sanctuary as congregants sang a chorus, which was followed by a reading from Matthew 21:1–11, an account of Jesus' triumphal entry into Jerusalem. The priest and his entourage then processed down the center aisle carrying palm branches.

Catholic congregations follow a lectionary—a set of scriptural passages assigned for each Sunday of the year. The reading for Palm Sunday about Jesus' passion—Matthew 26:14–27:66 (108 verses)—is the longest of the year. Three readers—Stubna, a layman and a laywoman—alternated reading the words of Jesus, the disciples, the Jewish authorities and the narrative.

Following the scriptural reading, Stubna delivered a homily. The day of Jesus' triumphal entry into Jerusalem, he asserted, involved contrasts and contradictions because in the ancient world, emperors were crowned and victors in war were feted with palm branches. The crowd enthusiastically welcomed Jesus to the city, hailing Him as a king. Many Jews wrongly assumed, Stubna asserted, that Jesus was coming to Jerusalem to demonstrate His power, expel the Romans and become their earthly king. It soon became clear, however, that He would not be the kind of king they desired. Instead of simply freeing the Jews from their bondage to Rome, Jesus would much more significantly liberate them from their enslavement to sin and Satan.

We can identify with the Jerusalem crowd's rejection of Jesus later in the week, Stubna argued. It is tough for us to stand with Jesus today; when difficulties arise, many desert Him. Although we often turn away from Jesus, Stubna maintained, He always invites us to come back. Christ wants us to lay down our lives in service, humility, compassion and love. To truly be Christ's disciples, we must take up our crosses. Stubna exhorted listeners to stand with Jesus and give Him the "total gift of ourselves."

After the homily, worshippers recited the Nicene Creed. A few short songs and prayers followed, including ones for political leaders, church leaders and persecuted Christians. Stubna then blessed the Communion elements, which Catholics believe become through the words of consecration the real and true presence of Jesus (His body and blood given to us at the Last Supper). The service ended with a prayer and benediction.

Stubna is committed to making Pittsburgh famous for God. The city, he argued, has a long, rich religious history, and its various Christian communities enjoy great camaraderie and cooperation. Stubna pointed out that since the 1980s, pastors, priests and parachurch leaders have held a prayer service on Good Friday at St. Paul, and the next day, they go to Mount Washington to ask God to bless the city.[47] "Christ wants the light of truth to shine more brightly in the world" through the lives of Christians, Stubna declared.[48] Through the ministry of St. Paul Cathedral, the light of Christ is strongly affecting Oakland and other parts of Pittsburgh as well.

Calvary Episcopal Church: Advancing Shoemaker's Vision

Calvary Episcopal Church, on the border of East Liberty and Shadyside, was founded in 1855. The church is in a socially, economically and racially diverse area that includes a dozen neighborhoods, and it is close to Carnegie Mellon University and the University of Pittsburgh. In the late nineteenth century, Calvary founded several missions that eventually became flourishing parishes, including St. Stephen's in Wilkinsburg, Fox Chapel Episcopal Church, Church of the Ascension in Oakland and St. Paul's in Mount Lebanon.[49] As described in chapters 1 and 4, many of Calvary's members have actively engaged in social ministry since the 1880s.

Calvary's current building, designed by renowned architect Ralph Adams Cram, a beautiful Gothic Revival church, opened in 1907. Constructed in the form of a cross, the exquisite, largely stone church has magnificent stained-glass windows, lovely polished woodwork and a sanctuary that seats 1,200. In 1907, Calvary was the largest and most important parish in the Diocese of Pittsburgh. Prominent Pittsburgh industrialists and many families who either established or worked for influential companies, banks, universities, hospitals and other enterprises belonged to Calvary. The congregation had several thousand members, large adult and children's choirs and ample finances. The first radio broadcast of a church service occurred at Calvary in 1921.[50]

After Samuel Shoemaker's highly successful ministry during the prosperous 1950s (described in chapter 4), Calvary faced many challenging social issues and demographic changes in the 1960s and 1970s. Its membership decreased and became more geographically and culturally

Calvary Episcopal Church. *Courtesy of Calvary Episcopal Church.*

diverse. Throughout its history, Calvary's parishioners have worked energetically to assist the poor and minorities. Since the 1980s, the church has ministered to many Pittsburgh-area residents who are HIV-positive or have AIDS. More recently, it has promoted racial reconciliation, challenged the city to improve its policing and welcomed gay worshippers. Prominent bishops in both the Episcopal Church and the global Anglican Communion have preached at the church. Its first African American senior pastor, Harold T. Lewis, who served from 1996 to 2012, was a strong advocate of social justice.[51]

When debates over theology and the ordination of gay bishops produced a major schism in the Episcopal Church in 2008, many Pittsburgh congregations, led by Bishop Robert Duncan, formed a new diocese that joined the Anglican Church in North America. Calvary led opposition to this action and worked to preserve the Episcopal Church's assets, governance and heritage in the Pittsburgh area. Today, it is the largest and most prominent of the thirty-six Episcopal congregations in the Pittsburgh diocese.[52]

Calvary's current rector, Jonathon Jensen, began his ministry in 2014. As a child, Jensen did not go to church. In high school and during his first two years of college at Transylvania University in Lexington, Kentucky, he attended services at various Christian denominations, Jewish synagogues and Buddhist temples. He majored in religion at Transylvania, but he was personally not rooted in any faith tradition. His junior year, Jensen attended an Episcopal church near campus where Kentucky senator Henry Clay had worshipped. He soon was attending regularly, helping with the youth group, leading a Sunday class for college students, reading theological tomes and working as the church janitor. Jensen gradually accepted God's grace and love and was confirmed in the Episcopal Church that academic year.[53]

Following his college graduation in 1993, Jensen attended Virginia Theological Seminary in a Washington, D.C., suburb. After completing his MDiv degree in 1996, Jensen did a two-year stint with an Episcopal congregation in Potomac, Maryland, and then served as the canon for pastoral care and outreach at Christ Church Cathedral in New Orleans from 1998 to 2002. Jensen spent the next seven years as the pastor of an Episcopal church in Lawrence, Kansas, which doubled in size during his tenure. From 2009 to 2014, he was the dean of Trinity Episcopal Cathedral in Little Rock, Arkansas.

Jensen's primary roles as Calvary's lead pastor are overseeing the church's staff, worship and building; setting a vision and policies; directing the vestry (the congregation's governing body); and raising funds. In his preaching,

Jensen seeks to explain to worshippers why the Bible matters today and how God acts in people's everyday lives. Jensen tries to develop one main point in depth and insists that every sermon can be summarized in two sentences. When preparing his sermons, he pictures three people: a man who has a PhD in theology, a woman who attends every Bible study the church offers and a man who comes to church only because his fiancée wants to be married there. In his ministry, Jensen seeks to help individuals encounter God and find and fulfill their callings. He strives to be present in people's lives when it matters the most, especially when they experience crises.[54]

Calvary plays a pivotal role today in the Episcopal Diocese of Pittsburgh. When half of the diocese's congregations and two-thirds of its priests left the denomination in 2008 after a long, messy, public divorce to join the Anglican Church of North America, Calvary remained. It hosts an annual Thanksgiving service for area Episcopal churches, ordination services for the diocese's new bishops and numerous diocese meetings. Calvary also gives 11 percent of its budget to support other Episcopal congregations in the Pittsburgh area.[55]

Because other congregations are now larger and more influential, Calvary is not the flagship church it once was in Pittsburgh. However, it still has 1,500 members, with 800 to 900 people attending on Easter and 350 on an average Sunday. Its parishioners come from all walks of life and include all ages: "Gay and straight, families with young children and empty nesters, descendants of Europeans, Africans and Asians; couples, single, married or divorced persons; students and retirees, all make Calvary" their church home and "contribute to the vitality, diversity and openness of the parish."[56] About half of Calvary's members live within a ten- to fifteen-minute car ride of the church; quite a few walk or bike to services; 300 to 400 members, however, live at least thirty minutes away. Jensen argued that people are attracted to Calvary primarily because of the quality of its music and its numerous social outreach programs.[57]

Calvary sponsors an adult forum on Sunday morning between its two worship services to help its members deepen their "knowledge and understanding of Christian life," "learn how to love God" and be better equipped to serve others. Taught by Jensen and a lay leader, the forum focuses on topics such as prayer, theology, social justice and the sacraments. Many members meet weekly to study the Bible or religious books, pray, engage in social activities or minister to the community.[58]

Associate rector T.J. Freeman explained that Calvary has a variety of activities for young adults who are either graduate students at Pitt or CMU or are young professionals. They go to brunch once a month after the morning service, meet once a month at a restaurant for a happy hour, have two four- or five-week book or Bible studies each year and do several service projects each year. These fellowship activities, Freeman asserted, help build relationships that facilitate spiritual discussions.[59]

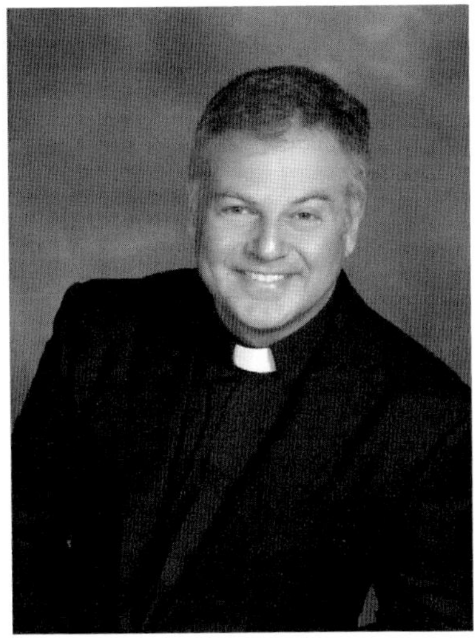

Jonathon Jensen. *Courtesy of Calvary Episcopal Church.*

Calvary's strengths, Jensen maintained, are its strong lay leaders, fruitful outreach ministries, impressive building and music, worship style, warm welcoming of visitors and the harmony of its church family. The church is at a crossroads, Jensen argued. For the past ten years, it has been engrossed internally because of the controversy and schism in the denomination. Now, in keeping with its illustrious heritage, it must again focus on serving and aiding the surrounding community.

Social ministry, Jensen noted, is a part of Calvary's DNA. The church states that its mission "is to challenge and enable" every member "to apply his/her faith beyond the walls of the parish" and "collaboratively assist people in need." Its members seek to be faithful to Christ's admonition in Matthew 25:40: "Truly I tell you, just as you did it to the least of these who are members of my family, you did it to me."[60] Many of its members currently participate regularly in the East End Cooperative Ministry (EECM), the Pittsburgh Interfaith Impact Network (which works to improve healthcare and transportation, aid immigrants and low-income employees and stop racial profiling by the police), Off the Floor Pittsburgh (a ministry that provides free furniture to poor families and individuals) or Habitat for Humanity. Founded in 1970, the EECM provides meals, shelter and groceries to low-income community residents. Numerous Calvary members work with people from more than fifty other congregations to operate the EECM's educational enterprises, drug and alcohol and violence prevention programs, summer day camp and winter coat drive. Calvary's members volunteer in the EECM's food pantry (the second-largest one in Pittsburgh), shelter dinners and community kitchen and tutor students in grades K–12. Calvary also helps fund the EECM's various programs. In addition, Calvary founded Alpha House, which furnishes accommodations and resources to people suffering from addiction, and Sheldon Calvary Camp, which provides a rich spiritual experience for eight hundred youth each summer.[61]

Jensen stressed that Calvary was one of the first Episcopal congregations in the Pittsburgh area to employ women priests, welcome homosexuals to worship and perform gay marriages. Calvary does not perform straight weddings and gay weddings, Jensen explained, but simply weddings.[62]

The Church Visit

On October 9, 2016, Alexia Skoria and I visited Calvary. I attended an open forum during the Sunday school hour that featured a report by vestry member Mark Rust about the church's stewardship campaign and a "state of the church discourse" by Pastor Jensen. Rust announced that members would be sharing about how they use their gifts of time, talent and treasure to advance the ministry of Calvary at morning services throughout the fall. Like many mainline congregations, Calvary had a budget deficit the last four years. Three-quarters of its income comes from pledges, while one-fifth comes from the interest on its $5 million endowment. A quarter of Calvary's budget is used to pay clergy salaries; 43 percent goes to parish support and administration. Jensen insisted that the church's programs are going well and argued that the only congregations that do have enough money (usually because of their huge endowment) are spiritually dead. To improve its financial situation, Calvary encourages its members to set up bequests to give their assets to the church after their death. Contrary to a common assumption, Jensen declared, industrialist Henry Clay Frick did not pay for building Calvary Church by himself; hundreds of people contributed, and many givers are needed today to carry out its mission. While Calvary's beautiful building is a great blessing, Jensen argued, it is very expensive to maintain.

Calvary's fifty-member church choir, consisting of both men and women ranging in age from eighteen to eighty, is very accomplished. Their anthem, "There Is a Balm in Gilead," brought tears to my eyes. The liturgically rich service consisted of readings from the Old Testament, the Epistles and the gospel, the standard Episcopal practice. The morning prayers included petitions for the victims of Hurricane Matthew in Haiti, people suffering from AIDS and the peace process in Colombia.

A worship service at Calvary Episcopal Church. *Courtesy of Calvary Episcopal Church.*

Jensen's sermon focused on Luke 17:11–19, which describes Jesus healing ten lepers. Although we would all like to be healed instantaneously as these lepers were, Jensen declared, healing is normally a process that requires a person's willingness to change and work hard. These ten lepers asked Jesus for money, but they received a much greater blessing. In biblical times, lepers were shunned by family, had no jobs or friends, could not participate in religious life and had to rely on charity. Only one of the ten lepers, a Samaritan, Jensen emphasized, returned to thank Jesus. The other nine, he argued, may have not wanted to become whole again. Our life circumstances are usually beyond our control, but we choose how to respond to them. Only the Samaritan recognized the full extent of what had happened—that he had been healed and made whole, that he was spiritually, physically and emotionally a new person.

All ten men were changed physically, but only one of them was holistically healed. Nine lepers were cured of their affliction, Jensen asserted, just as we can be cured of an addiction, a disease or depression. Only the Samaritan, however, recognized that he was freed to do something. He alone understood his responsibility to praise God and become a whole and holy person. Each of us, Jensen argued, has the same opportunity. We probably will not be physically healed from our health problems, but we can still become spiritually healed, whole and well. Through making moral choices and leading righteous lives, Jensen concluded, we thank God for His presence and power in our lives.

A special room at the church displays all of Samuel Shoemaker's and his wife Helen's books and numerous photos of them. Many parishioners, Jensen explained, are therefore aware of Shoemaker's quest to make Pittsburgh as famous for God as for steel. Calvary Episcopal Church, one of Pittsburgh's leading congregations for a century, is still playing a major role in fulfilling Shoemaker's vision by working to reduce the city's poverty, promote racial reconciliation and provide justice for all residents.[63]

Chapter 8

FOUR PITTSBURGH MEGACHURCHES

Four megachurches (defined as churches that have two thousand or more worshippers each weekend)[1] are significantly advancing Shoemaker's quest to make Pittsburgh famous for God. Allegheny Center Alliance Church, affiliated with the Christian and Missionary Alliance, began in 1894. The other three, which are all nondenominational—The Bible Chapel, North Way Christian Community and Victory Family Church—were founded in 1964, 1981 and 1993, respectively. ACAC meets on the North Side and in Homestead, Victory Family Church is in Cranberry and The Bible Chapel and North Way Christian Community have multiple sites in the Pittsburgh area. All four churches follow the same pattern of worship—twenty to thirty minutes of spirted singing led by a praise band, announcements and a thirty-five- to forty-five-minute sermon. All are evangelical and accentuate helping individuals develop a personal relationship with Christ, grow in their faith, share the gospel with others and meet material and social needs in the Pittsburgh area.

Allegheny Center Alliance Church: Proclaiming Jesus' "Compassion, Justice, Transforming Power, and Liberating Truth"

Allegheny Center Alliance Church (ACAC) was established in Pittsburgh in 1894. ACAC is affiliated with the Christian and Missionary Alliance

(C&MA), a denomination that traces its roots to the activities of A.B. Simpson in 1887 and currently has more than 2,000 congregations and 500,000 members in the United States and 6 million members worldwide. E.D. Whiteside, a businessman who directed the city's first rescue mission, initially led the congregation. ACAC's members erected their first building on Arch Street on the North Side in 1911. When it purchased the property of Christ Episcopal Church on Union Street on the North Side in 1950, ACAC had about 700 members. Ten years later, ACAC was "widely known as a center of missions and evangelism" and had contributed more than $1 million to foreign missions, and 118 of its members had become ministers or missionaries.[2]

ACAC grew rapidly in the 1950s and 1960s, and in the late 1960s, the congregation built its current sanctuary. In the 1970s, however, the neighborhood around the church changed dramatically. Crime and poverty became prevalent, thousands of residents moved to the suburbs and many North Side properties physically deteriorated. ACAC's membership declined from more than 900 in 1970 to less than 400 in the early 1980s. Few of its members lived in the local neighborhood; most were older whites who resided in the suburbs. Morale was low, and the future appeared to be bleak. Moreover, the church "had a bad reputation in the community," caused by the bigotry of some of its leaders and members and the church's indifference to the problems of a predominantly black community.[3]

Under the leadership of pastor Rockwell (Rock) Dillaman, who came in 1984, ACAC was rejuvenated and today is a vibrant multiethnic congregation with a median attendance of 2,223 for its four weekend services (the ninth-highest attendance of any C&MA church in the country). During the past thirty years, hundreds of people have committed their lives to Christ through its ministry. Today, Caucasians constitute 69 percent of its members, African Americans 27 percent and Asians and Latinos 4 percent. ACAC is a geographically diverse church, with 22 percent of its members living on the North Side, 16 percent in other Pittsburgh neighborhoods and 62 percent residing in the suburbs and rural areas. The median age of regular attendees is thirty-four; 37 percent of them are under eighteen, 52 percent are between eighteen and sixty-four and 11 percent are over sixty-four. ACAC is also an economically diverse congregation, with 45 percent of households earning less than $50,000, 30 percent earning between $50,000 and $70,000 and 25 percent earning more than $70,000. The church's operating budget for the 2016–17 fiscal year was $6.357 million.[4]

Allegheny Center Alliance Church. *Courtesy of Allegheny Center Alliance Church.*

ACAC currently has forty-five full-time staff, thirteen of whom are pastors, working in various areas—administration, missions, youth ministry, adult life, senior citizen life, visitation, visitor care and advancement. About half of the pastors are ordained. After two years of service and some basic academic work, male Alliance Church members can take an exam to receive ordination status. The C&MA does not ordain women as pastors (although they can be consecrated and hold the title of pastor). Women direct ACAC's children's and women's ministries, work in its worship, missions or counseling activities and serve as administrative assistants. ACAC's two governing boards are composed exclusively of men; thirteen men supervise the church's administration, while twenty-eight elders provide spiritual oversight.[5]

ACAC continues to meet at the Union Street site, but it now owns three adjacent buildings. Its main building contains the sanctuary, Connections Hub, a prayer room and nursery, toddler, adult and student meeting rooms. Youth meet in the three-story Whiteside Building. The six-floor Union Place building houses a chapel, offices, adult meeting rooms, the church's counseling ministries and the offices of the Urban Impact Foundation. These three church buildings are situated between Allegheny Center, an elementary school, a subsidized housing complex and a small park. Parking is limited, and partnering with nearby Allegheny General Hospital, ACAC plans to build a parking garage, which the two institutions will share. In the spring of 2018, ACAC planted a satellite church in Homestead.[6]

ACAC seeks to convey Jesus' "compassion, justice, transforming power, and liberating truth by our deeds and words" and to model God's kingdom as an ethnically, socially and economically diverse community of believers. ACAC's mission is to "communicate God's life-changing truth," win people to Christ and promote "God's worldwide mission." ACAC also seeks to help members become spiritually mature, serve, share and "model authentic unity in Christ." ACAC wants to help renew the North Side and "collaborate with other Christian ministries as God directs." Its staff and members strive to "replicate the ACAC model of ministry" in other Pittsburgh neighborhoods that face the same challenges as the North Side does.[7]

Dillaman grew up in a Christian home in Butler, thirty miles north of Pittsburgh. After World War II, his father suffered from post-combat stress disorder and could barely function. While he was hospitalized for his condition, God "saved him and healed him." Thereafter, he spent more than thirty years "selling vacuum cleaners door-to-door, sharing Jesus every time he went into a home, and leading over 3,000 people to the Lord." In high school, Rock rebelled against his background, vowing that he "would never darken a church door" again. Soon abandoning this pledge, he surrendered his heart to Christ at age nineteen. Initially wanting to be a jazz musician, Dillaman majored in music at Duquesne University. After his conversion, however, he felt called to enter the pastoral ministry and transferred to C&MA-sponsored Nyack College, north of New York City. Following his graduation from Nyack, he completed an MDiv degree at Asbury Theological Seminary in Kentucky in 1976 and pastored a C&MA congregation for seven years in Northeast, Pennsylvania, near Erie.[8]

Dillaman had no cross-cultural ministry experience when he came to ACAC in 1984. "God delights in doing things through people who don't know what they're doing," he asserted, "because then they don't get in the way of His glory." God impressed on him that He had strategically placed ACAC on the North Side. Strong evangelical churches abounded in the suburbs, but few existed in the city.[9]

Dillaman strove to restore the hope of his discouraged members and create a congregation that could minister effectively to its community. ACAC adopted a new children's curriculum "to be sensitive to our multi-ethnic neighborhood," and Dillaman changed his preaching style. He does not try to mimic the style of black preachers, but he does use illustrations and language with cultural markers to assure urban African Americans that he understands their life circumstances. His approach caused some members to leave, but by 1994, about one thousand people were attending ACAC each Sunday. Soon after Dillaman came, many African Americans began to participate in ACAC's children and youth ministries, but it took eleven years for an appreciable number of black adults to begin attending Sunday morning worship services. This trickle eventually became a steady flow, and ACAC's membership was about 30 percent nonwhite by 2000.[10]

When Dillaman arrived, he and his wife bought a home in the North Hills. After a few years, however, he concluded that "to incarnate the Lord's presence" on the North Side and to gain credibility with its residents, they needed to live in the community. They moved to the North Side when their three children were in either middle school or high school. Today, hundreds of ACAC members and most of its staff live in the neighborhood near the church.[11]

The Bible's social message was new to Dillaman when he became ACAC's pastor. He read the books of John Perkins, the founder of the Christian Community Development Association, and other authors who had a "holistic understanding of the Gospel." Dillaman also began to recognize how much "Scripture addresses doing works of justice and compassion." Living on the North Side altered what he noticed in the Bible. His basic theology did not change, but his practical theology and application of scriptural teaching did; he began to focus much more on social justice.[12]

Dillaman had to convince his members that this social justice focus was biblical, part of the C&MA's heritage and consistent with ACAC's overall mission. In the 1980s, most C&MA pastors and parishioners in the United States saw the Social Gospel as highly suspect because of its long-standing association with liberal theology. For them, Christianity primarily entailed winning souls to Christ and practicing personal piety. Dillaman, therefore, sought to "create a whole new understanding of what it means to be God's servant in a city."[13] For the last twenty-five years, he has often preached about social issues and exhorted his parishioners to assist the hurting, oppressed and victims of injustice. Justice, he argued, involves both creating enterprises "that enhance a community" and attacking things that destroy it.[14]

To promote vibrant community development, ACAC seeks to implement the "three Rs"—relocation, reconciliation and redistribution—that Perkins identified in *Restoring At-Risk Communities*. Relocation entails moving to a low-income community to build relationships with its residents and share the gospel with them more effectively. Reconciliation involves breaking down racial, ethnic and economic barriers. Redistribution occurs when "God's

Rock Dillaman. *Courtesy of Allegheny Center Alliance Church.*

people with resources" live in a poor community and use their skills and means to remedy the community's problems and reallocate income.[15]

Of ACAC's thirteen pastors, four are African Americans. Staffed by seventeen therapists, ACAC's counseling ministry assists hundreds of individuals, couples, families and children (8,116 counseling sessions were held in 2016). In addition, Christian Legal Aid of Pittsburgh, which supplies free legal advice and guidance on civil and family matters to people whose incomes are at or below 250 percent of the federal poverty guidelines, meets with clients at ACAC.[16]

In 2016, 835 women and men participated in ACAC's growth groups.[17] Each group consists of 8 to 12 individuals who either study specific topics or meet after the Saturday evening or Sunday services to discuss the sermon using study questions that Dillaman and other preachers provide. Many of the groups include people of different races, socioeconomic classes, ages and family structures. In addition, ACAC offers groups for couples who want to improve their marriages; individuals recovering from addictions and codependence or struggling with sexual and emotional problems in relationships; and women whose husbands are grappling with pornography, adultery or sexual addiction.[18] In 2015, 513 students from seventy-nine different schools participated in ACAC's middle and high school ministries under the supervision of 104 adult volunteers. That same year, 1,077 children (nursery to grade five) participated in ACAC's children's ministries.[19]

ACAC strongly supports missions, typically contributing about 17 percent of all donations received by the church, and currently twenty-eight of its former members are serving in foreign or domestic mission work and twenty-five more are preparing to do so. The church recently sponsored short-term mission trips to Kenya, Mexico and Ukraine and two to France and regularly hosts mission conferences and events. ACAC has also developed mission partnerships with organizations and congregations in Syria, Cambodia, Spain, Russia, Paraguay and Gabon.[20]

ACAC's pastors and members work diligently to improve the North Side through a variety of ministries. Two physicians from the congregation helped start the North Side Christian Health Center (NSCHC) in 1993 to provide primary care to the underserved living on the North Side and in surrounding neighborhoods. Its staff provide "whole-person spiritual and physical" healthcare each year to about five thousand patients, including cancer screenings, physical and gynecological exams, sick visits, well child visits, immunizations and vision and hearing screenings for children.[21]

Two other ACAC members established a Christian lending organization in 2007 called Grace Period to give low-income Pittsburghers an alternative to predatory payday lending. Grace Period required its four thousand members to establish a bank account through its partnership with a local credit union. ACAC members provided the initial capital for this venture. Grace Period members could borrow up to $500 to pay a bill. They had two options for repayment: if they repaid the loan in thirteen days, they paid no interest; if they did not do so, they had to devise a payment plan and put additional money into an "emergency fund" to help cover another potential financial crisis.[22] Sadly, despite its valuable service, Pennsylvania shut down Grace Period in 2014 because a clause in state lending laws that enabled it to serve the poor also enabled the worst predatory loan establishments to operate.

ACAC helped another member, Nikki Heckman, create a business called Bistro to Go in 2007 that currently employs forty-six community residents. This "Christ-centered business" serves "food that nourishes the body and delights the taste buds." Bistro to Go seeks "to initiate collaborative projects with faith-based and secular organizations" to "connect and revitalize the Northside." Heckman also wants to help community residents "get to know one another, have fun and volunteer together." Bistro to Go was named the city's "Best Comfort Food Restaurant" in a 2011 *Pittsburgh Magazine* readers poll.

ACAC partnered with Women's Choice Network (WCN) to open a clinic on the North Side on 2011. The clinic promotes the sanctity of life, gives women living on the North Side an alternative to abortion and provides pre- and postnatal care. ACAC provided the finances and manpower to build the clinic and the funds to operate it during its early years. WCN seeks to empower women who are at risk of having an abortion to instead carry their babies to term. Its clinic provides pregnancy tests, STD testing and treatment, medical consultation and sonograms for more than 1,500 women each year. WCN also furnishes childbirth, parenting and life skills classes and abstinence education.[23]

In 2007, ACAC paid $200,000 to shut down a North Side bar. Its rowdy patrons had long made the bar a nuisance in the community. Buying the bar, Dillaman argued, was the only way to end its negative influence on the community. A community group bought the facility from ACAC in 2017 and tore down the bar, and a bank is being constructed on the site.[24] Moreover, Ed Glover, one of ACAC's pastors, founded the Urban Impact Foundation (described in chapter 5) in 1995 to use arts, education and athletics to help at-risk North Side youth.

ACAC also dispenses about $150,000 a year to help North Side residents repair cars and pay utilities and rent. Its after-school program assists many young people academically. ACAC's summer day camps provide educational, recreational and spiritual enrichment to about three hundred youth a year. The church teaches single mothers about basic home repair and home improvement skills. ACAC also helps former inmates find accommodations and jobs and gives them a church home.[25] Some members are ministering to recently arrived Muslim refugees from Burundi and Somalia who live in Northview Heights, a low-income North Side community. Some of these Muslims have begun worshipping at ACAC. In addition, more than forty Nepalese immigrants attend a weekly Sunday afternoon service at ACAC, and the church is providing legal aid to many refugees and other immigrants.[26]

What "juices me most" about the ministry, Dillaman declared, is when people "grasp at a deeper level who God is and how to follow Him and be holy." His primary goal, he insisted, is to help ACAC members apply scriptural teaching to every facet of their lives. Instead of worshipping the God of the Bible, many Americans, Dillaman lamented, worship "the tribal war deity of the United States or the God of the American way." Dillaman repeatedly credits the work of the Holy Spirit for ACAC's success. "If you rely on the Spirit" and "advocate for your city," God will do "far more than we're seeing in American cities."[27]

Dillaman counsels pastors seeking to do cross-cultural, multiracial urban ministry to be patient, eager to learn and willing to be uncomfortable. They must reshape their preaching, teaching, Sunday school, curriculum and church administration to fulfill the expectations of their diverse congregants. Dillaman advises these pastors to view the Bible differently—keep going even if your minority parishioners do not trust you. Remember that they have their guard up because they constantly face both subtle and overt bigotry. Acknowledge that everything is more complicated and takes longer to accomplish than in a monocultural setting.[28]

The Church Visit

On Sunday, September 18, 2016, I visited ACAC, which is located about ten blocks from Heinz Field, where Steelers head coach Mike Tomlin, an ACAC member, would be seeking to lead his team to defeat the Bengals several hours later. I was accompanied by my student assistant Sarah Gibbs and my colleague Blair Allison, a mechanical engineering professor who is a member of ACAC. We met longtime member Sally Turnbull, whose property includes a lake that ACAC uses twice a year to do baptisms by immersion (119 believers were baptized in 2015 and 2016).[29]

The church has a Welcome Center, a special room for first-time visitors and information desks located beside several entrances. The Welcome Center provides free tickets that visitors can use to eat breakfast or lunch in the church's cafeteria. This facility doubles as a gymnasium where youth and adults play basketball, indoor soccer and other sports. Many church members eat in the cafeteria on Sundays. Visitors also receive free coffee, parking passes and Bibles. ACAC also sponsors a café for the public in its Union Place building (seventy-six thousand meals were served in the cafeteria and café combined in 2015).[30]

Among the numerous materials available to worshippers was a Pennsylvania Voters Registration Mail Application. Next to it was a synopsis of Dillaman's recent sermon titled "Guarding Your Soul in an Election." Many Christians, he asserted, believe that neither Donald Trump nor Hillary Clinton "incarnates the full scope of Scripture." Dillaman welcomed a party that comprehensively followed biblical morality, was consistently pro-life and "committed to the poorest and most vulnerable among us," cherished "service rather than power," promoted "justice rather than special interests" and strove to provide "a faithful moral example" rather than erect "a financial and military empire." Dillaman exhorted church members to follow three biblical principles during political campaigns: do not expect politics to provide "the identity, security, meaning, answers, power and hope" that can come only from God; do not equate faithfulness to God with being slavishly committed to a specific nation, party or agenda; and "don't demonize your opponents."

ACAC's sanctuary seats about nine hundred on its main floor and balcony in theater-type seats. During the service we attended, the sanctuary was two-thirds full. After saying the Apostles' Creed, we sang a praise chorus and the hymn "Christ, the Solid Rock." The music was upbeat, and the energetic singing was accompanied by lots of clapping. A praise band and a choir of forty-five members, about half of whom were African Americans, led worship. The choir's anthem repeatedly declared, "It will get better. Better. God is in control." While worshippers of all ages were present, blacks and whites in their twenties and thirties predominated. A video testimony from Jay Wilson, a former Steeler chaplain, and his wife, who attend ACAC, was used to publicize a marriage workshop.

Dillaman preached a thirty-five-minute expository sermon titled "It's Not About Us!" All his illustrations were drawn from Scripture, and he explicated numerous passages to argue that Christians can understand God's forgiveness only if they first comprehend God's covenants. Christians struggle to accept God's pardon, Dillaman averred, "because we make forgiveness all about us." Forgiveness, however, is first and foremost about God's faithfulness, not our failings. It is based on God's covenant, not our sinful human condition. Unfortunately, Dillaman asserted, many Christians incorrectly believe that God is disgusted by our sins, our sins can be forgiven only a limited number of times, Christians cannot overcome certain sins and our continued sinning indicates that we are not saved.

Those who try to win God's favor through their fervent religious activity, Dillaman asserted, often become angry, frustrated and disappointed with God. We must work from God's grace instead of for it. The devil, Dillaman declared, repeatedly reminds Christians about their sin. When he does, the pastor counseled, do not argue with him; simply point him to God's covenant and overcome him by the blood of the Lamb and the word of your testimony (Revelation 12:11). When Satan accuses us, point him to Jesus' scarred hands. Say to him, "Just talk to the hands." Satan has no rebuttal for this defense.

We usually focus on God's love and mercy, but I John 1:9 accentuates God's faithfulness and justice and explains why He forgives the penitent—

A worship service at Allegheny Center Alliance Church. *Courtesy of Allegheny Center Alliance Church.*

God cannot break His covenant. Worshippers repeatedly responded to Dillaman's points with Amens or applause. Dillaman ended his sermon by encouraging auditors to repeat a prayer to accept Christ as their savior. The service concluded with announcements, an offering and a benediction, all led by a black administrative pastor who looked like he could have played for the Steelers (who that afternoon beat the Bengals 24–16, bringing joy to many ACAC parishioners).

ACAC uses several means to foster diversity and enable people of different races, ages, socioeconomic status and educational backgrounds to feel comfortable: its multiracial staff, mixture of traditional hymns, gospel music and worship songs in its services, support of a wide variety of missions around the world and sermons that are intellectually stimulating but explain complicated concepts in simple terms that all worshippers can understand. ACAC appears to operate like a well-oiled machine. While remaining true to its core doctrines, every aspect of the church's ministry and services seems to be carefully planned to promote harmony and unity. ACAC's remarkable ministry is producing marvelous fruit for God's kingdom in Pittsburgh and other places.

THE BIBLE CHAPEL: DEVELOPING FOLLOWERS OF JESUS CHRIST

The Bible Chapel (TBC), a megachurch with five campuses, began in 1964 when nine couples met in a home in Upper St. Clair. Originally called the St. Clair Bible Chapel and then the South Hills Bible Chapel, TBC has roots in the Plymouth Brethren movement, which began in Ireland in the late 1820s. Originally led by John Nelson Darby, the Plymouth Brethren espouse dispensationalism, which teaches that God deals differently with the world in seven distinct eras.[31] Despite its background, TBC is completely independent; it is not part of any association of congregations. Dr. Ronald Moore, who has served as TBC's senior pastor since 1993, was familiar with the ministry of several large Bible churches in Dallas, where he attended seminary, but none of them served as a model for TBC. The Bible Chapel does take advantage of resources provided by other congregations: it has used Rick Warren's 40 Days of Purpose plan, and its staff regularly attend conferences sponsored by Willow Creek and other megachurches.

After meeting in Peters Township High School, TBC moved into a newly built facility in 1995 on a twenty-acre parcel in McMurray in the South Hills. This building included a 750-seat Family Life Center that served as its worship center, gymnasium and multi-purpose room for the next decade. During the next ten years, the church added more classrooms, a commercial kitchen and a youth activity center. In 2006, TBC completed a $9 million, fifty-three-thousand-square-foot project that doubled its size. The addition included a 1,400-seat worship center, fifteen classrooms, a recording studio and a large area for children's ministry.[32]

TBC leaders decided to establish other campuses in the Pittsburgh region. Typically, they target areas where solid biblical teaching is lacking, sizable numbers of current attendees live and/or opportunities to partner with parachurch organizations exist. They opened the Robinson Campus in 2009; the Washington Campus in Washington, Pennsylvania, in 2011; the Wilkinsburg Campus in 2013; and the Rostraver Campus in Westmoreland County in 2017. At the Washington Campus, TBC works in conjunction with the City Mission, a homeless shelter that supplies meals, counseling, legal services, job training and a medical clinic. In Wilkinsburg, TBC met at Pittsburgh Urban Christian School until 2016, when the congregation moved to a newly renovated church nearby, which includes a sixty-seat kitchen that offers free hot meals to community residents every Sunday morning.[33]

The Bible Chapel's main campus in McMurray. *Courtesy of The Bible Chapel.*

The average weekend attendance for The Bible Chapel is more than 4,000, with 3,000 worshipping at McMurray, 300 at Robinson, 300 at Washington, 175 at Rostrayer, 150 at Wilkinsburg and 250 online. According to Moore, 60 percent of the parishioners at the McMurray campus are between ages thirty-five and fifty-five, and families have an average of three children. Most adults are college-educated professionals. Young married couples predominate at both the Robinson Township and Washington campuses; many residents of the mission also attend the services at Washington. At the Wilkinsburg campus, the congregation typically consists of single adults and children who come without their parents; about 40 percent of the adults and 60 percent of kids are African Americans.[34]

Ron Moore has served as The Bible Chapel's senior pastor since 1992. He was raised in the Nazarene Church in Oklahoma and declares that "Christ got a hold of my heart" at age twelve. He received his BA at the University of Central Oklahoma, where he played on the baseball team. Moore earned Master of Theology and Doctor of Ministry degrees at Dallas Theological Seminary and a master's degree in education at Texas A&M at Commerce. He taught science, Texas history and computer literacy at a junior high school in Texas for four years after finishing his first degree at DTS.[35]

The Bible Chapel has grown rapidly from 1995, when it had three hundred members, until today. Moore asserted that the church's focus on teaching and preaching the word of God and providing "real answers for life's questions" has attracted many people. TBC's guiding verse is Jesus' prayer to His Father on behalf of His disciples: "Sanctify them by the truth; your word is truth" (John 17:17). The congregation has also increased in size, Moore contended, because it has helped members understand God's grace, become grounded in the Scriptures and become disciples, not simply converts.[36]

Moore's primary roles at The Bible Chapel are preaching, teaching and helping members enrich their marriages (his doctorate is in this area). He supplies the vision and leadership for TBC and is the only pastor on the church's eight-person board of elders. These godly elders, Moore explained, establish TBC's mission. If independent congregations implode, he argued, it is typically either because of battles over or lack of accountability about church finances or because the senior pastor has too much power. To prevent these problems, Moore does not know how much money any member gives and shares power with the other elders (he has only one vote on the eight-person board) and clergy. Moore praises the staunch commitment of the fifty members of the church's staff to Christ and to TBC's mission.[37]

Moore described his preaching style as exegetical and expositional. He preaches on various books of the Bible and on topics that are important to Christians. His ministry team chooses themes for sermons guided by the perceived needs of the congregation and its members. Moore recently did sermon series on Exodus, Hebrews and the life of Christ. His sermons explain and apply major biblical truths to the lives of his parishioners. Moore spends fifteen to twenty hours preparing each sermon and preaches most Sundays. He tackles controversial social issues unflinchingly, including homosexuality, divorce and unmarried couples living together. Many churches, Moore complained, fail to address provocative "topics that Scripture puts forth very clearly."[38]

Several books have significantly influenced Moore's life and ministry. C.S. Lewis's *Mere Christianity* gave him "a framework of the essentials of the faith." J.I. Packer's *Knowing God* helped him "comprehend the vastness of God's person and character." Reading Ray Pritchard's *Keep Believing* enabled him to trust God more fully when facing life's challenges. Scott Stanley's *A Lasting Promise* serves as a major resource for Moore's marriage enrichment sessions.[39]

What Moore loves the most about the ministry is seeing God transform people's lives. He is energized when his parishioners learn new biblical concepts and strive to follow them and collaborate to advance God's mission. "Nothing works quite like the church," Moore asserted, when its worship is inspiring and its impact in the community is great.[40]

Ron Moore. *Courtesy of The Bible Chapel.*

In 2016, Moore became the president of and Bible teacher for an international program called Back to the Bible. Following in the footsteps of renowned Bible instructors including Theodore Epp and Warren Wiersbe, Moore seeks to help the seventy-five-year-old organization "use the latest technology to reach the world with the life-transforming power of God's Word." The organization supplies speakers to discuss topics pertaining to family, faith and spiritual growth at worship services, women's and men's groups and on radio and TV shows. Its goTandem Bible study app has been downloaded by 200,000 people, most of whom are millennials. Moore devotes about five hours per week to Back to the Bible, recording Bible talks and speaking at various venues.[41]

Moore has written five books. Three are devotionals that focus on the entire Bible, the Psalms and the gospels, respectively. The fourth book, titled *Ignite*, examines various struggles of David. Moore's *Worn Out by Obedience: Recovering from Spiritual Fatigue* seeks to help people cope with the spiritual exhaustion that resisting temptation, dealing with difficult people and disappointment and ministering to others often brings.

The Bible Chapel's elders are all men, which has evoked criticism. Based on their understanding of Scripture, its leaders believe that only men should hold this position, even though they insist that women and men have equal worth and the same spiritual gifts. Women, Moore stressed, lead TBC's largest and most important ministry—to children. Moreover, women oversee male staff and volunteers in this area as well as in the church's worship ministry. Women also lead many of TBC's outreach endeavors.[42]

To produce disciples, TBC uses the Living Grounded curriculum that Moore developed. Before joining TBC, individuals are required to take this series of twelve foundational Bible studies that focus on people's relationship with God and how to positively influence others. About three thousand people have participated in this program. "Wherever a person is in his spiritual journey," Moore explained, "we want to help take him one step farther in his relationship with Christ." TBC also encourages new members to complete a Spiritual Gift Inventory to discern their gifts for ministry.[43]

The Bible Chapel's numerous ministries fit into one of three categories: engage, equip or employ. Engaging focuses on evangelism and teaching, equipping prepares members to serve and employing involves conducting ministries to aid individuals and communities. In Christ, TBC emphasizes, people are SSAFE: Significant, Secure, Accepted, Forgiven and Empowered. Growing believers do five essential tasks: they consistently study God's Word, worship God privately and corporately, develop close relationships with fellow Christians, use their gifts to serve God and others and share the gospel.[44]

Ministry to youth is paramount at The Bible Chapel. The staff ministers to students in three distinctive age groups: fifth through sixth grade, seventh through eighth grade and high school. Each group has its own student-led worship team and does numerous fun activities. For many years, TBC has sponsored major outreach events such as Teen Madness, a weeklong summer camp, and Color Wars. Kids often go home covered in mud or paint. More importantly, every event accentuates that Jesus transforms people's lives, and each summer, more than one hundred youth typically accept Jesus as their savior.[45]

On Sunday mornings, children participate in their own programs instead of the church's worship services; about one thousand children come every Sunday—seven hundred from birth to fourth grade and one hundred each in the three youth divisions. The junior high meeting room has a ping-pong table, a foosball table, a snack shack, a stage that a band uses to lead worship and tables where youth discuss the talks given during the services. On Wednesday nights, about five hundred people have dinner together in the church's Family Life Center. Afterward, younger children engage in Bible-based activities, youth have meetings and adults study Scripture.

The Bible Chapel also reaches out to youth through its Upward Sports ministry. About 70 percent of participants in its activities are not church members. One of its key programs is Upward Basketball; in 2016, 250 children participated in this league at the South Hills Campus and 40 children at the Wilkinsburg Campus through which they received exercise, fellowship and Christian nurture. At the closing ceremonies, more than 1,000 people heard a gospel presentation, and 80 children either accepted Christ as their savior or rededicated their lives to Him.[46]

The Bible Chapel's ministry to individuals with special needs is especially impressive. To do this, TBC provides a Sunday school class (about 18 attend on average), a Wednesday night program (for a maximum of 25 children), a Wednesday evening support group for parents and a monthly respite program that enables parents of special-needs children to have a date night.[47] The Bible Chapel also hosts Night to Shine, a prom for special-needs individuals in association with the Tim Tebow Foundation. In 2016, 122 people from ages fifteen to seventy-two attended the event at the South Hills Campus. They all received a partner for the evening. Women had their hair styled at a local salon or the church, were given gowns to wear and had makeup applied professionally. The evening featured limousine rides, dancing, dinner and karaoke. Many parents testified that it was "the best night of our kids' lives."[48]

TBC strongly promotes missions at home and abroad. Its members financially support and volunteer at three local missions: Light of Life Rescue Mission, Human Coalition Women's Clinic in the South Hills and the City Mission in Washington. Since 1992, TBC has operated a residential program in Panama for abandoned or orphaned children. The congregation helps fund the educational, medical and religious work of Africa Inland Church Zion in Mathare, a desperately poor section of Nairobi, Kenya. Each year, TBC sends about ten short-term mission teams of adults or youth to various locales around the world.[49]

Small groups are very important to TBC. About one thousand adults participate in groups that meet either in homes in the evening or at lunchtime at various businesses throughout the Pittsburgh area. About three hundred people participate in the six to ten adult Sunday school classes offered each semester, while two hundred adults participate in TBC's Wednesday night program.[50]

The Bible Chapel conducts numerous ministries in the Pittsburgh area. Members of TBC's Care Giving Ministry visit, pray with, furnish meals to and do minor home repairs for those who have lost loved ones or are in recovery programs. TBC provides support groups for individuals coping with the death of family members, going through the pain of divorce and struggling with addictions. Its Mercy Fund aids dozens of individuals and families undergoing financial emergencies. TBC's orphan care ministry assists adoptive and foster families. TBC's Outreach Ministry does mission work and projects in the local community and across the globe. The Men, Women and Sages ministry sponsors Bible studies, support groups, special events, a mentoring program and retreats.[51] In March 2016, 180 students in seventh through twelfth grade and adult volunteers spent a day repairing nonprofit shops, homes and ministries throughout the Pittsburgh area.[52]

Moore works to prod more members to get involved in TBC's life and ministry. Too many people, he complained, only attend worship services. TBC has recently developed a shepherding process through which highly committed members coach and mentor newcomers. TBC strives to create strong bonds among members and help them use their gifts to minister to others in the church and community.[53]

The Bible Chapel's strengths, Moore contended, are its commitment to God's inerrant word, its focus on teaching the Bible and developing disciples and its dedicated elders and young, energetic staff. TBC's website asserts, "We believe that the Bible is complete, authoritative, and true for everyone at every time" and "that 'all Scripture is inspired by God.'"[54] During the next ten years, The Bible Chapel plans to establish more campuses using a hub-and-spokes model as its current campuses launch other ministry sites in their vicinity.[55]

Recent statistics testify to The Bible Chapel's priorities, vitality and influence. In 2015 and 2016, 231 people joined TBC, 2,123 individuals attended for the first time, 103 individuals were baptized, 100 children were dedicated, 255 youth attended the senior high retreat and 1,453 children attended Vacation Bible School (in 2015, 209 of them trusted Christ as their savior). TBC's 2016 budget was $5,023,667. Illustrative of the church's commitment to social causes is that in 2015, 108 members participated in the March for Life in Washington, D.C., twenty-seven thousand diapers were given to 100 needy local families and almost $150,000 was dispensed to help families cope with sickness, death and financial crises.[56]

The Church Visit

Sarah Gibbs and I visited the South Hills campus of The Bible Chapel on October 30, 2016. Associate pastor Scott Arvay gave us a tour of the church's impressive facilities. Arvay grew up in an unchurched Pittsburgh family and became a Christian through the ministry of TBC. Arvay, who earned an MDiv degree at Dallas Theological Seminary, supervises the work of about ninety paid staff—some full time and some part time, including four campus pastors, the church's preschool (which has about eighty children) and the directors of the TBC's varied ministries.

At the 10:45 a.m. worship service we attended, the large auditorium was about two-thirds full with people from age eighteen to their eighties. The worshippers were almost exclusively Caucasian. Six large tapestries with scenes associated with the series Moore was preaching on the book of Exodus decorated the auditorium. As in other megachurches, the service had three main components: singing led by a praise band, announcements and a substantive sermon (about forty minutes). The young adult worship team, accompanied by a thirty-member youth choir, led the music.

Announcements highlighted various aspects of The Bible Chapel's program. In November, the church was sponsoring a Corn Hole tournament, a Thanksgiving breakfast for men and retreats for junior high and senior high students. TBC was hosting a luncheon to honor families that "have answered God's call to care for the orphaned." Other announcements highlighted the church's support of Samaritan Purse's Operation Christmas Child program, Upward Sports' basketball and cheerleading programs and TBC's upcoming tour of Italy and the sites of the seven churches in the Book of Revelation.

Worshippers sang five songs, including Kristian Stanfill's "Even So Come," Craig and Dean Phillips's "Great I Am" and the hymn "Holy, Holy, Holy." Before preaching, Moore exhorted worshippers to carefully evaluate the issues in the 2016 election and vote. He encouraged auditors to go to one of TBC's campuses on Election Day to pray for the electoral process.

Moore's sermon focused on the Israelites' escape from Egypt. Using a PowerPoint map, he pointed out that both the Egyptian army and the Philistines prevented the Israelites, who had no weapons, from taking the direct route to Palestine. The Israelites were hemmed in by mountains and the Red Sea, Moore declared; six hundred of the Egyptians' finest chariots and large numbers of soldiers were bearing down on them. It would have been better, many frightened Israelites lamented, to remain slaves in Egypt than to die in the desert. Like them, Moore asserted, we often want to return to the "good old days" when we are in difficult straits or feel tempted. Moore repeatedly accentuated the key verse in the story, Exodus 14:14: "The Lord will fight for you and you need only to be still."

Moore discussed three "transferable truths" from this episode. First, God does not always take His people on the shortest or easiest route. God led the Israelites on a circuitous path to demonstrate His power. Some of you, Moore proclaimed, "may be waiting on God to provide a spouse, and it is tempting to take a shortcut; some of you have difficult marriages, but don't give up; depend on God." Some of you are on demanding career paths, but

A worship service at The Bible Chapel. *Courtesy of The Bible Chapel.*

God has lessons for you to learn. He urged worshippers to depend on God who "is more than capable" in all circumstances.

Second, God never abandoned the Israelites; he continually led them by a pillar of cloud and fire. While it would be amazing to see such tangible signs of God's presence today, Christians have something even better. Jesus is with believers through the ministry of the Holy Spirit. Moreover, Jesus promises that the Holy Spirit "will teach you all things." Sadly, Christians often ignore the Holy Spirit's presence and power in our lives.

Third, God tells us to trust Him. When the Israelites saw the Egyptian army approaching, they panicked. They did not remember the promise: "The Lord will fight for you." God knows your situation, Moore proclaimed; He is in you and with you. Moore challenged worshippers to trust God. We must fight diligently to accomplish God's will, but ultimately the battle belongs to the Lord. Worshippers were invited to come to the front after the service ended to pray with a pastor or elder.

As it fulfills its mission "to develop followers of Jesus Christ," The Bible Chapel is having a tremendous impact for the gospel and helping make Pittsburgh famous for God.[57]

North Way Christian Community: "Making a Kingdom Impact" in Pittsburgh

North Way Christian Community, founded in 1981 by John (Jay) Passavant III in Wexford, is the Pittsburgh area's first nondenominational megachurch. With almost four thousand people worshipping each week at one of its six campuses, North Way is one of the region's largest, most vibrant and most active congregations. Passavant earned his BS at Washington and Lee University and an MDiv and DMin from Fuller Theological Seminary and then served as a commissioned officer in the Marine Corps. After being ordained in the Presbyterian Church (USA) in 1974, Passavant worked as a youth pastor for seven years before founding North Way. He led North Way in promoting both domestic and foreign missions, especially by chairing the board of the South East Asia Prayer Center (SEAPC). Passavant focused on developing strong families through various North Way programs and his involvement in a nationally broadcast television show called *Reality Talks*. In 2011, Passavant began a five-year process to pass on the lead pastor role to Scott Stevens.[58]

Stevens grew up in the Homestead-Munhall area of Pittsburgh. His involvement in the youth group of the Homestead United Presbyterian Church led him to commit his life to Christ. After completing a teaching degree at Edinboro University, he took a sales job in Pittsburgh and for seven years volunteered in Homestead's Children's and Student Ministries. Stevens served as the director of this program for six years and then spent six years ministering to students and young adults at Pleasant Hills Community Church. In 2002, North Way Christian Community hired Stevens to minister to children, students, young adults and families. In 2008, he became the church's executive pastor. Stevens is currently completing a master's degree in evangelism and church leadership at Trinity Evangelical Divinity School.[59]

As lead pastor, Stevens directs North Way's staff and teaching team and helps establish the church's strategic vision and future direction. His primary responsibilities include directing North Way's six campuses; he works closely with other pastors to help them increase the membership of their congregations to become financially sustainable. Stevens also determines North Way's sermon topics and preaches most Sundays at the Wexford campus. His sermons are aired live at the other five sites. In addition, Stevens leads North Way's Executive Leadership Team and the Elders' Council, which oversees worship, discipleship, community ministries, human resources and facilities.[60]

North Way Christian Community's main campus in Cranberry. *Courtesy of North Way Christian Community.*

In many cases, Stevens noted, churches, especially nondenominational ones, have struggled mightily in passing leadership from the founding pastor to his or her successor; he and Passavant worked very hard for five years to make this transition successful. Passavant, now seventy-one, concluded in 2011 that he wanted to direct some special projects, but he no longer wanted to oversee day-to-day operations.[61]

North Way strives, Stevens declared, "to be a healthy and growing church that makes a Kingdom impact in this region." Its three core values express its vision and mission. First, North Way aspires to be a church whose members love Jesus. Attendees engage in twenty-five minutes of expressive, Spirit-inspired worship at every service and hear about Jesus in every sermon. North Way members, Stevens asserted, are eager to express and share their deep love for Jesus. "North Way is centered on Jesus Christ as Savior and our Lord." North Way partners with parents to raise their children "from cradle to college…to know and love Jesus." Throughout its history, North Way has "focused on following Jesus" with "the Bible as our guidebook."[62]

Second, Stevens stated, North Way wants its members to engage in life together. North Way uses the term "Christian Community" rather than "church" to describe itself because of its commitment to fellowship and collaborative ministry. Its website states, "We desire to create community as we live and walk together to seek, find, and know the living God." The church, Stevens explained, urges members to join home groups. Both Stevens and Passavant participate in one. Many groups do volunteer work together. North Way also strives to help individuals and families when they struggle with crises, sin or suffering "to experience God's love by providing hope, encouragement and instruction."[63]

North Way's third priority is to engage with and influence the culture; its members seek both to learn from their culture and to base social institutions and practices on biblical values. North Way wants to be known for what its members are for, not what they are against. It strives to follow Jesus, do life together and provide "spirit-led worship" and "strong Biblical teaching" to "advance God's love and kingdom" in the Pittsburgh area.[64]

Stevens described his preaching style as conversational, engaging and confrontational. In every sermon, he analyzes a biblical text to explain its context, principles and application to listeners' lives. Stevens especially loves three aspects of the ministry: helping staff deepen their faith and work more effectively as a team, assisting people to cope with crises and preparing couples for marriage. Stevens directs North Way's Emerging Leaders Program to prepare its members (currently twelve men and women who are all in their twenties) for future ministry as pastors or youth leaders. Stevens seeks to improve their character and competency through courses he teaches them.[65]

North Way rapidly became a megachurch in part because it was one of the first nondenominational congregations in the Pittsburgh area. Today, North Way averages about four thousand worshippers on Sundays, with about half of them attending the Wexford campus. About seven thousand people attended Easter services in 2017. North Way, Stevens asserted, was fresh, new and attractive. It appealed to hundreds of people, many of whom were Christians but were mired in religiosity rather than enjoying a relationship with Christ. North Way's three core values as well as its multi-site approach, which began in 2006, Stevens contended, also fueled its growth.[66]

The age, race, socioeconomic class, jobs and places of residence of those who attend North Way vary from campus to campus. As a multi-site church, Stevens contended, North Way appeals to people of different classes, ages and interests. The Wexford campus attracts many young families because of its strong children's and student ministries. Most Wexford members are middle- and upper-middle-class; many have earned college degrees and hold white-collar jobs. Today, the Wexford campus also has a sizable senior citizen population. The Oakland campus draws many students and men and women in their twenties and thirties. The East End is the most racially and socioeconomically diverse North Way site; people who work for Google, physicians and the homeless all worship there. Both Sewickley Valley and Dormont are undergoing transition as younger families move in, which is reflected in the North Way campuses there. North Way's leaders expect the Beaver Valley campus, which opened in 2018, to be a blend of all generations. North Way members' differing ages, socioeconomic statuses and political views sometimes cause tension that requires pastors to work diligently to prevent dissension and preserve unity.[67]

As noted, small groups are extremely important at North Way. About 2,500 people, approximately half of the church's regular attenders, participate in small groups. This is a higher percentage than at any of the other eight profiled churches. Many small groups are composed of individuals who are in a similar stage in life. Some groups study the Bible, others study books by popular Christian authors, while still others revolve around doing ministry together. Groups meet on different days and in numerous places throughout the Pittsburgh area, including homes, coffee shops and North Way's campuses.[68]

North Way offers a wide array of opportunities for community service. North Way partners with other congregations and parachurch organizations to aid disenfranchised, abandoned and orphaned children locally, nationally and globally.[69] North Way helps children through its Orphan Care program, which was founded in 2006. Orphan Care also works to educate church members about abortion, support women and families financially and emotionally who choose to have babies and provide counseling and spiritual support for those affected by abortion. North Way also sponsors respite nights to enable parents of adopted and fostered children to enjoy a date night while their kids participate in fun activities at its campuses. In addition, North Way hosts a two-day Imagine Conference each year to engage, educate and equip believers to foster justice and express God's love through mentoring, ministering to refugees, supporting adoption and foster care and combating human trafficking.[70]

North Way members collaborate with the Pittsburgh Public Schools, Family Guidance Inc. and area congregations through the Learning and Mentoring Partnership to assist high-risk, gang-prone youth attending middle and elementary schools in the East End and supply them with educational resources. Since 2006, hundreds of North Way members have worked with students at the Faison K–5 School in Homewood who greatly need a (or another) caring adult in their lives. They help students with their homework, eat with them, take them on excursions, discuss their problems and provide emotional encouragement. Through the Family Mentoring program, all members of a North Way family assist one young person in these same ways.[71]

In 2012, North Way established a Community Justice Team to increase awareness about the plight of the oppressed and vulnerable (including victims of human trafficking), motivate church members to advocate on their behalf and assist needy individuals through educational and outreach endeavors. The team also partners with social agencies and other congregations.[72] Through North Way's Open Table program, groups of ten members partner with a low-income individual or family for one year to help them improve their financial circumstances.[73]

North Way members also work with Open Hand Ministries to renovate homes in Garfield and East Liberty to provide accommodations for low-income families. To help members learn about local mission opportunities, North Way sponsors a two-day Urban Immersion Serving Event each year. Participants are challenged to serve the marginalized, spend a day working with a local mission and then discuss their experience to better equip them for future service.[74]

North Way also operates a counseling service for couples, families and individuals. Since 2003, it has aided more than twenty thousand clients to improve their parenting, build stronger relationships and participate more actively in their communities. Its counselors have helped couples refrain from divorcing, many children to cope with developmental problems and hundreds of adults to overcome addictions. North Way subsidizes the center, so many clients receive counseling at either a reduced rate or for free.[75] North Way also sponsors a Support and Recovery Ministry to assist people who are struggling with drug and alcohol problems, marital discord, divorce, grief, codependency and other problems.[76] In addition, the members of North Way's Community Care Ministry visit, pray for and furnish meals for individuals and families who are dealing with illness, hospitalization, a death or a birth. Another North Way program provides single mothers with minor house and car repairs, lawn care, snow removal and help with filing taxes and making financial decisions.[77]

North Way strongly supports foreign missions. Many members sponsor children through SEAPC's partnerships with various ministries, which enables hundreds of abandoned children in Cambodia, India and Myanmar to receive food, shelter, clothing, education, medical care and loving nurture from Christian caregivers and to know Jesus personally.[78] North Way regularly organizes short-term mission trips for both adults and youth. Mission teams work with orphanages and churches in Haiti; they teach, build relationships and do service and building projects.[79] In 2017, teams ministered in Haiti, India, Honduras, Cambodia and Thailand.[80] In addition, North Way partners with missionaries in twenty countries to care for at-risk children, plant churches and equip indigenous leaders to reach their own people with the gospel.[81]

A seven-member Elders Council of "biblically qualified men called by God" led by Stevens directs North Way's ministry. The council provides spiritual and operational oversight, including hiring and supervising pastors. These elders, who belong to various campuses, serve up to three two-year terms. North Way also has a Financial Council that oversees its fiscal affairs. In addition, each campus has elders who govern and shepherd its ministry. The number of elders varies depending on the size and needs of each site, ranging from three at the East End to twenty-five at Wexford. All elders are currently men; some North Way members believe that women should be allowed to serve as elders and even pastors, and church leaders periodically evaluate this position.[82]

Stevens contends that North Way's primary strengths are its commitment to its core values and its passion for evangelism. The congregation's major challenges are managing its staff of one hundred and paying off its $5 million debt. North Way has not done as good a job of developing older staff as it has younger ones and plans to create a leadership development program for the entire staff.[83]

North Way's goal for the next ten years is a lofty one: to reach twenty-three thousand people for Jesus Christ—1 percent of the Pittsburgh region's total population. To do this, North Way will develop more disciples who reproduce "the character, ways and mission of Jesus" in others, produce additional leaders, increase its local and global mission outreach and launch new campuses.[84]

Stevens learned about Samuel Shoemaker's quest to make Pittsburgh as famous for God as for steel from Reid Carpenter, who helped mentor him. Stevens has read several of Shoemaker's books and has been inspired by the ministry of Saleem Ghubril (see chapter 6), who has worked energetically to accomplish Shoemaker's goal. North Way wants to establish a campus within twenty minutes of all area residents to provide them with a "solid, Christ-loving family" and seeks to work closely with other congregations who share their core values.[85] North Way members

Scott Stevens. *Courtesy of North Way Christian Community.*

are united by their belief that Jesus is the Son of God and that "love can transform a city." Pittsburgh's "vibrant, dynamic neighborhoods" make it an ideal place to fulfill their "multi-site church vision."[86]

The Church Visit

On Sunday, March 19, 2017, Sarah Gibbs and I visited North Way's Wexford campus. The church's massive building with its prominent steeple towers above the nearby restaurants, small office buildings and a health and wellness center. A sprawling parking lot surrounds the building. Built in 1995 and enlarged in 2007, North Way's Wexford church has ample space for its many programs for children, youth and adults. It also houses one of the two elementary school campuses of Eden Christian Academy, the largest nondenominational preschool through high school in the Pittsburgh area. The church's spacious main lobby contains a small welcome center with brochures and booklets and a shop that serves free coffee on Sundays.

In addition, North Way has a gymnasium where it has held services every Sunday for the past twenty years for about forty special-needs individuals. North Way also sponsors "You're a Star Prom!" events for such individuals who are fourteen or older that features a red carpet entrance, dancing, desserts, a photo booth and entertainment.[87] Several large, well-designed rooms and open spaces are used for North Way's children's and youth ministries. A "Kidz Church" is held for students in kindergarten to fifth grade during the 11:00 a.m. worship service.

We also toured North Way's food pantry. Primarily using donations from Whole Foods and Trader Joe's, it dispenses bread, produce and meat to several groups of people. Some low-income individuals and families pick up groceries every Sunday after the services. Food is distributed every week day through the local meals on wheels program and once a month to community residents who qualify financially.

At precisely 11:00 a.m., a praise band—consisting of three guitarists, two keyboard players, one drummer and a primary vocalist—began to play, and the worship pastor, Billy Bob White, led about 1,300 people in a nearly full sanctuary in singing four praise songs, including Kristian Stanfill's "The Lord Our God." Fog and colored lights enhanced the worship experience. The congregation consisted principally of youth, young adults and families with young children. Every Sunday, newcomers are invited to a meeting after the service to learn more about North Way.

A worship service at North Way Christian Community. *Courtesy of North Way Christian Community.*

A brief video introduced North Way's current sermon series on the Gospel of Mark. It highlighted how three groups—religious leaders, large crowds and Christ's disciples—interacted with Jesus. The series focused on the question, "Will we find a little bit of us in these groups?" Stevens preached a forty-five-minute sermon based on the story of Jesus healing a paralytic in Mark 2. He avoided theological jargon and explained concepts and events in an easily understood way.

Jealous of Jesus' popularity, the religious authorities, Stevens pointed out, went from questioning Jesus to condemning him. The large crowds whom Jesus attracted moved from listening closely to him to calling for his crucifixion. The disciples went from following Jesus to abandoning and denying him. Stevens confessed that he had some of each of these three groups in himself. Like the religious leaders, he sometimes questioned Jesus' authority and power. Like the crowds, he could be astonished and amazed by Jesus' teaching and miracles but then become complacent. Like the disciples, he could faithfully follow Jesus in the morning and act like a fool by the evening. Stevens urged listeners not to be indignant like the religious authorities, indifferent like the crowds or uncommitted like the disciples.

Mark 2:1–12 tells the story of Jesus healing a man who had been paralyzed from birth. Because the house where Jesus was teaching was very crowded, the man's four friends cut a hole in the roof to lower him in front of Jesus. When Jesus forgave the man's sins, the scribes accused him of blasphemy because they failed to realize that he was God, as healing the paralytic demonstrated. Unfortunately, Stevens added, unlike the man's friends, we often assume that people are so ensnared by financial problems, fear, anger, negative thinking or addiction that God cannot do anything to help them. We all know people, Stevens declared, who are broken and need God's healing touch. Invite them to come to church so they can meet Jesus.

Stevens had recently returned from visiting numerous pastors and churches with whom North Way has a long relationship during a three-week trip to India. While Americans worship in comfortable seats in climate-controlled buildings, Indian Christians often sit on the floor in sweltering heat. Many of them are extremely poor and endure persecution, and some are disowned by their families. Whereas many American Christians grumble if the Sunday service lasts more than an hour, Indian Christians worship enthusiastically for two hours. An India pastor told seminary graduates who would undoubtedly be hounded and harassed, "Evangelism is not an option; it is a command." Stevens exhorted his parishioners to emulate Indian Christians who joyfully share the gospel with others.

Since 1981, North Way Christian Community has faithfully proclaimed the gospel, developed disciples, ministered to community residents and worked to advance God's kingdom in the Pittsburgh area. It has sown many seeds and reaped much good fruit.

Victory Family Church: Influencing and Changing the World

Victory Family Church in Cranberry, north of Pittsburgh, advertises itself as "a full Gospel, non-denominational church, preaching the Word of God with an emphasis on the love of God."[88] Its mission is to "minister the love of God to the whole person, the whole family, and the whole community." VFC relentlessly shares the gospel "in truth and love" to help people "experience victory in everyday life," become spiritually mature and "influence and change the world."[89]

Founded and led by John Nuzzo, the church currently has five other pastors, a worship director and two marriage resource directors. The son of a steelworker, Nuzzo grew up in Midland in Beaver County. He graduated in 1981 with a degree in ministry from Rhema Bible College in Tulsa, Oklahoma (a school started in 1974 by Kenneth Hagin, a Pentecostal evangelist and author). After a short stint as a youth minister in Ohioville, near Midland, Nuzzo spent eight years speaking at evangelistic and Christian growth events in churches across the country. In the early 1990s, he engaged in evangelism and church growth with the Word of Life World Outreach, also founded by Hagin, in South Africa, Botswana and Zambia.[90]

As Nuzzo and his wife, Michelle, drove through Cranberry shortly before leaving for Africa, they sensed God telling them to plant a church in this community. John initially assumed that he would assist another more seasoned pastor in doing this. While they were ministering in Africa, however, John and Michelle felt called to return to Cranberry to establish a church on their own. They did so in 1993, calling it Victory Family Church. Its members worshipped for five years in Cinema World at the Cranberry Mall before building a church on Mystic Pine Trail in Cranberry; about four hundred people typically attended their services by this time.[91]

After adding hundreds of more members, VFC built a second facility on Route 19 in Cranberry, which opened in 2006. This immense structure of 103,000 square feet houses the original sanctuary (now a meeting room), more than two dozen classrooms, a bookstore, a large open area that includes a café and an auditorium that seats 2,400. About 3,000 people now attend either the church's four weekend services or the children's classes conducted during these services.[92]

Nuzzo insists that several factors explain its "phenomenal growth" from 1993 to the present: the sovereignty of God; the church's visibility; its attractive facilities; its events that attract community residents; its members, who are "committed to reaching and ministering to people"; its discipleship programs and small groups that connect people to the church; "the momentum created" as "thousands of people give their lives to Jesus Christ"; and the provision of "an environment where people experience the unconditional love of God" in "their everyday life."[93]

VFC's parishioners are diverse in age, family structure and socioeconomic status. The church has a sizable number of older members, many of whom mentor younger ones, but its predominant demographic is families with children. The church's youth attend schools in forty different districts. Spiritually mature members work with divorced individuals, blended

Victory Family Church. *Courtesy of Victory Family Church.*

families and engaged couples. Couples are required to be mentored for six weeks before getting married; some couples continue this relationship after their weddings.[94]

The church's chief priorities, Nuzzo explained, are evangelism, discipleship and spiritual care. Emulating Jesus, VFC seeks to reach the lost. It strives to make disciples by immersing members in the Bible, which is "a living guide for everyday life." "We believe," the church website states, that everyone "should be treated with the highest degree of love, care, dignity, respect, and honor."[95]

Nuzzo focuses on providing a vision, leading the staff and congregation and preaching. What Nuzzo loves most about the ministry is walking with people "through their pain and helping them grow in Christ." The mission of the church, Nuzzo asserted, "is not to make people happy; but to help them grow in Christ and serve others." "Too many Christians focus on 'what's in it for me?' instead of on building God's kingdom." Everything that VFC does aims to motivate and equip people to "make a great impact" for God's kingdom. The chief challenges his congregation faces, Nuzzo maintained, are combating "the destruction of the family," resisting "the throwaway nature of relationships" and working to "build godly families."[96]

To promote fellowship and Bible study, the church began offering a wide variety of small groups in 2013. In the fall of 2017, 1,234 adults belonged to one of these groups (500 people belonged to two groups each), which provide "friendship, fun, and support" and connect them with others who share their interests such as motorcycles, single parenting, financial planning, theater or flag football or face similar challenges in life. Some groups engage in recreational activities, while others study the Bible. Groups meet at homes, businesses, restaurants, athletic fields or other locations. "Broken Soldiers/Victorious Warriors" strives to help men who are struggling with sexual sin. The composition of groups changes three times a year so that people can continually try something new.[97]

VFC strongly supports both foreign and local missions and promotes civic engagement. Many members volunteer with Urban Impact and Light of Life Rescue Mission. VFC's weekly addiction recovery ministry provides love and support for those who are suffering from personal or family struggles through discussion groups, shared meals, food and clothing donations and free childcare. The church gives school backpacks (1,300 in 2016) and supplies to needy kids. During the 2016 election campaign, VFC worked to get people registered to vote and created a voter guide to explain where local, state and federal candidates stood on key issues; its pastors also encouraged members to vote for those who espoused biblical views.[98]

John Nuzzo. *Courtesy of Victory Family Church.*

In 2013, Nuzzo created an initiative to help revitalize three hundred congregations within a 250-mile radius of Pittsburgh. Presently, about seventy congregations representing a variety of theological traditions, most of which have 100 to 150 members, are participating. Nuzzo has monthly conference calls with the pastors of these churches and hosts an annual conference at VFC. The initiative focuses on three goals: evangelism (to double the size of their congregations), discipleship (to strengthen believers and operate more effectively as a church) and care (to respond to needs in their communities). Nuzzo urges pastors to "date" their methods and "marry" their message. Unfortunately, he argued, most congregations reverse this. Any method, he insisted, can become too restrictive; pastors begin with a passion to reach individuals for Christ, but many soon become preoccupied with incidentals. VFC supports other local congregations in additional ways, including helping fund their building projects.[99]

Nuzzo's background is Pentecostal, and the church identifies with this tradition. Nuzzo stressed that VFC follows the I Corinthians model—speaking in tongues and interpretation occur only in small groups, not in the main worship services. VFC's website states that the Holy Spirit guides, comforts and empowers Christians and teaches them to emulate Jesus. "The presence and baptism of the Holy Spirit [a major Pentecostal doctrine] are gifts from the Father, available to all believers. The confirmation of receiving the baptism of the Holy Spirit, which is received subsequent to salvation, is speaking in other tongues." In the spring of 2016, 150 worshippers came forward one Sunday to receive the baptism of the Holy Spirit after Nuzzo preached on the subject. The church also has a room where many go to pray with others for healing.[100]

Several times a year, VFC sponsors "a time of dynamic, Spirit-filled worship and teaching by gifted nationally and internationally known speakers." For example, clinical psychologist Henry McCloud, the author of twenty-five books, including the best-selling *Boundaries*, spoke in November 2016.[101]

The Church Visit

On Sunday, September 11, 2016, Alexia Skoria and I visited Victory Family Church. We were warmly greeted by several members of the Connections Team who effusively shared why they loved their church and how it had helped them grow spiritually. They offered us coffee and doughnuts, pointed us to many pamphlets that described church programs or focused on healing and the power of the Holy Spirit and gave us a coupon for free smoothies or lattes at their café.

VFC's youth room is housed in its original sanctuary. This large room has a section of church-style seating and an area for youth to socialize, which has a trendy, coffee shop feel, but is larger and more extravagant. While there, we overheard Alyssa Preston, VFC's communications director, assure a family she was escorting around the church, "We're not the mafia….If you feel that this is not the right place for you, we will help you find another Bible-believing church that is a better fit for you."

VFC's mammoth sanctuary looks like a concert venue and was filled with stage fog when we walked in. As we waited for the 11:00 a.m. service to begin, videos played on the three screens above the stage advertising church events and programs. In addition, messages projected on huge screens at the front of the auditorium declared, "You are accepted. You are loved." The lights faded when the thirty-five-member worship band and choir stepped onto the stage. Most worship team members were attractive people in their twenties. An impressive light show accompanied their music. The auditorium was about one-fourth full—roughly six hundred worshippers of varied ages, most of whom were in their twenties or thirties.

A praise band leader acknowledged that worship at Victory could feel overwhelming because of the lights, screens and cameras but insisted that the primary focus is on God's presence. "We are passionate about God," he proclaimed. "He responds to the praise of His people. God went all in for us; let's go all in for Him." As we sang, the words of the songs displayed on the screens were interspersed with biblical passages and adjectives and titles describing God and Jesus. During the announcements, an associate pastor encouraged worshippers to "do life together" by joining a small group to study the Bible or participating in a recreational activity.

A worship service at Victory Family Church. *Courtesy of Victory Family Church.*

Nuzzo's forty-five-minute sermon on homosexuality and transgender issues was the first in a series on topics that members had requested in a recent survey. He began by asking: How can we love those who live a gay or transgender lifestyle despite disagreeing with their practices? How can Christians honor God and obey His teachings about homosexuality without being considered bigots? How would Jesus relate to these people? We live in a world, Nuzzo lamented, where tolerance has been redefined. However, people can affirm some common American sexual practices only by rejecting God. Many Christians, Nuzzo averred, go to one of two extremes: either they redefine God's teachings so that society will view them as tolerant and loving or they act hatefully toward those whose sexual practices they repudiate.

Nuzzo discussed a variety of sexual practices or identities that evangelical Christians censure: premarital sex, adultery and pornography, as well as homosexuality and transgenderism. Citing Genesis 1:26–27, Nuzzo argued that people are made in God's image, an image that Satan seeks to distort. Although God condemns other forms of sin more harshly than sexual sin, Nuzzo contended, sexual sin alienates individuals from God and does not bring fulfillment.

Nuzzo empathized with people battling sexual sin and insisted repeatedly that God can heal sexual brokenness. "If I had lived your life [referring to some people he had talked with in the congregation who have difficult life stories]," Nuzzo declared, "I wouldn't be half as normal as you are." It is very easy, he added, to criticize and judge people if you have not lived their life. Nuzzo discussed two biblical texts that focus on "sexually broken" individuals: the story of the woman caught in the act of adultery (John 8:1–11) and Jesus' encounter with a Samaritan woman who had been married five times and was currently in a cohabiting relationship (John 4). Jesus did not shame either of these women, but He did challenge them to change their behavior.

Nuzzo urged worshippers to walk alongside sexually broken individuals to help free them. The church, he insisted, is an emergency room, not a museum. It should be a safe place where people are loved, cared for and made whole by Jesus, he declared, prompting applause from congregants. Nuzzo compared how we treat those with a broken leg and those with sexual addictions. We do not ask people with a broken leg, "What's wrong with you?" or tell them to "change." Instead, we walk with them and help them. At VFC, Nuzzo asserted, "We're not here to see through you, but to see you through." Willpower, Nuzzo contended, cannot fix people's sexual brokenness; only the Holy Spirit can.

While guilt is a positive emotion, Nuzzo asserted, shame is not. Jesus bore both our guilt and shame on the cross. Christians should not shame people. In relating to gay and transgendered individuals, he exhorted parishioners to focus on redemption rather than judgment. Nuzzo also insisted that Christians should love gay and transgender individuals while repudiating their sexual practices, but he did not discuss how Christians should respond to people who contend that their lifestyle is consistent with scriptural teaching rather than a form of sexual brokenness.

Nuzzo ended his sermon by challenging listeners to receive Christ as their personal savior. He invited congregants to pray with him aloud, and dozens did. Nuzzo urged those who had accepted Jesus as their savior to talk with a prayer partner after the service and pick up a booklet titled *I Have Decided!: Beginning Your New Life with Jesus*. This booklet discusses forgiveness, the Bible, prayer, the church, witnessing and the baptism of the Holy Spirit.

Through its vibrant, Spirit-led worship, focus on studying and applying the Bible, strong support of local and overseas missions and John Nuzzo's innovative program to help other congregations, Victory Family Church is significantly influencing the Pittsburgh region and many places beyond.

Chapter 9

TWO AFRICAN AMERICAN PITTSBURGH CHURCHES

Among Pittsburgh's numerous African American congregations, two have an especially powerful presence today: Macedonia Baptist Church in the Hill District and Mount Ararat Baptist Church in the East End. Both founded in the first decade of the twentieth century, the two churches have thriving ministries that lead many to Christ, produce dedicated disciples and substantially improve the social and material welfare of Steel City residents.

Macedonia Baptist Church: Developing "Dynamic Disciples"

Macedonia Baptist Church was founded in 1903 in the lower Hill District and today is loosely affiliated with the American Baptist Church and the National Baptist Convention of America (a predominantly African American denomination). Its members have included jazz great Stanley Turrentine and former Steeler defensive back J.T. Thomas and quarterback Kordell Stewart. Josh Gibson, the black Babe Ruth, was married at Macedonia, and the baseball field behind the church bears his name.[1]

An influx of black migrants from the South who came to Pittsburgh to find better jobs, combined with pastor James Robinson's dynamic preaching and winsome pastoral care, swelled the church's membership to 1,600 by the end of World War II. During the 1950s and early 1960s, Macedonia's ministry flourished under the leadership of William Harvey III, who earned a PhD in systematic theology from the University of Chicago Divinity School. During the tenure of Alfred Pugh from 1967 to 1987, Macedonia's budget increased almost tenfold, and the church built a low-income housing complex in Pittsburgh, operated a food program for Hill District residents, created a radio ministry that shared the gospel with many Pittsburghers and established a school in Haiti.[2]

Under senior pastor Jason Barr Jr., who served from 1988 to 2012, Macedonia's membership increased to more than three thousand, making it the largest congregation in the Hill District and Pittsburgh's third-largest African American church. Macedonia began holding three worship services on Sunday mornings, expanded its staff significantly and founded both the Macedonia Family and Community Enrichment Center (FACE) to provide community programs and social services from a faith-based perspective and the Macedonia Development Corporation to promote economic development and improve housing in the Hill District.[3]

Brian Edmonds, Macedonia's senior pastor since 2012, grew up in Baltimore and attended a Baptist church where his father was a deacon. As an eight-year-old, he accepted Jesus as his savior and was baptized to publicly affirm his commitment to Christ. Edmonds earned a BS in systems engineering at the University of Virginia. As a student, he worked as a

Macedonia Baptist Church. *Courtesy of Macedonia Baptist Church.*

campus ministry intern for Campus Crusade for Christ (now Cru). In 2006, he received an MDiv from Duke Divinity School. While attending seminary, he served as master of ceremonies for numerous regional and national Cru conferences called the Impact Movement. Duke assigned him to Macedonia Church to do his field education, and he obviously impressed Barr and the church's lay leaders, who hired him in 2007 as their pastor of young adults and campus ministries.[4]

Before beginning this position, Edmonds did mission work in Guatemala, Nigeria, South Africa and Costa Rica. In addition, he traveled with Cru to minister to people in Syria, Lebanon, Jordan, Israel and Egypt. Edmonds also served as a mentor, coach, advisor and teacher and volunteered with varied religious, professional and civic organizations, all of which confirmed his call to the ministry and helped equip him for his pastoral role at Macedonia.[5]

Recognizing his exceptional gifts, Macedonia selected Edmonds to be its senior pastor in 2012, when health problems forced Barr to retire. During Barr's frequent hospitalizations and illnesses, Edmonds had preached powerful sermons. When Barr stepped down, church leaders quickly concluded that God had brought Edmonds to Macedonia to prepare him for this position.[6]

Edmonds preaches most Sundays, teaches various groups and supplies a vision for Macedonia's ministry. He directs a staff of eighteen full-time and part-time "servant leaders." Edmonds also chairs the board of Macedonia FACE and is one member of the church's ten-person governing body. Macedonia exists, Edmonds asserted, to "know Christ and make him known" and to "develop dynamic disciples." "Our vision," he declared, is to be a "community that lifts and leads God's people to live liberated lives." Macedonia seeks to be an "agent of change in our community by the power of God." Its members, Edmonds explained, strive to meet "the spiritual and physical needs of our community and help people to fulfill their purpose."[7]

"We accomplish this mission," the church's website declares, "through proclaiming Jesus Christ to the world, preparing believers to access the power that we have in Jesus" and helping "people to live victoriously." Macedonia's ministry rests on eight core values: scriptural authority, biblical teaching, loving relationships, spiritual development, cultural relevance, the exercise of spiritual gifts, church growth and the pursuit of excellence.[8]

Edmonds described his preaching style as expository. He uses humor, illustrations and stories to engross his parishioners and inspire them to love Jesus and live out their faith in every area of life. Edmonds typically preaches for thirty to forty minutes, depending on the leading of the Holy Spirit. He

Brian Edmonds. *Courtesy of Macedonia Baptist Church.*

spends ten to twenty hours a week preparing his sermon. Until a year ago, he took a complete manuscript of his sermon with him into the pulpit, but now he internalizes his sermons and preaches without any notes.[9]

Edmonds's favorite part of the ministry is seeing God transform people as he preaches, counsels and converses with them in everyday settings. Macedonia has grown substantially in the last two decades, Edmonds contended, because of its faithfulness to Scripture, consistent biblical teaching, engaging music, relevance to its community and ability to appeal to people of all ages. Macedonia's staff and members work diligently to attract the unchurched, win them to Christ and involve them in the congregation's fellowship and ministry.[10]

While all Macedonia Church's two thousand members are African Americans, they differ in age, occupation and income. Most worshippers are between thirty and sixty. They are almost evenly divided between white-collar and blue-collar jobs. Some members live below the poverty line. About 70 percent of members currently do not live in the Hill District, but many who come from other Pittsburgh neighborhoods were born and raised on the Hill. Numerous members, especially senior citizens, use buses to get to church. Macedonia uses two large vans to transport students from Duquesne University, Carnegie Mellon University, the University of Pittsburgh, Point Park University and the Art Institute to its Sunday services.[11]

Edmonds argued that small groups and local missions are very important in Macedonia's life and ministry. About 300 members currently participate in these groups. Macedonia's small groups usually meet at the church and use resources that the staff select. Edmonds and other pastors teach some groups, especially the midweek men's and women's Bible studies, which typically attract 50 and 150 attendees, respectively, and break into smaller groups to discuss the lesson, pray and share concerns.[12] Macedonia strives to be "a church without walls," serving the surrounding community in numerous ways through holding coat drives; community events; prayer walks; and furnishing school supplies, hats, coats and gloves to elementary school students and personalized boxes of goods to needy community members.[13]

Especially impressive is Macedonia's Family and Community Enrichment Center, a community-based social services organization, which operates a counseling center. Its mission is to help develop healthy families. Established in 1991, FACE has been much more effective at some times than at others, but its impact during the last five years has been very significant. FACE assists families in the Hill District and nearby neighborhoods who are dealing with financial, relational, emotional and spiritual crises because of poverty, unemployment, lack of housing and insufficient food. In 2010, Trisha Gadson became FACE's executive director. Under her leadership, the annual budget has almost quadrupled from $500,000 in 2010 to $1.9 million in 2018, and FACE's employees have tripled to include 21 full- and part-time counselors, mentors and support staff; 2 volunteers; and 4 consultants. During the 2016–17 fiscal year, FACE served about 1,500 different individuals.[14]

FACE provides immediate and long-term help to families in crisis, HIV/AIDS case management, bullying prevention, a truancy intervention project and a Girls Circle that endeavors to build self-confidence in female teens. Through its Lifeline Support Services, FACE aids families undergoing a short-term crisis by connecting them with community organizations to assist them with various needs. Its Families and Community Teaming program (FACT) helps families develop a plan based on their strengths and needs to equip them to deal more effectively with situations that are causing anxiety, fear and uncertainty. FACE helps each family assemble a team to support the plan it devises. The team may include friends, neighbors, teachers, coworkers and church members, as well as community organizations and resources to aid the family to implement its plan. FACE also provides training to members of other community organizations on HIV/AIDS prevention and education, HIV testing and case management, the prevention of bullying and dating violence and diversity and cultural competence.[15]

FACE's Community Truancy Intervention Project (CTIP) employs various community resources to reduce school truancy and chronic absenteeism in schools in the Hill District. Closely connected with CTIP is FACE's Family Capacity service, which works to alleviate socioeconomic barriers and family stressors that inhibit the performance of Hill District elementary and secondary students. Partnering with community organizations, Family Capacity helps about one hundred students to boost their academic performance each year.[16]

Macedonia Church's governing board consists of Edmonds and nine laymen and laywomen who oversee the church's worship, administration, finances, personnel decisions and programs. These elders, who serve terms of five to seven years, must be spiritually mature and have a record of consistent and effective service to the church. Macedonia also has thirty deacons who serve for life and help supply members' physical and material needs.[17]

The primary strengths of Macedonia, Edmonds claimed, are its robust biblical teaching, lively music, welcoming atmosphere and commitment to the local community. Its major challenges, according to Edmonds, are its inadequate facilities and struggle to get members actively involved in ministry. Although Macedonia has a swimming pool, recreational center, outdoor basketball court and four nearby auxiliary buildings, its main building has limited space and its sanctuary seats only 650. Macedonia wants to construct a new complex in the Hill District that would include a 1,500-seat sanctuary. The church works diligently to keep people connected to its ministry, Edmonds insisted; its staff strive to "close the back door" by plugging them into a small group or a ministry to provide fellowship and opportunities to serve.[18]

Edmonds hopes that during the next ten years, Macedonia will build a new facility to increase its membership, expand its ministry and energize more people to serve the Hill District and nearby neighborhoods. He wants to see Pittsburgh become "a city of hope" where revival breaks forth and people "encounter the power of God to transform lives and communities." Edmonds prays that the city's churches will "become major change agents in the lives of young men and women" and that "by the grace of God, the chains of poverty and hopelessness in the city" will be broken.[19]

Macedonia partners with the city's other African American (and, on some issues, white) congregations to alleviate poverty, improve housing and education, reduce racial discrimination and tension and provide blacks with greater educational, social and employment opportunities. Edmonds works closely with the senior pastors of Mount Ararat Baptist Church, Rodman Street Baptist Church in East Liberty and Central Baptist Church in the Hill District to advance these aims, sometimes exchanging pulpits with them.[20]

Recently, Macedonia's members have been particularly concerned about the rash of shootings of African Americans by police officers in Ferguson, Missouri; Baton Rouge, Louisiana; St. Paul, Minnesota; and other locales, as well as the gunning down of police officers in Dallas. At a Sunday service in July 2016, hundreds of worshippers placed index cards at the base of a large wooden cross at the front of the sanctuary bearing the names of the victims of these atrocities. Other cards requested prayers for local congregations, the Hill District and an end to racism. "We need a place to lament," Edmonds declared, but also a place where we can find hope. Macedonia, he noted, included both police officers and people who were fearful of what might happen if they were stopped by the police. Edmonds challenged his parishioners to transcend their gloom and fear and "be the hands and feet of God" by praying for people, mentoring someone and registering to vote to help improve social conditions.[21]

The Church Visit

On Mother's Day 2017 (May 13), Alexia Skoria and I attended the 10:00 a.m. service at Macedonia Church. As discussed in chapter 3, the Hill District has long been one of Pittsburgh's poorest and most problem-plagued neighborhoods, but significant gentrification has occurred in the area near the church. The church was built in 1927 and is the smallest and most modest structure of the nine profiled congregations. Several rooms on the first floor are used to provide care and instruction for about thirty young children during the 10:00 a.m. service; the second floor has a small bookstore and gift shop, offices and an open area for fellowship; the third floor houses the sanctuary. Signs over the two doors on the second floor proclaim Macedonia's mission, "We Exist to Develop Dynamic Disciples," and state its guiding philosophy, "Faith, not Money, is the most powerful currency we have."

The sanctuary was packed with about 700 worshippers (1,200 attend Macedonia's two services on a typical Sunday). Six large banners, each containing a single word—Power, Peace, Hope, Grace, Love and Faith, accompanied by a relevant biblical verse—adorned the sanctuary. Before the service began, announcements were projected on two large screens at the front of the church. These announcements were repeated during the service in a video called the "Macey Minute." Five events were highlighted: weekly men's and women's Bible studies; an upcoming Graduation Sunday to honor the congregation's high school seniors and award $15,000 in college scholarships; a series of two-hour classes in June and July for dating, engaged and married couples; and an October bus trip for senior citizens to see *Jonah and the Whale* in Lancaster, Pennsylvania. Both the men's and women's groups were beginning a new series using Rick Warren's Bible study guide titled *Everything Is Possible with God.*

At precisely 10:00 a.m., a thirty-person choir, consisting mostly of middle-aged women, led worshippers in singing Chris Tomlin's "Our God Is Greater" accompanied by two keyboard players and a drummer. We then sang Michael W. Smith's "The Enemy Has Been Defeated." After a pastor shared the names of twenty people on the church's prayer list, a woman led the congregation in a prayer that focused on mothers as worshippers held hands. A lay leader reminded worshippers that Edmonds was celebrating his five-year anniversary as the congregation's senior pastor.

Edmonds invited mothers to have their photographs taken after the service with their families in front of a picturesque backdrop. Edmonds urged his parishioners to vote in the primaries on Tuesday. Using "I don't know who is running" as an excuse for not voting was unacceptable. People could check out the qualifications and positions of candidates online. Voting for community leaders, Edmonds argued, was just as important as voting for the president. The pastor insisted that he was not endorsing specific candidates, but he did stress that four of them—one running for mayor, one for judge and two for the local school board—had recently worshipped at Macedonia, which seemed to be a tacit endorsement.

Edmonds also announced that he would be giving quarterly updates on Macedonia's expansion plans. Because the congregation has outgrown its facilities, its members want to build a new church, but the cost of a parking garage—$12 million for four hundred spaces—is a major deterrent. Although the challenge of building new facilities is tremendous, Edmonds declared, God's provisions are amazing. In response, congregants shouted, "Hallelujah! You've seen him work! God's a provider!"

Edmonds urged worshippers to pray for current and prospective mothers. Mothers, he declared, vividly portray God's love through their willingness to forego careers to bear and raise children and to care for their husbands and homes. Their actions pointed people to Christ's sacrifice on the cross to atone for human sin.

After the deacons served communion, visitors were welcomed, and ushers gave us cards to fill out. When we turned in our cards after the service, we received devotionals, a CD containing a sermon by Edmonds, other literature about the church and candy. After the offering, the choir sang "How Much Do I Owe Him?" Worshippers stood, clapped, swayed with the music and sang along. Edmonds encouraged people to cry out to God, who is worthy of our praise. "Nobody can talk to him like you can," he avowed. "Don't hold back!" Worshippers shouted, danced and prayed loudly, proclaiming "glory to your name" and other phrases of adoration. Edmonds closed this time of prayer by asserting that Christ is Lord of everything—our bodies, families and careers.

Edmonds used Joshua 24:14–18 as the text for his thirty-minute sermon, focusing on verse 15: "But as for me and my household, we will serve the Lord." When he was preparing to marry nine years earlier, Edmonds received lots of advice, including "don't go to bed angry," be kind to each other when you disagree and "happy wife, happy life." Edmonds urged all Christians to make their families their chief ministry. Christian service should not be done at the expense of one's family. He had recently turned down a speaking engagement, Edmonds explained, to spend more time with his family. "Can you imagine what kind of world we would have," Edmonds asked, "if all those who know Christ as their Savior and Lord made their families their first ministry?"

As he was preparing to preach, Edmonds shared, God asked him three questions, which he, in turn, asked worshippers. The first was: Are you ministering to or managing your family? Many marriages are failing apart, he lamented, because men are trying to master rather than minister to their wives. Many children, Edmonds added, are using illicit drugs and acting irresponsibly because their parents are trying to control them instead of loving and serving them.

Second, Edmonds inquired, can we practice both "grace and truth in relationship to our families?" Jesus dispensed grace and spoke the truth. Some Christians, Edmonds claimed, focus only on grace, while others emphasize only truth. To have healthy marriages and help their children thrive, Christian parents must simultaneously embody grace and truth.

Finally, Edmonds asked parents, "Are you willing to lead by example?" At a critical juncture as the Jews prepared to enter the Promised Land, Joshua testified that he and his family pledged to follow the Lord. Parents should focus on being good role models rather than on trying to force their children to follow rules. Jesus, Edmonds asserted, is the greatest example of all time; He spoke and lived the truth. By exemplifying both grace and truth, Edmonds promised, Christians can affirm and celebrate mothers, create flourishing families, regenerate communities and change the world.

Given the high rate of children born out of wedlock in the African American community (about 70 percent), the fact that one-third percent of black men in their twenties are either in prison or jail or on probation or parole and the fact that at least 75 percent of the worshippers at the service we attended were women, Edmonds's message was very timely and important.[22]

Before pronouncing the benediction, Edmonds invited congregants to come to the front of the sanctuary and meet with deacons to receive Christ as their savior, pray about their concerns or learn more about Macedonia. After the benediction, Edmonds urged worshippers to "give somebody a hug and tell them God is good."

By faithfully proclaiming the gospel, nurturing believers, developing dynamic disciples and operating numerous fruitful ministries, Macedonia Church is having a tremendous impact for Christ in the Hill District and surrounding Pittsburgh communities.

Mount Ararat Baptist Church: Making Pittsburgh a More Just, Prosperous and Compassionate City

With 7,500 members, Mount Ararat Baptist Church, founded in 1906 in the East End, is the largest Protestant congregation in the Pittsburgh area. Dr. William Curtis, its senior pastor, grew up in Baltimore and received his BA in religious studies and philosophy at Morgan State University. After earning his MDiv at Howard University School of Divinity in Washington, D.C., he served for seven years as the senior pastor at Shiloh Baptist Church in York, Pennsylvania. In 1997, he became the senior pastor at Mount Ararat. While holding this position, he completed a Doctor of Ministry degree at United Theological Seminary in Dayton, Ohio, where he has also been an instructor.[23]

Since Curtis's arrival, the church has grown from 400 members to its current size, with 5,500 people attending one of its four worship services each weekend. Under his leadership, the congregation formed a community development corporation to minister to the Pittsburgh area, paid off its mortgage and implemented a tithing program that gives 10 percent of its revenue to the community. Curtis created The Church Online, an innovative technology firm that supplies live video streaming, mobile app development and website development assistance to ministries throughout the world. Curtis has also written *Faith: Learning to Live without Fear* (2012) and *Dressed for Victory: Putting on the Full Armor of God* (2015). He serves on the board of numerous organizations, including Amachi Pittsburgh, Pittsburgh Theological Seminary, the Interdenominational Theological Center and the Baptist School of Theology.

Curtis's primary roles at Mount Ararat are preaching (he spends fifteen to twenty hours per week preparing his sermons and preaches all but five Sundays each year), teaching, administration and management of facilities and properties. He also directs the church's staff which includes four other pastors, two administrative assistants, a director of communications and a chief financial officer.[24]

Martin Luther King Jr., Curtis asserted, influenced him in several ways. Curtis tries to emulate King's passion for intellectual rigor and his pursuit of "pulpit excellence." Curtis has also been inspired by the civil rights activist's vigorous effort to improve American culture and "his embrace of all races while seeking to empower his own." King's quest to promote justice serves as a model for Curtis's leadership of Mount Ararat. Curtis counsels pastors to love and nurture their parishioners, "wrestle with great ideas," "trust God for the growth and success" of their ministry and handle "the favor of God…with extreme care."[25]

Mount Ararat's chief priorities, Curtis explains, are evangelizing the lost, equipping the saints, edifying the body of believers and advancing the kingdom of God.[26] Through the Mount Ararat Community Activity Center (MACAC), established in 1990, the church works "to improve the quality of life of families and individuals" throughout the Pittsburgh area by "empowering individuals and families" to be independent and productive, fostering conditions that promote economic stability and providing programs to support and encourage family values. To help achieve these goals, MACAC operates a food and clothing bank for church members and neighborhood residents. Its Computer Technology Center gives people free use of computers with Internet access and offers classes that teach basic and

William Curtis. *Courtesy of Mount Ararat Baptist Church.*

advanced computer skills. MACAC's Early Childhood Development Center furnishes "a nurturing and stimulating" day care experience to help 25 to 40 children between birth and five years of age develop cognitively, emotionally and physically. Its BRIDGES (Build Relationships to Inform, Develop, Guide and Equip Students for Success) After School Program instructs 55 to 75 children in math, reading and science. Through its Mentoring Project, Mount Ararat members help about 150 local middle school students attend classes regularly, improve their academic achievement and social skills, enhance their self-esteem, develop spiritually and serve others. MACAC's ministries are housed in a new community center in Garfield, about five minutes by car from the church, that opened in March 2018. This three-story building, a renovated former school, has a large gym. MACAC's board includes men and women who work for or are retired from IBM, H.J. Heinz, Highmark, PNC Bank, UPS, KDKA, Carnegie Mellon University and other leading Pittsburgh companies and nonprofits.[27]

Mount Ararat also operates a counseling center staffed by eight therapists that assists about two hundred culturally diverse individuals, couples and families each year. Clients receive from one to eight counseling sessions. The center seeks to provide biblically based psychological guidance, emotional support and social services to both the church's members and community residents. Clients receive help to deal with depression, anxiety, stress, physical abuse, alcohol and substance abuse, relationship and family problems and grief and loss.[28]

Curtis's sermons combine narrative and exposition. Typically forty-five minutes long, they elaborate on the context and contemporary meaning of biblical texts while using a story form to apply key points to the lives of his parishioners. Curtis brings a full script of every sermon to the pulpit, but he often feels led by God to add extemporaneous insights as he preaches. Curtis says he loves to preach, which he does four times each weekend, and his passion is apparent. He is energized by seeing church members become mature disciples of Jesus.[29]

Mount Ararat has grown rapidly during the last twenty years, Curtis contended, because of its Christ-centering preaching, ministry to the whole person, emphasis on spiritual formation and strong sense of community. While embracing the traditions of the African American Baptist church, Curtis explained, Mount Ararat's worship style is charismatic. Its parishioners come from many different neighborhoods in the Pittsburgh area (about 30 percent of members live within a five-mile radius of the church) and every economic status, educational background and age group. They are teachers, small business owners and blue-collar workers.[30]

Curtis insisted that both small groups and local missions are extremely important to Mount Ararat's ministry and growth. Each week, twenty-one groups of ten to fifteen people each meet to study the Bible, grow spiritually and prepare to share the gospel through their words and deeds.

Group members are usually similar in age, spiritual development and/or life experiences. They meet year-round (often for several years), spend time together outside of their weekly meetings and develop strong bonds. Their leaders receive intensive training from Curtis and other pastors, but groups emphasize peer learning.[31]

Mount Ararat supports local missions through its community tithing program and its own ministries that focus primarily on feeding the hungry and assisting the poor in the surrounding neighborhood. One church program provides recreational, educational and social opportunities for Pittsburghers who are sixty-five and older through health and literacy activities, quilting and craft classes and computer instruction. Every year, members of the tithing committee decide which ministries, arts programs, schools and struggling smaller congregations to assist through the 10 percent of its revenue Mount Ararat gives to various enterprises in Allegheny County.[32]

Mount Ararat's governing board consists of twenty-five to thirty male and female deacons who are selected and trained by the senior pastor and make key decisions pertaining to both spiritual and practical matters. Curtis chairs the group and is the only pastor who is part of this body. All the board's financial decisions must be approved by congregational vote.[33]

Curtis identifies Mount Ararat's primary strengths as its focus on evangelism, vibrant worship, loving care of community members and strenuous efforts to improve the lives of African Americans living in the Pittsburgh area. He argued that everything the church does has an evangelistic component and insisted that his sermons and church programs strongly encourage parishioners to share their faith as part of their everyday lives. Mount Ararat works to reduce discrimination and promote social justice in Allegheny County through the weight of its numbers and its members' active participation in the NAACP, the Urban League and various ecumenical social ministries. The congregation's greatest challenge, Curtis contended, is dealing with "the distraction of cultural noise"—the proliferation of news, people's preoccupation with social media and society's exaltation of speed and self-gratification.[34]

During the next decade, Curtis wants to "continue to expand Mount Ararat's footprint in East Liberty," cooperate more fully with other congregations and community groups to improve social conditions in the East End, renovate the church's building to expand its ministry and pay off its debt. Mount Ararat seeks to make Pittsburgh a more just, prosperous and compassionate city by proclaiming the gospel, placing its people in strategic positions, participating in pivotal organizations and promoting constructive social changes.[35]

The Church Visit

Alexia Skoria and I visited Mount Ararat on Palm Sunday 2017 (April 9). Mount Ararat's church building is considerably smaller than the other profiled churches except for Macedonia and ACAC. Its sanctuary, however, seats about 1,800. The building also houses some classrooms and meeting rooms and a café, which is open from 9:00 a.m. to 2:00 p.m. on Sundays and during special church events. Mount Ararat uses several vans and small buses to transport worshippers from nearby locales.

People of all ages packed the sanctuary. More than at the other eight churches, worshippers, especially older ones, were formally dressed. Most men over age fifty wore sports coats and ties; most women over age fifty wore colorful dresses and hats; the ushers who collected the offering wore formal jackets and white gloves. The service began with video announcements called "Mount TV," which highlighted upcoming events, including a seminar on dating for young adults and collections for the church's food and clothing center. Another announcement accentuated the work of the Neighborhood Academy—"a faith-based, college preparatory, independent school" for grades six through twelve located near the church that seeks to "break the cycle of generational poverty by preparing low-income youth to attend college and be good citizens."[36]

A praise band consisting of eight members who played a variety of instruments and fifteen vocalists led congregational singing. We sang the 1895 hymn "At Calvary" and Kirk Franklin's 2011 praise song "At the Altar You Can Tell Jesus All about It." Many worshippers shouted "Hallelujah," "Amen" and "Yes, Lord" while we sang. A middle-aged woman led the congregation in prayer as we held hands with worshippers beside us and across the aisles. As we sang "Awesome God," the worship leader accentuated its key phrases, including "Mighty God," "Healing God" and "Sovereign God," which were echoed by other members of the worship team. During this song, many worshippers yelled, danced, raised their hands and jumped up and down.

Of all nine churches we attended, the worshippers at Mount Ararat and Macedonia were by far the most energetic, effusive and engaged. At Mount Ararat, first-time visitors were asked to stand, and we were serenaded with a song that declared, "We are the ministry that cares; we care about you." During the five-minute fellowship period that followed, we received hugs and handshakes from a few dozen worshippers and greetings such as "God bless you" and "Glad you are here."

A worship service at Mount Ararat Baptist Church. *Courtesy of Mount Ararat Baptist Church.*

Curtis rejoiced that the church was unveiling its new projection screens that morning. He urged parishioners to give enough money on Palm Sunday and Easter to pay for this $30,000 improvement. He exhorted them to "give something extra" and reported that he had pledged $1,000 to help cover the cost. He called on several people by name whom he was confident would give sizable gifts. "We're at a stage as a church" where "long campaigns to pay off improvements" are not needed, he declared, so let's "just get it done." A youth choir (ages ten to fifteen) then sang "We Worship You, O Lord" and "We Magnify Your Name."

Curtis's sermon, titled "Declare Your Devotion," based on John 12:12–15, described Jesus' triumphal entry into Jerusalem at the beginning of the last week of His earthly life. Curtis instructed congregants to turn to one another and say, "You've got to declare your devotion," which many people did.

While Jesus came into the city riding on a donkey, Curtis pointed out, Pilate and his entourage entered Jerusalem from the opposite side. Crowds had assembled to celebrate Jesus' arrival because they had heard that He had raised Lazarus from the dead and many believed that the miracles He had performed confirmed His claim to be the Messiah. The Jews had a choice to make: they could wave palm branches to openly declare their devotion to the Son of God or they could pay their homage to Rome on the other side of the city. You cannot be amused by Pilate, Curtis maintained, and amazed by Jesus at the same time.

Are we, Curtis asked, unapologetic followers of Jesus who is Israel's hope, God's Son and the Savior? Are we excited about Jesus because we know Him personally? Are we devoted enough to Him to oppose our secular, hedonistic culture? Will we allow Jesus to determine our motives and follow His direction? Are we committed to Jesus even if it offends Pilate? Faith involves not just confidence in God, but dedication to Him; it declares, "I ain't switching." "I'm going to follow Jesus," Curtis promised, "because of who He is rather than what He has done, even if He never blesses me again." Many, Curtis lamented, refuse to make a firm commitment to Jesus. Parishioners stood, clapped and shouted encouragement such as "C'mon, pastor" and "Amen" as Curtis built to rhetorical climaxes.

Curtis told a gripping story about a woman during the Great Depression who needed food for her family but had no money. A local grocer mockingly promised that he would give her the same weight in groceries as the weight of her grocery list. But as he placed various food items on the scale, her list continued to balance them. He did not realize that the scale had broken the night before. Her list contained no groceries, simply the prayer, "Dear Lord, you know what I need and I'm putting it all in your hands." The moral of the story, Curtis insisted, is that if we are devoted to God, His weight will help us overcome our problems. "Life will push you," Curtis contended, "until you have to declare" your allegiance to someone or something. If you are devoted to God, He can change your circumstances. Turn your life over to Jesus and watch Him work to meet your needs.

Curtis ended his sermon by asking worshippers who had never accepted Christ as their savior to repeat his prayer asking Jesus to forgive their sins and come into their hearts and then walk to the front of the sanctuary to meet with lay counselors at the end of the service. A few people came forward.

The energy, enthusiasm, excitement and engagement of Mount Ararat's members was palpable and contagious. Gripped by the Holy Spirit, people worshipped joyfully, grateful to experience God's presence and one another's company. Through its fervent worship, biblically based sermons, classes, small group meetings and ministries that provide material assistance, therapeutic counseling and opportunities for personal spiritual growth, Mount Ararat is faithfully promoting justice, compassion, economic advancement and spiritual development in the Steel City.

Chapter 10

FAITH AND THE PITTSBURGH PIRATES

[No city] *has used sport in the United States as much as Pittsburgh to tell its story to the world.*
—*Rob Ruck, professor of history at the University of Pittsburgh*[1]

The importance of faith in baseball has a long history. Many of the game's greatest stars are well known for their Christian commitment, including Christy Mathewson, Jackie Robinson, Duke Snider, Bobby Richardson, Lou Brock, Mike Schmidt, Paul Molitor, Gary Carter, Dale Murphy, Orel Hershiser, John Smoltz, Tom Glavine, Mike Piazza, Curt Shilling, Andy Pettitte, Mariano Rivera, Albert Pujols and Clayton Kershaw.[2] The founding of Baseball Chapel in 1973 and the creation of Faith Nights in the early 2000s have contributed to the faith of players becoming more pronounced and prominent. Today, 210 teams, including every Major League Baseball team and many in the minor leagues and independent leagues, have a chapel program.[3] In 2016, thirteen MLB teams hosted faith nights that featured Christian bands, worship and players' testimonies.[4]

The Pirates also have a long and rich association with Christianity that includes future evangelist Billy Sunday playing for the club from 1888 to 1890 and the 1951 movie *Angels in the Outfield*, in which celestial beings help the perennially hapless Pirates win the pennant. Over the years, the Pirates have had a sizable number of Christians, including manager Danny Murtaugh; catchers Smokey Burgess and Manny Sanguillen; outfielders

Roberto Clemente, Al Oliver, Mike Easler, Andy Van Slyke and Matt Diaz; first basemen Sid Bream, Kevin Young and Adam LaRoche; shortstops Tim Foli, Jay Bell and Abraham Nunez; and pitchers Randy Tomlin, Zack Duke, Matt Capps and Paul Maholm. The importance of faith to the team reached its zenith after the arrival of outfielder Andrew McCutchen in 2009 and manager Clint Hurdle in 2011. Hurdle initiated the Pirates' Faith Night in 2013, and the franchise had a host of outspoken Christians, including infielders Neil Walker, Pedro Alvarez, Josh Harrison, Sean Rodriguez, David Freese and Jordy Mercer; pitchers Mark Melancon, Jason Grilli, Jared Hughes, Charlie Morton and Gerrit Cole; catchers Mike McKenry and Chris Stewart; outfielders Matt Joyce and Adam Frazier; and coach Dave Jauss. Players testified that their faith helped give them proper priorities, purpose, peace of mind, composure and confidence. Their relationships with God enabled them to resist temptations, control their anger and deal with adversity and frustration. Many of them used their success on the diamond as a platform for sharing the gospel.

The Miracle on the Diamond

The Pirates' victory over the mighty New York Yankees in the 1960 World Series was a David and Goliath event that ended more than three decades of baseball frustration in Pittsburgh. The Pirates had not won a world championship since 1925 and had the worst record in baseball in the 1950s, winning only 40 percent of their games. As the city strove to cast off its gritty, grimy past and experienced a civic renaissance, many residents were hungry for sports success. The Pirates had nine straight losing seasons from 1949 to 1957. The Steelers had never won a playoff game, and the Penguins had not yet begun skating. Far from a city of champions, Pittsburgh was a site of sports futility. Nevertheless, the city had thousands of loyal, passionate sports fans.

As children went back to school in September 1960, both anxiety and excitement were palpable. Americans were engaged in a space race and an arms competition with the Soviets. The presidential campaign between Vice President Richard Nixon and Senator John F. Kennedy was heating up. Amazingly, the Pirates were in a pennant race that culminated in their winning the National League pennant and going to the World Series.[5] Their improbable triumph helped change perceptions of Pittsburgh as a sports city.

The series was played in two iconic ballparks: Yankee Stadium, "the house that Ruth built," and Forbes Field in Pittsburgh. For many years, the park was the home of the Pirates, the Steelers and the University of Pittsburgh football team. Babe Ruth hit his last three home runs at Forbes Field in 1935. Josh Gibson, the black Babe Ruth, launched some towering shots over the fences at Forbes Field while playing with the Homestead Grays of the Negro Baseball League.[6]

The Pirates had a very good team in 1960, led by right-fielder Roberto Clemente and shortstop Dick Groat, the NL's MVP. The Pirates scored more runs than any other team in their league. However, the Yankees had won eight of the last thirteen World Series, had MLB's best record in 1960 and featured Mickey Mantle, Roger Maris and other Bronx "bombers." Their collective power rivaled that of the 1927 "Murderers Row" Yankee squad that starred Babe Ruth and Lou Gehrig and swept the Pirates in four games in the World Series. Las Vegas bookmakers made the Yankees 15-1 favorites to win the series. In the seven games, the Yankees outscored the Pirates 55–27, had a team batting average of .338 to the Pirates' .256 and had a team ERA of 3.54 compared with the Pirates' 7.11. The Pirates, however, won four close games, and Bill Mazeroski's ninth-inning blast over the left-field fence brought a flood of joy to Pittsburghers, releasing years of pent-up frustration. ESPN still ranks it as the greatest home run in history, and watching the ball soar over the left-field fence was a deeply moving experience for many Pittsburghers, matched only by Franco Harris's 1972 "immaculate reception." Jubilant fans celebrated late into the night.

Danny Murtaugh. *Courtesy of the Pittsburgh Pirates.*

Unlike the Pirates' current team, the 1960 squad did not have a large group of outspoken Christians. The Baseball Chapel program had not been established, and although Billy Graham had begun recruiting born-again athletes to give their testimonies at his crusades, few Major Leaguers spoke openly about their Christian commitment. Nevertheless, the Pirates had a devout Catholic manager in Danny Murtaugh; a Catholic champion of the downtrodden in Roberto Clemente; Vernon Law, a dedicated Mormon pitcher nicknamed "The Deacon"; and other committed Christians, including Smokey Burgess.[7] Murtaugh, the Pirates' second-winningest manager, was widely respected for his military service in World War II, commitment to his family, faithfulness to the church, knowledge of baseball and ability to inspire players. He sent all his children to Catholic elementary and high schools and Catholic colleges. They testified that his faith was central to his life. "Even on road trips," his daughter Kathy related, "my dad always made it to Sunday Mass, and he encouraged his coaches to join him."[8] Sportswriter Matt Zibitka described the Pirates' skipper as "deeply religious." Father Francis O'Reilly extolled Murtaugh as a dedicated, loving "man of God."[9]

Clemente, "The Great One," who played for the Pirates from 1956 to 1972, is arguably the franchise's most beloved star. He and Murtaugh helped the Pirates win a second world championship in 1971. Clemente was the youngest of seven children born to a Catholic family in Puerto Rico. His mother, Luisa, a devout Christian, taught her children that "only God makes man happy."[10] Clemente's faith motivated his zealous efforts to aid the indigent, oppressed and vulnerable. Clemente died when a plane on which he was flying to deliver food and medical supplies to Nicaragua after the country experienced a devastating earthquake crashed on New Year's Eve 1972. "The athletic world has lost a superstar," the *New Pittsburgh Courier* declared. "The world generally has lost a fine Christian gentleman."[11]

The film *Baseball's Last Hero: 21 Clemente Stories* details his struggles to overcome racism, quest to help the indigent and fabulous baseball career. Clemente recorded three thousand hits, was named to twelve all-star teams, won an MVP award and four NL batting championships, arguably had the best throwing arm in MLB history and is enshrined in the Hall of Fame. Clemente saw his fame and wealth as a tool to aid the less fortunate. His final mission of mercy exemplified his compassion and commitment to sacrifice his life for others. Clemente, the filmmakers contend, was inspired by Jesus' words in John 15:13: "Greater love has no man than this, that he lay down his life for his friends."[12] His teammate Al Oliver declared that Clemente "preached like a Baptist minister." "How can the rich have so much" when people are starving, he repeatedly asked. To many, Clemente's name "is synonymous with moral excellence, compassion and charitable work."[13] Every September, MLB celebrates Roberto Clemente Day, and each year, it presents the Roberto Clemente Award to honor "the player who best represents the game of baseball through sportsmanship, community involvement and positive contributions, both on and off the field."[14]

Roberto Clemente. *Courtesy of the Pittsburgh Pirates.*

Among the many players Clemente influenced was Manny Sanguillen, the starting catcher on the 1971 World Championship squad. Sanguillen thanked Clemente for helping him become a good baseball player.[15] Sanguillen, who played baseball "to glorify God," was scheduled to fly with Clemente to aid earthquake victims in Nicaragua on the plane that crashed shortly after taking off, killing all its passengers. Because of a last-minute mix-up, Sanguillen missed the flight.[16] Undoubtedly speaking for many Pirates, Neil Walker, whose father, Tom, had also planned to join Clemente on that ill-fated flight, declared in 2014, "It's not just what he meant for the game of baseball and the City of Pittsburgh, but for humanity"; "he changed so many lives."[17]

Vernon Law, a devout Mormon, was the ace of the Pirates' pitching staff in 1960, winning twenty games during the regular season and two in the World Series. His faith informed all aspects of his life. "Law cannot be fully understood," John Moody argued, "without a knowledge of his religion." The Deacon did not drink alcohol, smoke or use drugs. He consistently attended church, gave 10 percent of his income to the church, spoke to many groups about his faith and served others through many means.[18] "I prayed for strength. I prayed that I would do my best. I prayed that no one would be hurt," he asserted.[19]

The 1979 World Champions

The Pirates captured another world championship in 1979, storming back from a 3-1 deficit to win the final three games against the Orioles, the last two of which were played in Baltimore. Led by first baseman Willie Stargell, the team's all-time home run leader, outfielders Dave Parker and Omar Moreno, shortstop Tim Foli, starting pitchers John Candelaria and Bert Blyleven and closer Kent Telulve, the Pirates adopted Sister Sledge's "We Are Family" as their theme song.[20] Philadelphia Phillies slugger Mike Schmidt insisted that the Pirates had a solid contingent of Christians.[21] Pirate manager Chuck Tanner frequently attended the team's chapel meetings. His quiet faith was most evident in his friendliness, kindness and optimism. "I played for a lot of managers," testified Grant Jackson, a relief pitcher on the 1979 squad, "and I never knew anyone who treated people like Chuck." If they asked baseball players to choose the game's "all-time nicest man," Pittsburgh sportswriter Ron Cook insisted, "Tanner surely would win." A manager, Tanner declared, should be judged "by whether he gets the most out of the twenty-five men he's been given," which Tanner did very effectively while leading the Pirates from 1977 to 1985.[22]

A Catholic priest at a downtown church entreated God to help the Pirates tie the series at two games each, but they lost 9–6, going down three games to one. Although some Las Vegas bookmakers at this point made the Pirates 100-1 underdogs to win the series against the Orioles, a Lutheran minister from Johnstown, near Pittsburgh, jokingly predicted that the Pirates would triumph because Genesis 1:28 declared that humanity had "dominion over the birds."[23] At this dark moment, right before Game 5, Tanner's mother died, prompting the manager to tell his players, "My mother is a great Pirates fan. She knows we're in trouble, so she went upstairs to get some help."[24] Her "assistance" paid off, as the Pirates won the last three games. Testifying to Tanner's winsome approach to his players, Phil Garner quipped after Tanner died in 2007, "Chuck's at the big ballpark in the sky—guarantee you he's up there patting somebody on the back saying, 'Hey, you're doing okay man.'"[25]

In addition to Sanguillen, the 1979 Pirates most recognized for their faith were Tim Foli and Mike Easler, both of whom played fourteen years in the majors with six different teams. Previously known for his frequent fights with opposing players, umpires, managers and even teammates, Foli's life changed radically after he accepted Christ as his savior. Prior to his conversion, Foli "made more headlines with his arguments and fights than he did with his fielding or hitting." Foli was "a legendary bench jockey" who routinely derided opponents. After making God "the Number 1 priority in my life," Foli explained, "He gradually turned things around for me." Foli's anger abated, and he stopped feuding with umpires and ridiculing opponents. Foli thanked God for changing his attitude, redirecting his life and giving him "peace of mind." Whenever autographing a picture for a fan, Foli added a reference to one of his favorite New Testament verses.[26] He strove to do his best for God because the Bible teaches "us [to] run the race to win."[27]

Mike Easler became a Christian as a minor leaguer. While feeling frustrated by his failure to get to the majors, he read a magazine article stating, "Is your back against the wall? There's nowhere else to go? Try Jesus." In response, he asked Christ to come into his life and sought to "live by faith." Easler's attitude, approach to baseball and relationship with wife, children and parents all changed dramatically.[28] "If you're living only for yourself," Easler declared in 1980, it is easy to lose hope. But surrendering his life to Jesus gave him "the strength and the peace to accomplish many great things."[29] Easler argued that God, not baseball or his family, was first in his life. While with the Pirates and other teams, he participated regularly in Baseball Chapel and was known for his "ringing testimony" for Christ. Jesus came to give us abundant life, Easler argued, and commanded Christians to promote the kingdom of God.[30]

Challenging Times, 1980–92

The early 1980s were a tough time for Pittsburgh. The area lost 130,000 jobs as the steel industry jettisoned 90 percent of its employees. The region's population declined by 176,000. The Pirates, who had a working-class fan base, struggled both to attract spectators and win games. By the early 1990s, economic and social conditions were improving in Pittsburgh, and the Pirates experienced a resurgence led by the killer Bs: Barry Bonds, Bobby Bonilla, Sid Bream, Jay Bell and Wally Backman. They won the National League Eastern Division in 1990, 1991 and 1992, but they did not go to the World Series in any of these years. In 1992, they lost the decisive Game 7 of the National League Championship Series to the Atlanta Braves 3–2, despite entering the ninth inning with a 2–0 lead.[31]

Many Christians played on these teams, including Bream, Bell, Randy Tomlin, Andy Van Slyke, Don Slaught, Roger Mason, Jeff King, Gary

Redus, Bob Patterson, Tim Wakefield, Jerry Don Gleaton and Kevin Young, all of whom participated regularly in a team Bible study led by Chaplain Jay Wilson. From 1989 to 2001, Wilson also held chapel services for the Pirates and members of the visiting team on Sundays and talked with players individually about their faith, while his wife, Candi, led a Bible study for Pirate wives. Eight players wrote testimony cards that were distributed under the auspices of the Baseball Chapel.[32] The cards listed players' favorite Bible characters and verses, Old and New Testament books and Christian authors. Players briefly described their conversions, insisted that sin separated people from God and urged readers to commit their lives to Christ. "I accepted Christ as my Savior," Van Slyke asserted. "Do you know Him as Savior and Lord?" "No decision," Bell contended, "is more important than where we are going to spend eternity." Bell urged readers to "trust Christ for your salvation rather than good works" or church attendance. Players also stressed that God had helped them deal with the pressure of the game and various trials. Christ gives me "contentment and real peace," Wakefield declared. Knowing the Lord enabled him to be composed in tough situations. "The peace and fulfillment" Christ provides, Tomlin argued, "is greater than any baseball highlight."[33]

Bell and Bream especially stand out for their faith. Bell, the Pirates' shortstop from 1989 to 1996, played seventeen years in the majors for five teams and had almost two thousand hits. He accepted Christ as his savior as a twelve-year-old at a Christian concert in Pensacola, Florida. Thereafter, Bell sought to bring others to Christ and disciple them in the faith. When you publicly "claim Jesus Christ as Lord and Savior, you're going to be watched very closely," Bell observed. Christians "need to conduct ourselves" in a worthy manner. Like many other Christian players, Bell insisted that he had more opportunities to witness during bad times than good ones.[34]

Bream, who played for the Bucs from 1985 to 1990 and for three other teams during his twelve-year career, grew up in a family that actively participated in the Methodist Church. He accepted Christ when he was thirteen, played baseball at Liberty University and as a young adult attended three church services a week. Nevertheless, during his first two full seasons in the majors (1986–87), when he suffered through hitting slumps, Bream frequently asked God, "Why are you doing this to me? I'm trying to be [a good Christian example]." At that point, Al Worthington, his baseball coach at Liberty, reminded Bream that he had "promised to honor and glorify" Christ. Bream realized that succeeding in baseball rather than serving God

Left: Jay Bell. *Courtesy of the Pittsburgh Pirates.*

Below: Sid Bream. *Courtesy of the Pittsburgh Pirates.*

had become his primary goal, prompting him to prioritize his relationship with God over his performance on the diamond.[35] "Because I went to a Christian university," Bream reported, "I was automatically deemed" the team's chapel leader.[36]

When he was with the Pirates, ten to fifteen players typically attended the team's chapels. Bream also was very involved in a nondenominational congregation in Harmony, north of Pittsburgh. For two years, he participated in clinics at Geneva College with Pirates and Atlanta Braves to teach eight- to fourteen-year-old children how to play baseball and share the gospel with them.[37] "Bream was greatly admired throughout baseball," Mike Roteman contended, "for being a tremendous person." He often signed autographs "Sid Bream Eph. 2.8," a verse that states, "For by grace you have been saved through faith; and this is not your own doing, it is the gift of God."[38] "My faith is what my life is all about," Bream asserted.[39] MLB players, Bream noted in 1990, have great material wealth, but they "feel a need for something more secure and lasting," which he sought to supply by introducing them to Jesus.[40]

Ironically, the Pirates lost Game 7 of the NL Championship Series when Bream, playing for Atlanta, slid across home plate ahead of a throw from left fielder Barry Bonds. While Pirate players and fans were devastated by "the slide," Bream saw it as providential. His slide, which has been ranked as the fourth most exciting play in MLB history, has given Bream a great "platform to share my faith." "I truly believe that God scripted it that way."[41] Despite receiving death threats from irate Pirate fans, Bream decided to live in the Pittsburgh area after he retired from baseball. He never dreamed that his slide would help propel the Pirates into twenty years of futility.[42] In recent years, Bream has proclaimed the gospel primarily through his work as the national spokesman for Pittsburgh-based Christian Sports International.[43] Bream declared, "God has orchestrated my life to give glory to Him" and "has provided the opportunities to share my faith."[44]

The Desert, 1993–2009

After the Pirates lost the final game of the 1992 NL Championship Series, they entered the desert, the drought. The Pirates set a deplorable record: the longest stretch of consecutive losing seasons, twenty, by any team in the four major American professional team sports—baseball, football, basketball and hockey. During these years, Pirate owners frequently threated to relocate the team, but Kevin McClatchy rescued the franchise, and the team began playing in beautiful PNC Park in 2001. Their losing streak provided ample opportunities for Christian Pirates to strengthen their character and testify to their faith. During this period of wandering in the wilderness, several players stand out for their Christian commitment, especially Abraham Nunez, Matt Capps, Adam LaRoche and Zach Duke.

Abraham Nunez played several positions for the Pirates from 1997 to 2004. He grew up destitute in the Dominican Republic, but he was not aware of his spiritual impoverishment. At age fifteen, Nunez went with friends to deride a street preacher. The preacher's message, however, pricked his heart. Realizing that Jesus could forgive his sins, Nunez surrendered his life to Christ and abandoned the gang activity and alcohol consumption that threatened to destroy him. As a Pirate, Nunez participated regularly in Bible studies and chapel services. In January 2000, he went to Nicaragua under the auspices of Athletes in Action to share how God had changed his life and to help young people experience God's grace.[45]

Matt Capps prayed to accept Christ at a church when he was ten, but his faith took a back seat during his teenage years. In 2004, at age twenty, Capps pitched very poorly for the Hickory Crawdads in the Class A minors and drank excessively. The next season, David Daly, his team's Baseball Chapel chaplain, discipled Capps and challenged him to align his actions with the faith he privately professed. Capps studied the Bible, invited "Jesus to completely take over my heart" and became the Crawdads' spiritual leader and influenced many teammates for Christ.[46] That year, Capps catapulted all the way to the Pirates. While pitching for the Pirates from 2005 to 2009, before every inning he worked, Capps walked to the back of the mound, removed his hat and prayed. He hoped that spectators would notice his prayer.[47] In 2009, Capps was appointed to the Fellowship of Christian Athletes (FCA) Board of Directors. Throughout his career, Capps frequently visited hospitals and hosted baseball clinics for inner-city kids.[48]

Adam LaRoche played first base for the Pirates from 2007 to 2009 and averaged twenty-one home runs per season during his twelve-year MLB career. LaRoche was raised in a Christian home and as an adult faithfully attended Sunday school, church services and a midweek Bible study. However, while with the Pirates, LaRoche reassessed his life and concluded that God had placed him on earth to spread His word, which put playing baseball in perspective. LaRoche was challenged when a chaplain asked whether he wanted his tombstone to say, "'Adam LaRoche: Gold Glove, batting average, hit so many homers, and has a million dollars in his bank account,' or do you want 'Adam LaRoche: Man of God, integrity, raised a great family, loving.'" As a Pirate and later as a Washington National, LaRoche served as a spiritual leader for his teammates. He spearheaded the Nationals' hosting of a faith night and spoke at it and at one the Chicago White Sox held.[49] In November 2015, LaRoche spent ten days undercover visiting brothels in Southeast Asia to help rescue sex slaves and felt called by God to continue this ministry. Concluding that he could not continue playing baseball while sexual trafficking was destroying the lives of young girls, he abruptly retired. In 2016, the nationwide Christian radio network K-Love gave LaRoche its Sports Impact Award for his labors for Christ on and off the baseball field.[50]

Zach Duke has pitched for nine MLB teams, including for the Pirates from 2005 to 2010. As a high school student in Waco, Texas, Duke committed his life to Christ. His relationship with God filled a void in his life and brought him a sense of fulfillment and immense joy. He strove "to be a model Christian"—to consistently practice his faith and not allow setbacks on the diamond to distance him from God. Duke participated in faith days with the Diamondbacks, Nationals and White Sox.[51]

Revival by the River, 2009–15

Although the Pirates' record-breaking losing streak did not end until 2013, the foundation for both success on the diamond and a stronger Christian presence on the team was laid when center fielder Andrew McCutchen arrived in 2009 and Clint Hurdle became manager in 2011. In 2011, about ten Pirates met for a chapel service before every Sunday game to worship and discuss their faith. When the Pirates were at home, the services were led by Brad Henderson, the team's volunteer chaplain. McCutchen, Neil Walker and pitchers Daniel McCutchen and Paul Maholm were among the regular attendees. Maholm, who hurled for the Pirates from 2005 to 2011, also occasionally organized a Bible study for his teammates and their wives. In addition, Catholic priests administered Mass and preached a sermon before every Saturday home game attended by Pirate players and staff and members of visiting teams.[52]

Andrew McCutchen: "Living in the Zone Spiritually"

Because of the quality of his play (five selections as an All-Star and the National League MVP in 2013), staunch Christian commitment, highly respected character and charitable work, McCutchen has been interviewed often about his faith. Because of these interviews, his outspokenness about his faith and his frequent tweeting of prayers, no current MLB player is better known as a Christian.[53]

McCutchen's parents, Lorenzo McCutchen and Petrina Swan, were both seventeen when he was born in Fort Meade, Florida. Lorenzo promised to help raise his son. When playing football at Carson-Newman College in Tennessee made this too difficult, he returned home and juggled three jobs. Petrina, a devout Christian, refused to marry Lorenzo until she was convinced that he had given his heart to Christ. When Andrew was five, Petrina was finally satisfied with the depth of Lorenzo's Christian commitment, and they married. She did data entry at a sheriff's office, while Lorenzo worked as a youth counselor at a nondenominational church in Fort Meade. Six years later, Lorenzo became a minister at this church. McCutchen's life was strongly shaped by the spiritual nurture he received at home and church. He participated in church activities almost every day. "I was baptized at age 16 and have been learning and growing in my faith ever since."[54] Relationships with FCA staff while playing in the minors further strengthened McCutchen's faith.[55]

Like Sid Bream, McCutchen had to decide if his career or relationship with God was more important. In McCutchen's case, the question arose at the pinnacle of his success in 2014. He decided to give his entire life, including baseball, to God. "The closer I got to God," McCutchen discovered, "the easier it was to play" baseball. Following God faithfully, McCutchen insisted, does not guarantee success on the field. However, having an identity that is rooted in God rather than his batting average, he maintained, enables him to play better. "The MVP is nothing," McCutchen avowed, compared with God's love and "what He can do for your life."[56]

His relationship with the Lord, McCutchen averred, gives him a purpose in life and confidence. "God created me" to "spread His message of love." He strives to "'follow Christ's exhoration to love your neighbor as yourself' and 'love the Lord with all your heart, soul and mind.'"[57] By playing baseball, McCutchen seeks to glorify God and "make a difference for Him."[58] Because God has given him much, McCutchen argued, He expects much from him. "Living in the zone spiritually," McCutchen

Andrew McCutchen. *Courtesy of the Pittsburgh Pirates.*

declared, "definitely helps me as a baseball player." "If we have faith just the size of a mustard seed, we'll be able to do amazing things."[59]

McCutchen reads the Bible daily (with his wife, Maria, since they married in 2014), knows its teachings well and tries to follow them faithfully. Since being called up to the Pirates at age twenty-two, he has displayed a spiritual maturity that transcends his age. His favorite verse is Romans 8:28, which promises that whether a situation appears to be good or bad, God will make it "work out for your good."[60]

Like many other Christian MLB players, McCutchen frequently testifies that he feels closer to God and grows more spiritually when undergoing trials. "Sometimes we experience more downs than ups in life, but if you" trust "God, continue to believe and work hard every day, those things will pay off eventually."[61] Whether "I go 5-for-5 or 0-for-5 at bat, I can still be a witness for Christ" by acting "in a way I know the Lord would be pleased."[62] In 2015, McCutchen did not get a hit in twelve of his first twenty-five games—the worst slump of his career. "Earlier in my career," he confessed, "it would have been totally demoralizing." "I prayed…not for God to help me get a hit" but rather for understanding. "What was I supposed to learn from this experience?" Struggles, McCutchen concluded, "can be our greatest blessings."[63]

Throughout his career, McCutchen has participated regularly in chapel services and Bible studies with teammates. The Pirates, he insisted, had many players "who are devoted to Christ" and held one another spiritually accountable.[64] McCutchen sometimes prayed with Christians on other teams. One of them, Milwaukee Brewers second baseman Scooter Gennett, declared, "Andrew is an outstanding baseball player, but he is a better Christian."[65] FCA president Les Steckel also praised McCutchen: "Cutch's commitment to Christ and to his family, fans and city makes him a wonderful role model for young athletes."[66]

Off the field, McCutchen contributed substantially to improving life in Pittsburgh. As the spokesperson for Habitat for Humanity of Greater Pittsburgh, he hosted a gala that raised more than $100,000; he also worked with Habitat crews to help remodel houses for low-income families. McCutchen helped raise money through various venues to benefit Light of Life Rescue Mission, the Homeless Children's Education Fund and Children's Hospital.[67] In 2010, he created Cutch's Crew to mentor inner-city youth baseball players and at-risk children. When Oliver and Perry High Schools merged in 2012, McCutchen worked with the players from the schools' previously competing baseball teams to make their transition as classmates and teammates a smooth one. He prodded them to practice baseball and study diligently.[68] In both Bradenton and Pittsburgh, McCutchen assisted children through the Make-A-Wish Foundation and visited many children in hospitals.[69] These endeavors earned him the prestigious Roberto Clemente Award in 2015. In accepting the honor, McCutchen declared, "What was most important to Clemente was helping others," which has had "a big impact on me."[70]

Clint Hurdle: "Look at What Jesus Has Done"

As important as McCutchen was to the Pirates, the hiring of Clint Hurdle in 2011 as the team's manager has had an even greater impact on both the Bucs' rejuvenation on the diamond and the flourishing of the team's faith. "We've had 19 straight losing seasons," McCutchen insisted in 2012, but if the Pirates can "break through and have a great year and end the streak of losing seasons…it would give people hope."[71] Under Hurdle's leadership, the Bucs halted the streak the next year, made the playoffs and won the NL wild card game over the Cincinnati Reds. They made the playoffs the next two seasons as a wild card, winning ninety-eight games in 2015, the third-highest total in team history.

Clint Hurdle. *Courtesy of the Pittsburgh Pirates.*

"I accepted Jesus Christ as my Savior and Lord at the age of 17 and recommitted to Jesus at age 40," Hurdle explains, but "in between was an obstacle course." Hurdle grew up in a working-class family in Merritt Island, Florida, and regularly attended church services and Sunday school. Sermons convinced him that he had sinned, fallen short of the glory of God and needed a savior, prompting him to commit his life to Jesus and be baptized.[72] In high school, Hurdle starred in baseball, football and basketball and signed with the Kansas City Royals, who drafted him in the first round in 1975. Featured on the cover of *Sports Illustrated* at age twenty with the title "This Year's Phenom," he was supposed to be the next great baseball star. The expectations for him were astronomical. "If I'd done everything I was supposed to," Hurdle reportedly declared, "I'd have led the league in homers, had the highest batting average, given $100,000 to the Cancer Fund, and married Marie Osmond." Instead, the brash, loud-mouthed Hurdle wandered away from Jesus, pursued pleasure, frequented bars with other Royals and drank excessively. "He lived fast. He lived hard," teammate Jamie Quirk asserted.[73]

Hurdle's baseball career was a bust: he played in only 515 Major League games during ten seasons, hitting .259. By the age of forty, he had been divorced twice and was battling alcoholism. Although his alcoholism contributed to his problems, Hurdle insisted, it also served as "a defense mechanism for not living up to the expectations of other people." "I used Jesus as an ATM card" to try to get out of trouble, Hurdle has repeatedly explained. He went to God to get filled up, but when everything seemed to be going well, he relied on himself. Hurdle refused to relinquish control of his life to Christ.[74]

While managing the Mets' minor-league team in Williamsport, Pennsylvania, in 1991, Hurdle met accountant Karla Yearick. After they dated for six years, Hurdle proposed. Yearick said she loved him, but she refused his offer because he still had much reforming to do. Her refusal prompted Hurdle to stop drinking and reaffirm his faith. Hurdle decided "to become a servant....Before then, I wanted to be served."[75] Attending AA meetings, reading the Bible and his relationship with Keli McGregor, the Colorado Rockies president from 2001 until 2010, contributed significantly to Hurdle's recommitment to Christ and growth in his faith. Convinced that Hurdle was a new man, Yearick married him in 1999.The struggle of their daughter, Maddie, born in 2002 with Prader-Willi syndrome—a rare genetic disorder that prevents people from feeling full after eating and leads to behavioral problems—both tried and strengthened their marriage and their faith.[76]

Hurdle managed the Colorado Rockies from 2002 to 2009. During these years, many Rockies' management personnel and players had a strong faith, which attracted national attention in 2007 when the team won twenty-one of its last twenty-two games and went to the World Series. The Rockies, declared two sportswriters, are "the closest thing Major League Baseball has to a faith-based club. The front office runs the franchise based" on "Christian principles" and recruits players known for their moral values and character.[77] Hurdle insisted that the Rockies would not hide or deny their devotion to Christ.[78] "We believed as long as we remained faithful we'd be blessed." In making decisions, we asked, "Would this be pleasing to God?"[79]

After the Rockies lost the 2007 World Series to the Red Sox, finished 74-88 in 2008 and struggled at the beginning of the 2009 season, they sacked Hurdle. "Fourteen months after our greatest victory," Hurdle noted, "I was fired by the two people [the Rockies' general manager and president] I admired most." The next year, Hurdle received offers to manage both the New York Mets and the Pirates. Hurdle had managed a Mets' minor-league team, and the Mets had a new ballpark, lots of money to buy players and a large fan base. The Pirates were mired in an eighteen-season losing streak and strapped for cash. Impressed by General Manager Neal Huntington's plan to build the team through its farm system, Hurdle chose Pittsburgh. More important was that Pittsburgh was the home of The Children's Institute, one of the premier facilities in the nation for treating Prader-Willi, which could enable Maddie to thrive.[80] Hurdle became a spokesman for the association that works to combat this disease and sees his daughter's condition as an opportunity to help other children.[81] But the "biggest reason I came to Pittsburgh," Hurdle explained, "was because I knew that this is where God wanted me."[82]

As the Pirates' manager, Hurdle has served as a Christian mentor to many players and testified often about his faith, including at the Faith Nights he introduced in 2013. In speaking in churches, high school baccalaureate services and men's conferences and sending daily e-mails to over a thousand people, Hurdle has been very forthright about both his mistakes and Christ's transformation of his life. To help others who are struggling with failure and frustration, he often confesses, "I am a loser, married three times, but when people see me they can say: 'look at what Jesus has done for that man.'"[83] A longer version is: "I'm an alcoholic. I've been married three times. I've been in a World Series as a manager, coach and player. I've lost all three. I've been called up. I've been sent down. I've been the can't-miss, did-miss."[84] In 2013, the Pirates not only ended their twenty-season losing streak, but they also made the playoffs for the first time since 1992, and Hurdle was named the NL Manager of the Year. Nevertheless, he asserted at that year's Faith Night that relationships are more important than titles: "We are here together to make a difference in Pittsburgh."[85] From 2013 to 2015, the Pirates, with one of the lowest payrolls in MLB, won more games than any NL team except the Cardinals, thanks in large part to Hurdle's innovative managing style, which included "radical defensive shifts, aggressive platooning and creative lineup construction and his ability to relate to and motivate his players."[86]

The Bucs' skipper served as a shepherd to numerous Pirates, including McCutchen, Josh Harrison, Pedro Alvarez and Gregory Polanco. When Polanco was struggling at the plate, Hurdle exhorted him to give his problems to the Lord. Hurdle "knows what God can do," Polanco testified. Hurdle empathized with his players: like McCutchen, he was drafted in the first round; like Harrison, he had to fight to stay in the majors; "like Alvarez, he was supposed to be The Next Big Thing"; and like Polanco, he had immense talent. "I remind them," Hurdle explained, that using my "faith like an ATM card…never worked out well." Hurdle assured players that their "ups and downs in baseball are part of God's plan." They draw strength from a manager whose relationship with God sustains him in his daily battle against alcoholism. Speaking for many Pirates, Polanco declared, "He prays for me. I pray for him."[87]

Succinctly summarizing his approach to life, Hurdle asserted, "I'm a big, big fan of making people feel loved."[88] "I want them to know I'm there," he added, "if they need a hand."[89] Hurdle has devoured books by evangelical pastor John Maxwell to improve his leadership skills. Huntington praised Hurdle's ability to reach his players.[90] Hurdle exhorts them to make good decisions and serve others. "We talk about transparent leadership" and the Golden Rule, he explained.[91] Hurdle's "love for Christ has infiltrated" the Pirate organization, Brad Henderson contended; his openness has prompted other Christians to talk freely about their faith. The Pirate management has strongly supported the club's chapel program through which some players have committed their lives to Christ. In 2015, fifteen players regularly attended chapel services, the most in Henderson's thirteen years as the Pirates' chaplain.[92]

For many years, Hurdle has sent more than one thousand people, including Rockies, Rangers and Pirates, a daily inspirational e-mail that contains quotations, stories and advice. Through these e-mails and texts, Hurdle strives to motivate players to live out their faith on and off the field.[93] Every message ends: "Make a difference today. Love, Clint."[94] In a typical e-mail, Hurdle wrote:

> *Regardless of your strengths, training or church tenure, you can love the overlooked. You see Jesus every day: The kid in your office with thick glasses, outdated clothing and a sad face. He's Jesus. A woman walks into your classroom. She's late and tired and pregnant. She's Jesus. "Whenever you did one of these things to someone overlooked or ignored, that was me—you did it to me"—Matthew 25:40. Make a difference today.*[95]

Hurdle's "signature Scripture" is II Corinthians 12:9: "Through my weaknesses, His [Christ's] strength is glorified." "Every day, humbly, I ask Him to give me the strength to move forward" and make "a difference in the lives of others."[96]

Hurdle sees himself principally not as a baseball manager, but as an ambassador of Christ. "Christ has given me the strength, endurance, and courage to live a sober life for the last 16 years," he declared in 2015.[97] "We are directed in the Bible to go and tell, to go and represent," to "put Jesus first." Rejecting celebrity and money, we must focus on serving others.[98] Those who "truly develop" a "relationship with Christ," Hurdle argued, "cannot keep quiet about it." He tries to express "his faith in a very real and public way," which, Henderson argued, he does very well.[99]

Hurdle and Henderson initiated Pirate Faith Nights in 2013. They have included testimonies by current Pirates (both in person and by video), their wives and former Pirates, as well as Henderson's interviews of players. Every Faith Night has ended with Hurdle giving his testimony and exhorting fans to follow Jesus more faithfully. The first year, 2,500 fans attended.[100]

In 2015, about twelve thousand fans watched a video of McCutchen explaining how his Christian convictions "strengthened him as a person and a baseball player" and heard inspirational talks by Hurdle, Coach Dave Jauss, Neil Walker, Chris Stewart and other players. Billie Jauss, Lindsey Stewart, Keli Alvarez and Maria McCutchen also discussed their faith.[101] Faith Night, Henderson insisted, enables players to "share how important their faith is" and helps fans get to know them as people.[102]

In July 2016, eighteen thousand fans remained after an extra-innings game with the Brewers to hear players from both teams and Pirate wives talk about their faith in Christ. Listening to players acknowledge God's control of their lives amid their struggles, Billie Jauss asserted, was powerful and inspiring. In addition, children from the Pittsburgh Kids Foundation asked the players questions.[103] As

Brad Henderson. *Courtesy of the Pittsburgh Pirates.*

a Cardinal, third baseman David Freese "made a dramatic decision" in 2009 "to turn his life over to Christ." After being involved in an off-field incident that embarrassed him, his family and his team, he told God, "Do with me what You will."[104] Hearing Freese and others "share the joy and fulfillment" they had in Christ, Dave Jauss declared, "was amazing."[105] Hurdle ended the event by urging fans "to take a stand for Jesus."[106]

Numerous people extol Hurdle's faith. Milwaukee Brewers coach John Shelby calls him "a very dedicated, godly man."[107] Among the coaches and managers Henderson has known during more than twenty years of sports ministry, Hurdle "stands alone in his ability to integrate his strong personal faith in Christ into his coaching philosophy. He is a man of great devotion to Christ whether he is leading his family or leading his team."[108]

Other Faithful Bucs

In addition to McCutchen and Hurdle, several other Pirates testified strongly about their faith in the 2010s. Catcher Mike McKenry, who was with the Bucs from 2011 to 2013, became a Christian in high school. At the 2013 Faith Night, Henderson called McKenry "our true spiritual leader." Like Bream, McKenry added Bible verses beside his autograph, including Colossians 3:23: "Whatever you do, work at it with all your heart, as working for the Lord."[109] "The No. 1 priority in life," he asserted, is to "grow as a Christian."[110]

Second baseman Neil Walker, who played for the Pirates from 2009 to 2015, attributed his deep faith to his family and his Catholic education, which taught him the "values of commitment, trust and belief." Walker lives in Gibsonia in the off-season and regularly attends Mass at St. Alphonsus Church. In 2010, Walker, his father, Tom, and Pirate broadcaster Greg Brown organized a Catholic Mass for players at PNC Park on Saturdays.[111] Walker, who also attended the Pirates' Sunday chapels, asserted that both services helped combat the temptations he faced as a baseball player.[112]

Jason Grilli, who pitched for the Pirates from 2011 until mid-2014, produced a player testimony for Baseball Chapel. "Growing up," he stated, "I knew about Jesus Christ in my head but my self-centered attitudes and beliefs kept me from accepting Him into my heart and life." As a student at the University of Hawaii, his life was "lonely and empty," and the islands' beauty constantly reminded him of God's creative power. Through participating in a Bible study, Grilli received Christ as his savior, which gave him meaning and purpose. Since then, whenever he experienced triumphs or trials, including two major arm surgeries, he was "no longer alone."[113] Grilli worked hard and "let God take care of the results."[114]

Mark Melancon hurled for the Pirates from 2013 to mid-2016 and was named the NL Relief Pitcher of the Year in 2013. He grew up in a Christian home, attended church regularly and committed his life to Christ at age eight. He told the fans at the 2013 Faith Night that without "Jesus Christ in your life, I don't know how you" cope with the constant pressure, frequent failure and periodic trades. "God puts adversity in your life," he argued, to make you a stronger disciple of Jesus.[115] "I say a prayer before I pitch, not for success," Melancon explained, but "that I glorify God in how I play."[116]

Josh Harrison, who has played a variety of positions for the Pirates from 2011 to the present, and Jordy Mercer, who has been the Bucs' shortstop since 2012, are also devoted Christians. In high school, Harrison was an active member of the Fellowship of Christian Athletes and of the Bible Fellowship Church in Ventura County, California.[117] "My faith," Harrison insisted, has enabled "me to get where I am today." Mercer testified that his relationship with God is more significant than his baseball career.[118]

Another committed Christian, utility man Sean Rodriguez, who played for the Pirates in 2015, 2016 and part of 2017 and 2018, made headlines in 2015 by offering a humorous apology for punching a Gatorade cooler in anger at a game. In a tweet, Rodriquez shared two Bible verses and wrote, "I want to apologize for allowing my emotions to control my actions in a negative manner. I also spoke to the cooler, apologized personally, and he's forgiven me as Christ forgives all."[119] At the Pirates' Faith Night the next year, Rodríguez described how difficult it is for many Christian baseball players to balance their "fierce passion for competition and a turn-the-other-cheek mindset."[120] In January 2017, Rodriguez, his wife and their two sons were all seriously hurt when a man rammed a stolen police car into their SUV in Florida. Rodriguez required surgery to repair labrum damage, a rotator cuff tear and a dislocated bicep tendon and did five months of rehab before returning to baseball. Rodriguez profusely thanked God that he came back to play so quickly.[121]

Every year, the Pirates as an organization and individual Pirate players, coaches and executives support a wide array of charitable causes to help children, the impoverished and groups with special needs. For example, the Pirates' *2016 Community Report* highlights the club's programs to provide sports opportunities for inner-city children, benefits for veterans and education for children and to fund cancer research and treatment. It also featured the "extraordinary" philanthropy and community service of Hurdle, McCutchen, Harrison and Gerrit Cole.[122]

The Pirates have a second chaplain, Jesus Origel, who ministers to Spanish-speaking players. The thirty-year-old Origel was raised by his Mexican immigrant mother in government-subsidized housing in Tempe, Arizona. He quit a gang and stopped dealing drugs after coming to know Christ through the witness of high school football teammates. He conducts four chapel services every Sunday the Pirates are at home for Spanish-speakers—for the Pirates, members of the visiting team, umpires and PNC staff; five or six Pirates typically attend. Origel and Henderson hold a joint chapel service for Pirate players once a month. During the season, Origel also leads a Bible study for Spanish-speaking players when the Pirates are at home (the average attendance is six) that deals with issues such as marriage, parenting and serving the community. In 2016, participants discussed Tony Evans's *Kingdom Man: Every Man's Destiny, Every Woman's Dream.* The most outspoken Christian during Origel's tenure as chaplain has been Venezuelan relief pitcher Jeanmar Gómez, who was with the Pirates in 2013–14. Origel contended that players' faith helps keep them grounded in a game where failure is common because they base their identity in Christ rather than in their accomplishments on the field.[123]

Conclusion

Despite the trades of McCutchen and Cole before the season, the Pirates finished 82-79 in 2018. Their prospects, however, do not appear as rosy as they did during their three-year playoff run. Many Pirates have testified that adversity offers a great opportunity to express their faith through their words and deeds. The future may afford such a platform. Nevertheless, Pirate fans can hope that the Jolly Roger is raised often in the years to come.

Chapter 11

FAITH AND THE PITTSBURGH STEELERS

The importance of faith, family and football permeates the entire [Steeler] *organization.*
—Benedictine Archabbott Douglas Nowicki

I am certain if Jesus was from Pittsburgh, he would refer to the Steelers in his talks as well.
—Dean Ward, pastor of The River, A Community Church, New Kensington

While baseball and hockey are very important in Pittsburgh, football is king. The Pirates and Penguins have a substantial fan base, but the Steeler Nation is unsurpassed in the United States. The loyalty and passion of many Steeler fans approaches a mania. From the early 1970s to today, a chain of faith runs from coaches Chuck Noll (1969–91) through Tony Dungy (assistant coach, 1981–88) to Bill Cowher (1992–2006) and Mike Tomlin (2007–present). "I remember as a young boy, after every game," stated Brian Rooney, the Steelers "would come into the locker room, take a knee, and recite the Lord's Prayer. Only after the prayer would Coach Chuck Noll, another man of great Christian faith, say his postgame comments." "Noll's quiet faith and leadership style shaped" the approach of Dungy. And today, coach Mike Tomlin, Dungy's protégé, "leads the team in line with how Noll and Dungy led. This has always been the Steelers' way," which "is founded upon the rock of our Christian faith." "The Steeler culture has been shaped by the Rooney family's Christian faith," argued former Steeler offensive guard and current radio commentator Tunch Ilkin. "The enduring leadership principles" promoted by the Rooneys, Chuck Noll, Bill Cowher and Mike Tomlin "apply as much now as they did 40 years ago," Damian Williams contended.[1]

The Rooneys and Chuck Noll shared the values of "family, faith, football, loyalty, and hard work," which Art Rooney instilled into the Steeler organization. Noll proved that a team could win championships abiding by these values, and they "remained firmly in place under Dan Rooney and Bill Cowher, and still define the Steeler organization under Art Rooney II and Mike Tomlin."[2]

A link of faith also stretches from players on the 1970s championship squads to the present team. Over the years, the Steelers have had a solid core of Christian players who have witnessed to their teammates, testified to their commitment to Christ in various settings and worked to aid the local community. After discussing the faith foundation laid by the Rooney family, who have owned the Steelers since 1933, this chapter will examine how Christianity influenced the Steelers in four different periods: the pinnacle years of 1974 to 1980, when the Steelers won four Super Bowls under Noll; the troubled years of 1981 to 1991, when the team floundered; the Steelers under Cowher (1992–2006); and their history during Tomlin's tenure (2007–present). Each of the four sections will profile coaches and players whose faith was strong, influential and, in some cases, controversial. Dozens of Steeler coaches and players have regularly attended Bible studies and chapel services, and many have shared their faith through television, radio and print interviews and speeches to church and community groups.

The Importance of the Steelers to Pittsburgh

From Seattle to New England and many cities in between, millions of Americans are passionate about and loyal to their professional football teams. The relationship of many fans and their teams takes on a quasi-religious ethos as they employ semi-sacred values, objects and memories to ascribe meaning to their teams' players, places and plays.[3] Arguably, this occurs with greater intensity in Pittsburgh than anywhere else because of the peculiar history of the city, the success of the Steelers and the character of the fans. No other team has risen so rapidly and spectacularly from the mire of mediocrity to the zenith of football attainment, celebrates an "immaculate reception" or has "Terrible Towels" to which some ascribe semi-mystical power. "With a creation narrative rooted in a miraculous event, a people scattered in other lands but bound to their homeland by a common creed, ethic, and dialect, and a sacred icon [Terrible Towels], Steelers Nation is a seriously religious place."[4]

On the fortieth anniversary of Franco Harris's seemingly miraculous catch of a ricocheted pass to beat the Oakland Raiders in a December 23, 1972 playoff game, the *Pittsburgh Post-Gazette* labeled it "the play that changed a city." The signs of Pittsburgh's impending economic decline were clear. Japan's steel mills were more efficient than Pittsburgh's, and European countries were subsidizing the production of steel.[5] At this troubled time, the city's football team rose from four forgettable decades of futility to become the most storied franchise in NFL history, injecting new vitality into Pittsburgh.

Terrible Towels are cherished by Steeler fans and commonplace throughout the region. Thousands wave them passionately at Heinz Field and other stadiums when the Steelers play on the road, many newborns are wrapped in towels in Pittsburgh-area hospitals, couples display them at their weddings and towels adorn funeral caskets.[6]

Since the early 1970s, Pittsburghers and their professional football team have been powerfully bonded. For many area residents, the Steelers are the heart and soul of Pittsburgh. Between 1970 and 1990, about 30 percent of the area's population departed as the steel industry collapsed. Many of them, however, retain a strong connection to the Steelers. Today, the website SteelerBar.com lists 844 bars and restaurants across the nation where the Pittsburgh diaspora assemble to watch the Black and Gold play. Wherever one goes—California, North Carolina or even Dallas—one can find sizable numbers of Steeler fans.[7] Geographically and culturally, the reputation and image of the franchise, argued a sportswriter, is best described not as the Steeler Nation but as the Steeler Planet.[8]

The Importance of Religion in Football

The NFL is America's most popular sports league, and almost 43 percent of Americans say that either college or professional football is their favorite sport.[9] About one-third of the players in America's three major professional team sports—football, baseball and basketball—are born-again Christians, with a little higher percentage in the NFL. Athletes in Action estimates that

35 percent to 40 percent of NFL players are evangelicals, compared to about 25 percent of Americans.[10] Postgame interviews of players, postgame prayer huddles, print and online testimonies and Hall of Fame acceptance speeches demonstrate how important Christian faith is in pro football culture. Moreover, every NFL team has a chaplain, almost always an evangelical, and leading coaches, including Tom Landry, Joe Gibbs and Tony Dungy, and star players, including Roger Staubach, Steve Largent, Kurt Warner, Reggie White, Mike Singletary, Aaron Rodgers, Drew Brees, Russell Wilson, Jared Allen, Darrell Green, Dallas Clark, Art Monk, Chris Carter, Shaun Alexander, LaDainian Tomlinson and Emmitt Thomas, are known for their Christian commitment. Other players whose careers were much shorter or less spectacular, most notably Tim Tebow, have also promoted the gospel.

The NFL has been ambivalent toward Christians testifying about their faith. Some Christian coaches and players say that they "feel free to talk about their faith, and even evangelize," if they do so discerningly, while others declare that the league prefers players to act like Christians but not explicitly say that they are Christians. The NFL has no rules prohibiting personnel from discussing their faith or even evangelizing, but it forbids players from displaying religious symbols or messages on their apparel during games or in postgame interviews. Many owners, coaches and league executives are delighted by the NFL's large numbers of Christians because they generally act morally, have strong marriages, are a positive influence on their teammates and do community service. Chapel services, Bible studies and religious instruction, Curtis Eichelberger maintained, provide "counseling and therapy to keep players mentally and emotionally at the top of their game." Many coaches see faith as "a steadying influence" in a profession where careers, friendships, marriages and self-identity can be destroyed by injury or poor performance.[11] Their faith also keeps Christians from using drugs and engaging in behaviors that "would diminish their competitiveness."[12] Many evangelicals are thrilled about the large numbers of vocal Christians playing in professional sports. Moreover, the Christian witness of players helps mitigate concerns about concussions, greed, drug usage and acts of domestic violence and sexual assault committed by players that plague both major college football programs and the NFL, leading many to demand reform and some to advocate abolishing the sport all together.

The Steelers are among the NFL's most faith-oriented franchises because of its owners, coaches, players and fans. For many years, a blog that bills itself as "the Home for Christian Fans of the Pittsburgh Steelers" has discussed matters of interest to this group.[13]

The Rooneys and Saint Vincent College

Art Rooney and his sons, Art Jr. and Dan, all devout Catholics, built and operated a franchise based on faith, integrity and family values. Throughout the Steelers' history, the Rooneys have sought to field a team that is closely connected to the Steel City and to hire coaches and draft players who excel at their craft and live virtuously.[14] Art Sr., the son of a North Side saloon owner, was a baseball barnstormer, ward leader and sports promoter. He bought the NFL's Pittsburgh Pirates in 1933 for a whopping $2,500 and in 1940 renamed them the Steelers after the city's leading industry.

Art Rooney Sr. regularly attended Mass and often discussed his Catholic faith. Speaking for many, safety Donnie Shell declared that the Rooney family has "great faith in God" and has done much to help the Pittsburgh community. They are "a great role model for the players, their families and the NFL."[15] The infectious faith of his grandfather Art Rooney, asserted Brian Rooney, "still sets the tone for the team today."[16] His faith, Rooney's son Dan declared, "meant everything to him."[17] For seven years, acclaimed actor Tom Atkins portrayed Art Rooney's commitment to his faith, family and football in the play *The Chief* several times a season at Pittsburgh Public Theater, and the play was adapted to the movie screen in 2010.[18]

In his 2008 memoir, Dan Rooney, who also served as the U.S. ambassador to Ireland, asserted that faith, family and football were his priorities.[19] "I pray each morning and go to mass," declared Rooney, "and say, 'let the Holy Spirit guide us and make the right'" decisions, including which college players we draft.[20] Steeler defensive tackle Joe Greene claimed that all Rooney's decisions were "based on faith."[21] "From top to bottom," the Steeler organization, argued Heinz History Center CEO Andrew Masich, reflected Rooney's "values, integrity, and character."[22] Rooney was inducted into the Pro Football Hall of Fame and selected as the NFL Executive of the Year and the Dapper Dan's Sportsman of the Year. Cardinal Donald Wuerl lauded his "strong faith" that undergirded "his commitment to and love for Pittsburgh."[23]

Since 1965, the Steelers have held their summer training camp at Saint Vincent College, America's oldest Benedictine archabbey and seminary, in Latrobe, one hour east of Pittsburgh. The Rooneys' relationship with Saint Vincent is long and strong. Several times during the Great Depression, the Chief bailed the college out of financial troubles. Art Rooney Jr. graduated from the college in the 1950s; and Art Rooney II, the Steelers' current president, serves on Saint Vincent's board of trustees.[24] Today, the college is home to 175 Catholic monks, many of whom interact with Steelers staff and players during camp. Numerous Steelers attend either Mass at the chapel or basilica with the monks or other religious services while at camp. Saint Vincent's president, Brother Norman Hipps, and thirty to forty other monks typically watch Steeler games on television during the regular season and pray daily for the team.[25]

The Glory Years: The Steel Curtain and Four Super Bowls, 1974–80

As the 1970s began, Pittsburghers were experiencing financial and emotional trauma. The steel industry, which for decades had been the city's lifeblood, was hemorrhaging as 150,000 laborers lost their jobs. Pittsburghers longed for heroes, hope and respect. And then the inconceivable occurred: the Steelers, one of the most hapless franchises in the NFL, quickly became its dominant team, winning an unprecedented four Super Bowls in six years and helping rejuvenate the spirit of the region's residents.[26] While numerous players helped build the Steelers' football empire, the Steel Curtain—Joe Greene, L.C. Greenwood, Dwight White and Ernie Holmes, all southerners who had endured the pain of racial segregation, arguably the most dominant defensive front four in NFL history—played a pivotal role. Colorfully nicknamed "Mean Joe," "Hollywood Bags," "Mad Dog" and "Fats," these "masters of mayhem" terrorized opposing quarterbacks and slammed runners to the turf, limiting the Vikings in the Steelers' first Super Bowl win to less than a yard per carry. *Time* magazine featured them on its cover, and advertisers showcased them in commercials.[27]

While the story of the Steelers' success on the gridiron is well known, the importance of their faith to many coaches and players is relatively unknown. Offensive lineman Jon Kolb (1969–81); quarterback Terry Bradshaw (1970–83); defensive backs Donnie Shell (1974–87), J.T. Thomas (1973–81) and Mel Blount (1970–83); and wide receiver John Stallworth (1974–87) were the team's most vocal Christians, but numerous others also had a strong faith: head coach Chuck Noll (1969–91), center Mike Webster (1974–88), offensive lineman Ted Petersen (1977–83, 1987), defensive tackles Ernie Holmes (1972–77) and L.C. Greenwood (1969–81), linebacker Loren Toews (1973–83), running back Rocky Bleier (1968, 1970–80), offensive tackle and tight end Larry Brown (1971–84) and wide receiver Lynn Swann (1974–82).

Chuck Noll: Teaching Men How to Win on the Football Field and in Life

Under Chuck Noll's leadership, the Steelers catapulted from a doormat to a dynasty, winning 88 regular season games from 1972 through 1979 while losing only 27 and winning four Super Bowls. Noll's overall record is 209-156-1 (.572), and his 16-8 postseason record is one of the best in league history. "He set a new standard for the Steelers that still is the foundation of what we do and who we are," Art Rooney II proclaimed in 2012. He built a sense of family among the players, teaching them "the importance of sacrifice, humility, and winning both on and off the field."[28]

Noll was a cradle-to-grave Catholic. He grew up in a staunch Catholic family in Cleveland and graduated from Benedictine High School in the city. He earned a degree at the University of Dayton, operated by the Marist order, and attended church faithfully as an adult. Noll was a devout Catholic, Tony Dungy declared, who "often used Bible verses to inspire" a team that "included some really solid Christians."[29] Dungy called Noll one of his two spiritual mentors. Noll was a Christian and a good coach, Bradshaw maintained. Many praised Noll for stressing the "proper priorities—faith, family and football…in that order." Catholic bishop David Zubik argued that in many ways Noll's life was modeled after Christ's. While Jesus showed people how to be "a light to the world," Noll taught us "to do our best and encourage others to do the same."[30]

Chuck Noll. *Courtesy of the Pittsburgh Steelers.*

Noll repeatedly insisted that pro football was a steppingstone to players' life's calling. He told rookies, Dungy recalled, that "you have to find your life's work, while you're working at this."[31] This phrase became closely associated with Noll and served as the subtitle for Michael MacCambridge's 2016 biography, *Chuck Noll: His Life's Work*, and Gary Pomerantz's *Their Life's Work: The Brotherhood of the 1970s Pittsburgh Steelers* (2014), which describes how the remarkable group of Steelers, motivated by their coach's philosophy,

Tony Dungy. *Courtesy of the Pittsburgh Steelers.*

excelled on the field and contributed substantially to society after their playing days ended. Noll set an example for his players; he was devoted to his family and was a licensed pilot, a sailor and a scuba diver; spoke French; and loved to cook, garden and do home repairs.

Numerous players and coaches testified that Noll profoundly influenced their lives. Almost every one of his players asserts that "I learned more from Chuck about life off the field than on," a journalist declared. "The later-life success of so many of his former Steelers is testimony to this." George Perles, who served on Noll's coaching staff from 1972 to 1982, argued that he "could have been a priest." He taught us, Mel Blount stated, "how to win on the football field and win in life." "If it hadn't been for Chuck," asked J.T. Thomas in 2014, "where would we all be?" Noll, Donnie Shell avowed, is "a great example of a servant leader."[32] "I learned from him," Dungy asserted, how "to be a complete person." "The Lord," Dungy contended, used Noll to prepare "me to be a coach." He taught the Steelers to "be better men." Noll changed our approach to life, maintained Rocky Bleier. "The truths that Chuck Noll taught me," Tunch Ilkin added, apply to me "today as a men's pastor and as a broadcaster, as a dad and a husband, as much as they did as a football player."[33]

Dungy, who played for Noll for two years and coached with him for eight, has highlighted his own faith in several books and many speeches and interviews. Because of Noll's and Shell's influence, during his second year in the NFL, he recommitted to following the Christian values his parents instilled in him. Shell proclaimed that Dungy "loves the Lord, is a great family man, great coach and has influenced so many people across the country." Like Noll, Dungy, who compiled a 139-69 record (.668) during the regular season while coaching Tampa Bay and Indianapolis from 1996 to 2008 and winning the Super Bowl in 2007, constructed his adult life around the three pillars of faith, family and football. Dungy sought to heed Matthew 16:26: "What will it profit a man if he gains the whole world and forfeits his soul?"[34]

Chaplain Hollis Haff

Hollis Haff, who worked with Athletes in Action, a division of Campus Crusade for Christ (now Cru), served as the Steelers' chaplain from 1974 to 1989. In 1974, Haff began holding chapel services before games, and soon 80 percent of Steelers were attending. He also started a Bible study for players and their wives attended by many of the team's stars—Shell, Kolb, Thomas, Webster, Greenwood, Holmes, Blount and Stallworth. His chapel talks and Bible studies focused on "basic Christian growth concepts." Haff also discipled numerous players individually. His "life-changing relationship with Christ" impressed and interested many Steelers. The Steelers' management valued his work because of his positive influence on players. During the 1970s, J.T. Thomas asserted, many Steelers were Christians—"we were a praying team." "Some think that the team's success in the past five years," a journalist wrote in 1979, is because of its players' "commitment to the Lord." The team, Bradshaw asserted in 1980, had a great awareness of God's presence.[35]

Haff also started two programs to present the gospel to community residents. Kolb, Thomas, Greenwood, Holmes, Blount, Shell, Stallworth, Webster, Pederson, Dungy, Toews, Wolfley, Ilkin and Dwayne Woodruff joined him in doing programs at about 350 area high schools between 1977 and 1982 modeled on the *Superstars* competition then popular on television. Three Steelers competed against schools' best three athletes in a tug of war, a relay race, a sit-up contest and a short volleyball game. Between events, Haff asked the Steelers questions about their careers and faith.[36] At these high school assemblies, Haff and Steeler players explicitly discussed their commitment to Christ and planted numerous seeds. Many who attended these assemblies have told Ilkin that the testimonies deeply touched them.[37]

From 1976 to 1986, Haff also operated a summer football camp at Geneva College in Beaver Falls in conjunction with the college's football coaches. At the four-day camps, 150 high school players as well as several dozen players from Geneva, Penn State and the University of Pittsburgh interacted with the same Steelers who did the high school assemblies. These ten to twelve Steelers led Bible study groups at the camps and discussed their faith with the high school and college players.[38]

Many NFL players respond positively to the gospel, Haff argued, because after they achieve their dreams and goals, they realize that success, fame and wealth are not ultimately fulfilling. Everyone has a God-shaped vacuum, an inner emptiness that no accomplishments or fame can satisfy; only a personal relationship with God can fill this void. Moreover, Haff maintained, their faith in Christ gives players a sense of stability and security that being traded, injured or performing poorly cannot take away.[39]

Campus Crusade's approach was "win, build, send": its staff strove to convert individuals to Christ, help them become dedicated disciples and equip them to "penetrate different worlds, including professional sports." Seeing so many Steelers profess faith in Christ and strive to live consistent Christian lives, Haff explained, was immensely gratifying.[40]

Haff argued that professional athletes who "become genuine Christians… can have a great impact" for God's kingdom, especially if, after they retire, they live and work in the cities where they played. Haff contended that Christian Steelers helped lead many children and youth and some adults to Christ by participating in high school assemblies, volunteering at the summer football camps, speaking to churches and community groups and developing personal relationships. At the height of the team's success, Haff addressed church groups about one hundred times per year, often using stories about the Steelers to share the gospel.[41]

The Spiritual Journey of Terry Bradshaw

The Steelers' key offensive player in the Super Bowl years was Hall of Fame quarterback Terry Bradshaw. During his playing years (1970–83) and since retiring, Bradshaw has sometimes expressed a very deep Christian faith, while at other times he has gone through periods of doubt and depression. Bradshaw grew up in a Christian home, attended a Southern Baptist church regularly and had a born-again experience as a teenager. While attending Louisiana Tech University, Bradshaw actively participated in a Fellowship of Christian Athletes chapter.

As a Steeler, Bradshaw participated in chapel services and Bible studies, often hosting the latter in his apartment. He frequently testified to his born-again faith, most notably in *No Easy Game* (1979), *Terry Bradshaw: Man of Steel* (1980) and a 1980 interview in *Playboy*. Bradshaw experienced substantial adversity on the field and in his personal life. His marriage to Melissa Babish, the 1969 Miss Teenage America, ended in divorce after "eighteen miserable months." The press labeled him a hayseed, "the Bayou bumpkin" and "Li'l Abner in football shoes." His erratic performance during his first four seasons led Steeler fans to frequently boo him. Bradshaw and Noll did not get along well, and he was benched for the first six games of 1974. In

Terry Bradshaw. *Courtesy of the Pittsburgh Steelers.*

addition, Bradshaw was deeply hurt by the media's portrayal of him. He "stood for Mom and apple pie, and God bless America." "I love God and I tote my Bible and I pray," Bradshaw declared. "I was too good to be true," and this led the media to attack him relentlessly.[42] Bradshaw also complained that reporters and journalists refused to talk with him about his faith.[43]

Ironically, *Playboy* gave him his largest platform for discussing his Christian commitment. When asked why, given his fundamentalist background, he was willing to be interviewed for such a periodical, Bradshaw responded that "if Jesus were on earth today, he'd want to be interviewed by *Playboy*," and it enabled him "to witness to 22,000,000 people." Bradshaw explained that in 1974, he hit rock bottom. He was recently divorced, his shoulder was injured and he had been benched. One night, Bradshaw reported, he had an encounter with the Lord that rejuvenated his faith. "I had separated myself from God," he confessed. "I lived only for Terry Bradshaw, not for God." He "chased women" and behaved erratically. "My whole life was out of control."[44] He asked God "to take my life and straighten me up." After recommitting his life to Christ, Bradshaw played football because he believed it was "what the Lord wants me to do."[45]

Although she insisted that their "mutual Christian faith" had been a major reason they married in 1976 and that their faith had served as a "Rock of Gibraltar" to "keep our priorities right," Bradshaw's second wife, U.S. Olympic figure skater JoJo Starbuck, filed for divorce five months after his *Playboy* interview was published.[46] To try to save their marriage, they prayed together, studied the Bible and went to counselors, but Starbuck finally concluded that their marriage was "irretrievably broken."[47]

During his playing career, Bradshaw suffered from attention deficit disorder and clinical depression, which were not diagnosed until 1999. That year, attorney Charla Hopkins, to whom he had been married for sixteen years and with whom he had two daughters, divorced him, sending Bradshaw into a tailspin. His anxiety attacks increased, he had insomnia and he drank heavily.

Once again, his faith eventually pulled him out of the doldrums.[48] Bradshaw insisted that he got his life back on track by renewing his commitment to God and seeking help to overcome his anxiety attacks and depression. Despite his earlier professions of faith and involvement in Christian activities, Bradshaw stated that at this point, "I really got saved." "I knew that God's spirit had moved into my heart" and "taken control of me."[49]

Since his playing days ended, Bradshaw has been a horse breeder, a cattle rancher, a motivational speaker and a spokesman for various products. He has worked as a television football commentator; appeared in several films, including *Smoky and the Bandit II* and *Failure to Launch*; and written additional books. He has spoken to hundreds of audiences across the country, repeatedly arguing that his faith in God has enabled him to defeat the disease of depression.[50]

Other Faithful Steelers

In addition to Noll, Dungy and Bradshaw, the 1970s Super Bowl teams included numerous other vocal Christians, several of whom remained in Pittsburgh after their playing days ended. Two members of the Steel Curtain testified to their faith in Christ. L.C. Greenwood was a six-time Pro Bowler who ranks second on the Steelers' all-time sack list. "Greenwood's faith was strong as a player and grew deeper after his days on the field," declared J.T. Thomas. Blount simply said that Greenwood "loved the Lord." After retiring in 1981, Greenwood was actively involved in the Pentecostal Temple Church of God in Christ in East Liberty and then Bethany Baptist Church in Homewood and also served on the board of the Coalition for Christian Outreach and other ministries.[51]

His wife's request for a divorce, fear that he would lose his sons and financial problems caused Ernie Holmes to snap in March 1973 following his first season with the Steelers. While driving on a highway in Ohio, a deluded Holmes thought that truckers were trying to hurt him. He fired shots at the trucks and a police helicopter that he thought were chasing him. Holmes was charged with several felonies and sentenced to five years' probation.[52] One night two years later, Holmes accidently walked into a chapel meeting held before the team's pregame meal; he liked the service, kept coming to them and soon accepted Christ as his savior.[53] Holmes's second wife, Yvonne, a Liberian he met at a Christian Athletes Association conference in Phoenix, reported in 1976 that "since Ernie accepted Christ, he's changed." "I'm a kid nourishing on the milk of the Bible," Holmes explained.[54] After his NFL career, Holmes worked as a professional wrestler, a bodyguard and a minor actor and then became a Baptist youth pastor and assistant minister.[55]

Donnie Shell, Jon Kolb, John Stallworth and Larry Brown, Tony Dungy declared, strove "to put God first in everything they did." They asked, "What would Jesus do?" before that expression became popular. During his rookie year in 1974, Shell asked "Jesus to come into his life" and forgive his sins. "The emptiness he had been feeling despite his football success immediately vanished."[56] Three years later, Dungy found Shell to be "one of the most fired up Christians I had ever met." Shell served as Dungy's spiritual mentor, challenging him to put his faith above football and teaching him to trust God more fully. Shell and Dungy studied the Bible together as diligently as they studied the Steelers' playbook. After retiring from football, Shell founded a consulting agency that furnished public speaking training, program development and life coaching.[57]

Jon Kolb was one of the Steelers' most fervent Christians. The offensive tackle played on all four 1970s Super Bowl squads, was named to the Steelers' All-Century Team in 2000 and served as the Steelers strength and conditioning coach from 1981 to 1991. During his playing and coaching career, Kolb participated faithfully in team chapels and Bible studies, and as a Steeler and since leaving the squad, Kolb has spoken extensively about his faith.[58] We must practice Christianity, he asserted, the same way people practice medicine and law.[59]

Wide receiver John Stallworth also regularly participated in team chapels and Bible studies and repeatedly discussed his relationship with Christ. Noll taught him that true leadership involved denying "personal fame and glory for the sake of the team." How we use our talents, Stallworth added, is "our gift back to Him."[60] Shortly before retiring from the Steelers, Stallworth founded Madison Research, an engineering and IT company based in Huntsville, Alabama, which today has about five hundred employees.[61]

When the Steelers drafted him in 1970, Mel Blount, another cornerback, was crestfallen because they were "the worst team in the league." "I didn't want to go to Pittsburgh," he admitted, but God had a different plan for his life. Blount—who played on four Super Bowl teams, was a five-time Pro Bowler and was inducted into the Hall of Fame—grew up as the youngest of eleven children on a farm near Vidalia, Georgia. His athletic prowess, strong work ethic and Christian faith, he avowed, propelled him to and sustained him in the NFL. After retiring, Blount founded youth homes in Vidalia and Claysville, south of Pittsburgh, to help troubled children "develop mentally, physically and morally," build strong Christian character and "become productive citizens." No matter how difficult children's circumstances are, Blount argued, accepting "Jesus Christ as your Lord and Savior" provides "a way out."[62] Since 2009, Steeler rookies have talked with about fifty youth each summer from several organizations that partner with Blount's youth home in Claysville about football and their life experiences. In addition, many former and current Steelers help raise hundreds of thousands of dollars every year to support Blount's youth homes.[63]

Another Fall of Fame receiver, Lynn Swann, has had an illustrious career after football. Called "the Baryshnikov of the gridiron for his acrobatic catches during his Super Bowl–studded years," Swann attended a Catholic high school in California and thanked his parents for instilling in him a strong faith in God. Stallworth praised his "strong sense of integrity." Swann's commitment to community service led to his selection as the NFL Man of the Year in 1981.[64] After his playing days ended, Swann worked for twenty-six years as a sideline commentator for *ABC Sports*, performed bit parts in movies, served as the nation's fitness czar under George W. Bush and currently is the athletic director at the University of Southern California. Running as the Republican candidate for governor of Pennsylvania in 2006, Swann labeled himself a prolife Christian.[65]

Years of Mediocrity, 1980–91

After winning their fourth Super Bowl in six years in January 1980, the Steelers descended into mediocrity for twelve seasons, going 93-91 and winning only two playoff games. It was a hard pill to swallow for a franchise that had risen so high so fast and for frenetic Steeler fans. The constant cry of "one for the thumb," a fifth Super Bowl ring, was not fulfilled. The Steeler brass painfully decided to let their legendary coach, Chuck Noll, go. While the teams during these years did not have as many outspoken Christians as the Super Bowl champion squads, coach Tony Dungy and several players stand out for their faith—offensive linemen Tunch Ilkin (1980–92) and Craig Wolfley (1980–89), linebacker Robin Cole (1977–88), defensive lineman Tim Johnson (1987–89) and defensive back Dwayne Woodruff (1979–90). Other Christians who attended Bible studies and chapels included guard Steve Courson (1978–85), linebacker Hardy Nickerson (1987–92) and defensive end Keith Willis (1982–91).

Tunch Ilkin: Playing for an Audience of One

Tunch Ilkin was born in Istanbul, Turkey, and raised as a Muslim. As a child, he immigrated to the United States with his parents. As a teenager, Ilkin drank heavily and used drugs, but he felt empty. "I fell for the lies of false manhood: that men partied, did drugs, drank, and chased women." His success in playing football in college and the NFL did not bring him fulfillment. When he came to Pittsburgh in 1980, football was his god, and he was still using drugs. "I was a dark, broken Muslim," an agnostic "who thought Christians were weird and wimpy and weak."[66]

However, he met a group of Steelers "who loved the Lord, loved each other, and loved me." Some of them shared the gospel with him. In October 1980, center Mike Webster asked him, "If you died today, where would you spend eternity?" Islam emphasizes doing good works to please God, prompting Ilkin to reply, "If God grades on a curve, I figure I'm ok." To have his sins forgiven and be admitted to heaven, Webster explained, Ilkin must accept Christ as his savior.[67] Two years later, Ilkin's roommate, Craig Wolfley, asked him, "Would you like to pray to receive Christ?" Ilkin declined, but later that evening, he said "the sinner's prayer" in Hal Lindsey's *The Late Great Planet Earth* and accepted Christ as his savior.[68]

Tunch Ilkin. *Courtesy of the Pittsburgh Steelers.*

Webster, Wolfley, Kolb, Shell and Stallworth all mentored Ilkin in the Christian faith. Wolfley and Ilkin frequently prayed together. Ilkin gradually concluded that a Christian "could still be intense and competitive" and became much more "serious about walking with Jesus." He started "to play football for the Lord instead of myself" and "to use the platform that God had given me as a professional athlete to share the good news of the Gospel." Doing this was liberating because "all you've got to do is give your best."[69] Ultimately, you play "for the audience of one—God." Christians recognize that God loves them whether they win, lose or draw.[70]

Ilkin and his wife, Sharon, regularly attended Bible studies led by Steeler chaplains Hollis Haff and Jay Wilson. Ilkin also organized a Bible study in South Hills, which he led for several years and Steve Courson, Wolfley and other members of the Ilkins' church—South Hills Bible Chapel—attended.[71] Ilkin also began to witness to individuals and to speak to church groups. In church settings, Ilkin typically gave his testimony and a brief gospel message. After retiring from the NFL, Ilkin has spoken at chapel services for the Steelers, Colts and Patriots and preaches a sermon every year to two to three hundred participants at the Steelers Fantasy Camp at Saint Vincent College.[72]

Ilkin contended that so many NFL players today are Christians because they "realize that there is more to life" than football. Ilkin cites a 2009 *60 Minutes* interview in which Patriot quarterback Tom Brady asked, "Why do I have three Super Bowl rings and still feel like there is something greater out there for me?" Many would say, Brady added, that "I've reached my goal," but "I think, 'God, it's got to be more than this.'"[73] People have a void, a heart disease, that they cannot fill with money, Super Bowl victories, being the MVP or being voted into the Hall of Fame, Ilkin insisted; "it can only be filled by the person of Jesus Christ" because "that's how God wired us."[74]

Today, Ilkin is both an analyst on Steelers radio broadcasts and the director of men's ministries at The Bible Chapel. "We talk about Jesus a lot on our radio show," he explained. Ilkin reported that thirteen current or former Steelers have spoken to the men's group at his church, including Mel Blount, Aaron Smith, Antwaan Randle El and Landry Jones.[75]

Wolfley, Cole, Woodruff and Johnson

While playing with the Steelers, Craig Wolfley, who was selected to the Steelers All-Century Team in 2000, attended South Hills Bible Chapel along with Ilkin, Courson, Webster and Ted Petersen. "Jesus is my savior," Wolfley declared. "What would we do without him?"[76] Both Wolfley and Ilkin frequently serve meals at Light of Life Rescue Mission and help raise money for the mission. All-Pro linebacker Robin Cole grew up in a gang-dominated neighborhood in Compton, California, and escaped this life because of his faith in Jesus Christ. As a player, Cole attended Allegheny Center Alliance Church on the North Side. Today, he shares his faith in churches and speaks to elementary and high schools about the importance of values.[77] "My wife and I are Christians," Dwayne Woodruff avowed. "We believe we're here" to "help our fellow man." After his playing days ended, the defensive back earned a law degree and has been elected to two ten-year terms on Allegheny County's Court of Common Pleas, where he works to aid children.[78] While in the NFL, Tim Johnson's love for God and people led him to serve churches as a teacher, small group leader and elder. His faith "was the anchor for everything" he did. Since retiring from the NFL, Johnson has pastored congregations in Nashville and Orlando.[79]

The Bill Cowher Years, 1992–2006

In 1992, the Steelers hired thirty-four-year-old Bill Cowher, a former NFL linebacker, to replace Noll as their head coach. Filling the shoes of Noll, who had led the Steelers from the outhouse to the penthouse in the 1970s, was a daunting task, but Cowher's tenure was a smashing success. "While the laconic, iconic Noll was stoic to a fault, Cowher coached with the same frothing fervor he demanded from his players." He brought "Cowher Power" to Pittsburgh, and during fifteen years as the Steelers' head coach, the team went 149-90-1, the best overall record in the NFL during this period.[80] The Steelers made the playoffs in ten of these seasons and won the 1995 AFC Championship and the 2006 Super Bowl. Although he rarely spoke to the media about it, Cowher had a strong Christian faith. Both head coaches in Super Bowl XL, reported a Baptist publication in February 2006, "are believers in Jesus Christ" who support their team's chaplain programs.[81] "Cowher felt comfortable interacting with his players on a spiritual level," Ilkin asserted. He regularly attended team chapels, thanked speakers for their messages and talked about their themes afterward with players.[82] The services were "a great release for me," Cowher explained.[83]

During Cowher's years as head coach, Christian coaches and players included Steelers' director of player development Ray Jackson (2005–14), defensive coordinator Dick LeBeau (2003–14), tight ends coach James Daniel (2004–), special teams coach Kevin Spencer (2002–6), center Jeff Hartings, tight end Mark Bruener, cornerback Rod Woodson, wide receiver Antwaan Randle El (2002–5, 2010), linebacker Levon Kirkland (1992–2000), fullback Tim Lester (1995–98), fullback Dan Kreider (2000–2007), quarterback Tommy Maddox (2001–5), cornerback Willie Williams (1993–96, 2004–5), linebacker Jason Gildon (1994–2003), offensive lineman Barrett Brooks (2003–6), quarterback Kordell Stewart (1995–2002), tight end Mitch Lyons (1997–99), linebacker Larry Foote (2002–8, 2010–13), cornerback Dewayne

Washington (1998–2003), safety Mike Logan (2001–6), defensive end Travis Kirschke (2004–9), wide receiver Hines Ward (1998–2011) and several others who will be discussed in connection with Mike Tomlin's tenure as head coach.

Muscular Christians: Hartings, Woodson, Bruner and Randle El

Jeff Hartings (2001–6), a two-time Pro Bowl selection, was "one of the most devout Christians" on the Steelers team during the first decade of the twenty-first century.[84] Dan Rooney called him "a tremendous role model both on and off the field."[85] While playing with the Detroit Lions, Hartings discovered that wealth did not bring him happiness or personal peace. "The pressure to perform on the field was turning me into a miserable, self-absorbed husband who feared failing as an athlete." "I went to church weekly," Hartings explained, "but I didn't have a relationship with God."[86] Following his third season in the NFL, Hartings finally found peace and purpose when he "asked Jesus Christ to forgive me of all my sins."[87] After doing so, Hartings played for God's glory, which removed "the pressure to perform for people."[88] When he came to Pittsburgh in 2001, Steeler chaplain Jay Wilson helped Hartings "understand what obedience to God means."[89] While on road trips, Christian Steelers frequently met in Hartings's hotel room on Saturday nights to pray and discuss their faith.[90] In 2004, Hartings shared the gospel during a mission trip in Nicaragua.[91] Hartings claimed that their prayer sessions, Bible studies and "giving everything to God helped the Pittsburgh Steelers win" the 2006 Super Bowl.[92] After retiring, Hartings stayed in Pittsburgh, spoke to numerous congregations and civic groups about his faith and volunteered with several organizations. "Being a Super Bowl champion," he asserted, "gives me opportunities to share my love of Christ with others" throughout the country.[93] Hartings helped found Play Ball for Kids, a partnership between Urban Impact Foundation, Steeler players and Pittsburgh businesses.

Cornerback Rod Woodson played seventeen seasons in the NFL, including ten (1987–96) with the Steelers. He was named to the Pro Bowl eleven times and to the NFL's 75th Anniversary Team. Introducing him before his Hall of Fame induction speech, emcee Rich Eisen insisted that faith, humility, kindness and love characterized Woodson's life. Woodson began his speech by thanking "my Lord, Jesus Christ. He's my savior. He died for my sins and my salvation." Woodson ended by exhorting the audience to "choose to love rather than hate"; "choose to heal rather than wound"; "choose Jesus Christ over the world."[94]

Mark Bruener, a committed Catholic, played tight end for the Steelers from 1995 to 2003 and later worked as a team scout. Bruener thanked his parents for grounding him strongly in the Catholic faith. The Mass held for team members every Saturday night before games, he insisted, "was a great help to us." Bruener spoke to students at several Pittsburgh-area Catholic schools about how "faith guided me in all that I do." "If you remember who your Savior is," Bruener declared, what He requires and "the grace he gives you" to follow Him, "then everything is certain to turn out fine."[95]

As with Barack Obama, Antwaan Randle El's name has led many to misidentify him as a Muslim. His devout Christian mother took him to a Pentecostal church near Chicago several times each week, but in high school and college, Randle El drifted from his faith in Christ and put "himself in the forefront." While at Indiana University, he partied and had sex with numerous women. Having a child out of wedlock his senior year brought him back to God.[96] Thereafter, he "tried to live for the Lord" both on the field and in raising his children.[97] Playing in the NFL, Randle El insisted, provided many chances to bask "in your own glory," but this was Satan's ploy to distract Christians from focusing on "Kingdom business," including the responsibility to "witness for the Lord."[98] As a Steeler, he attended Bible studies when the team was on the road and went to church services before home games.[99] Randle El saw football as his platform for reaching out to people who did not know Christ personally.[100] The weekend after the Steelers won the 2006 Super Bowl, he spoke at South Hills Bible Chapel. The 1,200 worshippers who typically attended its three services swelled to 2,800. Randle El asserted that the Bible provided "the game plan of life" and that his priorities were his "faith in God, love of family" and "playing professional football, in that order."[101] After retiring from the NFL, he helped found the Virginia Academy, a Christian high school where he serves as the athletic director, and, through his own foundation, supplies scholarships for underprivileged students to attend.[102]

Seven Steelers who played for Cowher—Hartings, Jason Gildon, Kent Graham, Tommy Maddox, Mitch Lyons, Dewayne Washington and Travis Kirschke—shared their testimonies at thegoal.com. Gildon, a three-time Pro Bowler linebacker, tried to give God part of his life while in college but made many bad decisions and felt "unbearable" guilt. Sick of his lifestyle, Gildon "asked Jesus Christ to forgive me of all my sins and make me the person He wants me to be." Quarterback Kent Graham (2000)

Antwaan Randle El. *Courtesy of the Pittsburgh Steelers.*

declared that the Bible pointed people to "the greatest relationship" they can have—"one with Jesus Christ." Tight end Mitch Lyons invited Christ to be his Savior and Lord at an NFL chapel service. Cornerback Dewayne Washington "felt empty" despite his success, prompting him to invite Jesus Christ to take control of his life.[103]

Quarterback Tommy Maddox thought that his career would flourish after he rededicated his life to Christ, but instead, the money, fame and fulfillment the NFL could potentially provide "were taken away, one by one, until there was nothing left." After working as an insurance agent and playing in the Arena League, Maddox signed with the Steelers and spent two seasons as the starting quarterback. "Hard times," Maddox insisted, "are necessary" to bring people "to a place where we trust God alone." His relationship with Jesus as his savior and Lord, asserted defensive end Travis Kirschke, "gives me a sense of peace" and a purpose.[104]

The 2006 Super Bowl

In interviews the week preceding the 2006 Super Bowl, Chaplain Jay Wilson, several coaches and numerous players shared their testimonies. At this point, Wilson, who worked full time for Athletes in Action, had been serving as the Steelers' chaplain for seventeen years. Sometimes twenty players came to the Bible study he led, but the average attendance in 2006 was ten to fifteen.[105] Participants shared their hurts and joys and discussed how to spread God's Word. Among the players who actively attended Bible studies and chapel services were Hartings, Randle El, Kreider, Kirschke, Maddox, strong safety Troy Polamalu, tight end Heath Miller, cornerback Willie Williams, offensive lineman Barrett Brooks and tackle Max Starks. These players often also prayed together before games. "We pray for God's will to be done," "for our families" and "for the safety of the team," Randle El explained.[106] Wilson's wife, Cindi, led prayer meetings for Steeler wives, and a Catholic priest led a Bible study for players every Friday the team was in Pittsburgh and a chapel on Sunday mornings when the Steelers played at home.[107] In addition, Wilson counseled many Steeler players and prayed with them in person and over the phone. He also organized summer clinics in various Pittsburgh neighborhoods, where players taught football skills and shared the gospel, and he took players on overseas mission trips.

Wilson urged Christian Steelers to use the Super Bowl as an opportunity to share the gospel with 20 million people. A Super Bowl ring, he argued, would not be worth nearly as much as "a testimony to Jesus in public will be."[108] Numerous Steeler players did discuss their relationship with the Lord. Randle El explained that he sought to focus on God and His word. "I've been praying every day that I would honor" God, Hartings stated, and use this platform for Him. Praying and reading the Bible and going to team Bible studies, Dan Kreider insisted, helped him "overcome temptations connected with the Super Bowl." Max Starks saw the annual media gathering, which involved more than three thousand participants, as "a world stage" for Christian players to share their faith. Polamalu urged listeners and readers to "Keep God No. 1 in your life all the time."[109] His career in football would end someday, Ray Jackson acknowledged, but Jesus' death on the cross for humanity's sin would last forever. Coaches Kevin Spencer and James Daniel asked God to keep them grounded in His Word and direct their words.[110]

Several Steelers, including Hines Ward, used the 2006 Super Bowl victory as a springboard for Christian witness. In fourteen seasons with the team, the four-time Pro Bowler set Steeler records in catches, yards gained and touchdowns. In April 2006, Ward went to South Korea, from which his mother brought him as a two-year-old to the United States with her American serviceman husband. There he announced the creation of the Hines Ward Helping Hands Foundation to fight discrimination against mixed-race South Korean children. After arriving in the United States and being abandoned by his father, Ward had "learned what it meant to live a life with God." "My mother taught me to believe in the Lord and everything will be alright," he declared. At his press conference in Seoul, Ward asserted, "The Bible says all people are brothers and sisters," which is "why God called me to come to Korea."[111] After his playing days ended, Ward won a season of *Dancing with the Stars*, appeared in *The Walking Dead* and *The Dark Knight Rises* and opened a restaurant in Pittsburgh.

Mike Tomlin at the Helm, 2007–Present

A substantial number of Christians have played for the Steelers during the tenure of Mike Tomlin, who is known for his strong faith. Tomlin began his career as the Steelers' head coach at age thirty-five. Like Cowher, he had a huge challenge. Cowher's stellar coaching career included winning the team's fifth Super Bowl two seasons before Tomlin took over. To date, Tomlin's regular season career record is 122-62-1 (his .662 winning

Mike Tomlin. *Courtesy of the Pittsburgh Steelers.*

percentage is higher than Cowher's .623 percentage), and the Steelers have made the playoffs in eight of his eleven seasons and played in two Super Bowls, winning the one in 2009. Despite his success as a coach, Tomlin places faith and family above football.

During the Tomlin years, Christian coaches and players have been plentiful: in addition to Ray Jackson, coaches Dick LeBeau and James Daniel and receivers Heinz Ward and Antwaan Randel El, there are special teams coach Amos Jones (2007–12), offensive coordinator Todd Haley (2012–17), defensive coordinator Keith Butler (2003–), defensive back Deshea Townsend (1998–2009), defensive end Aaron Smith (1999–2011), linebacker James Farrior (2002–11), safety Troy Polamalu (2003–14), defensive back Ike Taylor (2003–14), offensive lineman Max Starks (2004–12), quarterback Ben Roethlisberger (2004–), tight end Heath Miller (2005–15), cornerbacks Bryant McFadden (2005–10) and Anthony Madison (2006–10), defensive back Ryan Clark (2006–13), defensive end Nick Eason (2007–10), punter Daniel Sepulveda (2007–11), running back Mewelde Moore (2008–11), quarterback Brian Leftwich (2008, 2010, 2012), safety Ryan Mundy (2009–12), wide receivers Tyler Grisham (2009–11) and Antonio Brown (2010–), safety Will Allen (2010–15), offensive lineman Tony Hills (2010), defensive back Cortez Allen (2011–15), offensive tackle Kelvin Beachum (2012–15), fullback Will Johnson (2012–15), center Cody Wallace (2013–15), quarterback Landry Jones (2014–18), linebacker Arthur Moats (2014–17), cornerback Kevin Fogg (2014–15) and offensive tackle Alejandro Villanueva (2015–).

A Servant's Heart

Mike Tomlin was reared primarily by his grandparents, who were devout Christians and strongly influenced Tomlin's faith formation. At the College of William and Mary, he participated regularly in Athletes in Action.[112] Tampa Bay head coach Tony Dungy mentored Tomlin in his faith while Tomlin was the team's defensive backs coach. Like Dungy, he strives "to lead with a servant's heart."[113] To do this, Tomlin explained, a coach must know his players well enough to provide godly guidance and direct them in ways that most benefit them.[114]

Tomlin rejoiced that the Steelers' participation in the 2009 Super Bowl gave him an international forum to "speak about his faith in Jesus Christ." "I want people to know," he proclaimed, that "the most important thing" in my life is "my relationship with Jesus Christ. Football is what we do; faith is who we are all the time."[115] "Coaching is what I do," Tomlin added, which he loved, but "being a father, husband and follower of Jesus Christ is who I am."[116] Like Noll, Dungy and Cowher, Tomlin insists that helping players grow as people is a major part of his job. Tomlin asks God to give him "consistent real humility," which is "confidence properly placed in Christ."[117] He attends Allegheny Center Alliance Church, a racially integrated megachurch on the North Side.

Numerous players testify to Tomlin's faith and character. Tomlin "looks through a Christian lens at the world," declared Ilkin, and "has a heart for fathering the fatherless."[118] "It's a great blessing when a man of God is leading your team," asserted defensive end Nick Eason. "Having a Christian head coach has made a big difference to the team," argued Amos Jones, and "contributed to the Steelers' Super Bowl run." The spiritual messages Tomlin delivered in team meetings, Jones added, were "a blessing."[119] Daniel Sepulveda insisted that Tomlin's "godly principles" and example helped players deal with numerous adversities.[120]

In Pittsburgh, Tomlin has worked to aid youth, especially boys who do not have a father in their homes. Tomlin is an "All Pro Dad," one of fifty-three NFL coaches, players and alumni who are dedicated to their families and advocate for the importance of fatherhood. He has spoken several times at the Man Up conference in Pittsburgh about the importance of men serving as mentors for fatherless boys.[121] Tomlin and his wife, Kiya, received a community service award for their efforts to improve the city's educational system.

In 2018, Tomlin announced that the Steelers were supporting Operation Underground Railroad, a group composed of former Navy Seals and former law enforcement personnel who work to rescue children from sex trafficking. After praying about it, Tomlin brought OUR leaders to talk to the Steelers players, who enthusiastically agreed to partner with the organization.[122]

Other Steeler Coaches and Chaplains

As noted, several Christians served on Tomlin's staff, including Dick LeBeau, Keith Butler and Todd Haley. Faith, Hall of Fame defensive coordinator LeBeau avowed, is "almost a necessity" to help coaches and players "stay the course" because of the ups and downs in this profession."[123] LeBeau was happy to be "known as a spiritual dad to the players and other coaches."[124] While playing ten seasons with the Seattle Seahawks, Keith Butler was the faith leader who mentored teammates and shared Scripture with them. Winning the Super Bowl, he insisted, paled in comparison to helping people prepare to spend eternity with God in heaven.[125] "My faith in Christ," declared offensive coordinator Todd Haley, is crucial to getting "through every day."[126]

Kevin Jordan, an Athletes in Action staffer, worked for ten years as a chaplain for the UCLA football team before serving as the Steelers' chaplain from 2008 to 2012. Jordan appreciated the staunch support for his work and the access to players Tomlin provided. Tomlin considered the chaplain to be as "important as any high draft pick for the team." Jordan spent many hours with players to develop close relationships and build trust. Jordan led Sunday morning chapel services, typically attended by twenty-five players and coaches at which he and guests spoke. Jordan also led a weekly Bible study for couples and one for coaches on Saturday mornings.[127]

Chad Johnson has been the Steeler chaplain since 2012. Johnson became a Christian as a teenager and played point guard for Arizona Christian University. While working with at-risk youth and families in two megachurches in Phoenix, Johnson also was the chaplain for the Arizona Cardinals from 2003 to 2011.[128] As did Jordan, he provides spiritual guidance to players as they vent about family issues, deal with interpersonal problems and recover from injuries. Johnson visits players and their family members in the hospital, prays with players and mentors and disciples players. He leads Saturday night chapel services, pregame prayers, a meeting for players and coaches and their spouses once a week and a coaches' Bible study on Fridays. About thirty to thirty-five players and coaches regularly attend the chapel services. At chapel talks and Bible studies, Johnson reminds players about "the potential pitfalls of NFL fame" and their unique platform for sharing the gospel.[129] Johnson has helped many Steelers develop a plan to achieve their life goals, and he consults with them weekly to monitor their progress.[130]

The 2009 and 2011 Super Bowls

As in 2006, Steeler coaches and players used their appearance in the 2009 and 2011 Super Bowls to witness for Christ. Travis Kirschke thanked God for giving him a fantastic "platform to speak for Him."[131] Running back Mewelde Moore, like several other Steelers, declared that God is "No. 1 in my entire life." Defensive end Aaron Smith testified that he relied on his faith as his five-year-old son, Elijah, battled leukemia. Fellow defensive end Nick Eason avowed that John 3:16—"For God so loved the world"—directed his life. "Faith is the foundation of everything I do on the field and off," declared Polamalu.[132]

Having a personal relationship with Christ, Randle El argued at the media day in 2011, "is crucial to surviving the stresses of the NFL." "Because of Christ's death," safety Ryan Clark averred, people can be saved. Defensive back Anthony Madison urged Christians to reject false idols and stand strong in their faith. Ben Roethlisberger insisted that he was relying on his childhood faith for guidance. Their Christian fellowship, Moore maintained, increased the Steelers' confidence, provided a bond and enabled them "to communicate on a spiritual level." Offensive lineman Tony Hills, who was baptized at the Steelers' practice facility in 2010, wore Matthew 10:28 on his left arm to remind him to fear only God.[133]

Hundreds of Pittsburgh-area clergy referred to the Steelers' appearances in the Super Bowls in their sermons. They drew parallels between the effort required to get to football's biggest game and that needed to persevere in the journey of faith. Some pastors stressed the importance of teamwork. "The beauty of the Steelers," argued Father Aaron Kriss of Tarentum, is that each player's gifts help the team win. In religion, as in football, a Methodist minister from Greensburg averred, "we need to function like a team" following the directions of Coach Jesus.[134] Randall Bush, pastor of the East Liberty Presbyterian Church, insisted that the "energy and spirit" connected with the Steeler's Super Bowl appearance in 2011 could help Pittsburghers transcend racial and economic boundaries. Sean Kealy, a Duquesne University theology professor, by contrast, warned that the devotion of many Pittsburghers to the Steelers teetered "on the brink of idolatry."[135]

Troy Story

Troy Polamalu's "combination of speed, anticipation, and toughness" made the eight-time Pro Bowler one of the best at his position in the early twenty-first century. Polamalu was named a first-team All-Pro four times and the NFL's MVP in 2010.[136] Many football pundits argue that he revolutionized the safety position. For a dozen years, Polamalu was the public face of the Steelers franchise because of his stellar performance and his television commercials for Head & Shoulders shampoo.[137]

While playing with the Steelers, Polamalu was also widely known as one of the NFL's most devout Christians. Patton Dodd, author of *The Tebow Mystique*, reported that Polamalu was "mentioned by fellow players for his spiritual devotion" more than anyone else.[138] The NFL, David Kamp wrote in a *Gentleman's Quarterly* article, abounded with "Bible-study groups and postgame prayer circles. But even in this context, Polamalu stands out." Polamalu, Kamp argued, was different from other Christian stars such as Roger Staubach and Reggie White. He was "a mystic, a man more fourth century than twenty-first, living in constant dialogue with the Deity." "What truly marks Polamalu as a man apart," Kamp concluded, "is his godliness."[139]

The youngest of five children, Polamalu was raised by a single mother on welfare in an impoverished, crime-ridden Los Angeles neighborhood. Polamalu spent more time on the streets than with his mother. By third grade, he was stealing lunch every day from a local grocery store. However, he attended fourth to twelfth grade in Oregon, while living with his uncle, Salu Polamalu, and his wife. As a child, Polamalu attended a Samoan church in Los Angeles and went to a Catholic high school in Oregon. He developed a personal relationship with God and believed in the power of prayer.[140] By high school, Polamalu reported, "I was almost constantly in prayer."[141]

After joining the Steelers, Polamalu undertook a spiritual quest that led him and his wife, Theodora, to become Orthodox Christians in 2007. For several years, Polamalu read books and talked with priests, pastors and Roman Catholic, Greek Orthodox and Buddhist monks to develop "a deeper, more consistent experience of God." His study of Scripture and church history reaffirmed his childhood faith in Christianity and persuaded him that Eastern Orthodoxy, which split from the Catholic Church in 1054, was the most biblical and spiritually meaningful form. During his investigation, Polamalu spent four days in a 1,500-year-old monastery conversing with Orthodox monks in Greece. This experience and his wife's

Troy Polamalu. *Courtesy of the Pittsburgh Steelers.*

Greek heritage contributed to their decision to join the Greek Orthodox Church. After studying with a Greek Orthodox priest in Pittsburgh for a year, they were baptized into the faith.[142] Polamalu began to understand Scripture more clearly and fully.[143] Thereafter, Polamalu attended worship services at several parishes in Pittsburgh, and he journeyed periodically to meet with his spiritual mentor Abbot Ephraim at St. Anthony's Greek Orthodox monastery near Phoenix.[144] Ephraim's *Counsels from the Holy Mountain*, a collection of his homilies and sermons, guided Polamalu in football and in life.[145]

For Polamalu, the essence of faith is surrendering to God. "I try to serve God, through football, with passion," he declared. "As Mother Teresa said, God calls us not to be successful but to be faithful," Polamalu asserted.[146] The "idea that the more pious" people were, the more successful they will be, was "very dangerous." "If you look at faith in that way," he added, "you're bound to fail" both "spiritually and in your career."[147] For Polamalu, winning two Super Bowls paled compared to the fulfillment God provided.[148]

The Christian disciplines of prayer, Bible reading and worship are all very important to Polamalu. Polamalu strove to pray constantly to remain deeply rooted in his faith, strengthen his moral compass and help him overcome temptations. Through his thought, speech and work, he strove to glorify God.[149] Polamalu has an impressive knowledge of Scripture.[150] He frequently spent more time praying in the basilica at the Steelers' training camp than he did practicing.[151] During the season, Polamalu regularly attended the team's chapel services and the Catholic Masses led by Father David Bonnar.[152]

Polamalu often crossed himself on the field to offer "a wordless prayer for help, thanks, focus." Doing this, he explained, brought comfort when he encountered adversity and stress.[153] He also sometimes mouthed the simple "Jesus prayer": "Lord Jesus Christ, Son of God, have mercy on me a sinner."[154] In addition, Polamalu and other defensive backs usually prayed in a huddle on the sidelines between each series.[155]

Trying to reconcile the Samoan warrior spirit of his ethnic heritage with Greek Orthodox teachings, Polamalu admitted, was challenging. He strove, however, "to be a valiant Christian warrior" who controlled his passions.[156] "Football," Polamalu avowed, has "its demons—prestige, ego, avarice"—that players must battle.[157] He also had to combat jealousy, materialism, sexual immorality and pride.[158] Football, Polamalu argued, is "a very spiritual sport" because players must deal with "the fear of failure," pride and being criticized for making mistakes.[159] What set Troy apart, argued Gina Mazza Hillier, was his ability to keep "love at the center of his sport." Many players, Polamalu asserted, think that hatred "drives football," "but love overcomes all things."[160]

During the extensive publicity about Tim Tebow's religious rituals on the gridiron and references in interviews to his "Lord and Savior Jesus Christ," Amy Frykholm wrote about "The Other Devout Christian on the Field" in *Christian Century*. "I wish I could capture Polamalu's very different kind of spirituality amid the football season's endless hype," she declared, but "a rich and complex life of faith is hard to sum up."[161]

Many teammates and opponents expressed great admiration and affection for Polamalu. They respected his temperament, character, compassion and Christian faith. "I don't know anybody in the NFL who doesn't like Troy," declared Steeler cornerback Bryant McFadden.[162] "He is quiet, humble, [and] accountable," avowed safety Tyrone Carter.[163] Numerous teammates testified that Polamalu positively influenced their faith. He "taught me the most about life off the field," maintained safety Mike Logan, and "helped me spiritually mature."[164] When Steeler safety Shamarko Thomas asked him how to be great, Polamalu replied that greatness is about "putting God first and just doing the right things in your life." Polamalu's response revolutionized Thomas's life.[165] When we need guidance, linebacker James Harrison asserted, "he's the guy we go to."[166]

Off the field, Polamalu made weekly unpublicized visits to cancer patients at Pittsburgh's Children's Hospital and created a foundation to aid the needy.[167] Many hospital staff "marveled at Polamalu's attentiveness." "When he comes in," observed a child life specialist, "he makes the kids feel like they are the most important person in the room." His foundation helps fund the hospital, provided housing for residents of American Samoa who were displaced by a 2009 tsunami and supports the initiatives of Focus+ Pittsburgh, an Orthodox organization that fights poverty in Western Pennsylvania.[168]

Play for Jesus: Pathos and Redemption

While Polamalu's NFL career featured sterling character, a consistent Christian testimony and deep spirituality, Ben Roethlisberger's faith journey has been bumpy and controversial. Like Terry Bradshaw, he has experienced spiritual highs and lows. Roethlisberger holds the Steeler records for passes attempted, passes completed, passing yards gained and touchdown passes and is a likely candidate for the Hall of Fame. During his rookie season, the NFL threatened to fine him for painting "PFJ" ("Play for Jesus") on his cleats, and in a 2005 interview, Roethlisberger expressed thanks for "the opportunity to glorify God in all that I do."[169] Numerous players agreed that the quarterback "was sold out for Christ when he entered the League."[170]

Three years after the Steelers won the 2005 Super Bowl, however, Roethlisberger's off-the-field life took a nosedive. In 2008, Andrea McNulty, a former VIP hostess at Harrah's Lake Tahoe casino hotel, accused him of "luring her into his penthouse suite and forcing her to have sex with him." Roethlisberger denied her allegation and eventually settled her civil suit against him.[171] About one year after his heroic performance in the Steelers' 2009 Super Bowl win, Roethlisberger spent a night drinking, partying and carousing in a bar in Milledgeville, Georgia. The friends of a twenty-year-old Georgia College and State University sophomore told the police that Roethlisberger went into the public restroom with her while she was very inebriated. She accused him of sexual assault. Roethlisberger faced no criminal charges in either case, but after this incident, the NFL suspended him for the first four games of the 2010 season for violating its personal conduct policy.

Although no court convicted Roethlisberger, "the verdict of public opinion," journalist Tom Krattenmaker argued, was "loud and clear": he was guilty "of reckless partying" and "aggressive sexual conduct" that was "highly immoral and highly un-Christian, if not downright illegal." "Roethlisberger's half-hearted 'apology' and his success dodging criminal charges," Krattenmaker added, made a mockery "of the Christian piety" that had "been a big part of his persona." Roethlisberger's behavior discredited the faith he professed and required "a new catch phrase: Partying for Jesus."[172] David Kuo went even further. The quarterback, he contended, should receive jail time for his action—a "new kind of PFJ—Prison for Jesus."[173] The 2010 premiere of *South Park* skewered Roethlisberger in a scene showing him with Bill Clinton, Michael Jordan and David Letterman at a meeting for sex addicts.

Ben Roethlisberger. *Courtesy of the Pittsburgh Steelers.*

Football fans around the nation, including many in Pittsburgh, demanded that Roethlisberger be banished from the game. Their star's "repulsive behavior, the ultimate expression of athletic entitlement run amok," wrote Jack McCallum in *Sports Illustrated*, "has forced even the most diehard [Steeler] fans to question their team and their football faith." Many Steeler fans deplored Big Ben's behavior that ranged from "civic boorishness to borderline criminality," and his retention strained the long-standing close connection between the city and the Rooney family. The quarterback's escapades brought dark and divisive days in Pittsburghers' love affair with the Steelers. Expressing the inner turmoil and torment of many Steeler fans, the owner of Yinzers in the Strip District commented, "We love Ben like a brother who's a drug addict. You love him, you want him, you need him, but he's on thin ice. Our football team is our life."[174]

To be accused of such horrific acts, Roethlisberger confessed, "was devastating." He lamented that his actions had caused him, his family, teammates, friends and fans great pain. Roethlisberger regretted that he had put himself "in bad situations." He wanted to show that he had changed, "to settle down and grow up" and become again the person his "amazing family" had reared him to be. The road back was "was tough," he admitted, "but it brought me closer still to the Lord."[175]

The Steelers stuck with Roethlisberger in part because they were convinced that he was still the man they had drafted in 2004 who had pointed upward after touchdown passes and testified about his faith in interviews. Roethlisberger came from a strong Christian family but had strayed from the path. The Steelers were rewarded for their faith in Big Ben. He did begin to change. Roethlisberger recognized that only upright actions could "restore his name and reputation." During the summer of 2010, Roethlisberger began to reembrace the evangelical culture of his youth; he again listened to Christian artists and sought spiritual guidance.[176] Aided by his fiancée, Ashley Harlan, and Christ Church at Grove Farm, which they joined in 2010, his life began to turn around. They also announced that their religious convictions precluded them from living together before their wedding in 2011.[177]

During this tumultuous time, Roethlisberger was struck one day by the lyrics of TobyMac's song "Lose My Soul": "I don't want to gain the whole world, and lose my soul." He had fame and two Super Bowl rings, but he had lost his soul and hurt many people. Sobbing, Roethlisberger admitted that he needed God's grace. Roethlisberger apologized profusely to his father for his behavior. "I thought I lost my son," he declared, "and now you're back."[178]

In interviews before the 2011 Super Bowl, Roethlisberger asserted that he wanted to be perceived as a moral person who put "family and God first." He declared that Jesus meant "everything" to him and that rekindling his faith had brought forgiveness and inner peace.[179] Some questioned, however, whether the "humbled, chastened" Ben had truly changed.[180] Journalist David Gibson predicted that if the Steelers won the 2011 Super Bowl, Roethlisberger would "thank God for his remarkable pilgrimage from pariah to hero," and many would see him as "another scandal-tarred bad boy using Jesus" to "position himself for some sponsorship deals."[181] The Steelers lost to the Packers, so Gibson's prediction was never tested.

In a 2017 speech at Liberty University, Roethlisberger credited his wife, Ashley, for helping rejuvenate his faith. She had blessed "his life in immeasurable ways." "She's awesome," he effused.[182] Their involvement at Christ Church also aided Roethlisberger's spiritual rehabilitation. "Ben and Ashley have been very consistent and genuine in their worship," reported Bruce Cote, the church's senior associate pastor.[183]

Fatherhood and his faith prompted Roethlisberger to be more kind and caring. The quarterback reached out to teammates Martavis Bryant and Le'Veon Bell who were suspended for using banned drugs. He called Bryant every day while he was in rehab and told Bell that people would eventually forget his misdeeds if he became "a better person and player." Roethlisberger also brought several teammates to services at his church.[184] In 2017, Roethlisberger stated that he had devotions every day and asked "the Lord to help me, to make me better" as "a father, a husband, [and] a Christian."[185] Big Ben's actions since 2010 indicate that he has indeed come back to the fold.

Stalwarts of the Faith

Several other Steelers who played for Tomlin also had a strong faith. After becoming a starter in 1999, defensive end Aaron Smith realized that even though he was "living the dream," he was not happy. His wife attended a Bible study for players' wives and soon accepted Christ as her savior. The remarkable change in her life, especially her contentment, prompted Smith, who felt miserable, to attend church services at North Way Christian Community and give his life to Christ. After that, Smith was one of the most devout Christians on the Steelers' squad. "The joy Christ gives me," he avowed, cannot be taken away.[186] Smith's faith was strongly tested. In 2007, he ripped his bicep; in 2008, his five-year-old son, Elijah, was diagnosed with leukemia; in 2009, he tore his rotator cuff; in 2010, a midfoot strain ended his season. After his son's diagnosis, Smith declared that without his faith in the Lord, he would have been devastated. You have to trust that God is "going to help you" survive the storm.[187] Smith and his wife relied on prayer in dealing with these problems.[188]

Punter Daniel Sepulveda accepted "the grace of Jesus Christ" as a high school student. While playing with the Steelers, he frequently testified to his faith in interviews and talked at local churches and colleges. Scripture, he declared, "has anchored me."[189] His trust "in God's sovereignty" helped Sepulveda keep the demands of football in perspective.[190] Offensive tackle Kelvin Beachum led his teammates in prayer in the locker room before every game from 2012 to 2015. If "you put your life in Jesus' hands, He'll take care of you," Beachum promised.[191] He serves as a spokesperson for Bread for the World, a Christian organization that works to alleviate poverty and hunger around the world. "Knowing what it's like to be hungry" as a child and that many children today are malnourished motivates him to help end hunger.[192]

Landry Jones, the Steelers' backup at quarterback from 2014 to 2018, started only a few times when Roethlisberger was injured. His strong faith, Jones asserted, "keeps him grounded and focused" and enables him to be joyful despite playing very little. His Twitter profile declares, "In everything you do, work as if you are working for the Lord." He recorded a five-minute message for the I Am Second campaign to exhort people to live for Christ.[193] At six-foot-nine and 320 pounds, offensive tackle Alejandro Villanueva is large even by NFL standards. The West Point graduate led a platoon of thirty-eight soldiers in a war zone in Afghanistan and received a Bronze Star for rescuing wounded soldiers. God's preservation of his life led Villanueva to develop a close relationship with the Lord that centered on helping others. "Everything I have I owe to God," he declared. Villanueva, a Catholic, enjoys saying the Lord's Prayer with teammates before each game and attending Mass and chapel services.[194]

Wide receiver Antonio Brown grew up in a crime-ridden, impoverished neighborhood in Miami where drugs were prevalent. He was homeless during his senior year of high school after his mother kicked him out of her house when she remarried. "I couldn't have left" Miami and gone to prep school in North Carolina, he declared, "without God."[195] Brown's faith, which became much deeper after he joined the Steelers, helped him avoid trouble, become a star in the NFL and repair the rift with his father.[196] Brown's motto, which he tweets every morning, is "Chest up. Eyes up. Prayed up." His tweets often feature Christian messages such as "Have faith in God constantly!" Brown created a foundation to aid disadvantaged children in Miami's low-income neighborhoods.[197]

Conclusion

The Steeler story involves suffering, sadness and tragedy. The Steeler family and fans have experienced an extraordinary amount of loss. Of the seventy-seven men who played in the NFL in the 1970s and 1980s and died between 2000 and 2006, sixteen—more than one in five—were former Steelers. Ten of these sixteen played for the 1970s championship teams. Several of these deaths were especially tragic, including Mike Webster's in 2002. As featured in the 2015 movie *Concussion*, Webster suffered from brain damage, was addicted to Ritalin and was homeless for a while after his retirement. The deaths of Ernie Holmes and Dwight White in 2008 increased the members of Steeler Super Bowl teams who had died before the age of sixty to twelve.[198]

Overall, however, the tale of the Steelers since 1974 is one of triumph, exhilaration and camaraderie. The love affair, sometimes stormy but always passionate, between the city and the team has been at the heart of the story. The faith of Steeler owners, coaches, players and fans has been a major part of this relationship. Arguably, faith has played a very positive role in the Steelers' success on the field and has inspired many of the contributions former and active players have made off the field to enrich Pittsburgh and other locales. As historian Eric Miller wrote, "At its best," sport leads us to experience more fully health, community, play and joy—"all good gifts of the Creator." For this to happen, however, sport must be placed in "a grander, richer participation in life" that takes us "more deeply into gratitude and grace, sourced in the Creator and centered on the Cross."[199]

CHAPTER 12

FAITH AND THE PITTSBURGH PENGUINS

There is a common misconception that being a Christian hockey player means you are weak and nerdy. In reality, being a Christian... makes you strong and courageous.
—Joe Vitale

HOCKEY AND CHRISTIANITY

Considerably fewer Christians play in the National Hockey League than in Major League Baseball, the National Football League or the National Basketball Association. Thegoal.com features the testimonies of more than 150 MLB players and more than 150 NFL players, but only 3 NHL players. MLB, the NFL and the NBA, a sportswriter argued, "have institutionalized religion in a way the NHL seemingly never will."[1] Religion is a major part of the sporting world, former NHL star Paul Henderson declared, but hockey is "the least influenced by the Christian faith."[2] Whereas religious display is common in professional baseball, basketball and football—pitchers point fingers skyward, NBA players have tattoos of crosses, entire NFL teams often kneel to pray at midfield at the end of games and players in all three sports praise God in postgame interviews—hockey has remained "almost aloof" from religion.[3] NHL players have said much less about faith than their counterparts in other major sports.[4]

Four factors contribute to this. One is the climate of the NHL. In "the tough and hard-hitting sport of hockey," identifying oneself as a

Christian is challenging. Players' desire to be perceived as macho has long made religion a somewhat taboo topic in the NHL.[5] "Any sign of religion," reported Mike Gartner, who played in the NHL from 1979 to 1998, "raised eyebrows and hackles in equal measure."[6] "There's not a lot of Christians in the hockey world," declared Brad Thiessen, who was a goalie with the Penguins in 2011–12. "It's definitely a tough place to be a Christian." Sometimes Thiessen has been the only outspoken Christian on his team. "Wild partying and drinking" are common among NHL players," he asserted, who often "use their hockey status to get things they want."[7] Doing anything unusual in a hockey dressing room, from wearing a funny hat to having a bad haircut, explained Vancouver's Dan Hamhuis, attracts negative attention. NHL players often poke fun at Christians, so "if you're not real mature in your faith, you might not be comfortable defending it."[8] Christians long "had a reputation," NHL veteran Matt Cullen contended, for "not being tough enough to play the game."[9] As a result, the faith of players has often been "a closely guarded secret in the NHL." Even today, a sportswriter maintained, it is not easy to reveal your faith "to teammates willing to mock your every move or to a not-always-friendly front office."[10]

Some trace the long-standing reluctance of many NHLers to speak publicly about their faith to an episode that occurred in the early 1980s. Harold Ballard, the curmudgeonly Toronto Maple Leafs owner, attacked his team's center, Laurie Boschman, for his "soft" play, which he blamed directly on Boschman's Christian beliefs. Ballard's criticism reverberated across hockey-crazed Canada, compelling Boschman to defend his faith. The center argued that Ballard accused him unfairly because he misunderstood Christianity. Nevertheless, the charge that Christian faith prevented players from competing effectively in a tough sport did much damage and left a legacy that still persists. During the years when Boschman played (1979–93), the NHL's attitude toward religion "ranged from standoffish to downright distrustful." Despite this incident, Boschman had a stellar career with four teams and today is the team chaplain of the Ottawa Senators and coordinates chapel programs for the entire NHL.[11]

Two other factors that contribute to smaller numbers of Christians in the NHL are the countries of origin of the players and the opportunities for organized Christian fellowship. Unlike MLB, the NFL and the NBA, many hockey players grew up in Canada, eastern Europe, Scandinavia or Russia—places where Christians are much less numerous than in the United States or Latin America. Some analysts also refer to the reserved nature of many Canadians to explain why many Christians in the NHL remain quiet about their faith. In addition, institutional support for Christians came later in the NHL than in the other three sports. Hockey Ministries International was founded only four years after Baseball Chapel began in 1973, but it took much longer to gain acceptance. The Penguins, joked Hollis Haff, who served as their first chaplain, had the largest Bible study in the NHL in the early 1980s, consisting of three players: Michel Dion, Paul Baxter and Marc Chorney.[12] Only in the last fifteen years have NHL teams permitted chapel programs to meet on their property. HMI "is slowly but surely making a difference in how the hockey world views Christianity," insisted ESPN analyst Barry Melrose, but some coaches and the general managers are still reluctant to allow HMI to hold chapel services.[13] Some teams provide players with real estate agents and recommend car services but deny them access to a team chaplain or religious service.[14]

Nevertheless, Christian players are becoming more accepted in the NHL, and their reputation is improving. Cullen argued that because of the work of HMI and the Fellowship of Christian Athletes, more players coming into the NHL are strongly "established in their faith." Today, HMI holds chapel services for twenty-three of the thirty-one NHL franchises, although only sixteen of them are officially sanctioned by the team's management. More Christians are not "afraid or embarrassed or shy" about discussing their faith.[15]

Moreover, Christians are dispelling the label that they are soft. "Our team fighter" and its other "tough guys," Cullen reported, consistently attend chapel.[16] "Some great Christian NHLers," argued Mike Rupp, play "just as hard as anyone." "Once you experience Jesus," he added, you have "a fierce passion" and "there's nothing soft about it."[17] "Any Christian player I've ever known is always the toughest guy on the team and the best teammate," Melrose maintained. "A lot of people in the hockey world feel you can't be a big tough physical hockey player and be a Christian," but Christians are some of the fiercest competitors in the sport.[18] In addition, some recent and current NHL stars are Christians, including Jarome Iginla, Shane Doan, Mike Fisher, Eric Staal, Dan Hamhuis, Mike Gartner, Ryan Smyth, Joe Sakic, Cam Ward, Dean Prentice, John Vanbiesbrouck, Markus Naslund and Wayne Gretzky.

The Penguins and Faith

During the last decade, the Penguins have been one of the NHL's premier franchises, making the playoffs every season since 2006–7 and winning the Stanley Cup in 2009, 2016 and 2017. Several devout Christians have been with the Pens, most notably coach Dan Bylsma (2008–14), center Max Talbot (2005–11), center Jordan Staal (2006–12), left winger Matt Cooke (2008–13) and centers Mike Rupp (2009–11), Joe Vitale (2010–14), Eric Fehr (2015–17) and Matt Cullen (2015–17).

During Bylsma's six seasons as the Penguins' head coach, the team captured a Stanley Cup and went to the playoffs every year. He reached both the 200- and 250-win levels in his coaching career faster than any other coach in NHL history and directed the United States hockey team at the 2014 Winter Olympics. His parents, Bylsma asserted, "centered our family around their religious beliefs." Church, Sunday school and Christian schools were very important to his family. The discussion around the family dinner table often focused on religious, philosophical or ethical issues. Bylsma graduated from Western Michigan Christian High School, where he excelled in hockey. Hearing a sermon as a fifteen-year-old on the obligation to use one's talents to serve God inspired him to pursue playing professional hockey.[19] Bylsma's upbringing helped him develop a moral compass that determined his decisions. God revealed a code of conduct in the Bible, he argued, that should direct how Christians lived.[20]

Bylsma's players appreciated his "positive and creative" approach. He expressed his quiet faith through his demeanor and by donating money to Pittsburgh's Children's Hospital and visiting patients there.[21] In *So Your Son Wants to Play in the NHL*, Bylsma and his father, Jay, tell the story of Dan's daughter, who died at birth, to describe how people can survive "difficult times through perseverance, faith and a solid support system."[22] "The love and support of family and friends," Bylsma insisted, enabled us to experience more deeply God's presence and compassion.[23] He and Clint Hurdle became good friends after Hurdle came to Pittsburgh in 2011, in part because of their shared Christian commitment. Bylsma, Matt Cullen testified, helped him grow in his faith.[24]

Max Talbot scored both goals in the Pens' win in Game 7 of the 2009 Stanley Cup finals, and throughout his NHL career he was respected for "his character and locker room presence." He strove to be a good teammate by supporting them on and off the ice.[25] His "playful demeanor and natural exuberance" helped his teammates cope with the rigorous NHL schedule.

Left: Dan Byslma. *Courtesy of Michael Miller, Wikimedia Commons.*

Below: Max Talbot. *Courtesy of Lisa D. Gansky.*

Talbot frequently visited youngsters at Children's Hospital in Lawrenceville and patients at the Hillman Cancer Center in Shadyside to lift their spirits.[26] In addition, he and his wife, Cynthia Phaneuf, a two-time Canadian figure skating champion and a 2010 Olympian, established a foundation that has raised more than $900,000 to support the Make-A-Wish Foundation and charities that aid sick and hungry children.[27]

The NHL player who most "lets his faith guide every aspect of his career," wrote journalist Scott Taylor, "is Eric Fehr." Fehr recognizes that "there is a lot more to life than hockey." Throughout his career, Fehr's relationship with God has helped him cope with injuries, disagreements with coaches and pressure-filled games. Guided by Philippians 4:6–7, he has striven not to "worry about anything; instead pray about everything. Tell God what you need and thank him for all He has done." The foundation for Fehr's faith was laid by his parents, who read him Bible stories and taught him to make serving God his top priority, and by his regular attendance at Sunday school and church as a child.[28]

Matt Cullen, who has played for eight teams during his twenty-one-year career, including the Penguins' Stanley Cup–winning teams in 2016 and 2017, grew up in a "good, Christian household" and began reading the Bible at an early age. Attending Anaheim's chapel services during his rookie season helped reestablish his faith. From then on, he regularly went to HMI chapels and to church with his family. "Without my faith," Cullen confessed, "I don't know where I'd be." "Jesus was the most courageous man who ever lived," he asserted. Cullen's faith alleviates his fear of failing and disappointing others. His belief that God loves him unconditionally and is directing his life gives Cullen confidence and inspiration.[29]

While grappling with what would happen if he did not make the NHL, Matt Rupp became a Christian at age nineteen through the testimony of his future wife, who told him about her personal relationship with Jesus. Throughout his fourteen-year career, he strove to reflect "the image of Jesus" and avoid putting himself above his team. "Faith gives you the ability to bounce back up, dust yourself off and go at it again," Rupp insisted, "whether it's in life or on the ice. It's given me the ability to play with reckless abandon" and "the freedom to not fear anything."[30] Rupp has spoken to numerous Christian gatherings, including a faith breakfast at the 2015 NHL All-Star Game.

Joe Vitale's testimony is included in *Play to Win: Hockey New Testament* (2013). Surrendering his life to Christ brought Vitale purpose, strength, confidence and peace. "God has given me a job and goals," he argued, and the gifts to accomplish those goals. "My relationship with God," Vitale added, "has

Left: Eric Fehr. *Right*: Matt Cullen. *Courtesy of Michael Miller, Wikimedia Commons.*

strengthened every aspect of my life." Every day, Vitale explained, he faces frightening challenges, but when he puts his trust in Jesus, he can "do what seems impossible." "The best way to show my teammates the love of Christ," Vitale asserted, is to encourage them, spend time with them and help them learn new skills.[31]

Although his brother Eric is better known for his faith, Jordan Staal is also a devout Christian. Henry and Linda Staal furnished their four hockey-playing sons with a solid Christian foundation through their home, involvement in First Christian Reformed Church in Thunder Bay, Ontario, and education at Thunder Bay Christian School. At every dinner, the Staals had family devotions, and all four boys read devotional books before going to bed.[32] In a 2016 HMI testimonial, Staal thanked his parents for teaching him to make "time for God." His favorite Bible passage is James 1:2–4, which exhorts Christians to rejoice in their trials. Going through difficulties, Staal affirmed, strengthened his faith.[33] When hockey supplied his identity, he felt empty. After the Penguins won the Stanley Cup in 2009, fulfilling his foremost hockey dream, Staal understood more fully that only Jesus can fill the void in people's lives, prompting him to strive more diligently to glorify God through playing hockey.[34] He participated regularly in HMI's chapel services. His Penguin teammate Matt Cooke called Staal the "spiritual leader of our team."[35]

Right: Joe Vitale. *Courtesy of Michael Miller, Wikimedia Commons.*

Below: Jordan Staal. *Courtesy of Wikimedia Commons.*

The transformation of Matt Cooke is one of the biggest stories in hockey and religion and testifies to the power of God. Cooke was frequently derided as a "bum, goon, rat, pest, [and the] dirtiest player in the NHL." He was an agitator who sought to intimidate opponents and make space for star shooters to score. Cooke's overly aggressive play led the NHL to revise its rules to prohibit blindside hits.[36]

Growing up in Sterling, Ontario, Cooke occasionally attended Sunday school and worship services at an Anglican church. However, when he was twelve, Cooke blamed God for allowing his grandfather, with whom he shared a room, to die and became distant from Him. When he came to the Penguins, Chaplain Brad Henderson gave him a Bible, but he did not read it. His wife Michelle's life centered on her faith. For twelve years, she prayed that Matt would come to God and continually invited him to accompany her to church services. He saw no need to attend church because his life was going well: he had a beautiful wife and three healthy children, and his hockey career was flourishing, highlighted by the Pens winning the 2009 Stanley Cup.[37]

During the 2010–11 season, however, his life began to fall apart. He was suspended twice for illegal hits, and some called for him to be banned from hockey. Michelle had four surgeries in January 2011 to remove a mass that was hampering the functioning of her kidney, lungs and diaphragm. In desperation, Matt, who had not prayed in two decades, called on God to heal his wife. In March, he was suspended for the second time for what was judged to be an intentional elbow to the head of New York Rangers defenseman Ryan McDonagh. His hit disappointed his wife, who was battling to regain her health; his team, which lost its top penalty killer; and Mario Lemieux, the Pens' co-owner, who had recently chastised the NHL for "not cracking down on vicious blows to the head." The media reaction was scathing. For the first time in his career, Cooke publicly apologized for his action, but hockey analysts refused to take him seriously. Cooke "hit rock bottom." Several Christians worked to help him control the anger that was causing his aggression on the ice.[38]

During a three-week period, his life began to change; he finally understood the gospel message. When Scott Stevens, the lead pastor of North Way Christian Community where his family attended, asked at a service if anyone wanted prayer to establish a deeper relationship with God, Cooke raised his hand. He was impressed by the faith of Steeler defensive end Aaron Smith, who began to mentor him spiritually. Cooke gradually concluded that God controlled everything and placed his trust in the Lord, filling the void in his life. Thereafter, he sought to grow in his relationship with God.[39]

Cooke strove to alter his playing style. "He apologized publicly for his past sins," admitting, "I need to change." "He knew [that] to stay on the ice," Stevens explained, he must "change his style." "It wasn't just an overnight change," Bylsma declared. Cooke approached the game in "a different light" and with a different mindset and became "a better player and person." After going eighteen months without an infraction, Cooke was taken off the league's probationary list of "repeat offenders." His 2011–12 season with the Penguins was among his best—he scored thirty-eight points and had only forty-four penalty minutes (fewer than 220 other NHL players).[40]

Cooke's life was transformed. After Staal was traded, he strove to become the Pens' spiritual leader; he invited teammates to attend chapel services and talked with many church and community groups and individuals about his religious rebirth.[41] Becoming a born-again Christian "changed my approach," Cooke explained. If you practice and are prepared, "you can leave games up to God." "I believe that everything happens for a reason," he added. "I was meant to prove that change is possible....The biggest thing I gained" through "my relationship" with God is being patient with both "the highs and lows."[42]

From 2010 to 2012, several Pens, including Cooke, worked to help the indigent in Haiti. In August 2010, Rupp and Talbot traveled with Brad Henderson to Haiti to help victims of a devastating earthquake that had rocked the Port-au-Prince area eight months earlier. They were deeply touched by the children with whom they played ball hockey, soccer and basketball at an orphanage near Cap-Haïtien. Plagued by poverty, AIDS and an oppressive government, Haiti had an estimated 850,000 orphans before the massive earthquake killed more than 220,000 people, injured 300,000, displaced 1.5 million and reduced thousands of buildings to rubble. Henderson raised $350,000 to help build a second orphanage in the area.[43]

Matt Cooke. *Courtesy of Michael Miller, Wikimedia Commons.*

The next winter, Rupp and Talbot continued their efforts to help the children at the orphanage. Talbot had previously created a charitable organization to assist children and raised about $90,000 to help fund this second orphanage. During the 2010–11 hockey season, Talbot and Rupp received e-mails and reports from Henderson about developments in Haiti. Talbot hoped that orphans who received a home, an education, religious training and moral instruction would someday help improve life in Haiti.[44]

In August 2012, Jordan Staal, Joe Vitale and Matt Cooke went with Henderson to Haiti to celebrate the opening of a recycling store whose proceeds would support the two orphanages and to give their residents ball hockey and soccer equipment donated by Reebok, Wilson and other companies. Seeing widespread filth, sewage and trash in the ocean and thousands of children without adult supervision was both shocking and heartbreaking. Like Talbot, Cooke created a foundation to assist the indigent in Haiti and at home, which focused primarily on aiding women and children.[45]

Conclusion

The Pens have a large and enthusiastic following in Pittsburgh and many fans in other locales. After the team won the Stanley Cup in June 2017, 650,000 people viewed their championship parade, which was the largest crowd in the city's history, surpassing all the parades to celebrate the Steelers' six Super Bowl victories.[46] Pittsburgh's weather in June is much better than in February, but the size of the throng testifies to the Pens' popularity.

In 2012, Matt, an engineer from Greensburg, near Pittsburgh, created the Penguins Jesus Twitter account, which he runs with several friends. During the 2017 playoffs, they strove to ensure that fans "kept the faith" throughout the Pens' "trials and tribulations." The account averaged 1 million views a day during May and early June as social media–savvy fans flocked to the site. Before the Penguins won Game 6 in Nashville to wrap up their fifth Stanley Cup, Matt wrote that the championship was almost guaranteed. Sidney Crosby and Evgeni Malkin would not let Nashville win back-to-back games. "Not if Penguins Jesus' divine providence—or his Twitter followers—have anything to say about it," quipped a *Pittsburgh Post-Gazette* sportswriter.[47] With superstars Crosby and Malkin and a solid supporting cast, the Pens' future appears to be very bright. Win or lose, hopefully the Pens will have a strong contingent of Christians to contribute to the building of God's kingdom in Pittsburgh and beyond.

Chapter 13

PITTSBURGH

A FAITHFUL CITY

I will restore your leaders as in days of old,
your rulers as at the beginning.
Afterward you will be called
the City of Righteousness,
the Faithful City.
—Isaiah 1:26

You're the God of this city
Greater things have yet to come
And greater things are yet to be done in this city.
—Chris Tomlin, "God of This City"

Cities play a central role in the Bible. Jerusalem, Jericho, Babylon and Nineveh are important places in the Old Testament, while Jerusalem, Caesarea, Antioch in Syria, Rome, Athens, Corinth, Ephesus and Philippi are prominent sites in the New Testament where the gospel was proclaimed and congregations were planted. Their populations, prominence and potential leaders for the nascent church led Paul to focus on cities in his missionary journeys. The Bible insists that cities can thrive only if God directs their paths. "Unless the Lord watches over the city," the Psalms declare, "the watchman stays awake in vain" (127:1). Moreover, the Scriptures command Christians to promote the well-being of the cities where they reside. The prophet Jeremiah told the Jews to "seek the welfare of the city where I have sent you into exile, and pray to the Lord on its behalf, for in its welfare you will find your welfare" (Jeremiah 29:7).[1]

Jesus declared in the Sermon on the Mount that His followers are to be "a city on a hill [that] cannot be hidden" (Matthew 5:14). In his 1630 sermon "A Model of Christian Charity," John Winthrop, the governor of Massachusetts Bay Colony, exhorted his fellow Puritans to recognize that they were "a city on a hill" that many would look to as a model for building godly societies. This phrase has reverberated throughout American history, inspiring millions of believers to try to make their communities exemplars of Christian faith and biblical morality. In addition, like Abraham, Christians look "forward to the city with foundations whose architect and builder is God" (Hebrews 11:10). They rejoice that God has prepared a heavenly city for them—the New Jerusalem (Hebrews 11:16; Revelation 21:2).

From Boston to New York to Philadelphia to Washington, D.C., cities have been very important in American history. Many have labored to make them aesthetically appealing centers of commerce, culture, civility and opportunity. Pittsburgh—the first American city founded west of the Allegheny Mountains—has sought to promote these ends and has a long and rich Christian history.

In many ways, Pittsburgh's Christians have fallen short in their quest to make their city as famous for God as for steel. Nevertheless, their efforts have been remarkable. Resolutely and relentlessly, the city's Christians have worked to exalt God's name and spiritually revitalize their communities. Through hundreds of churches, dozens of parachurch ministries and their vocations and families, countless Christians have worked energetically, enthusiastically and effectively for more than two centuries to glorify God by saving souls and improving social institutions. They have created, funded and staffed numerous organizations and agencies that have fed the hungry, aided the unemployed to find jobs, housed the homeless, clothed the ill-clad, improved accommodations for low-income residents, provided medical care, assisted children to learn more effectively in schools, helped individuals fight substance abuse and combatted racial, ethnic and sexual discrimination. Pittsburgh's Christians have helped elevate public and private moral standards, reduce crime and redirect the lives of many juvenile and adult offenders. They have established numerous schools, colleges and hospitals. Their multifaceted endeavors have had many salutary consequences, served as a model for other cities and advanced God's kingdom.

Where the Allegheny and Monongahela Rivers meet to form the Ohio River, Christians have built a city in which compassion, righteousness, respect for differences and generosity have flourished. Their zealous efforts have produced much good fruit: transformed lives, innumerable acts of kindness, improved institutions and a more just society. Building on the solid foundation laid by many devoted followers of Jesus, may Pittsburghers continue to construct a city that honors God, reflects His attributes and uplifts the downtrodden and despised. For many years, Pittsburgh produced more steel than any other area in the world; for years to come, may its Christians help lead the world in building signposts for God's kingdom.

NOTES

Introduction

1. Darren Hartwell, "Boston Crowned as America's Most Successful Sports City; Pittsburgh Second," NESN, June 4, 2015, http://nesn.com/2015/06/boston-crowned-as-americas-most-successful-sports-city-pittsburgh-second.
2. D.J. Gallo, "So Good, They Donate Champions," ESPN, April 21, 2008, http://sports.espn.go.com/espn/titletown/news/story?id=3356716.
3. *Pittsburgh Business Times*, "Sporting News Names Pittsburgh Top Sports City," October 7, 2009, https://www.bizjournals.com/pittsburgh/stories/2009/10/05/daily17.html; Matt Mosley, "NFL's Best Fans? We Gotta Hand It to Steelers (Barely)," ESPN, August 29, 2008, http://www.espn.com/nfl/preview08/columns/story?id=3530077.
4. Kenneth J. Heineman, *A Catholic New Deal: Religion and Reform in Depression Pittsburgh* (University Park: Pennsylvania State University Press, 1999), 1.
5. Ibid., 209.
6. Roy Lubove, *Twentieth Century Pittsburgh: Government, Business, and Environmental Change* (New York: John Wiley and Sons, 1969), 1–2.
7. Explore Pennsylvania History, "David L. Lawrence Historical Marker," http://explorepahistory.com/hmarker.php?markerId=1-A-32E (Dickens, Steffens, British visitor and Mencken quotations); Joseph Frazer Wall, *Andrew Carnegie* (Pittsburgh: University of Pittsburgh Press, 1989), 386 (Spencer quotation); PBS, "Meet Andrew Carnegie: Welcome to Pittsburgh," http://www.pbs.org/wgbh/amex/carnegie/sfeature/meet_pittsburg.html (Parton, British economist and Carnegie quotations); S. Trevor Hadley, *Only in Pittsburgh* (Cincinnati, OH: Education Publishing Resources, 1994), 232 (Carson quotation).
8. *Pittsburgh Sun-Telegraph*, "This Is Pittsburgh—1953," November 8, 1953, B1.

9. *Pittsburgh Magazine*, "Pittsburgh Ranked Smartest City in America," June 25, 2013, http://www.pittsburghmagazine.com/Best-of-the-Burgh-Blogs/The-412/June-2013/Pittsburgh-Ranked-Smartest-City-in-America.
10. Sally Kalson, "30 Years: 'Hell with the Lid Off' to Most Livable—How Pittsburgh Became Cool," *Pittsburgh Post-Gazette*, http://www.post-gazette.com/local/region/2013/10/20/30-Years-Hell-with-the-lid-off-to-Most-Livable-How-Pittsburgh-became-cool/stories/201310200277.
11. Sean Posey, "Is Pittsburgh America's Most Livable City?," Hampton Institution, http://www.hamptoninstitution.org/pittsburgh-livable-city.html#.VpZigPkrJdh; *Pittsburgh Magazine*, "Pittsburgh Ranked Smartest City in America"; David Cross, "America's Smartest Cities," Motovo, http://www.movoto.com/blog/top-ten/smartest-cities.
12. *Metropolis*, "The Metropolis Guide to the Best Cities to Live, Work, and Play in (2015)," http://www.metropolismag.com/July-August-2015/The-Worlds-Most-Livable-Cities/index.php?cparticle=3&siarticle=2#artanc.
13. Linda Pritchard, "The Soul of the City: A Social History of Religion in Pittsburgh," in Samuel Hays, ed., *City at the Point: Essays on the Social History of Pittsburgh* (Pittsburgh: University of Pittsburgh Press, 1989), 327.
14. Leland Baldwin, *Pittsburgh: The Story of a City* (Pittsburgh: University of Pittsburgh Press 1937), 110, 249; Pritchard, "Soul of the City," 333; Keith Zahniser, *Steel City Gospel: Protestant Laity and Reform in Progressive-Era Pittsburgh* (New York: Routledge, 2013), 46–47 (quotations).
15. *Presbyterian Banner* 100, "Pittsburgh as a Center of Presbyterianism" (May 28, 1914): 8.
16. Tyler Flynn, "Presbyterians and Modernity: Developing a Public Ethic in Pittsburgh, 1900–1930," *Journal of Presbyterian History* 89 (Fall/Winter 2011): 67; George Swetnam, "All Ye That Labor," in William McKinney, ed., *The Presbyterian Valley* (Pittsburgh: Davis and Warde, 1958), 464.
17. George Swetnam, "Star in the West," *Pittsburgh Perspective* 4 (December 1963): 7. In 1914, the PCUSA's Pittsburgh Presbytery had 145 congregations, 190 ministers and 55,000 members. Pittsburgh was home to Western Theological Seminary, Pennsylvania College for Women, the Presbyterian Training School, Presbyterian Hospital and the offices of the General Assembly's Permanent Committee on Temperance (*Presbyterian Banner*, "Pittsburgh as a Center of Presbyterianism," May 28, 1914, 8).
18. O.M. Walton, *Story of Religion in the Pittsburgh Area* (Pittsburgh: Pittsburgh Bicentennial Association, 1958), 2.
19. Pritchard, "Soul of the City," 333. Also see Walton, *Story of Religion.*
20. Ann Rodgers, "Pittsburghers Can Honor at Least 16 Saints or Candidates for Sainthood with Ties to This Region," *Pittsburgh Post-Gazette*, October 31, 2010, accession no. 2W64255290945.

21. Daniel Marsh, *The Challenge of Pittsburgh* (New York: Missionary Education Movement, 1917), 227.
22. Quoted in Jeremy Bonner, "The Pittsburgh Paradigm: The Rise of Confessional Anglicanism in Southwestern Pennsylvania, 1950–2000," *Anglican and Episcopal History* 77 (September 2008): 283.
23. Joseph Casino, "From Sanctuary to Involvement: A History of the Catholic Parish in the Northeast," in Jay Dolan, ed., *The American Catholic Parish: A History from 1850 to the Present*, 2 vols. (New York: Paulist Press, 1987), 1:111.
24. *Observer-Reporter*, "Spotlight on the Valley," February 17, 2017, https://observer-reporter.com/living/spotlight-on-the-valley/article_798e01ac-1d53-505c-a0eb-526bdfd31fa9.html; Pritchard, "Soul of the City," 330; Walton, *Story of Religion*, 7, 17–19.
25. Laurence Glasco, "Double Burden: The Black Experience in Pittsburgh," in Hays, *City at the Point*, 71.
26. *Huffington Post*, "Most and Least Religious Cities in America: Pittsburgh, PA," http://www.huffingtonpost.com/2012/05/18/most-and-least-religious-cities_n_1522644.html?slideshow=true#gallery/226922/4.
27. Timothy Kelly, *The Transformation of American Catholicism: The Pittsburgh Laity and the Second Vatican Council, 1950–1972* (South Bend, IN: University of Notre Dame, 2009), 7.
28. City-Data, "Allegheny County, Pennsylvania (PA) Religion Statistics Profile," http://www.city-data.com/county/religion/Allegheny-County-PA.html; BestPlaces, "Pittsburgh, Pennsylvania," http://www.bestplaces.net/religion/city/pennsylvania/pittsburgh; Pew Research Center, "Adults in the Pittsburgh Metro Area," http://www.pewforum.org/religious-landscape-study/metro-area/pittsburgh-metro-area.
29. See Reid Carpenter, "Pittsburgh—A City as Known for God as for Steel: A Review of Four Decades," unpublished paper, August 1988.
30. Marsh, *Challenge of Pittsburgh*, vii, viii.

Chapter 1

1. On the cover of the *Pittsburgh Methodist* 3 (April 1914).
2. Gaius Glenn Atkins, *Religion in Our Times* (New York: Round Table Press, 1932), 156.
3. One exception is Zahniser, *Steel City Gospel*.
4. Tyler Flynn, "United Service in Divisive Times: The Pittsburgh Council of Churches, 1916–1929," *Pennsylvania History: A Journal of Mid-Atlantic Studies* 84 (Winter 2017): 62.
5. Zahniser, *Steel City Gospel*, 45.
6. Marsh, *Challenge of Pittsburgh*, viii.

7. Albert Jay Nock, "What a Few Men Did in Pittsburgh," *American Magazine* 70 (October 1910): 808.
8. William Scaife, "A Glimpse of Pittsburg," *Atlantic* 87 (January 1901): 83–87; Anthony N. Penna, "Changing Images of Twentieth-Century Pittsburgh," *Pennsylvania History* 43 (January 1976): 49–63.
9. H.L. Mencken, "Pittsburgh Dreams," *Baltimore Evening Sun*, 1910 (first phrase); Mencken, "Explaining the Returns," *Baltimore Sun*, 1910 (second phrase). See also Edward Muller, "Ash Pile or Steel City? H.L. Mencken Helps Mold an Image," *Pittsburgh History* 74 (Summer 1991): 51–61.
10. Lincoln Steffens, *The Shame of the Cities* (New York: McClure, Phillips, 1904), 102–4.
11. Lubove, *Twentieth Century Pittsburgh*, 6–10; Clarke Chambers, *Paul U. Kellogg and the Survey: Voices for Social Welfare and Social Justice* (Minneapolis: University of Minnesota Press, 1971).
12. Edward Devine, "Pittsburgh the Year of the Survey," in Paul Underwood Kellogg, ed., *The Pittsburgh District Civic Frontage* (New York: Survey Associates, 1914), 3–4.
13. John Fitch, *The Steel Workers* (New York: Charities Publication Committee, 1910), 223; Robert Woods, "Pittsburgh: An Interpretation of Its Growth," *Pittsburgh District*, 10; Pritchard, "Soul of the City," 343.
14. Zahniser, *Steel City Gospel*, 116.
15. Flynn, "United Service in Divisive Times," 13.
16. Fred B. Smith, 1926 address, quoted in Charles Zahniser, *Pittsburgh Council of Churches: A Historical Sketch* (Pittsburgh: Pittsburgh Council of Churches, 1943), ii.
17. Ronald Butera, "A Settlement House and the Urban Challenge: Kingsley House in Pittsburgh, Pennsylvania, 1893–1920," *Pittsburgh History* 66 (January 1983): 25–47; Zahniser, *Steel City Gospel*, 67–68; William Matthews, *Adventures in Giving* (New York: Dodd, Mead, 1939), 65.
18. *Pittsburgh Christian Outlook* 18, "Who's Who in Pittsburgh Churches: H.D.W. English" (June–July 1922): 3 (quotation); Arthur Burgoyne, *All Sorts of Pittsburghers Sketched in Prose and Verse* (Pittsburgh: Leader of All Sorts, 1892), 112–13; George Thornton Fleming, "Henry David Williams English," *History of Pittsburgh and Environs*, 5 vols. (New York: American Historical Society, 1922), 5:239–40.
19. Julia Shelly Hodges, *George Hodges: A Biography* (New York: Century, 1926), 99.
20. Zahniser, *Steel City Gospel*, 121.
21. *National Cyclopedia of American Biography* (New York: James White, 1922), 33:500–501.
22. Gary Scott Smith, "The Men and Religion Forward Movement of 1911–12: New Perspectives on Evangelical Social Concern and the Relationship Between Christianity and Progressivism," *Westminster Theological Journal* 49 (Spring 1987): 91–118.

23. Zahniser, *Steel City Gospel*, 161–62.

24. *Presbyterian Banner*, "Social Service Union," November 27, 1913, 7; *Pittsburgh Methodist* 3, "The Christian Social Service Union" (January 1914): 14–15; *The Survey* 33, "The Christian Social Service Union" (July 25, 1914): 435.

25. Zahniser, *Steel City Gospel*, 173. See also Emily Vandervelde, "Alcohol and the Social Problem," *Pittsburgh Christian Outlook* 10 (September 1916): 1–3; *United Presbyterian*, "The Police Courts," April 22, 1915; Marsh, *Challenge of Pittsburgh*, 185–89.

26. *Pennsylvania Outlook* 9, "Social Evangelism" (September 1915): 1, 5; *Pennsylvania Outlook* 9, editorial, (November 1915): 4; *United Presbyterian*, "Church Federation in Pittsburgh," July 15, 1915, 5.

27. These denominations were the Baptist, Brethren, Christian, Congregational, Evangelical, Lutheran, Methodist, Episcopal, Methodist Protestant, Presbyterian, German Reformed, Reformed Presbyterian and United Presbyterian. See Philip Mason Smith, "Protestant Comity in Metropolitan Pittsburgh," PhD diss., University of Pittsburgh, 1942, 70–71.

28. *Pittsburgh Christian Outlook* 11, "Great Simultaneous Evangelistic Campaign 1917" (January 1917); W.I. Wishart, "Why the Council of Churches," *Pittsburgh Methodist* 16 (July–September 1927): 5.

29. Carman Johnson, "The Social Service Commission Organizes," *Pittsburgh Christian Outlook* 11 (January 1917): 3.

30. H.D.W. English, "Address to the Churches," *Pittsburgh Christian Outlook* 12 (June 1918): 2–3, 5.

31. *Pittsburgh Christian Outlook* 26, "Is the Council of Churches Worthwhile?" (June 1928): 2.

32. Marsh, *Challenge of Pittsburgh*, viii.

33. Ibid., 1–24, viii (quotation).

34. Ibid., 67–107, 120–24.

35. Ibid., 110–29, quotations from 113–14.

36. Ibid., 211–25.

37. Ibid., 275 (first quotation), 293–97 (second quotation from 297), 305.

38. G. Herbert Ekins, "The Challenge of Pittsburgh," *Pittsburgh Christian Outlook* 11 (May 1917): 5 (quotation); Charles Zahniser, "The 'Challenge of Pittsburgh' Campaign," *Pittsburgh Methodist* 6 (April 1917): 11.

39. Charles Zahniser, "The Pittsburgh Council of Churches," *Pittsburgh Methodist* 6 (October/November/December 1917): 12.

40. *Pittsburgh Christian Outlook* 17, "Prohibition Progress in Pittsburgh" (February 1921): 2; *Pittsburgh Christian Outlook* 19, "Mass Meeting Against Lawlessness" (March 1923): 2 (quotations), 4.

41. *Pittsburgh Christian Outlook* 16, "Statement on Civil Liberties" (June 1920): 3; *Pittsburgh Christian Outlook* 17, "At the Legislature" (April 1921): 5.

42. Flynn, "United Service in Divisive Times," 78–82.
43. Zahniser, *Pittsburgh Council of Churches*, 30–33.
44. *Literary Digest*, "His Honor, the Greatest Gang Leader in the U.S.A." (August 29, 1925): 46.
45. *Literary Digest* 70, "Pittsburgh's Court of Morals" (September 3, 1921): 33–34; Theodore MacFarlane Knappen, "Tempering Justice with Common Sense: Pittsburgh's Experiment with a 'Moral Court,'" *Harper's Magazine* 141 (July 1920): 211 (quotation); Tensard De Wolf, "A Message from the Morals Court," *United Presbyterian*, December 30, 1920, 31; Gertrude Gordon, "De Wolf's Job Is More Difficult than Solomon's," *Pittsburgh Christian Outlook* 17 (September 1921): 6.
46. A.D. Brandon, "Morals Court of Pittsburgh," *Pittsburgh Methodist* 16 (April–June 1927): 11.
47. *Literary Digest*, "His Honor," 45; Knappen, "Tempering Justice," 211.
48. *Pittsburgh Christian Outlook* 11, "The Room Registry" (September 1917): 3; *Pittsburgh Christian Outlook* 13, "Our Hospital Service" (December 1919): 2; *Pittsburgh Christian Outlook*, "New Penitentiary Board" (August–September 1923): 3.
49. *Pittsburgh Christian Outlook* 20, "The Story of the Women's Department of Pittsburgh Council of Churches" (May 1924): 6; Zahniser, *Steel City Gospel*, 39–41, 186.
50. *Pittsburgh Christian Outlook* 12, "The New Negro Population" (February 1918): 3–7.
51. *Pittsburgh Christian Outlook* 13, "New Work for Negroes Established" (October 1919): 3, 5; Will Chappell, "Morgan Community House's First Year," *Pittsburgh Christian Outlook* 16 (August–September 1920): 3.
52. Flynn, "United Service in Divisive Times," 61.
53. Zahniser, *Steel City Gospel*, 88, 94.
54. *Pittsburgh Methodist* 1, "History of the Methodist Episcopal Church Union" (January 15, 1912): 3–5: *Pittsburgh Methodist* 2, "Report of the Superintendent of the Methodist Episcopal Union" (January 1913): 3 (quotation).
55. Daniel Marsh, "The Place, Activities and Relation of the City Societies to Methodism," *Pittsburgh Methodist* 9 (July 1920): 2–5; ibid., "History of the Pittsburgh Goodwill Industries," *Pittsburgh Methodist* 11 (January–March 1922): 2.
56. Zahniser, *Steel City Gospel*, 186; Swetnam, "All Ye that Labor," 452–75.
57. Zahniser, *Steel City Gospel*, 156; *United Presbyterian*, "Market Street Mission, Pittsburgh, PA," April 29, 1915, 4; Ernest Logan, *The Church that Was Twice Born: A History of the First Presbyterian Church of Pittsburgh, Pennsylvania, 1773–1973* (Pittsburgh: Pickwick-Morcraft, 1973), 151–57; Stanton Belfour, *Centennial History of the Shadyside Presbyterian Church* (Pittsburgh, PA, 1966), 32–33, 112–14; *Pittsburgh Christian Outlook* 17, "Dr. Snyder Elected Superintendent" (April 1921): 6.
58. For example: *United Presbyterian*, "The Compassion of Jesus," February 11, 1909, 6. See Wallace Jamison, *The United Presbyterian Story: A Centennial Study, 1858–1958* (Pittsburgh: Geneva Press, 1958), 27, 39, 53, 61, 97, 108, 109, 218.

59. R.A. Hutchison, "The United Presbyterian Church," in Marsh, *Challenge of Pittsburgh*, 269–72; *United Presbyterian*, "The Church and Community Service," April 26, 1917, 4.
60. H.C. Gleiss, "Baptist Churches," in Marsh, *Challenge of Pittsburgh*, 240–44; Walter Hand, "A History of the Background, Development, and Programs of the Pittsburgh Baptist Association," PhD diss., University of Pittsburgh, 1944, 138–58, 166.
61. *The Survey* 45, "Rankin" (November 20, 1920): 269; *Pittsburgh Christian Outlook* 19, "Rankin Christian Center" (October 1923): 1.
62. Zahniser, *Steel City Gospel*, 98, 12.
63. Ibid., 97–98.
64. Ernest Heissenbuttel and Roy Johnson, eds., *Pittsburgh Synod History: Its Auxiliaries and Institutions, 1845–1962* (Warren, OH: Pittsburgh Synod of the United Lutheran Church, 1963); Ambrose Hering, "Lutheran Church," in Marsh, *Challenge of Pittsburgh*, 246–50.
65. Zahniser, *Steel City Gospel*, 206.
66. Flynn, "United Service in Divisive Times," 92.

Chapter 2

1. Rodgers, "Pittsburghers Can Honor."
2. Gretchen Crowe, "Top 10 Catholic Cities, USA," Our Sunday Visitor, https://www.osv.com/osvnewsweekly/byissue/article/tabid/735/artmid/13636/articleid/9926/top-10-catholic-cities-usa.aspx?ref=top10.
3. Mary Ann Knochel, *Roman Catholic Diocese of Pittsburgh* (Charleston, SC: Arcadia Publishing, 2007). Since 1951, the diocese has consisted of six southwestern Pennsylvania counties.
4. James Garvey, "History," Epiphany Parish, https://epiphanychurch.net/history.
5. Paul Kleppner. "Government, Parties, and Voters," in Hays, *City at the Point*, 162.
6. Diocese of Pittsburgh, "A Brief History of the Diocese of Pittsburgh," http://www.dioceseofpgh.org/brief-history-diocese-pittsburgh.
7. Heineman, *Catholic New Deal*, 86–87; Jane Granatir Alexander, "The Laity in the Church: Slovaks and the Catholic Church in Pre–World War I Pittsburgh," *Church History* 53 (September 1984), 363–78.
8. Pritchard, "Soul of the City," 339; Casino, "From Sanctuary to Involvement," *American Catholic Parish*, 1:111.
9. Heineman, *Catholic New Deal*, 88–90, quotation from page 90.
10. John Bodnar, Roger Simon and Michael Weber, *Lives of Their Own: Blacks, Italians, and Poles in Pittsburgh, 1900–1960* (Urbana: University of Illinois Press, 1982), 77; *History of Sacred Heart Parish, Pittsburgh, 1872–1944* (n.p., n.d.), 54–55;

Golden Jubilee of Rev. Thomas Devlin, 1876–1926 (Pittsburgh, PA, 1926), 16–25, 56–57; *Saint Peter's Festival Days, March 18–21, 1989* (Pittsburgh, PA, 1989).

11. Heineman, *Catholic New Deal*, 1, 4–7, 13, xiii (first quotation), 1 (second quotation).
12. Ibid., 15–19, 27–29, 33, quotation from 28; Thomas Coode and John Petrarulo, "The Odyssey of Pittsburgh's Father Cox," *Western Pennsylvania Historical Magazine* 55 (July 1972), 217–38.
13. Heineman, *Catholic New Deal*, 44–45; *Pittsburgh Catholic*, "Bishops Assert Rights of Labor," April 26, 1934.
14. Heineman, *Catholic New Deal*, 46–54.
15. *Pittsburgh Catholic*, December 13, 1934.
16. Ibid., November 21, 1935.
17. Heinemann, *Catholic New Deal*, 109–10, 122. See also Patrick McGeever, *Rev. Charles Owen Rice: Apostle of Contradiction* (Pittsburgh: Duquesne University Press, 1989), and Neil Betten, "Charles Owen Rice: Pittsburgh Labor Priest, 1936–1940," *Pennsylvania Magazine of History and Biography* 94 (October 1970): 518–32.
18. Kenneth Heineman, "Iron City Trinity: The Triumph and the Trials of Catholic Social Activism in Pittsburgh, 1932–1972," *U.S. Catholic Historian* 22 (Spring 2004): 143, 127.
19. Charles Owen Rice, "CIO" radio address, KDKA, 1937, as quoted in Heineman, *Catholic New Deal*, 152.
20. Heineman, *Catholic New Deal*, 210–11, first quotation from 211; Heineman, "Iron City Trinity," 126 (second quotation).
21. Chuck Morris, *American Catholic: The Saints and Sinners Who Built America's Most Powerful Church* (New York: Times Books, 1997), 164.
22. Kelly, *Transformation of American Catholicism*, 60.
23. Ibid., 17–21 (quotation from 20), 62–64.
24. Ibid., 59 (quotation), 40–43, 157–60.
25. Ibid., 86–96.
26. Ibid., 77, 106.
27. Ibid., 108–9, 110, 116, 126, 128, quotation from 108.
28. Heineman, "Iron City Trinity," 132.
29. Kelly, *Transformation of American Catholicism*, 296–97.
30. Ibid., 5, 8. See also Patricia McElligott, *Irish Pittsburgh* (Charleston, SC: Arcadia Publishing, 2013), chapter 4.
31. David O'Brien, *Renewal of American Catholicism* (New York: Oxford University Press, 1972), 3; Jay Dolan, *The American Catholic Experience: A History from Colonial Times to the Present* (Garden City, NY: Doubleday, 1985), 425.
32. Kelly, *Transformation of American Catholicism*, x (quotation), xi; Timothy Kelly, "Essay: Pittsburgh Catholics," *National Catholic Recorder*, May 27, 2009, https://www.ncronline.org/news/parish/essay-pittsburgh-catholics.

33. Kelly, "Pittsburgh Catholics."

34. Kelly, *Transformation of American Catholicism*, 176–77, quotation from 176.

35. See Patti Gallagher Mansfield, *As by a New Pentecost: The Dramatic Beginning of the Catholic Charismatic Renewal* (Steubenville, WV: Franciscan University Press, 1992); Bruce Barron, *Famous for God: Great Christian Endeavors in Pittsburgh, 1952–2018*, chapter 4 (publication forthcoming); Vincent Synan, *The Century of the Holy Spirit: 100 Years of Pentecostal and Charismatic Renewal, 1901–2001* (Nashville, TN: Thomas Nelson, 2012).

36. Heineman, "Iron City Trinity," 134, 123, 138, 122, 142, 143 (quotation). See also Kenneth Heineman, "Model City: The War on Poverty, Race Relations, and Catholic Social Activism in 1960s Pittsburgh," *The Historian* 65 (Summer 2003): 867–900.

37. Heineman, "Iron City Trinity," 142.

38. Diocese of Pittsburgh, "Brief History"; Robert Lockwood, "Reorganization Meant to Ensure 'the Church Alive!'" Pittsburgh Catholic Publishing Associates Inc., http://www.pittsburghcatholic.org/News/reorganization-meant-to-ensure-the-church-alive (first quotation); Peter Smith, "Bishop Zubik: Bishop on a Mission," *Pittsburgh Post-Gazette*, https://newsinteractive.post-gazette.com/blog/bishop-zubik (second and third quotations); David Zubik, "The Church Alive!," Catholic Diocese of Pittsburgh, https://diopitt.org/documents/2017/8/Pastoral%20Letter_The%20Church%20Alive.pdf, 20.

39. Smith, "Bishop Zubik."

40. Zubik, "Church Alive!," 15–16, quotations from 15.

41. Melissa Pravlik, "Top 5: Largest Pittsburgh-Area Houses of Worship," *Pittsburgh Business Times*, http://www.bizjournals.com/pittsburgh/news/2013/12/27/largest-pittsburgh-houses-of-worship.html; David Wilson, "Largest Pittsburgh-Area Houses of Worship," Anglican Yinzer, January 15, 2013, http://anglicanyinzer.blogspot.com/2013/01/largest-pittsburgh-area-houses-of.html.

42. Kelly, "Pittsburgh Catholics."

43. Carol Kuruvilla, "Catholic Church Covered Up Child Abuse by 301 Priests in Pennsylvania: Report," *Huffington Post*, August 14, 2018, https://www.huffingtonpost.com/entry/pennsylvania-report-catholic-clergy-sex-abuse-scandal_us_5b2d4062e4b00295f15c56db.

44. Adalberto Toledo, "Pittsburgh Catholic Diocese Hires Hispanic Outreach Coordinator," *Pittsburgh Post-Gazette*, June 13, 2017, http://www.post-gazette.com/local/region/2017/06/13/Pittsburgh-Catholic-Diocese-Hispanic-outreach-coordinator-jorge-vela/stories/201706080137?utm_source=newsletter&utm_medium=email&utm_content=editors-picks-local-frontpage&utm_campaign=Headlines-Newsletter.

45. Peter Feuerherd, "Pittsburgh Plan Would Consolidate 188 Parishes into 48 Groups, *National Catholic Recorder*, September 27, 2017, https://www.ncronline.

org/news/parish/pittsburgh-plan-would-consolidate-188-parishes-48-groups (quotations).

46. Peter Smith, "Bishop Zubik Unveils Parish Reorganization Plans for Pittsburgh Diocese," *Pittsburgh Post-Gazette*, April 28, 2018, http://www.post-gazette.com/local/region/2018/04/28/Roman-Catholic-parishes-mergers-Bishop-Zubik/stories/201804280011.

47. Smith, "Bishop Zubik"; Lynne Hayes-Freeland, "Bishop Zubik Hopes Merger Will 'Help People See the Focus of Faith,'" *CBS Pittsburgh*, September 18, 2017, http://pittsburgh.cbslocal.com/2017/09/18/catholic-diocese-pittsburgh-merger.

48. Zubik, "The Church Alive!," 1, 2, quotations in that order.

Chapter 3

1. Breanna Smith, "Let's Talk About: Bethel AME Church," *Pittsburgh Post-Gazette*, http://www.post-gazette.com/life/lifestyle/2013/02/07/Let-s-Talk-About-Bethel-AME-Church/stories/201302070577; University of Pittsburgh University Library System, "Free at Last?: Slavery in Pittsburgh in the 18th and 19th Centuries," http://www.library.pitt.edu/freeatlast/abolition.html.
2. Laurence Glasco, ed., *The WPA History of the Negro in Pittsburgh* (Pittsburgh: University of Pittsburgh Press, 2004), 144.
3. Smith, "Let's Talk About: Bethel AME Church"; Glasco, *WPA History*, 364; Dorothy Sterling, *The Making of an Afro-American: Martin Robison Delany, 1812–1885* (Garden City, NY: Doubleday, [1971]).
4. Glasco, *WPA History*, 170, 150, 157, 193 (Douglass quotation).
5. Dennis Dickerson, "The Black Church in Industrializing Western Pennsylvania, 1870–1950," *Western Pennsylvania Historical Magazine* 64, no. 4 (1981): 331; Bodnar, Simon and Weber, *Lives of Their Own*, 74.
6. Sandra Levis, "Race and Renaissance: Showing the Tarnish on Pittsburgh's Gleaming Progress," *Pittsburgh Quarterly* (Fall 2010), http://www.pittsburghquarterly.com/index.php/Book-Reviews/a-checkered-past.html.
7. Lynette Clemetson, "Revival for a Black Enclave in Pittsburgh," *New York Times*, August 9, 2002, http://www.nytimes.com/2002/08/09/us/revival-for-a-black-enclave-in-pittsburgh.html?pagewanted=all.
8. Heineman, *Catholic New Deal*, 76–77; Bodnar, Simon and Weber, *Lives of Their Own*, 36, 159–60, 191, 200, 214.
9. Heineman, *Catholic New Deal*, 77; Bodnar, Simon and Weber, *Lives of Their Own*, 191, 198.
10. Levis, "Race and Renaissance."
11. Bodnar, Simon and Weber, *Lives of Their Own*, 75; *Pittsburgh Press*, "Notes for the Afro-Americans," August 19, 1900 (quotation).

12. Flynn, "United Service in Divisive Times," 89 (quotation); *Pittsburgh Christian Outlook*, "The New Negro Population" (February 1918): 3–7; *Presbyterian Banner*, "The Negro a Valuable Asset" (November 27, 1919): 1.
13. *Pittsburgh Christian Outlook* 12, "Negro Churches Unite for Service" (March 1918): 4.
14. *Pittsburgh Christian Outlook* 24, "Department of Work Among Negroes" (June–July 1927): 2; W.R. Brown, "The Outlook of Our Work in the Morals Court and City," *Pittsburgh Christian Outlook* (June–July 1927): 2, 7.
15. S.R. Morsell, "The Problems and Needs of the Newer Negro Population," *Pittsburgh Christian Outlook* 24 (June–July 1927): 3; Dickerson, "Black Church," 334.
16. Joe William Trotter and Jared Day, *Race and Renaissance: African Americans in Pittsburgh Since World War II* (Pittsburgh: University of Pittsburgh Press, 2013), 24.
17. Trotter and Day, *Race and Renaissance*, 15–16, 24–26, 215; Dickerson, "Black Church," 330–31, 337; Bodnar, Simon and Weber, *Lives of Their Own*, 199.
18. Trotter and Day, *Race and Renaissance*, 15.
19. Clemetson, "Revival"; Levis, "Race and Renaissance." See also Rob Ruck, *Sandlot Season: Sport in Black Pittsburgh* (Urbana: University of Illinois Press, 1987).
20. Heineman, *Catholic New Deal*, 78 (quotation); Bodnar, Simon and Weber, *Lives of Their Own*, 199–200.
21. Dickerson, "Black Church," 339, 341–42, quotation from 342; Trotter and Day, *Race and Renaissance*, 30.
22. Trotter and Day, *Race and Renaissance*, 14, 23, 39 (quotation). See also Glasco, "Double Burden," 70.
23. Levis, "Race and Renaissance."
24. Ibid.; *New Pittsburgh Courier*, "Community Mourns Lavelle," July 14, 2010, http://newpittsburghcourieronline.com/2010/07/14/community-mourns-lavellefamily-leaders-reflect-on-his-life-of-giving; Robert Wauzzinski, *The Transforming Story of Dwelling House Savings and Loan: A Pittsburgh Bank's Fight Against Urban Poverty* (Lewiston, ME: Edwin Mellen, 2003), 77; Trotter and Day, *Race and Renaissance*, 102.
25. Trotter and Day, *Race and Renaissance*, 93.
26. Ibid., 108; *Pittsburgh Post-Gazette*, "Rights Groups Divide on Coordination," September 15, 1967, section 2, page 1; *Pittsburgh Press*, "Realtors Okay Housing Accord," August 9, 1967, 2; *Pittsburgh Press*, "Rent Strike Boils Over at Meeting," *Pittsburgh Press*, July 20, 1967, 9.
27. Trotter and Day, *Race and Renaissance*, 190.
28. Levis, "Race and Renaissance."
29. Clemetson, "Revival."
30. TheHistoryMakers, "Business Makers: Robert R. Lavelle," http://www.thehistorymakers.com/biography/robert-r-lavelle-41; *New Pittsburgh Courier*, "Community Mourns Lavelle"; Chi-Ming Chien, "Robert Lavelle: Dwelling House Savings and Loan," *At the Corner of Church and Market* (blog), https://

churchandmarket.wordpress.com/2013/01/15/robert-lavelle-dwelling-house-savings-and-loan.

31. Wauzzinski, *Transforming Story*, 3, 2 (quotation).

32. Clemetson, "Revival."

33. Wauzzinski, *Transforming Story*, 46, 7, 9, 14.

34. Tim Grant, "Obituary: Robert R. Lavelle," *Pittsburgh Post-Gazette*, http://vwww.post-gazette.com/news/obituaries/2010/07/06/Obituary-Robert-R-Lavelle-Founder-of-Hill-District-s-Dwelling-House-Savings-Loan/stories/201007060168.

35. Chien, "Robert Lavelle"; Wauzzinski, *Transforming Story*, 3.

36. Wauzzinski, *Transforming Story*, 242, 18, quotations in that order.

37. Chien, "Robert Lavelle"; Wauzzinski, *Transforming Story*, 247.

38. Quoted in Chien, "Robert Lavelle."

39. Wauzzinski, *Transforming Story*, 21; Grant, "Obituary."

40. Chien, "Robert Lavelle."

41. Wauzzinski, *Transforming Story*, 19, 97 (first quotation), 105, 152, 36 (second quotation).

42. *New Pittsburgh Courier*, "Community Mourns Lavelle."

43. TheHistoryMakers, "Business Makers"; Legacy, "Robert R. Lavelle," http://www.legacy.com/obituaries/postgazette/obituary.aspx?n=robert-r-lavelle&pid=143958666; *New Pittsburgh Courier*, "Community Mourns Lavelle" (quotations); Thomas Merton Center, "Award Winners," http://thomasmertoncenter.org/about/history/past-merton-award-winners.

44. *New Pittsburgh Courier*, "Community Mourns Lavelle."

45. Tim Grant, "How Dwelling House Went from a Tight Ship to a Bookkeeping Nightmare," *Pittsburgh Post-Gazette*, http://www.post-gazette.com/businessnews/2009/08/24/How-Dwelling-House-went-from-a-tight-ship-to-a-bookkeeping-nightmare/stories/200908240101; Grant, "Obituary" (first quotation); Russ Pulliam, "Old-Fashioned Banker Meets New-Fangled Heist," *WORLD* magazine, http://www.worldmag.com/2009/09/old_fashioned_banker_meets_new_fangled_heist (second quotation).

46. Clemetson, "Revival."

47. Facebook, "Ebenezer Baptist Church: About," https://www.facebook.com/pg/ebcpgh/about/?ref=page_internal.

48. Jim Ritchie, "Church Had Roots in City's Black Community," Pittsburgh History and Landmarks Foundation, http://phlf.org/2004/03/14/church-had-roots-in-citys-black-community; Chris Ramirez, "Pastor Steps Away but Ministry Goes On," TRIBLive, May 5, 2012, http://triblive.com/lifestyles/family/1440717-74/church-winsett-ebenezer-says-pastor-ago-briscoe-cayce-eight-fire; *New York Times*, "2 Firefighters Die in Pittsburgh as Historic Black Church Falls," March 15, 2004, http://www.nytimes.com/2004/03/15/us/2-

firefighters-die-in-pittsburgh-as-historic-black-church-falls.html; Ashley Johnson, "Ebenezer Welcomes New Shepherd After a Year Search," *New Pittsburgh Courier*, November 1, 2013, https://newpittsburghcourieronline.com/2013/11/01/ebenezer-welcomes-new-shepherd-after-a-year-search/2.

49. Ervin Dyer, "Black Churches Banding Together to Battle AIDS, HIV," *Pittsburgh Post-Gazette*, http://old.post-gazette.com/healthscience/20010303churchaids3.asp; *Washington Times*, "Hundreds March from Black Churches in Pittsburgh," January 4, 2015, via AP, http://www.washingtontimes.com/news/2015/jan/5/hundreds-march-from-black-churches-in-pittsburgh.

Chapter 4

1. Michael Sider-Rose, *Taking the Gospel to the Point: Evangelicalism and the Origin of the Pittsburgh Leadership Foundation* (Pittsburgh: Pittsburgh Leadership Foundation, 2000), 15.
2. See Dick B., *New Light on Alcoholism: God, Sam Shoemaker, and A.A.* (Kihei, Maui, HA: Paradise Research Publications, 1999).
3. Helen Shoemaker, *I Stand by the Door: The Life of Sam Shoemaker* (New York: Harper and Row, 1967), xvii.
4. John Woolverton, "Evangelical Protestantism and Alcoholism, 1933–1962: Episcopalian Samuel Shoemaker, The Oxford Group and Alcoholics Anonymous," *Historical Magazine of the Protestant Episcopal Church* 52 (March 1983): 53, 62.
5. Quoted in Shoemaker, *I Stand*, 220.
6. Shoemaker, *I Stand*, 126, 134, 138, 135, 139, 141.
7. *Newsweek*, "Ten of America's Greatest Preachers," March 28, 1955, 56–57; Shoemaker, *I Stand*, 207, 217 (first quotation), 219 (second quotation), 218 (third quotation).
8. Don James, booklet, quoted in Shoemaker, *I Stand*, 203.
9. Sider-Rose, *Taking the Gospel to the Point*, 17–22; *Parade*, "How Pittsburgh Is Building 'a City Under God,'" as printed in *Charleston Daily Mail*, April 8, 1956, 67. See also *TIME* 65, "Religion: God & Steel in Pittsburgh" (March 21, 1955): 53; Pittsburgh Experiment, "30-Day Prayer Experiment," http://www.pittsburghexperiment.org/prayer-experiment.
10. Shoemaker, *I Stand*, 195–96 (first and second quotations from 195, third quotation from 196); *Parade*, "How Pittsburgh Is Building." See also *Christian Century*, "Pittsburgh Experiment Takes Christian Message to Young Businessmen," April 20, 1955, 484.
11. Sider-Rose, *Taking the Gospel to the Point*, 31.
12. Reid Carpenter, "Making Pittsburgh Famous for God," YouTube, April 24, 2015, https://www.youtube.com/watch?v=yMpA0qkTgzY.

13. Sider-Rose, *Taking the Gospel to the Point*, 16.
14. Shoemaker, *I Stand*, 205–7; Sider-Rose, *Taking the Gospel to the Point*, 23–28.
15. Brian Miller, "The Investor: The Pittsburgh Leadership Foundation," Center on Faith in Communities, http://www.centeronfic.org/articles/Pittsburgh.pdf, 148.
16. Sider-Rose, *Taking the Gospel to the Point*, 37–39.
17. Pittsburgh Experiment, "History," http://www.pittsburghexperiment.org/history. See also Peter Smith, "The 'Pittsburgh Experiment' at 60: Making Prayer an Everyday Presence," *Pittsburgh Post-Gazette*, February 22, 2015, http://www.post-gazette.com/local/2015/02/22/The-Pittsburgh-Experiment-at-60-Making-prayer-an-everyday-presence/stories/201502130196.
18. See Ed Wintermantel, "What Do You Say, Reid Carpenter," *Pittsburgh Press*, January 31, 1971, PE Archives 1971, 94, https://news.google.com/newspapers?nid=djft3U1LymYC&dat=19710131&printsec=frontpage&hl=en.
19. Sider-Rose, *Taking the Gospel to the Point*, 71.
20. Miller, "Investor," 148.
21. Ibid., 149.
22. Sider-Rose, *Taking the Gospel to the Point*, 30–31, 37; Ervin Dyer, "25 Years Ago, the Pittsburgh Leadership Foundation Sowed Seeds for Diverse Charitable Causes," *Pittsburgh Post-Gazette*, http://www.post-gazette.com/local/city/2003/11/27/25-years-ago-the-Pittsburgh-Leadership-Foundation-sowed-seeds-for-diverse-charitable-causes/stories/200311270074 (first quotation); Miller, "Investor," 148 (second quotation); Trinity Episcopal Cathedral, Pittsburgh, "Keynote Speaker," http://www.asmuhl.com/pghpc/conference-program/keynote-speaker.
23. Pittsburgh Leadership Foundation, "Mission, Vision & Values," https://plf.org/about/mission-vision-values.
24. Ibid., "Why We're Different," https://plf.org/why-were-different; ibid., "What We Do," https://plf.org/what-we-do (quotation).
25. John Stahl-Wert, "The Untapped Conviction and Belief in This City Personal Transformation," Pittsburgh Leadership Foundation, http://www.plf.org/Resources/Resource/Pdf/PT-01.pdf.
26. Miller, "Investor," 131–32.
27. Ibid., 141–43; Dyer, "25 Years Ago."
28. PR Newswire, "10,000 Wool Blankets Distributed at Pittsburgh Community Storehouse," http://www.prnewswire.com/news-releases/10000-wool-blankets-distributed-at-pittsburgh-community-storehouse-71020457.html; The Education Partnership, "History: Our Story," http://www.theeducationpartnership.org/history.
29. Miller, "Investor," 137–38.
30. Ibid., 133.
31. Ibid., 134–35. Today, the Pittsburgh Kids Foundation runs these programs. See https://www.pittsburghkidsfoundation.org/pittsburgh.

32. Points of Flight, "Reid Carpenter," January 4, 1999, http://www.pointsoflight.org/programs/recognition/dpol/awards/1283.
33. Miller, "Investor," 140–41; Coalition for Leadership, Education and Advocacy for Recovery, "CLEAR's History," http://www.clearrecovery.org/about-us/clear-history; Amachi: People of Faith Mentoring Children of Promise, http://www.amachimentoring.org/index.html.
34. Barbara Elliott, *Street Saints: Renewing American Cities* (West Conshohocken, PA: Templeton Foundation Press, 2004), 174.
35. Pittsburgh Leadership Foundation, *What Is Your Great Purpose?*, brochure, https://plf.org/uploads/2016/07/LC-brochure-2014-web.pdf; phone interview with Lisa Slayton, March 6, 2017; e-mail from Slayton, March 6, 2018.
36. Interview with Slayton.
37. Emily Jensen, "Gathering, Equipping, and Coaching at PLF with Terry Collier," Pittsburgh Leadership Foundation, July 29, 2015, http://plfblog.org/2015/07/gathering-equipping-and-coaching-at-plf-with-terry-collier.
38. Pittsburgh Leadership Foundation website.
39. Interview with Slayton.
40. Ibid. See Jessi Marsh, "Stories of Transformation," Pittsburgh Leadership Foundation, https://plf.org/what-we-do/organizational-consulting.
41. Pittsburgh Kids, https://www.pittsburghkidsfoundation.org (quotation); phone interview with Brad Henderson, October 6, 2016; Pittsburgh Youth Workers Conference, "2018 General Session Speakers," http://www.pywc.org/speakers.html.
42. PR Newswire, "Pittsburgh Leadership Foundation Opens Next Chapter, Launches 'Serving Leaders,'" http://www.prnewswire.com/news-releases/pittsburgh-leadership-foundation-opens-next-chapter-launches-serving-leaders-61838507.html; e-mail from Slayton, March 6, 2018.
43. Lisa Slayton, "Faith & Work 2.0—An Experiment," Part II, Pittsburgh Leadership Foundation, October 10, 2013, https://plf.org/who-we-are/blog/faith-work-2-0-an-experiment-part-ii-2.
44. Interview with Slayton.
45. Darrin Grove, "Stories of Transformation," Pittsburgh Leadership Foundation, https://plf.org/what-we-do/organizational-consulting.
46. Pittsburgh Leadership Foundation, "What We Do: Urban Leaders Project," https://plf.org/what-we-do/urban-leaders-project; ibid., "What We Do: Vocational Learning Community," https://plf.org/what-we-do/vocational-learning-community.
47. *Christianity Today*, "Pittsburgh 2015," http://www.christianitytoday.com/le/live/pittsburgh-2015.
48. Miller, "Investor," 146.
49. Interview with Slayton.

50. Ibid.
51. Ibid.; e-mail from Slayton, March 6, 2018.
52. Interview with Slayton.
53. Leadership Foundations, "Program Overview," http://leadershipfoundations.org/program-overview.
54. Miller, "Investor," 150; e-mail from Lisa Slayton, March 6, 2017.
55. Steve Garber, "The Way the World's Supposed to Be," Washington Institute, November 28, 2015, http://www.washingtoninst.org/10491/the-way-the-worlds-supposed-to-be.

Chapter 5

1. Coalition for Christian Outreach, "About," http://ccojubilee.org/about/who-we-are.
2. Phone interview with Dan Dupee, January 2017.
3. Coalition for Christian Outreach, "CCO History," http://ccojubilee.org/am-site/media/cco-history.pdf.
4. Ibid.; phone interview with Bob Long, June 15, 2016. I also thank Long for reading this section on the CCO and discussing it with me on November 6, 2017.
5. Coalition for Christian Outreach, "Where We Serve," http://ccojubilee.org/about/where-we-serve.
6. Interview with Long; e-mail from Amy Maczuzak, March 5, 2018.
7. Coalition for Christian Outreach, "CCO History" (first quotation); ibid., "What We Believe," http://ccojubilee.org/about/what-we-believe (second quotation); ibid., "About."
8. Coalition for Christian Outreach, "CCO History"; interview with Long; e-mail from Amy Maczuzak, March 2, 2018.
9. Coalition for Christian Outreach, "CCO History."
10. *Christianity Today*, "R.C. Sproul's Testimony," http://www.christianitytoday.com/ct/2002/decemberweb-only/12-30-21.0.html?start=2; Burk Parsons, "R.C. Sproul: A Man Called by God," Ligonier Ministries, May 1, 2007, http://www.ligonier.org/learn/articles/r-c-sproul-man-called-god.
11. Coalition for Christian Outreach, "CCO History."
12. Interview with Long.
13. Interview with Dupee; Coalition for Christian Outreach, "About" (quotation).
14. Coalition for Christian Outreach, "CCO History."
15. Ibid., "Celebrating 40 Years of the Jubilee Conference," booklet, 3.
16. Coalition for Christian Outreach, "CCO History: The Jubilee Conference."
17. "Celebrating 40 Years," 4, 7, quotations in that order.
18. Ibid., 6–11.
19. Jubilee Professional, "About," http://professional.jubileeconference.com/about.

20. See Bible Center Church, https://www.biblecenterpgh.org/outreach.
21. Best Christian Workplace Institute, "Certified Best Christian Workplaces—U.S. 2018," http://www.bcwinstitute.com/bcwlists.html.
22. Coalition for Christian Outreach, "CCO History."
23. Coalition for Christian Outreach, "What We Do," https://ccojubilee.org/about/what-we-do.
24. Coalition for Christian Outreach, "CCO History."
25. Ibid.
26. Coalition for Christian Outreach, "What We Do."
27. Interview with Dupee.
28. Interview with Long.
29. Interview with Dupee.
30. Jessica Whipple, "Renewal and Restoration on Pittsburgh's North Side," Christian and Missionary Alliance, https://www.cmalliance.org/alife/urban-impact-changes-lives; interview with Ed Glover, June 6, 2016; Urban Impact, "Our Founding," https://www.uifpgh.org/about/our-founding (quotation).
31. Urban Impact, "Our Team," https://www.uifpgh.org/about/our-team; interview with Ed Glover.
32. Interview with Ed Glover.
33. Urban Impact, "Our Beliefs," https://www.uifpgh.org/about/our-beliefs.
34. Interview with Ed Glover; interview with Nathan Glover, June 6, 2016.
35. Urban Impact, *Spring 2016 Newsletter*, https://www.uifpgh.org/wp-content/uploads/2016/12/Spring2016Newsletter.pdf; Amy Glover, "Urban Impact Values Our Volunteers!," *Spring 2016 Newsletter*, Urban Impact, https://www.uifpgh.org/wp-content/uploads/2016/12/Spring2016Newsletter.pdf.
36. Urban Impact, "Education Programs," https://www.uifpgh.org/programs/education; Amelia Shuppy, "Literacy Support Program—Pittsburgh Allegheny," *Summer 2017 Newsletter*, Urban Impact, https://www.uifpgh.org/wp-content/uploads/2016/12/Summer2017_Newsletter_Final_Box.pdf.
37. Urban Impact, "Athletics Programs," https://www.uifpgh.org/programs/athletics; interview with Nathan Glover.
38. Urban Impact, "Athletics Programs"; interview with Nathan Glover.
39. Olivia Ska, "2017 Football Clinic," *Summer 2017 Newsletter*, Urban Impact.
40. Cindy Dell, "Celebrating 12 Years of Play Ball for Kids," *Winter 2015 Newsletter*, Urban Impact, https://www.uifpgh.org/publicationsphotos/documents/Winter2015Newsletterv4-ADDTOWEB.pdf.
41. Urban Impact, "Program Options," https://www.uifpgh.org/programs/options; Whipple, "Renewal and Restoration"; Amy Glover, "2015 Weigand Scholarship Award Recipients," *Winter 2015 Newsletter*, Urban Impact.
42. Urban Impact, "Performing Arts Programs," https://www.uifpgh.org/programs/performing-arts; Ruth Cortese, "What It Means to Be a PrinciPAL,"

Spring 2016 Newsletter, Urban Impact; Adam Kennard, "Arts Showcase," *Summer 2017 Newsletter*, Urban Impact.

43. Alex Pursglove, "ManUp Pittsburgh—5 Year Anniversary," *Summer 2017 Newsletter*, Urban Impact.
44. Interview with Ed Glover.
45. Ibid.
46. Jeff Arnold, "One Amazing Mission: Aliquippa Impact," Your Beaver County, http://www.yourbeavercounty.com/one-amazing-mission-aliquippa-impact.
47. Whipple, "Renewal and Restoration"; Urban Impact, "Our Team."

Chapter 6

1. Light of Life Rescue Mission, "History," https://www.lightoflife.org/the-mission/about/history; Robert Schwartz, "Light of Life Celebrates 14th Anniversary," *Pittsburgh Press*, September 25, 1971, https://news.google.com/newspapers?nid=1144&dat=19710925&id=yhwcAAAAIBAJ&sjid=jlAEAAAAIBAJ&pg=7296,1739780&hl=en.
2. Interview with Jessi Marsh, September 26, 2016; Light of Life Rescue Mission, "FAQ."
3. Healing Community Statement on the wall at Light of Life.
4. Light of Life Rescue Mission, "FAQ."
5. Light of Life Rescue Mission, "Men's Residential Program," https://www.lightoflife.org/our-programs/mens-residential. Light of Life participants play in the New Horizons Sports League, which includes teams from the Salvation Army, the Adult Rehabilitation Center, Wood Street Commons and Mon Yough Community Services. See Kaitlynn Riely, "Sports Becomes a Part of Their Journey to Recovery," February 9, 2013, *Pittsburgh Post-Gazette*, via Light of Life Rescue Mission, https://www.lightoflife.org/the-mission/news/news-room/news-releases/news-release-subpage-1.
6. Light of Life Rescue Mission, "Women and Children's Program," https://www.lightoflife.org/our-programs/women-and-childrens; interview with Marsh.
7. Light of Life Rescue Mission, "Women and Children's Program"; interview with Marsh.
8. Light of Life Rescue Mission, "Women and Children's Program"; interview with Marsh.
9. Light of Life Rescue Mission, "Women and Children's Program"; interview with Marsh.
10. Interview with Kate Wadsworth, September 30, 2016.
11. Interview with Marsh.
12. Andrew Goldstein, "Light of Life Shines on Thanksgiving," *Pittsburgh Post-Gazette*, http://www.post-gazette.com/life/holidays/2015/11/27/Light-of-Life-shines-on-Thanksgiving-in-Pittsburgh-s-North-Side/stories/201511270038.

13. Goldstein, "Light of Life."
14. E-mail from Kate Wadsworth, March 27, 2018. Wadsworth read this section on Light of Life in late March 2018 and provided much helpful information.
15. Interview with Marsh.
16. Light of Life Rescue Mission, https://www.lightoflife.org/wp-content/uploads/2016/08/LOL-Summer-News-2016-web.pdf; ibid., https://www.lightoflife.org/wp-content/uploads/2018/02/LOL-WinterNews-2018-FFS.pdf.
17. WPXI News, "Light of Life Rescue Mission Holds Annual Day of Hope Picnic on North Side," http://www.wpxi.com/news/light-life-rescue-mission-holds-annual-day-hope-pi/32148765; Light of Life Rescue Mission, https://www.lightoflife.org/wp-content/uploads/2016/08/LOL-Summer-News-2016-web.pdf; Ashley Murray, "Light of Life Rescue Mission Serves Hot Holiday Meals," *Pittsburgh City Paper*, December 23, 2014, http://www.pghcitypaper.com/Blogh/archives/2014/12/23/light-of-life-rescue-mission-serves-hot-holiday-meals.
18. Light of Life Rescue Mission, "FAQ."
19. Light of Life Rescue Mission, "Annual Report, 2016," https://www.lightoflife.org/wp-content/uploads/2017/09/536385.pdf.
20. Light of Life Rescue Mission, https://www.lightoflife.org/wp-content/uploads/2016/08/LOL-Summer-News-2016-web.pdf; ibid., "Marathon," https://www.lightoflife.org/get-involved/events/marathon; ibid., https://www.lightoflife.org/wp-content/uploads/2017/11/LOL-17-Fall-News-v8.pdf.
21. Light of Life Rescue Mission, https://www.lightoflife.org/wp-content/uploads/2016/08/LOL-Summer-News-2016-web.pdf.
22. Citizens Bank, "Light of Life Rescue Mission Is New Champion in Action in Pittsburgh," April 22, 2009, https://www.citizensbank.com/about-us/news/citizens/2009/04-22-09-pitt-champion.aspx.
23. Murray, "Light of Life."
24. Henderson Brothers, "HBI Cares," https://www.hendersonbrothers.com/henderson-brothers'-day-of-service-at-the-light-of-life-rescue-mission.
25. Light of Life Rescue Mission, https://www.lightoflife.org/wp-content/uploads/2016/08/LOL-Summer-News-2016-web.pdf; ibid., https://www.lightoflife.org/wp-content/uploads/2017/11/LOL-17-Fall-News-v8.pdf.
26. Gene Collier, "A Noble Project," *Pittsburgh Post-Gazette*, http://old.post-gazette.com/magazine/19980823project1.asp; Ann Rodgers, "The Pittsburgh Project: Back from the Brink," *Pittsburgh Post-Gazette*, http://www.post-gazette.com/local/city/2012/08/05/The-Pittsburgh-Project-Back-from-the-brink/stories/201208050203 (quotation); *Pittsburgh Business Times*, "Personalities of Pittsburgh: Pittsburgh Promise's Saleem Ghubril," http://www.bizjournals.com/pittsburgh/print-edition/2016/01/29/personalities-of-pittsburgh-pittsburgh.html.

27. E-mail from Lauren Pfeiffer, February 16, 2016. See also Christian Community Development Association, "CCD Philosophy," http://www.ccda.org/about/ccd-philosophy.
28. The Pittsburgh Project, "Who We Are," http://pittsburghproject.org/about-us-2/who-we-are; The Pittsburgh Project, "About Our Campus," http://pittsburghproject.org/about-us-2/about-our-campus; Rodgers, "Pittsburgh Project" (quotation).
29. The Pittsburgh Project, "Who We Are."
30. Ibid.
31. Ibid., "Service Camps," http://pittsburghproject.org/programs/service-camps.
32. Phone call with Lauren Pfeiffer, March 22, 2018; e-mail from Pfeiffer, March 22, 2018.
33. Rodgers, "Pittsburgh Project."
34. Robin Suttell, "Lakewood Congregational Youth and Pastor to Take Plunge for Summer Mission Trip," *Lakewood Observer*, August 21, 2013, http://lakewoodobserver.com/read/2013/08/21/lakewood-congregational-youth-and-pastor-to-take-plunge-for-summer.
35. Rodgers, "Pittsburgh Project."
36. Interview with Pfeiffer, June 7, 2016; Rodgers, "Pittsburgh Project"; e-mail from Pfeiffer, March 22, 2018.
37. Interview with William Thompkins, June 7, 2016.
38. Ibid.
39. The Pittsburgh Project, "Who We Are."
40. The Pittsburgh Project, *Looking Up Since 1985*, brochure; The Pittsburgh Project, "Service Camps."
41. Rodgers, "Pittsburgh Project" (second and third quotations).
42. Pfeiffer e-mail.
43. LIVING Ministry, http://www.livingministry.org.
44. Northside Common Ministries, http://www.ncmin.org. See also North Side Street Guide, http://www.northsidestreetguide.com.
45. The Pittsburgh Project, "The Pittsburgh Project Appoints a New Executive Director," http://pittsburghproject.org/wp-content/uploads/2018/03/Press-Release-Wayne-Younger.pdf.
46. Quoted in Rodgers, "Pittsburgh Project."
47. Interview with Thompkins; Rodgers, "Pittsburgh Project."
48. See The Philadelphia Project, "About Us," http://www.thephiladelphiaproject.com/aboutus; Aldersgate United Methodist Church, "God's Helping Hands," http://www.aldersgatechurch.net/gods-helping-hands.

Chapter 7

1. Logan, *Church that Was Twice Born*, 23–24, 138, 34, 47–48; University of Pittsburgh, "About," http://www.pitt.edu/about.
2. Logan, *Church that Was Twice Born*, 59, 82, 63 (quotation), 64, 67, 69, 77, 79, 87, 84, 85, 88.
3. Ibid., 92–94, 97–99.
4. Ibid., 105–7, 111, 109.
5. Ibid., 133, 128–29 (first quotation from 129), 134, 150; Joseph Duff, *The Life of Maitland Alexander* (Pittsburgh: First Presbyterian Church, n.d.), 23 (second quotation from Logan, *Church that Was Twice Born*, 150).
6. Logan, *Church that Was Twice Born*, 129–31, 133, 151–52.
7. Ibid., 157, 159–60; Ernest Edwin Logan, *The Church that Kept on Being Born Again: A History of First Presbyterian Church of Pittsburgh, 1773–1997* (Pittsburgh: First Presbyterian Church, 1998), 43.
8. Bradley J. Longfield, *The Presbyterian Controversy: Fundamentalists, Modernists, and Moderates* (New York: Oxford University Press, 1991), 107, 116, 117 118 (quotation), 122, 124; Logan, *Church that Was Twice Born*, 169–89.
9. Logan, *Church that Was Twice Born*, 169–89.
10. Ibid., 194, 197, 201, 205, 213, 215–16; Robert J. Lamont, "The Heart of the Gospel for the Heart of the City," *First Church Life* (February 1954): 9 (quotation).
11. Logan, *Church that Was Twice Born*, 223–24, quotation from 223.
12. Robert J. Lamont, "From the Minister's Desk," *First Church Life* (Spring 1969): 1 (quotation); Logan, *Church that Was Twice Born*, 227–32, 240.
13. Logan, *Church that Was Twice Born*, 60–62.
14. Ibid., 76–80, 84–85.
15. Ibid., 96, 87, 86, 94.
16. Phone interview with Tom Hall, February 15, 2017; First Presbyterian Church of Pittsburgh, "Staff and Leadership," https://www.fpcp.org/staff-leadership; e-mail from Hall, December 11, 2017.
17. Interview with Hall; First Presbyterian Church of Pittsburgh, "Staff and Leadership."
18. Interview with Hall; First Presbyterian Church of Pittsburgh, "Staff and Leadership."
19. Interview with Hall (first two quotations); http://fpcp.org/about-us/our-mission (third quotation).
20. Interview with Hall.
21. First Presbyterian Church of Pittsburgh, "2017 Missions Team Recap," https://docs.wixstatic.com/ugd/3a8051_5c5e4e32e3fd41c2ba97bfbeaf945cb1.pdf.
22. Ibid., "The Cellar," https://www.fpcp.org/volunteer.

23. Interview with Hall.
24. Ibid.
25. Ibid.
26. Ibid.
27. See Logan, *Church that Was Twice Born*, 143–48.
28. St. Paul Cathedral, Roman Catholic Diocese of Pittsburgh, "History," http://stpaulpgh.org/parish/historical-information; phone interview with Kris Stubna, April 19, 2017.
29. St. Paul Cathedral, Roman Catholic Diocese of Pittsburgh, "TV Ministry," http://stpaulpgh.org/ministries/tv-ministry.
30. Interview with Stubna; St. Paul Cathedral, Roman Catholic Diocese of Pittsburgh, "Parish Rector" http://stpaulpgh.org/parish/rector.
31. Interview with Stubna; St. Paul Cathedral, Roman Catholic Diocese of Pittsburgh website (quotation).
32. Interview with Stubna; St. Paul Cathedral, Roman Catholic Diocese of Pittsburgh, "Parish," http://stpaulpgh.org/parish.
33. Interview with Stubna.
34. Ibid.
35. St. Paul Cathedral, Roman Catholic Diocese of Pittsburgh, "Bible Study," http://stpaulpgh.org/faith-formation/bible-study.
36. St. Paul Cathedral, Roman Catholic Diocese of Pittsburgh, "Adult Education," http://stpaulpgh.org/faith-formation/adult-education.
37. Ibid.; interview with Stubna.
38. St. Paul Cathedral, Roman Catholic Diocese of Pittsburgh, "St. Paul's Students," http://stpaulpgh.org/parish/st-pauls-students; interview with Stubna.
39. Interview with Stubna.
40. Ibid.
41. St. Paul Cathedral, Roman Catholic Diocese of Pittsburgh, "Social Service Outreach," http://stpaulpgh.org/ministries/social-service-outreach; Ed Blazina, "Obituary: Sharon Lewis / 'Always Joyful' Outreach Leader at St. Paul Cathedral," *Pittsburgh Post-Gazette*, December 13, 2015, http://www.post-gazette.com/news/obituaries/2015/12/13/Obituary-Sharon-Lewis-Always-joyful-outreach-leader-at-St-Paul-Cathedral/stories/201512130151.
42. St. Paul Cathedral, Roman Catholic Diocese of Pittsburgh, "Respect Life Group," http://stpaulpgh.org/organizations/respect-life-group.
43. Interview with Stubna.
44. Ibid.
45. Ibid.
46. Ibid.
47. Ibid.
48. St. Paul Cathedral, Roman Catholic Diocese of Pittsburgh website.

49. "Calvary Episcopal Church 2013 Parish Profile," http://deimel.org/commentary/b_pages/ccprofile.pdf, 4, 17.
50. Ibid., 4.
51. Ibid.; *Pittsburgh Post-Gazette*, "Rector of Calvary Episcopal in Shadyside Retires: The Rev. Harold T. Lewis Led through Painful Period for Diocese," November 26, 2012, http://www.post-gazette.com/life/lifestyle/2012/11/26/Rector-of-Calvary-Episcopal-in-Shadyside-retires/stories/201211260123.
52. *Calvary Episcopal Church 2013 Parish Profile*, 17.
53. Interview with Jonathon Jensen, October 5, 2016.
54. Ibid.; Peter Smith, "Calvary Episcopal Church Names New Rector: The Very Rev. Jonathon Wesley Jensen Is a Kentucky Native Arriving from Arkansas," *Pittsburgh Post-Gazette*, November 24, 2013, http://www.post-gazette.com/local/city/2013/11/24/Ark-pastor-new-rector-at-Calvary-Church.html.
55. Interview with Jensen.
56. "Calvary Episcopal Church 2013 Parish Profile," 6.
57. Interview with Jensen.
58. Interview with Jensen; Calvary Episcopal Church, http://www.calvarypgh.org/index.aspx?page_id=10&level=3 (quotation).
59. Interview with T.J. Freeman, October 9, 2016.
60. E-mail from Jonathon Jensen, October 11, 2018.
61. Ibid.; Cavalry Episcopal Church, "Serving Our Community," https://www.calvarypgh.org/serving-our-community.
62. Interview with Jensen.
63. Ibid.

Chapter 8

1. Hartford Institute for Religion Research, "Megachurch Definition," http://hirr.hartsem.edu/megachurch/definition.html.
2. Walton, *Story of Religion*, 56.
3. Phone interview with Rockwell Dillaman, September 2016.
4. Allegheny Center Alliance Church, *2016–17 Annual Report*, 2, 12, http://www.acac.net/images/uploads/Communications/ACAC_Annual_Report_Web.pdf; ibid., *2015–16 Annual Report*, 5.
5. Interview with Dillaman.
6. Ibid.; Allegheny Center Alliance Church, *ACAC in 2016 and Beyond: A Vision for Expanded Influence*, 2016 booklet, 12.
7. Allegheny Center Alliance Church, http://www.acac.net.
8. Interview with Dillaman.
9. Pittsburgh Urban Heroes, "Rockwell Dillaman," http://pittsburghurbanheroes.com/2013/heroes/dillaman.html.

10. Ibid.; interview with Dillaman.
11. Pittsburgh Urban Heroes, "Rockwell Dillaman."
12. Ibid. (quotations); interview with Dillaman.
13. Interview with Dillaman; Pittsburgh Urban Heroes, "Rockwell Dillaman" (quotation).
14. Kate Giammarise, "Forgive Us Our Debts," *Pittsburgh City Paper*, September 16, 2010, http://www.pghcitypaper.com/pittsburgh/forgive-us-our-debts/Content?oid=1378284.
15. Allegheny Center Alliance Church, http://www.acac.net/index.cfm/PageID/943/index.html.
16. Allegheny Center Alliance Church, *2016–17 Annual Report*, 8.
17. Ibid., *2016–17 Annual Report*, 6.
18. Ibid., *2016 Fall/Winter Guidebook*, 17.
19. Ibid., *2015–16 Annual Report*, 19–20.
20. Ibid., *2016 Fall/Winter Guidebook*, 18; ibid., *2015–16 Annual Report*, 8; *2016–17 Annual Report*, 12, 9.
21. North Side Christian Health Center, "Who We Are," http://www.nschc.org/index.php/about-nschc-mission/who-we-are. See also Kathleen Ganster, "Resume: A Newsmaker You Should Know/Doctor Mark W. Guy," *Pittsburgh Post-Gazette*, April 3, 2015, http://www.post-gazette.com/local/north/2015/04/03/Resume-A-newsmaker-you-should-know-Doctor-Mark-W-Guy-honored-for-his-dedication-to-patients/stories/201504030029.
22. Giammarise, "Forgive Us Our Debts"; Jesse James DeConto, "Lending with Grace: Breaking the Cycle of Payday Loans," *Christian Century*, June 19, 2012, http://www.christiancentury.org/article/2012-06/lending-grace; Tim Schooley, Neighborhood Alliance: Church on Pittsburgh's North Side Works to Its Community," *Pittsburgh Business Times*, http://www.bizjournals.com/pittsburgh/stories/2009/08/31/focus3.html; Amy Sherman, "An Ichthus in a Sea of Loan Sharks," *Christianity Today*, http://www.christianitytoday.com/thisisourcity/7thcity/loansharks.html?start=1.
23. Women's Choice Network, "About Us," http://mypregnancycenter.org/wordpress/?page_id=2. See also Ann Rodgers, "Women's Center in Pittsburgh's North Side Welcomes Ultrasound Machine," *Pittsburgh Post-Gazette*, August 18, 2012, http://www.post-gazette.com/local/city/2012/08/18/Women-s-center-in-Pittsburgh-s-North-Side-welcomes-ultrasound-machine/stories/201208180103; e-mail from Blaine Workman, November 14, 2017.
24. *Northside Chronicle*, "Nuisance Bar Shuttered after Years of Complaints," http://www.thenorthsidechronicle.com/rebels-closed.
25. Allegheny Center Alliance Church, *2016–17 Annual Report*.

26. Interview with Dillaman; Allegheny Center Alliance Church, *2016–17 Annual Report*; ibid., "Church Planting," http://www.acac.net/church-planting; e-mail from Workman.
27. Interview with Dillaman.
28. Ibid.
29. Allegheny Center Alliance Church, *2016–17 Annual Report*, 2.
30. Allegheny Center Alliance Church, *2015–16 Annual Report*, 21.
31. See F. Roy Coad, *A History of the Brethren Movement: Its Origins, Its Worldwide Development and Its Significance for the Present Day* (Vancouver: Regent College Publishing, 2001).
32. Bill Northrop, "See and Now We Are in the New Building," XP Astor, http://www.xpastor.org/wp-content/uploads/2012/12/2007_south_hills.pdf.
33. The Bible Chapel, *2016 Annual Report*, 4, 13, http://822ab18d4e8207be0029-275d1f2c7551aa7e2a0ece25ec8ebcd7.r51.cf2.rackcdn.com/uploaded/a/0e6086683_1491015895_annual-report-2016-vi.pdf; ibid., "History," http://www.biblechapel.org/about/history.
34. Interview with Ron Moore, October 13, 2016; The Bible Chapel, *2016 Annual Report*, 7.
35. Interview with Moore; Ron Moore, *Worn Out by Obedience: Recovering from Spiritual Fatigue* (Chicago: Moody Publishers, 2017), 180–81; The Bible Chapel, "Ron Moore, Senior Pastor," http://www.biblechapel.org/about/staff/member/1350062.
36. Interview with Moore.
37. Ibid.
38. Ibid.; Tom Fontaine, "Pastors Avoid 'Controversy' to Keep Tithes Up, Author Says," TRIBLive, August 24, 2014, http://triblive.com/news/allegheny/6643510-74/pastors-issues-moore.
39. The Bible Chapel, "Ron Moore, Senior Pastor."
40. Interview with Moore.
41. Back to the Bible, "About," https://www.backtothebible.org/about (quotation); interview with Moore.
42. Interview with Moore.
43. Life Letter Café, "7 Questions Sunday: Ron Moore and Living Grounded," http://lifelettercafe.com/2015/11/7-questions-sunday-ron-moore-living-grounded; Lynda Guydon Taylor, "Room to Pray," *Pittsburgh Post-Gazette*, May 21, 2006, http://www.post-gazette.com/local/washington/2006/05/21/Room-to-pray/stories/200605210226.
44. Interview with Moore; Moore, *Worn Out by Obedience*, 177–86; The Bible Chapel, "Mission," http://www.biblechapel.org/about/mission.
45. Ann Rodgers, "Some Churches Preach Fun to Attract Youths," *Pittsburgh Post-Gazette*, May 6, 2006, http://www.post-gazette.com/life/lifestyle/2006/05/06/Some-churches-preach-fun-to-attract-youths/stories/200605060104.

46. The Bible Chapel, *2016 Annual Report*, 8.
47. Interview with Jaclyn Royall, October 30, 2016.
48. Interview with Royall (quotation); The Bible Chapel, *2016 Annual Report*, 9.
49. The Bible Chapel, *2016 Annual Report*, 8; The Bible Chapel, "Outreach," http://www.biblechapel.org/outreach.
50. Interview with Moore.
51. The Bible Chapel, *2016 Annual Report*, 3; The Bible Chapel, "Care-Giving," http://www.biblechapel.org/connect/care-giving.
52. The Bible Chapel, *2016 Annual Report*, 9.
53. Interview with Moore.
54. The Bible Chapel, "Beliefs," http://www.biblechapel.org/about/beliefs.
55. Interview with Moore.
56. The Bible Chapel, *2015 Annual Report*; *2016 Annual Report*, 7, 11, 15, 26.
57. The Bible Chapel, "About," http://www.biblechapel.org/about.
58. Jay Passavant, "About," http://www.jaypassavant.com/about; North Way Christian Community, "About Us," https://www.northway.org/Pages/AboutUs/HistoryFuture.aspx.
59. Phone interview with Scott Stevens, July 14, 2017; Pittsburgh Kids Foundation, "Scott Stevens," https://www.pittsburghkidsfoundation.org/scott-stevens.
60. Interview with Stevens.
61. Ibid.
62. Interview with Stevens (first quotation); SuperPages, "North Way Christian Community," http://www.superpages.com/bp/wexford-pa/north-way-christian-community-L0003259442.htm (second and fourth quotations); North Way Christian Community, "Who We Are," http://www.northway.org/who-we-are (third quotation).
63. North Way Christian Community, "Connect," http://www.northway.org/connect; ibid., "Care Ministry," http://www.northway.org/care-ministry (quotations in that order); interview with Stevens.
64. North Way Christian Community, "Our Beliefs," http://www.northway.org/who-we-are/#our-beliefs-038-values; interview with Stevens.
65. Interview with Stevens.
66. Ibid.
67. Ibid.; e-mail from Randy Blincow, November 17, 2017.
68. Interview with Stevens; North Way Christian Community, "Small Groups," http://www.northway.org/small-groups.
69. North Way Christian Community, "Outreach," http://www.northway.org/outreach.
70. North Way Christian Community, "Short Term Mission Trips," https://www.northway.org/Pages/Outreach/ShortTermTrips.aspx; North Way Christian Community, "Respite Night Event," https://my.northway.org/portal/event_detail.aspx?id=27560.

71. North Way Christian Community, "Local Partners," https://www.northway.org/Pages/Outreach/lamp.aspx; ibid., "Outreach," https://www.northway.org/outreach.
72. North Way Christian Community, "Local Partners."
73. Ibid., "Serve," http://www.northway.org/campus/wexford-campus/?tab=serve#ministries.
74. Ibid., "Local Partners: Wexford Campus," https://www.northway.org/local-partners/#wexford; North Way Christian Community, "Upcoming Events," http://www.northway.org/events.
75. North Way Counseling Services, www.northwaycounseling.org; North Way Christian Community, "Upcoming Events."
76. North Way Christian Community, "Support Recovery Groups," http://www.northway.org/support-recovery-groups.
77. Ibid., "Care and Counseling," http://www.northway.org/campusministry/care-counseling-at-wexford.
78. SEAPC, "Parenting," http://seapc.org/how-we-serve/parenting.
79. North Way Christian Community, "Short Term Mission Trips."
80. Ibid.
81. North Way Christian Community, "Global Partners."
82. Interview with Stevens; North Way Christian Community, "Who We Are" (quotation).
83. Interview with Stevens.
84. North Way Christian Community, "Who We Are."
85. Interview with Stevens.
86. Student Guide to Pittsburgh, "North Way Christian Community," http://www.studentguidetopittsburgh.com/profiles/North-Way-Christian-Community; North Way Christian Community, "Who We Are," quotations in that order.
87. North Way Christian Community, "Upcoming Events."
88. Victory Family Church, http://www.victoryfamilychurch.org.
89. Victory Family Church, "What We Believe," http://www.lifeatvictory.com/beliefs.
90. Victory Family Church, "Leadership," http://www.lifeatvictory.com/leadership; interview with John Nuzzo, May 9, 2016.
91. Interview with Nuzzo.
92. Ibid.
93. E-mail from John Nuzzo, October 4, 2018.
94. Interview with Nuzzo.
95. Ibid.; Victory Family Church, "What We Believe."
96. Interview with Nuzzo.
97. Ibid.; Victory Family Church, "Small Groups," http://www.lifeatvictory.com/smallgroups; e-mail from John Spencer, November 14, 2017.

98. Interview with Nuzzo; Victory Family Church, "Serve at Victory," http://www.lifeatvictory.com/serve; http://www.lifeatvictory.com/questions.
99. Interview with Nuzzo.
100. Ibid.; Victory Family Church, "What We Believe."
101. E-mail from Nuzzo, October 4, 2018.

Chapter 9

1. Macedonia, Church of Pittsburgh, "Our Story," http://www.macedoniapgh.org/our-story-2; Abby Mendelson, Tim Fabian and Brian Cohen, *Pittsburgh Prays: Thirty-Six Houses of Worship* (Pittsburgh: Three Blind Mice Press, 2013), 99.
2. Macedonia, Church of Pittsburgh, "Our Story."
3. Ibid.
4. Phone interview with Brian Edmonds, July 6, 2017; Macedonia, Church of Pittsburgh, "Our Pastor," http://www.macedoniapgh.org/#!ourpastor2/c14o9.
5. Interview with Edmonds; Macedonia, Church of Pittsburgh, "Our Pastor."
6. Interview with Edmonds.
7. Ibid.
8. Macedonia, Church of Pittsburgh, "Mission, Vision, and Values," http://www.macedoniapgh.org/mission-vision-values.
9. Interview with Edmonds.
10. Ibid.
11. Ibid.
12. Ibid.
13. Ibid.
14. Joyce Gannon, "Program to Aid Citizen Enterprise Helps Nonprofits Tackle the Details," *Pittsburgh Post-Gazette*, August 15, 2016, http://www.post-gazette.com/business/development/2016/08/15/Launched-after-Martin-Luther-King-Jrs-death-Program-to-Aid-Citizen-Enterprise-helps-nonprofits-tackle-the-details/stories/201608140089; e-mail from Trisha Gadson, July 31, 2017.
15. Macedonia Family and Community Enrichment Center Inc., http://macedoniaface.org; ibid., "Family Engagement Services," http://macedoniaface.org/family.html.
16. Ibid., "Family Engagement Services"; e-mail from Trisha Gadson, November 16, 2017.
17. Interview with Edmonds.
18. Ibid.
19. Ibid.
20. Ibid.
21. Peter Smith, "Amid Grief, Worshipers Find Renewal in Hill District Church Service," *Pittsburgh Post-Gazette*, July 11, 2016, http://www.post-gazette.com/

local/city/2016/07/11/Amid-grief-worshipers-find-renewal-in-Hill-District-church-service/stories/201607110030?utm_source=newsletter&utm_medium=email&utm_content=editors-picks-local-frontpage&utm_campaign=Headlines-Newsletter.

22. Marc Mauer and Tracy Huling, *Young Black Americans and the Criminal Justice System: Five Years Later*, The Sentencing Project, October 1995, http://www.sentencingproject.org/wp-content/uploads/2016/01/Young-Black-Americans-and-the-Criminal-Justice-System-Five-Years-Later.pdf.
23. Mount Ararat Baptist Church, "Senior Pastor: Reverend Dr. William H. Curtis" http://www.mt-ararat.org/about/senior-pastor.
24. Ibid., "Church History," http://www.mt-ararat.org/about/church-history; phone interview with William Curtis, May 30, 2017; Mount Ararat Baptist Church, "Senior Pastor."
25. Jacqueline Trussell, "The BNC Interview—Dr. William H. Curtis," Black and Christian, http://blackandchristian.com/articles/exclusives/trussell-02-02.shtml.
26. Interview with Curtis, "BNC Interview."
27. E-mail from Denise Williams to author, June 5, 2017; Mount Ararat Community Activity Center, "About Us," http://www.macac-inc.org/about.html.
28. Mount Ararat Baptist Church, "Counseling Center (MACC)," http://www.mt-ararat.org/ministries/counseling-center-macc; e-mails to the author from Taunya Tinsley, June 11, 2017, and June 12, 2017.
29. Interview with Curtis.
30. Ibid.
31. Ibid.; e-mail to author from Lori Spears, June 7, 2017.
32. Mount Ararat Community Activity Center, http://www.macac-inc.org.
33. Interview with Curtis; Mount Ararat Community Activity Center, "Board of Directors," http://www.macac-inc.org/boardstaff.html.
34. Interview with Curtis.
35. Ibid.
36. GuideStar, "Educational Institutions: The Neighborhood Academy," https://www.guidestar.org/profile/25-1816609.

Chapter 10

1. Quoted in J. Brady McCullough, "Immaculate Reception: The Play that Changed a City," *Pittsburgh Post-Gazette*, September 9, 2012, http://www.post-gazette.com/steelers/2012/09/09/Steelers-Immaculate-Reception-The-play-that-changed-a-city/stories/201209090135.
2. See Dave Branon, ed., *Power Up! Diamond: Devotional Thoughts for Baseball Fans* (Grand Rapids, MI: Discovery House Publishers, 2009); Sports Speakers 360, "Christian

Athletes Speaker Fees," http://www.sportsspeakers360.com/christian-speakers.php?; Kevin Jackson, "Major League Baseball Stars Put Faith in the Spotlight," *Christian Post*, http://www.christianpost.com/news/major-league-baseball-stars-put-faith-in-the-spotlight-26498; Mike Yorkey, *Playing with Purpose: Baseball: Inside the Lives and Faith of Major League Stars* (Uhrichsville, OH: Barbour Publishing, 2012).

3. Baseball Chapel, "About Us," http://www.baseballchapel.org/index.cfm?Fuseaction=AboutUs&CFID=4971012&CFTOKEN=85db94e2a2c396e8-FA0AB18F-060A-FA3B-FFD916EB025A07E4.
4. Reid Cherner, "If You Billed It Around Faith, They Will Certainly Come," *USA Today*, July 21, 2005, http://usatoday30.usatoday.com/money/2005-07-21-faith-night_x.htm; https://theincrease.com/featured-articles/mlb-faith-night-2016.
5. Jack Doyle "'The Mazeroski Moment': 1960 World Series," Pop History Dig, http://www.pophistorydig.com.
6. Ibid.
7. Thad Mumau, *"Had 'Em All the Way": The 1960 Pittsburgh Pirates* (Jefferson, NC: McFarland, 2015), 157.
8. Colleen Hroncich, "A Great Manager, a Great Man," Knights of Columbus, July 1, 2016, http://www.kofc.org/en/columbia/detail/great-manager-great-man.html.
9. Quoted in Colleen Hroncich, *The Whistling Irishman: Danny Murtaugh Remembered* (Philadelphia: Sports Challenge Network, 2010), 239, 242.
10. Dave Maraniss, *Clemente: The Passion and Grace of Baseball's Last Hero* (New York: Simon & Schuster, 2007), 18–19, quotation from 18.
11. *New Pittsburgh Courier*, "Roberto Clemente: The Great One," January 13, 1973, http://www.pbs.org/wgbh/americanexperience/features/primary-resources/clemente-dec-1972.
12. Christian Film Database, "Baseball's Last Hero: 21 Clemente Stories," http://www.christianfilmdatabase.com/review/baseballs-last-hero-21-clemente-stories.
13. Danny Torres, "Roberto Clemente Day," National Baseball Hall of Fame, http://baseballhall.org/discover/roberto-clemente-day.
14. Major League Baseball Community, "Roberto Clemente Day: Honoring the Life of Roberto Clemente," http://web.mlbcommunity.org/programs/roberto_clemente_award.jsp?content=about. See also Phil Musick, *Who Was Roberto?: A Biography of Roberto Clemente* (New York: Doubleday, 1974); Jim O'Brien, *Remember Roberto: Clemente Recalled by Teammates, Family, Friends and Fans* (Pittsburgh: Geyer Printing, 1994); Bruce Markusen, *The Team that Changed Baseball: Roberto Clemente and the 1971 Pittsburgh* Pirates (Yardley, PA: Westholme, 2009).
15. Charlie Vascellaro, "My Clemente: Manny Sanguillen," La Vida Baseball, https://www.lavidabaseball.com/manny-sanguillen-roberto-clemente.
16. *Worldwide Challenge*, "The Happiest Man in Town," August 1973, 33, quoted in Shirl Hoffman, "The Athletae Dei: Missing the Meaning of Sport," University

of Pittsburgh, Program of Physical Education, http://library.la84.org/SportsLibrary/JPS/JPS1976/JPS03i.pdf.

17. Andrea Bosco, "Pittsburgh Pirate Neil Walker and Dad, Tom, Talk Baseball & Their Father-Son Bond," *Whirl* magazine (June 1, 2014), http://whirlmagazine.com/pittsburgh-pirate-neil-walker-and-dad.

18 See John Moody, *Kiss It Good-Bye: The Mystery, the Mormon, and the Moral of the 1960 Pittsburgh Pirates* (Salt Lake City, UT: Shadow Mountain, 2010), 23–24, 37, 100–1, 118–19, 145–46, 179, 181, quotation from 23.

19. Bill Donohue, "Baseball as Bellwether," Catholic League, March 20, 2017, http://www.catholicleague.org/baseball-as-bellwether (quotations). The most prominent Christian Pirate in the early 1970s was outfielder Al Oliver, a seven-time all-star. After retiring from baseball, Oliver became a minister. See Sports Celebrity Marketing, "Al Oliver," http://www.sportscelebs.com/sitebuildercontent/sitebuilderfiles/aloliverchristianweb.pdf; Al Oliver and Andrew O'Toole, *Baseball's Best Kept Secret* (Pittsburgh: City of Champions, 1997), and Al Oliver, *Life Is a Hit, Don't Strike Out* (Laplace, LA: VIP Ink, 2014).

20. John McCollister, *Tales from the 1979 Pittsburgh Pirates: Remembering "The Fam-A-Lee"* (Champaign, IL: Sports Publishing, 2014), 19.

21. George Vecsey, "Religion Becomes an Important Part of the Baseball Scene," *New York Times*, http://www.nytimes.com/1981/05/10/sports/religion-becomes-an-important-part-of-baseball-scene.html?pagewanted=all; William Kashatus, *Mike Schmidt: Philadelphia's Hall of Fame Third Baseman* (Jefferson, NC: McFarland, 2002), 131.

22. Ron Cook, "Tanner Has a Lot of Life Left," *Pittsburgh Post-Gazette*, May 28, 2007.

23. McCollister, *Tales from the 1979 Pittsburgh Pirates*, 150.

24. Dejan Kovacevic, "Obituary: Chuck Tanner/Manager Who Led Pirates' 'Family' to 1979 Championship," *Pittsburgh Post-Gazette*, February 12, 2011, http://www.post-gazette.com/sports/pirates/2011/02/12/Obituary-Chuck-Tanner-Manager-who-led-Pirates-Family-to-1979-championship/stories/201102120181.

25. *CBS Pittsburgh*, "Former Pirates Manager Chuck Tanner Has Died," February 11, 2011, http://pittsburgh.cbslocal.com/2011/02/11/former-pirates-manager-chuck-tanner-has-died.

26. Dan Donovan, "Faith Transforms Foli into a Winner," *Pittsburgh Press*, June 5, 1979, https://news.google.com/newspapers?nid=1144&dat=19790605&id=wY4qAAAAIBAJ&sjid=JVwEAAAAIBAJ&pg=4419,2319563&hl=en (all quotations); Bruce Markusen, "Card Corner–Tim Foli," *Bronx Banter* (blog), http://www.bronxbanterblog.com/2008/11/21/card-corner-tim-foli; McCollister, *Tales from the 1979 Pittsburgh Pirates*, 18.

27. Scott Robertson, "Play or Pray: Decision to Sit Out Difficult and Sometimes Impractical," *Pittsburgh Sports Report*, May 2004, http://www.pittsburghsportsreport.com/2004-Issues/psr0405/04050108.html.

28. Andrew Knox, "St. Louis Cardinals: The Hit Man," Christian Broadcast Network, http://www1.cbn.com/sports/st.-louis-cardinals%3A-the-hit-man.
29. Christian Mingle, "Christian World Series Icons," https://www.christianmingle.com/believe/Christian-World-Series-Icons/#bWfRLp0lWif4CDYR.97.
30. TeleMissions, "Focus on Faith," http://telemissions.com/focus-on-faith. See also *WORLD* magazine, "The 'Hit Man' Returns," September 5, 1998, https://world.wng.org/1998/09/the_hit_man_returns.
31. See Richard Peterson and Stephen Peterson, *The Slide: Leyland, Bonds, & The Star-Crossed Pittsburgh Pirates* (Pittsburgh: University of Pittsburgh Press, 2017).
32. Phone interview with Jay Wilson, September 29, 2016.
33. I am indebted to Wilson for sending me copies of these cards. See also Marvin Olasky, "How Beleaguered Baseball Players Find Inner Peace," Crosswalk, http://www.crosswalk.com/faith/men/how-beleaguered-baseball-players-find-inner-peace.html.
34. Ken Walker, "Jay Bell Again Aims for World Series, While Remaining Steady in His Faith," *Baptist Press News*, February 21, 2000, http://www.bpnews.net/5315/jay-bell-again-aims-for-world-series-while-remaining-steady-in-his-faith.
35. David Peck, "Sid Bream: Faith and Baseball at the Bible Church," *Lovell Chronicle*, March 22, 2014, http://www.lovellchronicle.com/2014/03/sid-bream-faith-and-baseball-at-the-bible-church.
36. Doug Gulasy, "Former Steelers, Pirate 'All In' for Men's Conference," *Pittsburgh Tribune Review*, October 6, 2011, https://www.highbeam.com/doc/1P2-29808401.html.
37. Phone interview with Sid Bream, September 13, 2017.
38. Mike Roteman, *Warning Track Power* (Bloomington, IN: AuthorHouse, 2010), 135.
39. Joseph Cress, "Mt. Holly Springs' Bream Slid His Way into Baseball History," *The Sentinel*, October 6, 2013, http://cumberlink.com/news/local/history/mt-holly-springs-bream-slid-his-way-into-baseball-history/article_90fa40ae-2ecc-11e3-a06e-001a4bcf887a.html.
40. Gary Swan, "Religion Making a Big Hit with Baseball Players," *San Francisco Chronicle*, http://articles.sun-sentinel.com/1990-09-22/features/9002150491_1_bible-studies-baseball-chapel-religion.
41. E-mail from Sid Bream, October 5, 2018.
42. Lee Jenkins, "Welcome to the Bandwagon," *Sports Illustrated*, http://www.si.com/vault/2013/09/09/106367109/welcome-to-the-bandwagon (quotation); Chauncey Ross, "Pirates' Bream to Deliver His Message of Faith," *Indiana Gazette*, April 14, 2014, https://www.indianagazette.com/news/indiana-news/pirates-bream-to-deliver-his-message-of-faith,19685129.
43. TEAMSCI, http://www.teamcsi.biz/index.php.

44. E-mail from Bream, September 12, 2017.

45. Interview with Wilson; Edgard Rodriquez, "Abraham Nunez: God Changed Me," *Deportes: El Nuevo Diario*, circa January 31, 2000. I thank Jessica Taylor for translating the newspaper accounts of Nunez's trip.

46. Joshua Cooley, "Capps Strives to Compete with Class and Dignity," *Baptist Courier*, August 19, 2010, https://baptistcourier.com/2010/08/capps-strives-to-compete-with-class-and-dignity.

47. Jill Ewert, "The Year of the Capper," *Sharing the Victory*, May 2009, https://archives.fca.org/vsItemDisplay.lsp&objectID=E87D16A4-C29E-BBE0-C3BC4868F49F0AB0&method=display.

48. Cooley, "Capps Strives to Compete."

49. Amanda Comak, "Team Spirit and Holy Spirit—for Nationals Religion Looms Large On and Off the Field," *Washington Times*, http://www.washingtontimes.com/news/2013/sep/26/for-washington-nationals-religion-looms-large-on-a.

50. Posted by Jeremy McGarity, "Adam LaRoche Quit Baseball to Follow His Faith, but What He Won't Say Is Heartbreaking," https://jeremymcgarity.com/2016/04/21/adam-laroche-quit-baseball-to-follow-his-faith-but-what-he-wont-say-is-heartbreaking; John Stonestreet, "The Peculiar Story of Adam LaRoche: Walking Away from the Game and $13M," Break Point, http://www.breakpoint.org/2016/04/the-peculiar-story-of-adam-laroche; *Sports Spectrum*, "Adam LaRoche Wins K-Love 'Sports Impact' Award" (June 7, 2016), http://www.sportsspectrum.com/articles/2016/06/07/adam-laroche-wins-k-love-sports-impact-award.

51. Chad Bonham, "A CSJ Conversation with Zach Duke," *Christian Sports Journal*, June 20, 2017, http://christiansportsjournal.com/a-csj-conversation-with-zach-duke; Colleen Kane, "For Faith Day, White Sox Say Come One and Come All," *Chicago Tribune*, August 27, 2015, http://www.chicagotribune.com/sports/baseball/whitesox/ct-faith-day-white-sox-spt-0828-20150827-story.html.

52. Michael Sanserino, "Players' Chapel at PNC Park Draws Faithful," *Pittsburgh Post-Gazette*, August 14, 2011, http://www.post-gazette.com/sports/pirates/2011/08/14/Players-chapel-at-PNC-Park-draws-faithful/stories/201108140146.

53. Matt Gajtka, "Friday Insider: Worlds of Baseball, Faith Mingle," DK Pittsburgh Sports News, July 22, 2016, http://dkpittsburghsports.com/2016/07/22/friday-insider-worlds-of-baseball-faith-mingle.

54. Bruce Darnall, "Pirate Slugger McCutchen Stays Humble Despite Accolades," Athletes in Action, May 7, 2014, http://athletesinaction.org/news/pirates-slugger-mccutchen-stays-humble-despite-accolades (quotation); Popular Pittsburgh, "Pittsburgh's MVP: Andrew McCutchen," http://popularpittsburgh.com/andrew-mccutchen; Andrew McCutchen, "The Faith to Follow Through," *Guideposts*, https://www.guideposts.org/positive-living/andrew-mccutchen-the-faith-to-follow-through.

55. Clay Meyer, "In the Zone: All-Star Center Fielder Andrew McCutchen Breaks Down FCA's 2012 Camp Theme," Fellowship of Christian Athletes, http://www.fca.org/magazine-story/2012/05/01/in-the-zone.
56. Stephen Copeland, "The Mind of McCutchen," *Sports Spectrum* (January 21, 2014), https://www.sportsspectrum.com/articles/2014/01/21/the-mind-of-mccutchen.
57. Darnall, "McCutchen."
58. YouTube, "Andrew McCutchen—My Story," https://www.youtube.com/watch?v=AXRCATcPyPk.
59. Meyer, "In the Zone."
60. Gregory Spaulding, "Cutch in the Clutch," *Sports Spectrum* (Spring 2011), http://www.sportsspectrum.com/articles/2013/10/02/cutch-in-the-clutch/andrew-mccutchen-spread.
61. Meyer, "In the Zone."
62. Darnall, "McCutchen."
63. McCutchen, "Faith."
64. *Sun-Gazette*, "All-Star Outfielder Andrew McCutchen Talks about His Faith," July 18, 2015, htttp://www.sungazette.com/page/content.detail/id/638980/All-Star-outfielder-Andrew-McCutchen-talks-about-his-faith.html?nav=5015 (quotation); Spaulding, "Cutch in the Clutch."
65. Darnall, "McCutchen."
66. *Sun-Gazette*, "All-Star Outfielder Andrew McCutchen."
67. See Crowd Rise, "Cutch's Crew: Pittsburgh 2016," https://www.crowdrise.com/cutchscrewpittsburgh2016.
68. Official Pittsburgh Pirates Website, "Cutch Sets Excellent Example for Young Players," http://pittsburgh.pirates.mlb.com/pit/community/nl_201208_cutch.jsp.
69. Nicole Barley, "Pittsburgh Pirates' Andrew McCutchen: 'Everything Happens for a Reason,'" *Whirl* magazine (June 1, 2013), http://whirlmagazine.com/walk-this-way.
70. Adam Berry, "McCutchen Named Clemente Award Winner," Major League Baseball, http://m.mlb.com/news/article/156011020/pirates-andrew-mccutchen-wins-clemente-award.
71. Meyer, "In the Zone."
72. Bruce Darnall, "Pirates Manager Hurdle Confronted by Tough Love," What Christians Want to Know, June 2015, http://www.whatchristianswanttoknow.com/pirates-manager-hurdle-confronted-by-tough-love.
73. Stephen Nesbitt, "Note to Self," *Pittsburgh Post-Gazette*, http://newsinteractive.post-gazette.com/pirates/2016/clints-climb.
74. Anthony Gutierrez and Mark Ellis, "Pirates' Baseball Manager Floundered until He Came Back to Jesus," God Reports, http://blog.godreports.com/2015/11/pirates-baseball-manager-floundered-until-he-came-back-to-jesus.
75. Ron Cook, "Once a Draft Bust, Clint Hurdle Has Been Pivotal as the Pirates Manager," *Pittsburgh Post-Gazette*, June 9, 2015, http://www.post-gazette.com/

sports/2015/06/09/Cook-Once-a-draft-bust-Clint-Hurdle-has-been-pivotal-as-Pirates-manager/stories/201506090113.

76. Tom Friend, "Love Clint," ESPN, http://espn.go.com/mlb/playoffs/2013/story/_/id/9726637/pirates-manager-clint-hurdle-inspiring-others-daily. See also Jorge Arangure Jr., "Former 'Phenom' Hurdle Finds True Calling as Manager," ESPN, October 23, 2007, http://www.espn.com/mlb/playoffs2007/news/story?id=3075136.
77. Dave Zirin and Tom Krattenmaker, "A Baseball Team Built on Faith," *Los Angeles Times*, http://articles.latimes.com/2007/oct/24/opinion/oe-krattenmaker24.
78. Bob Nightengale, "Baseball's Rockies Seek Revival on Two Levels," *USA Today*, http://usatoday30.usatoday.com/sports/baseball/nl/rockies/2006-05-30-rockies-cover_x.htm.
79. Mark Sanborn, "Clint Hurdle: Leading with Integrity," http://www.marksanborn.com/blog/clint-hurdle-leading-with-integrity. Sanborn is quoting Hurdle's remarks at the church the Rockies manager attended—Cherry Hills Community Church in Highland Ranch, Colorado.
80. Friend, "Love Clint."
81. Vicki Michaelis, "Clint Hurdle Balances Family Concerns with Baseball," *USA Today*, http://usatoday30.usatoday.com/sports/baseball/nl/rockies/2005-09-12-hurdle-family-cover_x.htm.
82. Clint Hurdle speaking at Chippewa United Methodist Church, November 14, 2013, YouTube, https://www.youtube.com/watch?v=F5-bhbhUq-w.
83. Ibid.
84. Nesbitt, "Note to Self."
85. YouTube, "Clint Hurdle—Faith Night at PNC Park," August 1, 2013, https://www.youtube.com/watch?v=mMB_LpYV1qQ.
86. Quoted in Albert Chan, "The Renaissance of Clint Hurdle," *Sports Illustrated*, https://www.si.com/vault/2015/03/30/106752180/the-renaissance-of-clint-hurdle.
87. Rob Rossi, "Pirates' Hurdle Finds Message Polanco Can Believe," TRIBLive, March 26, 2016, http://triblive.com/sports/robrossi/10202774-74/hurdle-polanco-god.
88. Meghin Delaney, "Pittsburgh Pirates Manager Clint Hurdle Inspires Community Leaders at Annual Leadership Prayer Breakfast in Bradenton," *Bradenton Herald*, http://www.bradenton.com/news/local/article34791777.html.
89. Cook, "Hurdle Has Been Pivotal."
90. Quoted in Chan, "Clint Hurdle."
91. Gajtka, "Friday Insider."
92. J.C. Derrick, "Pirates Revival," *WORLD* magazine (September 4, 2015), https://world.wng.org/2015/09/pirates_revival.
93. Brett Honeycutt, "Sports Spectrum's Co-Coach of the Year: Clint Hurdle," *Sports Spectrum* (January 21, 2014), http://www.sportsspectrum.com/articles/2014/01/21/sports-spectrums-co-coach-of-the-year-clint-hurdle.

94. Nesbitt, "Note to Self."
95. Faith in the Game, http://faithinthegame.tumblr.com/post/4638608302/pittsburgh-pirates-manager-clint-hurdle-is-a-great.
96. Darnall, "Pirates Manager Hurdle."
97. Gutierrez and Ellis, "Pirates' Baseball Manager."
98. John Bevere, "Dodgers' Clayton Kershaw Pitches for Christ," *Charisma* magazine (October 4, 2012), http://www.charismamag.com/spirit/devotionals/live-extraordinarily?view=article&id=15632:dodgers-clayton-kershaw-pitches-for-christ&catid=1559.
99. Chad Bonham, "A Conversation with Pittsburgh Pirates Manager Clint Hurdle," Beliefnet, http://www.beliefnet.com/columnists/inspiringathletes/2011/06/pittsburgh-pirates-manager-clint-hurdle-on-spiritual-transformation-dealing-with-criticism-and-sharing-gods-love.html (quotation); Gutierrez and Ellis, "Pirates' Baseball Manager."
100. See *CBS Pittsburgh*, "Beyond the Baselines: A Special Connection with the Pirates on Faith Night," August 3, 2013, http://pittsburgh.cbslocal.com/2013/08/03/beyond-the-baselines-a-special-connection-with-the-pirates-on-faith-night.
101. YouTube, "Faith Night 2015 Video: Pirate Wives Talk About Their Faith," https://www.youtube.com/watch?v=pR6PNgYdvA0.
102. Official Pittsburgh Pirates Website, "Impact of Pirates Faith Night Continues to Grow," http://pittsburgh.pirates.mlb.com/pit/community/nl_201512_faith_night.jsp.
103. The Increase Baseball, "Exceeded Expectations—Pirates Faith Night," July 26, 2016, http://theincreasebaseball.com/featured-articles/exceeded-expectations-pirates-faith-night.
104. Rob Rains, *Intentional Walk: Faith and the St. Louis Cardinals*, Chapter 1: David Freese, Faith Gateway, October 21, 2013, http://www.faithgateway.com/intentional-walk-faith-and-the-st-louis-cardinals/#.V6YHGfkrJdg.
105. The Increase Baseball, "Exceeded Expectations."
106. Gajtka, "Friday Insider."
107. Quoted in Darnall, "Pirates Manager Hurdle."
108. Quoted in Gutierrez and Ellis, "Pirates' Baseball Manager."
109. Michael Sanserino, "Michael McKenry"s Three-Run HR Sparks Pirates," *Pittsburgh Post-Gazette*, August 2, 2012, accession no. 2W63087055576; Michael Sanserino, "Pirates' McKenry Still Working to Prove Critics Wrong," *Pittsburgh Post-Gazette*, March 24, 2013, accession no. 2W6238484329.
110. Melissa, "Faith Night: A Summary and Reflection," *The Nice Guys* (blog), https://theniceguys2013.wordpress.com/2013/08/02/faith-night-a-summary-and-reflection (first quotation); Sanserino, "Players' Chapel" (second quotation).
111. Matthew Peaslee, "Walker's Faith Is Paramount in His Career," *Weirton Daily Times*, January 11, 2016, http://www.weirtondailytimes.com/page/content.detail/

id/656688/Walker-s-faith-is-paramount-in-his-career.html?nav=5014 (quotation); Trent Beattie, "Pittsburgh Pirates' Second Baseman on the Gift of Life: Neil Walker Lives His Faith On and Off the Diamond," *National Catholic Register*, http://www.ncregister.com/daily-news/pittsburgh-pirates-second-baseman-on-the-gift-of-life.

112. Sanserino, "Players' Chapel."

113. Baseball Chapel, "Jason Grilli—Pitcher," http://www.baseballchapel.org/index.cfm?Fuseaction=PlayerTestimonies.

114. Steve Popper, "Baseball: Jason Grilli, 36, Is Unlikeliest of All-Stars," North Jersey, July 16, 2013, http://www.northjersey.com/sports/baseball-jason-grilli-36-is-unlikeliest-of-all-stars-1.712691. See also Jason Grilli, *Just My Game* (Herndon, VA: Mascot Books, 2014).

115. YouTube, Faith Night 2013, https://www.youtube.com/watch?v=8jzjbRwr10o; *Sports Spectrum*, "Mark Melancon—Beyond the Ultimate" (September 10, 2014), http://www.sportsspectrum.com/articles/2014/09/10/mark-melancon-beyond-the-ultimate-by-athletes-in-action.

116. Jason Mackey, "Melancon an All-Star for the Third Time," DK Pittsburgh Sports News, July 5, 2016, http://dkpittsburghsports.com/2016/07/05/melancon-back-to-all-star-game-for-third-time.

117. Ventura County Sports Hall of Fame, 2007 Individual Biographies, www.vcshf.com [cached], http://www.zoominfo.com/p/Joshua-Harrison/1208668568.

118. Gajtka, "Friday Insider."

119. Marissa Payne, "Pirates Sean Rodriguez Tweets Elaborate Apology to Gatorade Cooler," *Washington Post*, https://www.washingtonpost.com/news/early-lead/wp/2015/10/08/pirates-sean-rodriguez-tweets-elaborate-apology-to-gatorade-cooler.

120. Gajtka, "Friday Insider."

121. Joe Trezza, "Rodriguez Has New Outlook Back in Pittsburgh," Major League Baseball, http://m.mlb.com/news/article/247593144/sean-rodriguez-talks-about-car-crash-aftermath.

122. *Pittsburgh Pirates 2016 Community Report*, https://www.digitalpublications-mlb.com/157005/157249/186082/PITCommunityReport2016/index.html.

123. Interview with Jesus Origel, December 1, 2016; Jim Salisbury, "Fueled by Faith, Phillies Closer Jeanmar Gomez Enjoys a Blessed Season," NBC Sports Philadelphia, August 15, 2016, http://www.csnphilly.com/philadelphia-phillies/fueled-faith-phillies-closer-jeanmar-gomez-enjoys-blessed-season; *A Lamp Unto My Cleats* (blog), "Jeanmar Gomez—Joshua 1:9," August 29, 2016, https://alampuntomycleats.com/2016/08/29/jeanmar-gomez-joshua-19.

Chapter 11

1. Rooney as quoted in John-Henry Westen, "A Super Bowl of Faith as Both Steelers and Cardinal Owners Are Deeply Committed Christians," LifeSite, January 30, 2009, https://www.lifesitenews.com/news/a-super-bowl-of-faith-as-both-steelers-and-cardinal-owners-are-deeply-commi; Tunch Ilkin and Damian Williams, *Forged in Steel: The Seven Time-Tested Leadership Principles Practiced by the Pittsburgh Steelers* (Beaver, PA: Minerd Publishing), 11; Rex Rutkoski, "Authors Link Steelers' Values to Community, Family Life," Theta Chi, October 3, 2014, https://www.thetachi.org/news/2015/04/21/national-eagle/life-s-lessons-resonate-beyond-the-football-field.
2. Homer J., "Chuck Noll and His Living Legacy," Behind the Steel Curtain, a Pittsburgh Steelers Community, September 5, 2014, http://www.behindthesteelcurtain.com/steelers-2014-preview-preseason-news-updates-roster-depth-chart-salary-cap/2014/7/24/5919987/chuck-noll-and-his-living-legacy.
3. Arthur Remillard, "Steelers Nation and the Seriously Religious Side of Football," Marginalia: A Review of Books in History, Religion and Culture, http://marginalia.lareviewofbooks.org/steelers-nation-and-the-seriously-religious-side-of-football.
4. Remillard, "Steelers Nation."
5. McCullough, "Immaculate Reception."
6. Remillard, "Steelers Nation"; *USA Today*, "Pittsburgh Newborns Getting Towel Treatment," February 1, 2011, http://web.b.ebscohost.com/ehost/detail/detail?vid=23&sid=b6a79674-1421-4d20-b292-30c585bd565c%40sessionmgr103&hid=123&bdata=JkF1dGhUeXBlPWlwLGNvb2tpZSx1cmwsdWlkJnNpdGU9ZWhvc3QtbGl2ZSZzY29wZT1zaXRl#AN=J0E067968093211&db=aph.
7. Remillard, "Steelers Nation."
8. Gene Collier, "Steeler Nation No Longer—This Is Steeler Planet," *Milwaukee Journal Sentinel*, January 29, 2011, http://www.jsonline.com/sports/packers/114877634.html.
9. Paul Putz and Hunter Hampton, "God and the Gridrion Game," *Christianity Today*, http://www.christianitytoday.com/history/2017/september/god-and-grid-iron-christianity-football.html?utm_source=ctweekly-html&utm_medium=Newsletter&utm_term=9581590&utm_content=535271229&utm_campaign=email.
10. M. Alex Johnson, "In Sports, God Is the Game," *NBC News*, February 4, 2005, http://www.nbcnews.com/id/6876708/ns/us_news/t/sports-god-always-game/#.V5vCIvkrJdg; David Plotz, "Are the Colorado Rockies Blessed?," *Slate*, http://www.slate.com/articles/news_and_politics/recycled/2007/10/are_the_colorado_rockies_blessed.html.

11. *Christianity Today*, "NFL Fumbles Religion," September 11, 2007, via Jesus Christ's Superstars, https://jcsuperstars.wordpress.com/2008/01/03/nfl-fumbles-religion (first quotation); Curtis Eichelberger, *Men of Sunday: How Faith Guides the Players, Coaches, and Wives of the NFL* (Nashville, TN: Thomas Nelson, 2012), 6, 8, quotations in that order.
12. Tom Krattenmaker, "Going Long for Jesus," *Salon*, May 10, 2006, http://www.salon.com/2006/05/10/ministries.
13. See *Christian Steelers* (blog), http://christiansteelers.blogspot.com.
14. Eric Miller, "Why We Love Football," *Christianity Today*, http://www.christianitytoday.com/ct/2007/september/18.26.html?start=5.
15. *Pittsburgh Sports Daily Bulletin*, "Donnie Shell, Steelers Safety, 1974–1987," http://pghsportsdaily.com/2015/03/12/donnie-shell-steelers-safety-1974-1987.
16. Westen, "Super Bowl."
17. Shawn Brown, "Dan Rooney: It's Not About the Money," Christian Broadcast Network, http://www1.cbn.com/dan-rooney-its-not-about-money.
18. On Art Rooney Sr., see Art Rooney Jr., *Ruanaidh: The Story of Art Rooney and His Clan* (Pittsburgh: Geyer, 2008); Rob Ruck, Maggie Jones Patterson and Michael Weber, *Rooney: A Sporting Life* (Lincoln: University of Nebraska Press, 2010).
19. See Dan Rooney, *My 75 Years with the Pittsburgh Steelers and the NFL* (Philadelphia: Da Capo, 2008).
20. Brown, "Dan Rooney."
21. Quoted in Rooney, *My 75 Years*, 248.
22. Andrew Masich and David Halaas, "Introduction," in Rooney, *My 75 Years*, xviii.
23. Catholic Philly, "Pittsburgh Steelers Chairman Dan Rooney, Lifelong Catholic, Dies at 84," http://catholicphilly.com/2017/04/news/obituaries/pittsburgh-steelers-chairman-dan-rooney-lifelong-catholic-dies-at-84.
24. Max Cohen, "Steelers Faithful: 50 Years at Saint Vincent," *Pittsburgh Post-Gazette*, July 24, 2015, Sports, A-1.
25. Ibid.
26. Chad Millman and Shawn Coyne, *The Ones Who Hit the Hardest: The Steelers, the Cowboys, the '70s, and the Fight for America's Soul* (New York: Gotham, 2010).
27. Gary Pomerantz, "The Curtain Falls on the '70s Steelers," *Black and Gold World* (blog), October 2, 2013, http://blackandgoldworld.blogspot.com/2013/10/the-curtain-falls-on-70s-steelers.html.
28. Keith J. Rothfus, Honoring Mr. Charles Henry "Chuck" Noll, of Sewickley, Congressional Record—Extensions of Remarks, June 26, 2014, E1084.
29. Tony Dungy, *Quiet Strength: The Principles, Practices, and Priorities of a Winning Life* (Carol Stream, IL: Tyndale House, 2008), 41.
30. Michelle Bearden, "Dungy Recalls Primary Role of Faith in His Life," *Tampa Bay Online*, http://www.tbo.com/news/dungy-recalls-primary-role-of-faith-in-

his-life-20140507; Maurice Levy and Samantha Stevenson, "Terry Bradshaw, a Candid Conversation with the Steelers' Country-boy, Christian Quarterback," *Playboy* (March 1980); John Franko, "Steelers Coach Chuck Noll: 'He Was Always About Others,'" Catholic Diocese of Pittsburgh, June 20, 2014, http://diopitt.org/pittsburgh-catholic/steelers-coach-chuck-noll-he-was-always-about-others (Zubik quotation).

31. Steve Schaefer, "Tony Dungy: Faith, Philanthropy and a Few Good Money Lessons from Dad," *Forbes*, February 11, 2015, http://www.forbes.com/sites/steveschaefer/2015/02/11/tony-dungy-faith-philanthropy-and-a-few-good-money-lessons-from-dad/#69a5eb0a7ea2.

32. Jim Campbell, "Commentary: Remembering Chuck Noll, the Consummate Teacher," Lancaster County, June 26, 2014, http://lancasteronline.com/sports/pittsburgh/steelers/commentary-remembering-chuck-noll-the-consummate-teacher/article_e7035372-fd9e-11e3-8e44-0017a43b2370.html; Scott Brown, "Remembering Chuck Noll: Their Words," ESPN, June 15, 2014, http://espn.go.com/blog/pittsburgh-steelers/post/_/id/7150/remembering-chuck-noll-their-words (Perles quotation); Mike Bires, "Bishop: Funeral Service Like Noll's Life—Simple, Direct, Positive," *Ellwood City Ledger*, http://www.ellwoodcityledger.com/news/local_news/bishop-funeral-service-like-noll-s-life--simple/article_005f6954-bb0e-5d78-b0b9-9481cac2b918.html (Blount quotation); Paul Zeise, "Noll's Funeral a Final Lesson on Greatness; Simple Ceremony for Former Coach," *Pittsburgh Post-Gazette*, June 18, 2014, Local, A-1 (Thomas quotations); "Statements on the Death of Former Steelers Coach Chuck Noll" (Shell quotation).

33. *Pittsburgh Post-Gazette*, "Patricia Sheridan's Breakfast with…Troy Polamalu," November 8, 2010, ascension no. 2W62954790968 (first Dungy quotation); Leah Marieann Klett, "Super Bowl 50 Breakfast: Tony Dungy Urges Athletes to Make Faith Ultimate Priority," *Gospel Herald*, http://www.gospelherald.com/articles/62047/20160210/super-bowl-50-breakfast-tony-dungy-urges-athletes-to-make-faith-ultimate-priority-if-you-follow-the-lord-youll-be-okay.htm (second Dungy quotation); "Statements on the Death of…Noll" (Bleier quotation); Rutkoski, "Steelers' Values" (Ilkin quotation).

34. Bearden, "Dungy Recalls"; Teresa Varley, "Shell Proud of What Dungy Has Done," Pittsburgh Steelers, August 4, 2016, http://www.steelers.com/news/article-1/Shell-proud-of-what-Dungy-has-done/94feb8e5-8f94-49b9-856a-88b23e8647e0.

35. Interview with Haff; *Pittsburgh Sports Daily Bulletin*, "J.T. Thomas, Steelers Cornerback, 1973–1982," December 16, 2011, https://pittsburghsportsdailybulletin.wordpress.com/2011/12/16/j-t-thomas-steelers-cornerback-1973-1982; Mike Bires, "Hollis Haff: The Steelers' Spiritual Coach," *Pittsburgh Steeler Weekly*, October 13, 1979, 26; Levy and Stevenson, "Terry Bradshaw."

36. Phone interview with Haff, September 14, 2016.
37. Phone interview with Tunch Ilkin, September 21, 2016.
38. Interview with Haff; interview with Ilkin.
39. Interview with Haff.
40. Interview with Haff.
41. Interview with Haff.
42. Levy and Stevenson, "Terry Bradshaw."
43. *Observer Reporter*, "Some Tidbits, and Such, on Super Steelers," January 15, 1980, https://news.google.com/newspapers?nid=2519&dat=19800114&id=H_NdAAAAIBAJ&sjid=Zl8NAAAAIBAJ&pg=1036,1968865&hl=en.
44. Encyclopedia, "Terry Bradshaw," http://www.encyclopedia.com/topic/Terry_Bradshaw.aspx.
45. Levy and Stevenson, "Terry Bradshaw."
46. *Lakeland Ledger*, "Terry Bradshaw's Wife Files for Divorce," August 7, 1980, https://news.google.com/newspapers?nid=1346&dat=19800807&id=5GdRAAAAIBAJ&sjid=NfsDAAAAIBAJ&pg=6595,1673123&hl=en.
47. Cable Neuhaus, "Even Prayer Couldn't Make the JoJo Starbuck–Terry Bradshaw Union a Marriage Made in Heaven," *People*, August 25, 1980, http://www.people.com/people/archive/article/0,20077269,00.html.
48. Elizabeth Forbes, "Terry Bradshaw: Quarterback Scramble," Esperanza—Hope to Cope, August 12, 2010, http://www.hopetocope.com/terry-bradshaw-quarterback-scramble-3. See also Terry Bradshaw with David Fisher, *Keep It Simple* (New York: Pocket Books, 2001), 6–10.
49. Christian Broadcast Network, "Terry Bradshaw Interview," http://www1.cbn.com/700club/interview-terry-bradshaw-0.
50. Jason Leopold, "Army's Prescription to Combat Soldier Suicides: Christianity," *Public Record*, May 11, 2009, https://www.militaryreligiousfreedom.org.
51. Sheldon Ingram, "Funeral Held for Steelers Defensive Great L.C. Greenwood," Pittsburgh's Action News 4, October 7, 2013, http://www.wtae.com/sports/steelers/lc-greenwood-former-steelers-great-dies/22182334 (quotations); UAPB News, "UAPB Officials Remember L.C. Greenwood as Ambassador and Legend," https://uapbnews.wordpress.com/2013/10/01/uapb-officials-remember-l-c-greenwood-as-ambassador-and-legend.
52. Gary Pomerantz, *Their Life's Work: The Brotherhood of the 1970s Pittsburgh Steelers, Then and Now* (New York: Simon & Schuster, 2013), 241, 243–44.
53. Interview with Haff.
54. *Jet*, "Christ, Wife Change Life for Troubled Ernie Holmes" (November 25, 1976): 44.
55. ESPN, "Former Steeler Holmes Called 'Fearsome' on Field, Gentle Off It," January 27, 2008, via AP, http://espn.go.com/espn/wire?section=nfl&id=3217253; Pomerantz, *Their Life's Work*, 242, 244. Roxannafirehall, "The Good, the Bad,

and the Ugly," Going Deep, November 24, 2015, https://goingdeepsteelers.org/2015/11/24/the-good-the-bad-and-the-ugly.

56. Donnie Shell, "Testimony," http://donnieshell.com.

57. Dungy, *Quiet Strength*, 41 (quotation); Tony Dungy, "When Mentors Mold the Man," *Guideposts*, https://www.guideposts.org/inspirational-stories/when-mentors-mold-man?nopaging=1; Tony Dungy, Lauren Dungy and Nathan Whitaker, *The Uncommon Marriage Adventure* (Carol Stream, IL: Tyndale House, 2015), 250; Alex Kubik, "Super Coaches," Our Faith in Action, http://ourfaithinaction.net/2007/super-coaches; *Pittsburgh Sports Daily Bulletin*, "Donnie Shell, Steelers Safety."

58. Rich Emert, "Pittsburgh Steelers: Where Are They Now?: Jon Kolb," *Pittsburgh Post-Gazette*, http://old.post-gazette.com/steelers/20010913where0914p5.asp; Alex Kozora, "Ledyard/Kozora,: Greatest Steelers Offensive Tackle," Steelers Depot, July 16, 2015, http://www.steelersdepot.com/2015/07/ledyardkozora-greatest-steelers-offensive-tackle.

59. *Pittsburgh Sports Daily Bulletin*, "Jon Kolb, Steelers Offensive Lineman, 1969–1981," February 23, 2012, https://pittsburghsportsdailybulletin.wordpress.com/2012/02/23/jon-kolb-steelers-offensive-lineman-1969-198.

60. Pro Football Hall of Fame, "John Stallworth's Enshrinement Speech Transcript," August 3, 2002, http://www.profootballhof.com/news/john-stallworth-s-enshrinement-speech-transcript.

61. John Stallworth, "How I Did It: John Stallworth, CEO, Madison Research," Inc., http://www.inc.com/magazine/20060801/hidi-stallworth.html.

62. Chris Gay, "NFL Hall of Famer Mel Blount Shares His Faith at Augusta Futurity," *Augusta Chronicle*, http://chronicle.augusta.com/sports/futurity/2012-01-25/nfl-hall-famer-mel-blount-shares-his-faith-augusta-futurity# (first, second and fourth quotations); Mel Blount Youth Home Mission, http://www.mbyh.org (third quotation). See also Mel Blount with Cynthia Sterling, *The Cross Burns Brightly: A Hall-of-Famer Tackles Racism and Adversity to Help Troubled Boys* (Grand Rapids, MI: Zondervan, 1993).

63. F. Dale Lolley, "Steelers' Rookies Teach Life Lessons at Blount Youth Home," *Observer-Reporter*, May 28, 2016, http://www.observer-reporter.com/20160528/steelersx2019_rookies_teach_life_lessons_at_blount_youth_home; Abby Dudley, "Mel Blount Youth Home All-Star Celebrity Roast," *Whirl* magazine (April 21, 2016), http://whirlmagazine.com/mel-blount-youth-home-star-celebrity-roast-2016.

64. Amy Worden, "Pols Apart Lynn Swann: With Star Power and a Storied Life of Successes, He Makes First Electoral Bid," *Philadelphia Inquirer*, http://articles.philly.com/2006-10-29/news/25418200_1_bill-scranton-lynn-swann-ridge-administration.

65. Ross Atkins, "Where Are Yesterday's Super Bowl Heroes?" *Christian Science Monitor*, https://www.csmonitor.com/USA/Sports/2013/0201/Where-are-yesterday-

s-Super-Bowl-heroes; Breaking Christian News, "Lynn Swann, Announces Candidacy for Governor—Describes Himself as 'Christian and Pro-Life,'" September 23, 2005, http://www.breakingchristiannews.com/articles/display_art.html?ID=1378.

66. *In Community Magazines*, "Tunch Ilkin: Man of Faith," interviewed by Jessica Marsh (Spring 2014), http://www.incommunitymagazines.com/faithpittsburgh/articles.php?page=archives/manoffaith-sp14.html.
67. Tunch Ilkin, "Faith and Football: Thirty Years Later," Bible Chapel, http://www.biblechapel.org/the-bible-chapel-blog/faith-and-football-thirty-years-later.
68. Ibid.
69. Ibid.
70. Interview with Ilkin.
71. Ibid.
72. Ibid.
73. Ibid.
74. Vincent Man, "Former Pro Bowler Talks Football, Faith," May 18, 2010, http://www.timminspress.com/2010/05/18/former-pro-bowler-talks-football-faith.
75. Interview with Ilkin.
76. Carl Kologie, "Wolfley's Life of Faith Takes Him from Gridiron to Gospels," *Indiana Gazette*, April 22, 2011, https://www.indianagazette.com/news/indiana-news/wolfleys-life-of-faith-takes-him-from-gridiron-to-gospels,98956.
77. *Pittsburgh Sports Daily Bulletin*, "Robin Cole, Steelers Linebacker, 1977–1988," https://pittsburghsportsdailybulletin.wordpress.com/2012/07/03/robin-cole-steelers-linebacker-1977-1988; http://www.teamcsi.org/index.php.
78. Gene Collier, "A Life's Work that Makes a Super Bowl Ring Pale by Comparison," *Pittsburgh Post-Gazette*, http://www.post-gazette.com/sports/gene-collier/2017/02/19; Jim O'Brien, "Ex-Steeler Woodruff Renders Positive Verdict on Life," *Pittsburgh Business Times*, http://www.bizjournals.com/pittsburgh/print-edition/2013/03/15/ex-steeler-woodruff-renders-positive.html?page=2; *Pittsburgh Sports Daily Bulletin*, "Dwayne Woodruff, Steelers Cornerback, 1979–1990," http://pghsportsdaily.com/2016/06/26/dwayne-woodruff-steelers-cornerback-1979-1990 (quotation).
79. *Pittsburgh Sports Daily Bulletin*, "Tim Johnson, Steelers Defensive Lineman, 1987–1989," http://pghsportsdaily.com/2014/06/13/tim-johnson-steelers-defensive-lineman-1987-1989.
80. Jason Keidel, "Bill Cowher, Steward of Steelers' Legacy," *CBS Pittsburgh*, http://sports.cbslocal.com/2017/05/08/bill-cowher-pittsburgh-steelers-coach-60th-birthday-legacy.
81. *Baptist Courier*, "Super Bowl Gives Players, Coaches Faith Platform," February 8, 2006, https://baptistcourier.com/2006/02/super-bowl-gives-players-coaches-faith-platform.

82. Interview with Ilkin.
83. Art Sticklin, "Chaplain Is Fan of Steelers Who Live Out Their Faith," *Baptist Press News*, January 31, 2006, http://www.bpnews.net/22555/chaplain-is-fan-of-steelers-who-live-out-their-faith.
84. Jonathan Barnes, "Power of Steelers' Prayer?" *Barnestormin* (blog), http://barnestormin.blogspot.com/2006/01/power-of-steelers-prayer.html.
85. Steelers UK, "Jeff Hartings," http://www.steelersuk.com/steelers/players/hartings.htm.
86. *Pittsburgh Sports Daily Bulletin*, "Jeff Hartings, Steelers Center, 2001–2006," https://pittsburghsportsdailybulletin.wordpress.com/2012/03/30/jeff-hartings-steelers-center-2001-2006.
87. The Goal, "Jeff Hartings," http://thegoal.com.
88. John Harris, "Steelers Center Jeff Hartings Maintains Perspective, Faith," TRIBLive, December 31, 2006, http://triblive.com/x/pittsburghtrib/sports/s_486451.html, "Jeff Hartings" (quotation).
89. Jonathan Barnes, "Spirit on the Sidelines: Steelers Chaplain Focuses on Individual Players, Not Team Success," *Pittsburgh Post-Gazette*, January 22, 2006, http://old.post-gazette.com/pg/06022/640800.stm.
90. Barnes, "Steelers' Prayer?"
91. Sticklin, "Chaplain Is Fan."
92. Nielsen, "Night with NFL."
93. Mike Mathison, "Former Steeler Hartings Eager to Share His Faith," *Herald Star Online*, April 10, 2014, http://www.heraldstaronline.com/page/content.detail/id/597434/Former-Steeler-Hartings-eager-to-share-his-faith.html?nav=5016.
94. Pro Football Hall of Fame, "Rod Woodson Enshrinement Speech," August 8, 2009, http://www.profootballhof.com/players/rod-woodson/enshrinement.
95. Trent Beattie, "Ex-Steeler Uses Faith to Balance Family and Football: Mark Bruener Finds Strength in Christ," Catholic Diocese of Pittsburgh, http://diopitt.org/pittsburgh-catholic/ex-steeler-uses-faith-balance-family-and-football.
96. Jerry DiPaola, "NFL Players Still Turn to Religion for Solace," TRIBLive, September 19, 2010, http://triblive.com/x/pittsburghtrib/sports/steelers/s_700270.html#axzz3uJMph2nI.
97. Jan Ackerman, "The Steelers' Antwaan Randle El Tells Peters Congregation Bible Is the 'Game Plan of Life,'" *Pittsburgh Post-Gazette*, February 13, 2006, http://www.post-gazette.com/pg/06044/654608.stm.
98. *Sports Spectrum*, "Athlete Testimonies: Antwaan Randle El/Jeff Hartings," http://sportsspectrum.com/resources/testimonies/?by_name=Antwaan+Randle+El+%2F+Jeff+Hartings.
99. *Sharon Herald*, "Randle El Speaks in Grove City," July 2, 2016, accession no. 2W64185323364.

100. Christine Thomasos, "Antwaan Randle El Praying About Long-Term Football Brain Injuries," *Christian Post*, January 23, 2016, http://www.christianpost.com/news/antwaan-randle-el-praying-nfl-football-brain-injuries-green-bay-packers-155675.
101. Ackerman, "Randle El."
102. J. Brady McCollough, "Former Steelers Receiver Antwaan El: 'If I Could Go Back, I Wouldn't,'" *Pittsburgh Post-Gazette*, January 19, 2016, http://www.post-gazette.com/sports/steelers/2016/01/19/If-I-could-go-back-I-wouldn-t-play-football/stories/201601190177.
103. The Goal, "Jason Gildon," http://www.thegoal.com/players/football/gildon_jason/gildon_jason.html; "Graham Kent," http://www.thegoal.com/players/football/graham_kent/graham_kent.html; "Mitch Lyons," http://www.thegoal.com/players/football/lyons_mitch/lyons_mitch.html; "Dewayne Washington," http://www.thegoal.com/players/football/washington_dewayne/washington_dewayne.html.
104. The Goal, "Tommy Maddox," http://www.thegoal.com/players/football/maddox_tommy/maddox.html; "Travis Kirschke," http://www.thegoal.com/players/football/kirschke_travis/kirschke_travis.html.
105. Barnes, "Sidelines."
106. Ackerman, "Antwaan Randle El."
107. Barnes, "Sidelines."
108. Ibid.; *Baptist Courier*, "Super Bowl Gives Players, Coaches Faith Platform," February 8, 2006, https://baptistcourier.com/2006/02/super-bowl-gives-players-coaches-faith-platform (quotation).
109. Art Stricklin, "Super Bowl Players Tell the World's Media of Their Faith," *Baptist Press News*, February 1, 2006, http://www.bpnews.net/22562.
110. Art Stricklin, "Steelers Coaches Cognizant of God's Hand in Their Lives," *Baptist Press News*, February 2, 2006, http://209.157.64.201/focus/f-religion/1571061/posts.
111. Kim Jin-Young, "Super Bowl MVP Hines Ward Confesses Life with God," *Christian Post*, April 4, 2006, http://www.christianpost.com/news/super-bowl-mvp-hines-ward-confesses-life-with-god-1561.
112. Mike Granovitz, "Faith, Fatherhood, and Football," *In Community Magazines* (Summer 2014), http://www.incommunitymagazines.com/faithpittsburgh/articles.php?page+archives/faithfatherhood-su14.html.
113. Art Stricklin, "Mike Tomlin, Steelers Head Coach, Talks about His Faith," *Baptist Press News*, January 29, 2009, http://www.bpnews.net/29752/mike-tomlin-steelers-head-coach-talks-about-his-faith.
114. Rebecca Rollett, "Character (Ac)Counts: Steelers Head Coach Mike Tomlin," Behind the Steel Curtain, http://www.behindthesteelcurtain.com/2013/12/4/5173134/steelers-mike-tomlin-sideline-fine-nfl.

115. Stricklin, "Tomlin."
116. Jerry Pierce, "Super Bowl: Football Fun, but Isn't 'Who We Are,' Steelers Coach Tomlin Says," *Baptist Press News*, February 2, 2011, http://www.bpnews.net/34575.
117. Granovitz, "Faith, Fatherhood, and Football."
118. Interview with Ilkin.
119. Stricklin, "Tomlin."
120. Pierce, "Super Bowl."
121. Jacob Klinger, "Pittsburgh Steelers Head Coach Mike Tomlin Shares Fatherless, Fatherly Perspectives," Penn Live, June 8, 2015, http://www.pennlive.com/steelers/index.ssf/2015/06/steelers_mike_tomlin_manup_fatherless.html.
122. Tom Buehring, "NFL Coach Takes on Human Trafficking," Christian Broadcast Network, http://www1.cbn.com/nfl-coach-takes-human-trafficking?cpid=socclub-fb&adbsc=social_700club_daily75004217&adbid=10155868074681668&adbpl=fb&adbpr=6445306667.
123. Art Stricklin, "Super Bowl: Tomlin Follows Dungy's Lead," *Baptist Press News*, February 3, 2011, http://www.bpnews.net/34585/super-bowl-tomlin-follows-dungys-lead.
124. Teresa Varley, "Smith Remains Goal Oriented," Pittsburgh Steelers, February 5, 2013, http://www.steelers.com/news/article-1/Smith-remains-goal-oriented/ea9f880e-a5c6-41eb-ad2d-6b0dc56f52ea.
125. Stricklin, "Tomlin."
126. Art Stricklin, "Cardinals' Haley Has 'God to Lean On,'" *Baptist Press News*, January 29, 2009, http://www.bpnews.net/29753/cardinals-haley-has-god-to-lean-on.
127. Art Stricklin, "Super Bowl: Steelers' Chaplain Benefits from Coach's, Team's Support," *Baptist Press News*, February 1, 2011, http://www.bpnews.net/34568/super-bowl-steelers-chaplain-benefits-from-coachs-teams-support (quotation); Art Stricklin, "Steelers Embrace New Chaplain," *Baptist Press News*, January 27, 2009, http://www.bpnews.net/29741/steelers-embrace-new-chaplain.
128. Chad M. Johnson, "About," http://www.chadmjohnson.com/contentpages/44489/4175802b-227f-4da6-bc4c-c7df9d919dd9/About.aspx.
129. Jeremy Fowler, "From Couples Counseling to Late-Night Calls, Team Pastor Chad Johnson Is There for Steelers," ESPN, February 22, 2016, http://espn.go.com/blog/nflnation/post/_/id/198468/from-couples-counseling-to-late-night-calls-team-pastor-chad-johnson-is-there-for-steelers (all quotations); Relationships-411, "Interview: Pastor Chad Johnson," https://relationships-411.com/2015/07/08/interview-pastor-chad-johnson.
130. Dani Bostick, "Meet Pittsburgh Steelers Chaplain Chad Johnson," Behind the Steel Curtain, August 12, 2015, http://www.behindthesteelcurtain.com/nfl-pittsburgh-steelers-news/2015/8/12/9134979/meet-pittsburgh-steelers-chaplain-chad-johnson.

131. Christian Broadcast Network, "Does God Care Who Wins the Super Bowl?," http://www.cbn.com/cbnnews/us/2009/february/does-god-care-who-wins-the-super-bowl-/?mobile=false.
132. Art Stricklin and Joni Hannigan, "Steelers' Polamalu: 'Faith Is Foundation,'" *Baptist Press News*, January 28, 2009, http://www.bpnews.net/29748/steelers-polamalu-faith-is-foundation.
133. Christian Broadcast Network, "Super Bowl XLV Media Day," http://www1.cbn.com/content/super-bowl-xlv-media-day (second quotation); Pierce, "SUPER BOWL," (first and third quotations).
134. Rex Rutkoski, "Clergy Draw Parallels between Faith, Football," TRIBLive, February 4, 2011, http://triblive.com/x/pittsburghtrib/sports/steelers/s_721437.html.
135. Ann Rodgers, "Praying Favorites?" *Pittsburgh Post-Gazette*, February 6, 2011, accession no. 2W63612026448.
136. MLive, "Steelers Safety, 8-time Pro Bowler Troy Polamalu Retires," via AP, http://www.mlive.com/sports/2015/04/steelers_safety_8-time_pro_bow.html.
137. Chris Adamski, "Polamalu Intercepted City's Heart by Doing 'Everything the Right Way,'" TRIBLive, April 10, 2015, http://triblive.com/news/allegheny/8145462-74/polamalu-steelers-troy.
138. Ben Maller, "Expert: Tim Tebow Overshadowing Several of NFL's Other Religious Players," ThePostGame, December 6, 2011, http://www.thepostgame.com/blog/dish/201112/nfl-star-beats-tim-tebow-most-religious-athlete-football.
139. David Kamp, "Troy Story," *GQ*, http://www.gq.com/story/troy-polamalu-pittsburgh-steelers-super-bowl.
140. Alex Kubick, "The Bigger Game: Troy Polamalu," Our Faith in Action, February 8, 2009, http://ourfaithinaction.net/2009/bigger-game-troy-polamalu; *Pittsburgh Post-Gazette*, "Patricia Sheridan's Breakfast"; Jim Klobuchar, "NFL's Samson: A Warrior in Prayer," *Christian Science Monitor*, http://www.csmonitor.com/2006/0120/p15s01-alsp.html.
141. Kamp, "Troy Story."
142. Mike Prisuta, "Finally Home: How Pittsburgh Won Over Troy Polamalu," *Pittsburgh Magazine*, http://www.pittsburghmagazine.com/Pittsburgh-Magazine/December-2014/Finally-Home-How-Pittsburgh-Won-over-Troy-Polamalu/#sthash.KxI6tSQL.dpuf.
143. Ann Rodgers, "Troy Polamalu Says 'Kala Christougena!,'" *Pittsburgh Post-Gazette*, January 7, 2011, http://www.post-gazette.com/steelers/2011/01/07/Troy-Polamalu-says-Kala-Christougena/stories/201101070228.
144. Thomas George, "In Faith and Football, Polamalu Is without Equal," National Football League, January 28, 2009, http://www.nfl.com/superbowl/story/09000d5d80e68a8d/article/in-faith-and-football-polamalu-is-without-equal.

145. Terry Mattingly, "Polamalu's Faith, Religion, Spirituality, Whatever," Get Religion, January 15, 2011, http://www.getreligion.org/getreligion/2011/01/polamalus-faith-religion-spirituality-whatever.
146. Christian Broadcast Network, "Steelers Safety Troy Polamalu: Put Pride Aside," http://www1.cbn.com/content/steelers-safety-troy-polamalu-put-pride-aside-0.
147. Rodgers, "Troy Polamalu."
148. DiPaola, "NFL Players."
149. Christian Broadcast Network, "Steelers Safety Troy Polamalu."
150. Gina Mazza Hillier, "Troy Polamalu: The Vertical Game of Football," *Point of Light: Western PA's Journal of Meaningful Living* (Autumn 2006), http://www.ginamazza.com/samples/troy_polamalu_by_gina_mazza.pdf.
151. Hillier, "Polamalu."
152. Gina Mazza Hillier, "Troy Polamalu: Player with a Passion for Jesus," *Pittsburgh Catholic*, January 23, 2009, http://www.olgscott.org/Resources/Articles/Troy_Polamalu_Player_with_a_passion_for_Jesus.pdf.
153. *Pittsburgh Post-Gazette*, "Patricia Sheridan's Breakfast."
154. Rocky Samuels, "Tim Tebow God-Talk Could Be Elevated by Troy Polamalu," Bleacher Reports, January 5, 2012, http://bleacherreport.com/articles/1012272-troy-polamalu-could-elevate-tim-tebow-god-talk-for-steelers-vs-broncos/page/2.
155. DiPaola, "NFL Players."
156. *Pittsburgh Post-Gazette*, "Patricia Sheridan's Breakfast."
157. Hillier, "Polamalu."
158. Gina Mazza, "The Mane Man," *Pittsburgh Magazine*, http://www.pittsburghmagazine.com/core/pagetools.php?pageid=11995&url=%2FPittsburgh-Magazine%2FAugust-2009%2FThe-Mane-Man%2F&mode=print.
159. Jerome Solomon, "Polamalu's Hair Makes Him Easy to Spot, but His Play Is What Makes Him Stand Out," *Boston Globe*, February 5, 2006, http://archive.boston.com/sports/articles/2006/02/05/the_steelers_mane_man/?page=full.
160. Hillier, "Player with a Passion."
161. Amy Frykholm, "The Other Devout Christian on the Field," *Christian Century*, January 9, 2012, http://www.christiancentury.org/blogs/archive/2012-01/other-devout-christian-field; Samuels, "Tim Tebow."
162. Adamski, "Polamalu Intercepted."
163. George, "Faith and Football."
164. *Pittsburgh Sports Daily Bulletin*, "Mike Logan, Steeler Safety, 2001–2006," December 10, 2012, http://pghsportsdaily.com/2012/12/10/mike-logan-steelers-safety-2001-2006.
165. Prisuta, "Finally Home."
166. Karen Crouse, "A Defensive Anchor Walks a Spiritual Path," *New York Times*, http://www.nytimes.com/2011/01/13/sports/football/13polamalu.html?_r=0.

167. Prisuta, "Finally Home."
168. Adamski, "Polamalu Intercepted."
169. David Kuo and Patton Dodd, "God's Quarterbacks: What Tebow and Roethlisberger Reveal about Evangelical Politics," *Washington Post*, https://www.washingtonpost.com/opinions/who-is-gods-quarterback-tebow-roethlisberger-and-american-evangelicalism/2012/01/05/gIQAS6VcfP_story.html.
170. Shaun Brown, "Ben Roethlisberger: Possible Trade?," Christian Broadcast Network, http://www1.cbn.com/thefinishline/archive/2010/04/22/ben-roethlisberger-possible-trade.
171. Beth Stebner, "Steelers Quarterback Ben Roethlisberger Settles Lawsuit with Woman Who Claims He Lured Her into His Hotel Suite and Raped Her," *Daily Mail*, January 22, 2012, http://www.dailymail.co.uk/news/article-2089883/Ben-Roethlisberger-settles-lawsuit-woman-claims-raped-her.html.
172. Tom Krattenmaker, "'Playing for Jesus': The Christian Rise and Fall of Ben Roethlisberger," *Huffington Post*, April 14, 2010, http://www.huffingtonpost.com/tom-krattenmaker/big-bens-fall-from-grace_b_537990.html.
173. David Kuo, "Play for Jesus, Ben," Beliefnet, http://www.beliefnet.com/faiths/christianity/2010/04/play-for-jesus-ben.aspx#Xifd5Au6IQdIes0Q.99.
174. Jack McCallum, "Ben: The Hangover," *Sports Illustrated*, May 10, 2010, https://www.si.com/vault/2010/05/10/105935652/the-hangover-roethlisberger.
175. Bryan DeArdo, "Teary Ben Roethlisberger on Early Struggles: 'I Lost My Soul,'" Pittsburgh Steelers NFL Football News, http://pit.247sports.com/Bolt/Teary-Ben-Roethlisberger-on-early-struggles-I-lost-my-soul—51876133.
176. Kuo and Dodd, "God's Quarterbacks."
177. Michael David Smith, "Religious Roethlisberger Won't Live with Fiancée before Marriage," ProFootballTalk, http://profootballtalk.nbcsports.com/2011/04/07/religious-roethlisberger-wont-live-with-fiancee-before-marriage.
178. DeArdo, "Roethlisberger."
179. Michael Bean, "Super Bowl XLV: Pittsburgh Steelers Tuesday Press Conference—Ben Roethlisberger Quotes," SB Nation Pittsburgh, http://pittsburgh.sbnation.com/pittsburgh-steelers/2011/2/1/1969488/ben-roethlisberger-media-day-quotes-steelers-packers-super-bowl-2011.
180. Martin Fennelly, "Hard to Cheer for Roethlisberger's So-Called Redemption," *Tampa Bay Online*, February 1, 2011, http://www.tbo.com/list/sports-columns-mfennelly/hard-to-cheer-for-roethlisbergers-so-called-redemption-10903.
181. Cathy Lynn Grossman, "Can Sheen, Lohan Follow Roethlisberger Path to Piety?" *USA Today*, February 6, 2011, http://content.usatoday.com/communities/Religion/post/2011/02/ben-roethlisberger-steelers-charlie-sheen-lindsay-lohan-/1#.V2FObLsrJdg.
182. DeArdo, "Roethlisberger."

183. Joanne Klimovich Harrop, "Roethlisberger, Fiancée Find Acceptance at Christ Church," TRIBLive, July 18, 2011, http://triblive.com/x/pittsburghtrib/sports/steelers/s_747216.html.
184. Dan Pompel, "How Ben Roethlisberger Grew Up and Became One of the NFL's Great Teammates," Bleacher Report, August 6, 2015, http://bleacherreport.com/articles/2505720-how-ben-roethlisberger-grew-up-and-became-one-of-the-nfls-great-teammates.
185. DeArdo, "Roethlisberger."
186. Shawn Brown, "Steelers' Defensive End: Aaron Smith," Christian Broadcast Network, http://www1.cbn.com/steelers-defensive-end-aaron-smith.
187. John Romano, "Son's Fight with Leukemia Holds Lessons for Pittsburgh Steelers' Aaron Smith," *Tampa Bay Times*, January 25, 2009, http://www.tampabay.com/sports/sons-fight-with-leukemia-holds-lessons-for-pittsburgh-steelers-aaron-smith/970454.
188. DiPaola, "NFL Players."
189. "Steelers' Daniel Sepulveda Talks Super Bowl XLV," Beliefnet, http://www.beliefnet.com/entertainment/2011/01/steelers-punter-daniel-sepulveda-talks-super-bowl-xlv.aspx?p=2.
190. Scott Brown, "Steelers Couldn't Resist Punter Sepulveda's Powerful Leg," TRIBLive, June 3, 2007, http://triblive.com/x/pittsburghtrib/sports/steelers/s_510761.html.
191. Lee Kann, "Observations from the Edge: GOD…and the NFL," *New Pittsburgh Courier*, January 12, 2016, http://newpittsburghcourieronline.com/2016/01/12/observations-from-the-edge-godand-the-nfl; Christian Broadcast Network, "Kelvin Beachum: Pittsburgh Steelers Lineman Is a Force to Be Reckoned With," http://www1.cbn.com/video/pittsburgh-steelers-lineman-is-a-force-to-be-reckoned-with (quotation).
192. Kelvin Beachum for Bread for the World, bread@bread.org.
193. Pittsburgh Steelers, "Inside the Steeler Locker Room," October 18, 2015, http://www.steelers.com/news/article-1/Inside-the-Steelers-locker-room/2cc0e8e8-344c-438a-aea8-0a02d121c199; Emily Pierce, "Can Faith Carry Landry Jones and Pittsburgh Past the Cleveland Browns?" The Inquisitr, http://www.inquisitr.com/2561148/can-faith-carry-landry-jones-and-pittsburgh-past-the-cleveland-browns (first quotation); Jeremy Fowler, "Meet Landry Jones," ESPN, November 8, 2015, http://espn.go.com/blog/pittsburgh-steelers/post/_/id/15833/meet-landry-jones-new-mexico-qb-husband-to-sooners-hoops-star-devout-christian; Cyd Ziegler, "Steelers Quarterback Landry Jones Talks about His Religion and Gay Athletes," Out Sports, May 22, 2013, http://www.outsports.com/2013/5/22/4356344/landry-jones-gay-christian-pittsburgh-steelers-nflpa (second quotation); I Am Second, "Landry Jones," http://www.iamsecond.com/seconds/landry-jones.

194. John Franko, "Faith Warrior: Steelers Lineman Builds Ties to God," Catholic Diocese of Pittsburgh, February 19, 2016, http://diopitt.org/latest-diocesan-news/faith-warrior-steelers-lineman-builds-ties-god.
195. Steelers Universe, "Steelers Universe Exclusive Interview with Antonio Brown," July 26, 2011, http://www.steelersuniverse.com/forums/showthread.php/8723-Steelers-Universe-Exclusive-Interview-With-Antonio-Brown-July-26-2011 (quotations); Peggy Bickerstaff, "Steelers Antonio Brown: Anatomy of a Fighter," Still Curtain, July 28, 2015, https://stillcurtain.com/2015/07/28/steelers-antonio-brown-anatomy-fighter; Stacy Carey, "Who Is Antonio Brown of Dancing with the Stars?" The Inquisitr, March 5, 2016, http://www.inquisitr.com/2858036/who-is-antonio-brown-of-dancing-with-the-stars-season-22.
196. *CBS Pittsburgh*, "Steelers WR Brown Has Taken Tough Road to Stardom," via AP, February 3, 2011, http://dfw.cbslocal.com/2011/02/03/steelers-wr-brown-has-taken-tough-road-to-stardom.
197. Twitter, Antonio Brown (@AB84), August 15, 2011, https://twitter.com/antoniobrown84/status/103078111729561600; STACK, "15 Things You Need to Know About Antonio Brown," March 10, 2015, http://www.stack.com/a/antonio-brown.
198. Gary Pomerantz, "Joe Greene, and the Three Who Aren't There," *Sports Illustrated—Pro Football*, October 31, 2014, http://mmqb.si.com/2014/10/31/joe-greene-steel-curtain-front-four-gary-pomerantz.
199. Miller, "Why We Love Football."

Chapter 12

1. Amalie Benjamin, "Religion Rarely on Display Across the NHL," *Boston Globe*, April 5, 2015, https://www.bostonglobe.com/sports/2015/04/05/religion-not-often-display-nhl/TgROsmqu1gFE4IIhB1thOO/story.html.
2. Greg Wyshynski, "Ex-NHLer Says Hockey's the Sport Least Influenced by Christianity," Yahoo! Sports, June 12, 2008, https://sports.yahoo.com/nhl/blog/puck_daddy/post/Ex-NHLer-says-hockey-s-the-sport-least-influence?urn=nhl,87601.
3. Jamie Hall, "Christians in the Hockey Coliseum: National Hockey League Tentatively Embraces Players' Religion," *Calgary Herald*, April 21, 2013, http://www.calgaryherald.com/life/Christians+hockey+coliseum+National+Hockey+League+tentatively+embraces+players+religion/8273238/story.html.
4. Benjamin, "Religion."
5. Daniel Schopf, "Religion in Hockey Part One: NHL Players," The Hockey Writers, November 12, 2012, http://thehockeywriters.com/religion-in-hockey-part-one-nhl-players.

6. Quoted in Benjamin, "Religion."
7. Jim Coggins, "Being a Christian in Pro Hockey Can Be Tough," Canadian Christianity, https://canadianchristianity.com/bc/bccn/0909/26tough.html.
8. Benjamin, "Religion."
9. Chad Bonham, "A Conversation with Minnesota Wild Center Matt Cullen," Beliefnet, http://www.beliefnet.com/columnists/inspiringathletes/2013/05/a-conversation-with-minnesota-wild-center-matt-cullen.html.
10. Benjamin, "Religion."
11. Hall, "Hockey Coliseum"; Benjamin, "Religion" (quotation)
12. Phone interview with Hollis Haff, September 14, 2016.
13. Hall, "Hockey Coliseum" (quotation); Benjamin, "Religion."
14. Benjamin, "Religion."
15. Bonham, "Conversation."
16. Ibid.; Benjamin, "Religion."
17. Beyond the Ultimate, "Mike Rupp," http://www.beyondtheultimate.com/athlete/Mike-Rupp.
18. Hall, "Hockey Coliseum."
19. Dan Bylsma and Jay Bylsma, *So Your Son Wants to Play in the NHL* (Chelsea, MI: Sleeping Bear Press, 1998), 77–78.
20. Dan Bylsma and Jay Bylsma, *So You Want to Play in the NHL: A Guide for Young Players* (Chicago: Contemporary Books, 2001), 31, 33.
21. J. Brady McCollough, "Blysma's Drive, Spirit May Win Over American Fans," BCSN Gameday Nation, February 13, 2014, http://www.bcsn.tv/news_article/show/349469; Jason Mackey, "For Many, Bylsma Served as More than Just Penguins' Coach," TRIBLive, June 14, 2014, http://triblive.com/sports/penguins/6269240-74/bylsma-coach-hockey; Joe Starkey, "The Book on Penguins Coach Bylsma," TRIBLive, April 12, 2009, http://triblive.com/x/pittsburghtrib/sports/penguins/s_620304.html (quotation).
22. Starkey, "Penguins Coach Bylsma." See also Bucky Gleason, "Backyard to Big Time: How Hard Work Drove Dan Bylsma to NHL Success," *Buffalo News*, Hockey, https://buffalonews.com/2015/08/21/backyard-to-big-time-how-hard-work-drove-dan-bylsma-to-nhl-success.
23. Bylsma and Bylsma, *You Want to Play*, 205–8, quotation from 208.
24. Bonham, "Conversation."
25. NESN, "Max Talbot Brings Positive Energy, Character to Boston Bruins," March 7, 2015, https://nesn.com/2015/03/max-talbot-bringing-positive-energy-character-to-boston-bruins-video.
26. Jason Seidling, "Talbot's Visit to Hillman Cancer Center Puts Smiles on Patients' Faces," National Hockey League, October 18, 2010, https://www.nhl.com/penguins/news/talbots-visit-to-hillman-cancer-center-puts-smiles-on-patients-faces/c-540857.

27. David Cabrera, "Max Talbot & Cynthia Phaneuf Canada's Coolest Parents On and Off the Ice," Garden of Life, December 20, 2015, https://www.gardenoflife.com/content/max-talbot-cynthia-phaneuf-canadas-coolest-parents-off-ice.
28. Scott Taylor, "More to Life than Hockey," Promise Keepers, September 2013, http://www.promisekeepers.ca/articles/more-to-life-than-hockey.
29. Bonham, "Conversation" (all quotations); Christian Broadcast Network, "NHL Champion Checks Fear of Failure," http://www1.cbn.com/content/nhl-champion-checks-fear-failure.
30. Beyond the Ultimate, "Mike Rupp."
31. Joe Vitale in *Play to Win: Hockey New Testament* (Carol Stream, IL: Tyndale House, 2013), unnumbered page between 175 and 176. See also JoAnne Viviano, "Many Players in Professional Hockey Find Solace with God," *Columbus Dispatch*, http://www.dispatch.com/content/stories/local/2015/01/21/locker-room-faith.html.
32. Christopher Page, "Christians in the NHL Playoffs—the Staal Brothers," http://christopherapage.com/uncategorized/christians-in-the-nhl-playoffs-the-staal-brothers; Phil de Haan, "CRC Man Wins Hockey's Highest Prize," *The Banner*, January 18, 2011, http://www.thebanner.org/news/2011/01/crc-man-wins-hockey-s-highest-prize; Jayne Thurber-Smith, "Focused on the Goal," *Salvationist*, http://salvationist.ca/2013/05/focused-on-the-goal.
33. "Jordan Staal—Upbringing & Favorite Bible Verse," Hockey Ministries International, December 1, 2016, https://www.hockeyministries.org/home-ice/videos/category/player-stories.
34. YouTube, "Jordan Staal—My Identity Is Found in Jesus," September 13, 2016, www.youtube.com/watch?v=Xnanqq6BBFA.
35. Doug Smith Live, "Matt Cooke," http://dougsmithlive.com/matt-cooke.
36. Jesse Marx, "Matt Cooke: The Soul of an Agitator," City Pages, October 2, 2013, http://www.citypages.com/news/matt-cooke-the-soul-of-an-agitator-6771025.
37. Matt Cooke interview with Doug Melder, November 11, 2012, Doug Smith Live, http://dougsmithlive.com/matt-cooke.
38. Cooke interview; Greg Wyshynski, "Wife's Health Scare Made Penguins' Matt Cooke a Changed Man," Yahoo! Sports, August 24, 2011, http://sports.yahoo.com/nhl/blog/puck_daddy/post/wifes-health-scare-made-penguins-matt-cooke-a-changed-man?urn=nhl,wp11087; Joel Peretic, "A New Recipe for Cooke," *Pittsburgh Sports Report*, December 31, 2012, http://www.pittsburghsportsreport.com/PSR/node/5248 (quotation).
39. Cooke interview.
40. Marx, "Matt Cooke."
41. Smith, "Matt Cooke."
42. Peretic, "New Recipe." After playing three years without being suspended, Cooke, while with Minnesota, had a knee-on-knee hit against defenseman Tyson Barrie that put him out for several weeks and resulted in a seven-game suspension. This caused

many to question whether Cooke had truly changed. See Dave Lozo, "Matt Cooke Suspension Will Serve as Reminder of Hockey's Perpetual Dark Side," Bleacher Report, April 23, 2014, http://bleacherreport.com/articles/2039649-matt-cooke-suspension-will-serve-as-reminder-of-hockeys-perpetual-dark-side. Cooke insisted that "it was not my intent to collide with him knee-on-knee. It was my intent to finish my check. Since March 20, 2011 [the elbow to Ryan McDonagh that resulted in a seventeen-game suspension], I've approached the game differently....The stats that I've collected over those three seasons prove that I'm a changed player." What happened "was not my intent." Quoted in Michael Russo, "Matt Cooke Makes Statement Regarding 7-Game Suspension," *StarTribune*, http://www.startribune.com/wild-s-matt-cooke-speaks-about-seven-game-nhl-suspension/256566441.

43. Shelly Anderson, "Three Pittsburgh Athletes Find Friendship and Hope among the Young Survivors of a Devastating Haiti Earthquake," *Pittsburgh Post-Gazette*, August 26, 2010, http://www.post-gazette.com/sports/penguins/2010/08/26/Three-Pittsburgh-athletes-find-friendship-and-hope-among-the-young-survivors-of-a-devastating-Haiti- earthquake/stories/201008260430.
44. Shelly Anderson, "Penguins' Rupp, Talbot Continue Work with Haitian Orphanage," *Pittsburgh Post-Gazette*, January 27, 2011, http://www.post-gazette.com/sports/penguins/2011/01/27/Penguins-Rupp-Talbot-continue-work-with-Haitian-orphanage/stories/201101270285.
45. Rob Rossi, "Pens' Cooke, Vitale Join Staal on Haiti Trip," TRIBLive, August 10, 2012, http://triblive.com/sports/penguins/2390154-85/cooke-vitale-staal-henderson-trip-foundation-penguins-join-kids-players; Shelby Anderson, "Trip to Haiti 'Life-Changing' Penguins," Questia, https://www.questia.com/newspaper/1P2-36611836/trip-to-haiti-life-changing-penguins.
46. Adam Bittner, "City Estimates Penguins Stanley Cup Parade Crowd at 650,000," *Pittsburgh Post-Gazette*, June 14, 2017, http://www.post-gazette.com/sports/penguins/2017/06/14/stanley-cup-parade-estimate-steelers-super-bowl/stories/201706140134.
47. Joshua Axelrod, "'Penguins Jesus' Blesses Team's Stanley Cup Run," *Pittsburgh Post-Gazette*, June 9, 2017, http://www.post-gazette.com/sports/penguins/2017/06/09/Penguins-Jesus-Stanley-Cup-Twitter/stories/201706090188.

Chapter 13

1. See Robert Cargill, *The Cities that Built the Bible* (New York: HarperOne, 2016); *Christian History Magazine* 124, "Faith in the City" (December 2017).

ABOUT THE AUTHOR

Gary Scott Smith taught for thirty-nine years at Grove City College, where he chaired the History Department and coordinated the Humanities Core. He earned his MDiv at Gordon-Conwell Theological Seminary and his PhD in American history at Johns Hopkins University. He received Grove City College's inaugural Professor of the Year award in 2000, and the next year, he was named Pennsylvania Professor of the Year by the Carnegie Foundation for the Advancement of Teaching and the Council for Advancement and Support of Education. He is the author or editor of thirteen books, including *Faith and the Presidency: From George Washington to George W. Bush* (Oxford University Press, 2006), *Heaven in the American Imagination* (Oxford University Press, 2011), *Religion in the Oval Office: The Religious Lives of American Presidents* (Oxford University Press, 2015) and *Suffer the Children: What We Can Do to Improve the Lives of the World's Impoverished Children* (Cascade Books, 2017). Smith is also an ordained minister in the PCUSA and currently is the co-director of the mission program and a parish associate at Saint Andrews–Covenant Presbyterian Church in Wilmington, North Carolina.